Airline Industrial Relations
Pilots and Flight Engineers

AIRLINE INDUSTRIAL RELATIONS
Pilots and Flight Engineers

JOHN M. BAITSELL
Associate Professor of Business Administration

DIVISION OF RESEARCH
GRADUATE SCHOOL OF BUSINESS ADMINISTRATION
HARVARD UNIVERSITY
Boston · 1966

Foreword

THIS quite comprehensive study of the industrial relations system of the Air Line Pilots Association, the Flight Engineers' International Association, and the United States scheduled airline companies contributes substantially to our knowledge of the various unique characteristics of collective bargaining in this industry. The primary value of the study is thus its analysis of this particular system of collective bargaining.

Beyond this immediate contribution is the perspective the study gives to the problems and consequences of recurring and varied government intervention in labor disputes. Collective bargaining can hardly be said to function in a "normal" fashion in most segments of transportation. Neither is it possible to generalize from one transportation industry to another nor even from one to another dispute. But the pilots and flight engineers and the airlines are worthy of special study because of their multi-sided involvement with government agencies and the difficult public policy questions thereby created. Finally, the pilots and flight engineers make an interesting subject for study because of their relative professional status and the probable future growth of unionism or near-unionism among at least some professional groups. Both because of their professional status and because of an almost tripartite relationship with the government, an understanding of the behavior of the pilots and flight engineers in their airline bargaining may give insights as to future developments in other bargaining relationships.

Professor John T. Dunlop's framework for the analysis of industrial relations systems provided important insights for this study. The substantive issues to which the parties have given almost continuous attention over the years, and the evolving resolution of these issues, have most obviously and interestingly grown from and been related to the technological and product market opportunities and constraints imposed by the environment. Adjusting work assignments to technological change, developing a most complex method of compensation, resolving the unique set of scheduling problems and their relationship to compensation, and building a unique and ambitious retirement system all reflect important environmental variables. While many facets of these issues could be singled out for comment, the scope and character of the pension system with its use of variable annuities has been a most creative resolution to a very special retirement problem. Professor Baitsell has done very creditable work in his analysis of these influences on this system.

A most interesting research finding is that "the airline managements and the pilots tend to emphasize the negotiation of agreements and to de-emphasize the filing and processing of grievances." More particularly, "for every two first-step grievances pilots file, they negotiate at least one new document." Various characteristics of the relationship probably contribute to this relative tendency to negotiate solutions to problems, a somewhat novel industrial relations situation.

Finally, the company-by-company structure of bargaining and other features of the environment create a power imbalance in which the relative costs of disagreement to the airline managements have appeared to outweigh the costs of agreement. No small part of the reason for this situation has been the very rapid growth of the industry. If managements attempted to modify this power balance through industry-wide negotiation, government intervention would be intensified even beyond its present dimensions. This balance of power problem, coupled with the government's strong desire to prevent transportation strikes, presents a very real dilemma with regard to the creation of a stable collective bargaining relationship.

E. ROBERT LIVERNASH
Albert J. Weatherhead, Jr., Professor
of Business Administration

Financial Acknowledgment

The financial support for continuing Professor Baitsell's research after the completion of his thesis came from an allocation from the Aviation Research Fund of the Harvard Business School. This fund was originally established more than twenty years ago by contributions from members of the aviation transportation and aircraft manufacturing industries for general research in aviation. Allocations to specific projects are made by the Dean. I express for all at the School our gratitude for this generous support of our research activities in this field.

BERTRAND FOX
Director of Research

Soldiers Field
Boston, Massachusetts
August 1966

Acknowledgments

THROUGHOUT the seven years that this book proceeded from doctoral work to its present form, countless individuals knowledgeable about the airline industry shared their information and their ideas with me. They included airline officials and employees, union officers, people in government, and private labor mediators. While concern for their interests necessitates my not thanking them by name, I do wish to acknowledge the fundamental contribution they made to this work.

A few individuals and one foundation made such important contributions to my doctoral dissertation that I wish to repeat my appreciation to them here. Professor James J. Healy gave me the initial idea for a study of the airline labor scene and as thesis supervisor helped me shape the detailed nature of the research. Also of great intellectual value were the training and advice I received from the late Professor Benjamin M. Selekman. During those early months I received important encouragement from Mr. Andrew Towl, the Director of Case Development, Harvard Business School, and from my close friends, Mr. and Mrs. Charles F. Blevins. The United States Steel Foundation generously provided the necessary financial support for that work.

As the research moved ahead, Professor Healy continued to provide sound advice, and additional people came to my aid. I am indebted to Professors Thomas Kennedy and Bertrand Fox, both of Harvard, who read through the manuscript and gave me very helpful comments. Professsor E. Robert Livernash also commented in detail on the entire manuscript and worked closely with me on several drafts of Chapters 4, 6, and 10 to the point where without having to accept the responsibility for their faults I would give him much of the credit for what they contain of value.

During the last four years this study has been sponsored by the Division of Research of the Harvard Business School, and, as a result, I have fallen heir gratefully to the sound counsel of its

Director, Professor Fox, to the incisive editing and esthetic skills of Miss Ruth Norton, its Editor and Executive Secretary, and to the additional outstanding editorial and indexing abilities of Mrs. Nina Dolben. The financial support of the Division provided the time free from other duties and the means to travel which were absolutely essential to update, expand, and complete this study of a rapidly evolving industrial relations system.

I am indebted to Mrs. Bea Siegel for excellent general secretarial assistance and for typing draft upon draft of this manuscript, some of which, incidentally, were much longer than the version which appears between these covers.

In very special ways I am grateful to two members of my family. I appreciate beyond words the help of my wife, Carol, who cheerfully ran our home while I was off working on this book in other cities, in my office, or, perhaps worse, while we were presumably talking together. I appreciate also the encouragement of my father, George Alfred Baitsell, Colgate Professor of Biology Emeritus, Yale University, who by his example led me to a scholarly career and who today with eyes grown dim over decades of writing and editing will still rifle through these pages and spot the inevitable instance of "the data is."

While I acknowledge all this help, I alone accept the responsibility for the shortcomings of this volume.

JOHN M. BAITSELL

Soldiers Field
Boston, Massachusetts
August 1966

Contents

Crews on Building Sequences; The Impact of Flight Crews on the Monthly Lines of Flying; The Impact of Flight Crews on the Daily Administration of Scheduling . . . The Decline in Flight Crew Utilization

List of Tables

PART I

General Background Information

THIS BOOK contains an analysis of the industrial relations system[1] which has evolved between the commercial airlines and the principal unions representing pilots and flight engineers. This system displays a number of interesting and unique characteristics.

Because it concentrates on pilots and flight engineers, this book deals with but one section of the total airline industrial relations system. Excluded from consideration are other flight crew members such as pursers, stewards, and stewardesses; as well as all ground personnel such as mechanics, office employees, and ticketing people.

The analysis is divided into three parts. Part I contains background information in three chapters which deal in turn with the characteristics, the history, and the determinants of this industrial relations system. In Part II the analysis concentrates on the following substantive contract areas: compensation, scheduling, pensions, and work assignment. Part III contains analyses of the processes by which the parties handle grievances and negotiate new contract terms. Part III ends with some concluding observations regarding the evolution of this industrial relations system.

---

[1] John T. Dunlop, *Industrial Relations Systems* (New York: Holt-Dryden, 1958). Much of the terminology of Professor Dunlop's excellent book has been used in this book, although the analysis does not conform to his model for viewing industrial relations systems.

CHAPTER 1

Characteristics of the Certificated Airline Industry

THIS CHAPTER on characteristics has been divided into two parts. The first half describes selected characteristics of the air carriers; the second half describes selected characteristics of the employees in the industry. The first half will treat four fundamental characteristics of the air carriers: (a) the types of certificated carriers, (b) the growth of the industry, (c) the current U.S. aircraft fleet, and (d) the management organization of the air carriers. The second half will discuss the following characteristics of the airline employees: (a) their types and numbers, (b) their wage levels, and (c) their unionization.

CHARACTERISTICS OF THE AIR CARRIERS

The Types of Certificated Route Air Carriers

The certificated route air carriers of this country are divided into eight categories according to the type of service they perform.[1] These categories have been established by the Civil Aeronautics Board (CAB) under existing legislation which requires carriers to qualify for a permanent "certificate of public convenience and necessity" prior to operating. The eight categories are presented in Table 1.1.

[1] The CAB recognized two other categories of air carriers in 1964; 15 supplemental carriers had been issued interim certificates pending permanent certification. These carriers could conduct unlimited interstate charters, certain foreign and overseas charters, and unlimited military planeload contract flights. In addition, some of these carriers could carry individually ticketed passengers or waybilled cargo until July 10, 1964. CAB, *Annual Report, 1963*, p. 76.

The 51 certificated route air carriers vary widely in size. One of the commonly used measures of size is a revenue ton-mile, which is defined by the CAB as one ton of revenue traffic transported one mile. Using this measure, these air carriers ranged in size during the twelve-month period ended September 30, 1964, from 70,000 revenue ton-miles for Western Alaska Airlines to 1.25 billion revenue ton-miles for Pan American World Airways. Table 1.1 presents the revenue ton-miles carried by the carriers in the eight categories during the twelve months ended September 30, 1964.

The domestic trunk carriers operate primarily within the continental limits of the United States and serve primarily the larger

TABLE 1.1.   CATEGORIES OF CERTIFICATED ROUTE AIR CARRIERS
AND REVENUE TON-MILES OF TRAFFIC CARRIED:
12 MONTHS ENDED SEPTEMBER 30, 1964

Reporting Unit		*Over-all Revenue Ton-Miles* (*in thousands*)		*Per Cent*
(1) Domestic trunk operations		4,754,060		61.7%
Big Four	3,373,210		43.8%	
Other trunks	1,380,850		17.9	
(2) Local service carriers		229,538		3.0
(3) Helicopter carriers		1,575		–
(4) Intra-Alaska carriers		17,982		0.2
(5) Intra-Hawaiian carriers		16,951		0.2
(6) Domestic all-cargo carriers		376,683		4.9
(7) International and territorial operations of passenger/cargo carriers		2,135,374		27.7
(8) International and territorial operations of all-cargo carriers		175,093		2.2
Total Certificated Route Industry		7,707,256		99.9%*

* Rounding variance.

SOURCE: CAB, *Air Carrier Traffic Statistics,* September 1964, pp. 1–8.

cities. In 1964 these carriers, flying domestically, accounted for 61.7% of the total revenue ton-miles carried by the certificated route airline industry.

Included among the trunk lines are the four largest domestic air carriers (American, Eastern, TWA, and United), which by themselves in their domestic operations accounted for 43.8% of the total revenue ton-miles carried by the certificated airline industry in 1964. If their international and territorial operations are added, they accounted for another 6.8% of the revenue ton-miles carried by the certificated route industry, making a total of 50.6%.

The local service carriers have been certified to operate within the continental United States over routes of lesser density than the trunk lines. Normally their routes are between the smaller cities or between those cities and the larger metropolitan areas. With the latter service, these carriers act as feeders for the trunk lines, bringing traffic into major terminals where it can be transferred to the trunk lines. For the most part providing local service has been a post-World War II experiment. Twelve of the 13 carriers in this category have been certified since 1945. In 1964 the local service lines accounted for 3.0% of the revenue ton-miles carried by the certificated route airline industry.

In 1964 five cities (New York, Chicago, Los Angeles, and San Francisco/Oakland) were served by scheduled helicopter service between the airport and the center of the city, the central post office building, and the suburbs. Despite the glowing predictions a few years back of the widespread use of helicopters for this type of service, only four carriers have been certified. In 1964 they accounted for only a negligible percentage of the industry's revenue ton-miles.

Intra-Alaska and intra-Hawaiian carriers operate wholly within either Alaska or Hawaii. Together, the carriers in both categories accounted for only 0.4% of the revenue ton-miles carried by the certificated route industry in 1964.

As the name implies, all-cargo carriers have been certified by the CAB to engage primarily in the transportation of freight and express. To a limited degree they may also conduct some non-scheduled passenger operations. The all-cargo carriers in this category conduct operations within the territory of the United States.

In 1964 they accounted for 4.9% of the revenue ton-miles of the certificated route industry.

The CAB defines international operations as follows: "In general, operations outside territory of the United States, including operations between United States points separated by foreign territory or major expanses of international waters."[2] In this category are included carriers which transport both passengers and cargo. Nine of the domestic trunk lines conduct some type of international and/or territorial operations. In calculating the revenue ton-miles of the carriers in this category, the traffic they carry domestically is excluded. Applying this exclusion, all the carriers in this category accounted for 27.7% of the revenue ton-miles of traffic carried by the certificated airline industry. One carrier, Pan American, really dominates this category. It alone carried 1.25 billion revenue ton-miles in 1964 which amounted to 58.8% of the revenue ton-miles carried in the operations under this category. TWA was the second largest carrier in this category, accounting for 14.1% of the revenue ton-miles carried in this category in 1964.

International and territorial all-cargo carriers accounted for 2.2% of the revenue ton-miles of the certificated industry in 1964.

This discussion of the categories of air carriers has presented the situation as of September 30, 1964. The point needs to be stressed, however, that this is not a static situation. Changes occur frequently as carriers adopt new names, enter or go out of business, merge, or gain or lose relative shares of the market. Another source of changes stems from revisions the CAB makes in the definitions and names of the various categories.

Perhaps the most interesting changes have occurred in the share of the market the various carriers have enjoyed over the years. For example, in 1954 the domestic trunks carried 72.9% of the revenue ton-miles of the certificated airline industry which was 11.2 percentage points higher than the comparable figure in 1964, given in Table 1.1. The Big Four have also lost ground. In 1954 they accounted for 54.1% of the revenue ton-miles.[3] The comparable figure was down to 43.8% in 1964. The failure of the Big Four to

[2] CAB, *Air Carrier Traffic Statistics,* September 1964, p. 46.
[3] CAB, *Certificated Air Carrier Traffic Statistics,* January 1955, p. 39. The 1954 figures are for the 12-month period ended January 31, 1955.

maintain their relative position in the certificated industry has resulted from an apparent policy of the CAB to award important new routes to the eight other trunk lines while being very slow to grant the Big Four significant additions to their route structures.[4] Allowing Capital and United to merge in 1961 represented a departure from this policy.

The Growth of the Certificated Industry

The tremendous growth of the certificated airline industry in the past 20 years can be shown by a few comparisons. Table 1.2 contains selected traffic figures for the scheduled domestic passenger/cargo service of the certificated route air carriers in the 20-year period from 1943 to 1963. The first row of figures shows that over-all revenue ton-miles rose from 209,893,000 in 1943 to 4,455,234,000 in 1963, increasing by a factor of 21.2. The next two rows present the growth in passenger service measured in terms of a revenue passenger-mile, defined by the CAB as the transporting of a revenue passenger one mile. Particularly interesting is the rapid growth in air coach and economy services which were started in 1948 and which by 1963 accounted for 64% of the passenger business. Over the 20-year period the total revenue passenger-miles increased by a factor of 23.6.

The fourth row introduces the concept of available service as opposed to revenue service. As the name implies, the available seat-miles for a flight are the number of seats available to revenue passengers multiplied by the length of the flight in miles. In other words, seats are counted regardless of whether they are filled or not. In the 20-year period available seat-miles rose by a factor of 38.9.

The total revenue passenger load factors are presented in row five because of the importance of load factor figures to the air carriers. They are not measures of growth. A revenue passenger load factor is obtained by dividing the number of revenue passenger-miles by the comparable available seat-miles and expressing the resulting quotient as a percentage. For any given flight the number

---

[4] *The Status and Economic Significance of the Airline Equipment Investment Program,* A Report by Dr. Paul W. Cherington to the Honorable E. R. Quesada, President Eisenhower's Special Assistant for Aviation, June 30, 1958, p. 9.

TABLE 1.2.　SELECTED TRAFFIC STATISTICS OF THE SCHEDULED DOMESTIC PASSENGER/CARGO SERVICE OF THE CERTIFICATED ROUTE AIR CARRIERS: 1943–1963

Year	1943	1948	1953	1958	1963
Revenue ton-miles (000)	209,893	720,042	1,690,901	2,838,760	4,455,234
Revenue passenger-miles (total) (000)	1,632,452	5,976,323	14,793,875	25,375,489	38,456,612
Revenue passenger-miles (coach plus economy) (000)	0	4,835	3,719,499	10,075,760	24,667,287
Available seat-miles (000)	1,857,837	10,374,485	23,337,498	42,723,508	72,254,533
Revenue passenger load factor (%)	88.0%	57.6%	63.4%	59.4%	53.2%
Number of employees	29,654	60,416	84,651	119,746	143,112
Number of aircraft	204	878	1,139	1,546	1,600

SOURCE: *FAA Statistical Handbook of Aviation*, 1962 and 1964 editions.

of miles is the same in both the divisor and the dividend and, therefore, cancels out, leaving the load factor as the number of seats filled divided by the number of seats available for revenue passengers in the plane. For example, it would be correct to speak of a plane that was half filled as having a load factor of 50% for that particular flight. The vital importance of its load factor to a carrier stems from the fact that costs are essentially constant for making a flight with no passengers or with a full load. The carrier will make money on a flight if it carries enough revenue passengers to cover this essentially constant cost. The number of revenue passengers for each aircraft type needed to cover this cost is known as that plane's "break-even load factor." Airline managers watch their load factor figures very carefully because the carrier profits directly in relation to them. In recent years load factors have dropped and by 1963 were only 53.2%.

The figures for the number of people employed show growth over the 20-year period for the entire employee group. This should not be interpreted to mean, however, that the two groups involved in this study, the pilots and the flight engineers, enjoyed a steady rise in employment. As will be discussed below, pilots experienced some periods of level or declining employment against a long-term upward trend.

The Current United States Aircraft Fleet

The number of aircraft in use by the domestic passenger/cargo air carriers rose from 204 in 1943 to 1,600 as of December 31, 1963. Table 1.3 shows how the make-up of the aircraft fleet changed from 1953 to 1963. Particularly interesting to this analysis is the increase in the number of turbojet aircraft from zero in 1953 to 353 by 1963.

The Management Organization of the Air Carriers

The task of organizing an airline so that efficient and workable lines of authority exist throughout a company is very difficult. Airlines must carry on a large variety of functions in many locations which may be spread over the globe, and at minimum are spread over a section of the country. A major carrier may have 20,000 employees working in over 80 locations.

Every air carrier, of course, must cover certain major line and staff areas. These include flight operations, aircraft maintenance, sales, personnel, finance, and legal. Countless ways exist, however, in which an airline may be organized to handle them. One important organizational question is whether to place the aircraft maintenance function under the flight operations department or to set it up as a separate line organization. At present all the carriers studied have done the latter.

TABLE 1.3. AIRCRAFT IN OPERATION BY DOMESTIC
PASSENGER/CARGO CERTIFICATED ROUTE AIR CARRIERS:
DECEMBER 31, 1953 AND 1963

Aircraft	*1953*	*1963*
Turbojets	0	353
Turboprops	0	229
4-Engine pistons	462	446
2-Engine pistons	660	501
Single-engine pistons	0	51
Helicopters	17	20
Totals	1,139	1,600

SOURCE: *FAA Statistical Handbook of Aviation,* 1957 and 1964 editions.

Perhaps a more knotty organizational problem is how to divide the responsibility for servicing the passenger. Essentially this is a question of trying to separate sales functions, such as making reservations and checking tickets at the terminal, from flight operations functions, such as flying a passenger from one city to another. For example, to whom should the stewardesses report? The scheduling of their flight assignments tends to be an operations function yet the nature of their work of servicing the passenger tends to be part of the selling function. The carriers surveyed have experimented with many different lines of authority to try to divide the passenger between sales and operations. At least one has established a customer service department which cuts across both sales and operations to follow the passenger from the time he makes a reservation until he picks up his baggage after the completion of the flight.

To find answers to the inevitable problems that airline organization causes, many air carriers have turned to reorganization as a panacea. They continually reassign functional areas among different divisions of their carriers. They increase the number of executives in some areas while cutting back in others. Some of them experiment with a different number of bases at which to have the flight crew members and their families live. A dominant characteristic of the organization of the airline industry is its state of continual flux.

In this changing situation it would not be accurate to call any particular organizational make-up "typical" of the air carriers. The organizational structure at one small trunk line is discussed below, but even as this information was being obtained a complete revision was being made by that carrier.

At this airline there is a vice president for each of the major areas which have to be covered with the exception of the legal area because this carrier obtains all its legal advice from a law firm. The treasurer's function has been separated from the finance department forming a treasurer's department. With a department headed by a vice president–services the carrier attempts to place under one vice president many of the services given the passengers.

While this organization in its entirety may not be called typical, certain aspects of the personnel department are typical of all but the largest air carriers. In the first place, the labor relations function usually falls under a personnel vice president. Of more importance is the small size of the personnel department staff. At this carrier only three men handle the entire range of personnel functions which include the selection and hiring of all new employees (including pilots) and the maintenance of all personnel records for the entire company. A labor relations assistant is nominally in charge of negotiations and contract administration with six unions representing different employee groups. In practice this man negotiates with all these unions except the pilots' union, with which the operations department negotiates. And contract administration is essentially in the hands of the appropriate line department; e.g., the maintenance department administers the mechanics' contract. The ramifications of having small personnel and industrial relations staffs at all but the largest carriers and the resulting transfer of their functions to line departments are widespread. They will be explored more fully later.

Characteristics of the Airline Employees

The Types and Numbers of Employees

The over-all increase in the total number of airline employees over the years from 1943 to 1963 has been presented in Table 1.2. In Table 1.4 these totals are divided into the eight broad types of employees found in the industry, and the absolute growth of each type over the same 20-year period is presented.

Table 1.4. Personnel Employed by Domestic
Passenger/Cargo Certificated Route Air Carriers:
1943–1963

Personnel	1943	1948	1953	1958	1963
Pilots and copilots	2,125	5,307	7,726	11,289	12,137
Other flight deck personnel	8	312	1,365	3,092	3,182
Pursers, stewards, stewardesses	845	3,038	4,954	8,262	10,829
Communications personnel	1,685	2,612	2,665	2,970	2,683
Mechanics	8,271	16,428	20,717	24,996	28,592
Aircraft and traffic servicing	3,356	9,222	14,249	30,454	39,215
Office employees	10,973	21,396	30,193	25,368	29,225
All others	2,391	2,101	2,782	13,317	17,249
Total	29,654	60,416	84,651	119,746	143,112

Source: *FAA Statistical Handbook of Aviation,* 1950 and 1964 editions.

The eight types of airline employees are fairly self-explanatory. The first three types include the personnel who actually are a part of the plane crew. Those listed under "Other flight deck personnel" are flight engineers. The personnel under the "Communications personnel" heading are ground communicators. The "Aircraft and traffic servicing" employees include the men who handle and load the aircraft around the ramps and also the people who handle all types of traffic at the airport, such as ticket takers. Of course all these categories may be subdivided into the hundreds of jobs airline employees perform. One study of just the clerical job classes at a major air carrier lists 207 jobs.[5] Such a detailed breakdown, however, would serve no useful purpose in this analysis.

Table 1.5 shows the number of "Pilots and copilots" and of "Other flight deck personnel" employed by the industry from 1954 to 1963. These data will be important in the later analysis because the flight crew members feared that technological unemployment would result from the arrival of jet aircraft after 1958. As can be seen, the number of pilots and copilots declined in 1960 relative to 1959 and had not reached the latter level again by 1963. During the period 1959 to 1963 the number of other flight deck personnel held relatively constant around 3,200.

TABLE 1.5. FLIGHT DECK CREW MEMBERS EMPLOYED BY THE CERTIFICATED ROUTE AIR CARRIERS IN SCHEDULED DOMESTIC OPERATIONS: 1954–1963

Year	Pilots and Copilots	Other Flight Deck Personnel	Year	Pilots and Copilots	Other Flight Deck Personnel
1954	7,803	1,624	1959	12,175	3,370
1955	8,721	1,721	1960	11,460	3,144
1956	9,143	2,241	1961	11,741	3,334
1957	11,430	3,135	1962	11,595	3,244
1958	11,287	3,092	1963	12,137	3,182

SOURCE: *FAA Statistical Handbook of Aviation, 1964.*

In Table 1.6 the numbers of airline employees used by the domestic certificated route passenger/cargo air carriers are presented along with the percentage each type is of the total group. Thus, the pilots and copilots, flying domestically, numbered 12,137 in 1963 and accounted for 8.5% of all airline employees used by these carriers. The flight engineers who comprised the "Other flight deck personnel" accounted for about 2.2% of the total

[5] George A. Fuller, *The Development and Installation of a Wage and Salary Structure for a Major Airline,* Ph.D. Thesis, State University of Iowa, 1953.

TABLE 1.6. PERSONNEL, PAYROLL, AND AVERAGE SALARY OF CERTIFICATED
DOMESTIC ROUTE PASSENGER/CARGO AIR CARRIERS: 1963

Personnel Classification	No. of Personnel	Per Cent	Annual Payroll (000's)	Per Cent	Average Annual Salary
Pilots and copilots	12,137	8.5%	$ 221,767	19.9%	$18,272
Other flight deck personnel	3,182	2.2	45,875	4.1	14,417
Stewards, stewardesses, pursers	10,829	7.6	52,103	4.7	4,811
Communications personnel	2,683	1.9	16,387	1.5	6,108
Mechanics and other maintenance personnel	28,592	20.0	212,540	19.1	7,434
Aircraft and traffic servicing personnel	39,215	27.4	247,833	22.2	6,320
Office employees	29,225	20.4	185,466	16.7	6,346
All other employees	17,249	12.0	131,547	11.8	7,626
Total Domestic Passenger/Cargo	143,112	100.0%	$1,113,518	100.0%	$ 7,781

SOURCE: *FAA Statistical Handbook of Aviation*, 1964, p. 135.

group. Thus the employees covered intensively in this study accounted for about 10.7% of the airline employees in domestic passenger/cargo operations.

Before turning to the payroll and salary information given in Table 1.6, it might be well to consider one further nonfinancial characteristic of pilots and flight engineers. This is their age distribution which becomes important when considering a man's chance for promotion.

Table 1.7 presents age distributions of men who held airline transport pilot ratings and of those who possessed a flight engineer's certificate as of January 1, 1964. The important point to note here is the relatively small percentage in both groups who were over 49 years of age. Fifteen per cent of the airline transport pilots and 4.0% of the men possessing flight engineers' certificates were

TABLE 1.7. AGE DISTRIBUTION OF AIRMEN HOLDING AIRLINE TRANSPORT PILOT RATINGS AND FLIGHT ENGINEER CERTIFICATES: AS OF JANUARY 1, 1964

Age Group	Airline Transport		Flight Engineer	
	Number	Per Cent	Number	Per Cent
20–24	7	*	23	*
25–29	293	1%	478	5%
30–34	1,660	8	2,250	25
35–39	3,232	16	2,324	26
40–44	7,039	35	2,462	28
45–49	4,969	25	1,044	12
50–54	1,907	9	284	3
55–59	920	5	101	1
60 and over	242	1	26	*
Total	20,269	100%	5,853	100%

* Less than 0.5%.

SOURCE: *FAA Statistical Handbook of Aviation*, 1964, pp. 57 and 58.

over 49 years of age. These figures indicate that within the next decade relatively few vacancies will open up because of normal retirements for age.

Airline Employee Wage Levels

Airline employees earn relatively high incomes. As shown in Table 1.6 their average annual salary in 1963 was $7,781. That figure compares favorably with the average annual salary of all production workers in manufacturing for 1963 of $5,168.[6]

The highest incomes among airline employees are earned by the pilot group (pilots and copilots) which averaged $18,272 in 1963. The average salary for flight engineers was $14,417 or 185% of the average for all airline employees. At the low end of the scale, the stewards, stewardesses, and pursers averaged only $4,811 in 1963.

Another way to view the high earnings of the pilot group and the flight engineers is to determine the percentages their wages are of the total airline payrolls. In 1963 the pilot group, although only accounting for 8.5% of the total number of airline employees, received 19.9% of the total payroll. Similarly, the flight engineers received 4.1% of the total payroll although representing only 2.2% of the airline personnel. Thus this study deals intensively with the two highest paid employee groups in this industry.

The importance of these wages to the airlines can be briefly stated. In 1963 the wages of the pilot group were 19.9% of the total annual payroll which was in turn 43.4% of total operating expenses and 40.9% of total operating revenues.[7]

The wages of the pilot group and of the flight engineers will be treated in detail in Chapter 4 (Methods of Compensation) but a brief word about them here is appropriate to dispel any idea that all pilots earn approximately $18,272 per year, or that all flight engineers earn roughly $14,417 per year. In the case of both groups there is a tremendous range in earnings. For example, one major airline will pay newly hired pilots a straight salary of $6,000 per year, whereas a senior jet pilot could earn over $30,000 a year.

[6] U.S. Bureau of Labor Statistics, *Monthly Labor Review*, May 1964, p. 602. Gross average weekly earnings in 1963 for all production workers in manufacturing was $99.38, which, multiplied by 52 weeks, gives $5,168 per year.

[7] *FAA Statistical Handbook of Aviation*, 1964, pp. 135, 138, and 139.

The Unionization of Airline Employees

The degree of unionization among the eight types of airline employees varies widely. At the high end of the scale are the pilots, the other flight deck personnel, the stewards, stewardesses, and pursers, the communications personnel, and the mechanics. As shown in Table 1.6, these five types of employees accounted for 40.2% of all domestic passenger/cargo airline personnel in 1963. At the other end of the scale with very little union representation are the aircraft and traffic servicing personnel, the office employees, and the balance of the airline personnel. They accounted for 59.8% of the airline personnel in 1958. These figures would indicate that somewhat less than 50% of all employees of all the domestic certificated route passenger/cargo carriers are represented by a union, and statements made by union and management officials reinforce this estimate. Although the degree of unionization varies carrier by carrier, it would appear to be higher among the large carriers. For example, nine of the largest carriers reported in 1961 the following figures for unionized employees as a percentage of total employees:[8]

American	54.4%	Northwest	70.3%
Braniff	88.5	Pan American	63.8
Continental	52.9	TWA	52.3
Eastern	55.0	United	64.4
National	85.8		

A more detailed look can be taken at the representation of employees at the 11 domestic trunks and the 13 local service lines, which are of primary concern to this study. The pilot groups are represented by the Air Line Pilots Association (ALPA) at 23 of these carriers and by the Allied Pilots Association at the 24th. Most of the pilots belong to one of these unions. The flight engineers are represented by one of three unions at every domestic trunk line. The Flight Engineers' International Association (FEIA) represents flight engineers at three trunk lines; ALPA represents them at seven

[8] CAB, Mutual Aid Pact Investigation, Docket 9977, "Joint Exhibits of the Airline Parties," Exhibit 10.

trunk lines; and the International Association of Machinists (IAM) is the bargaining agent for piston flight engineers at one of the trunks. Flight engineers are not employed by the local service lines because they do not use aircraft that require an engineer.

The next three types of airline employees are almost as thoroughly represented. The stewards, stewardesses, and pursers are represented at all but one trunk line and one local service line. The communications personnel are represented at nine of the trunks. The mechanics are represented at all trunks and at all but one of the local service lines.[9]

The degree of union representation is less among the other three categories. Clerical personnel have unions at five of the smaller trunks and six of the feeders, and partial groups at five other trunks and two other feeders. The dispatchers are represented at all the trunks and feeders, but only a handful of dispatchers are employed at any airline. Isolated groups of stock clerks, flight simulator operators, guards, cafeteria employees, and station employees are represented by unions. It is true, however, that the great majority of these employees lack representation.

One final characteristic of the airline employees needs to be discussed. This is the internal structures of the principal unions involved in this study.

In establishing an efficient internal structure the airline unions face a problem similar to that of the airline managements. How should they organize themselves to cover the many locations in which an airline will employ personnel? Fortunately for ALPA and FEIA their members at any one airline will be living at only a handful of locations. The Big Four typically will have flight crews at about ten locations, while the feeders will have them at about half that number or less. This limited number of membership groups permits these unions to have simpler internal structures than the managements.

The smallest unit in the internal structure of ALPA is composed of a group of members working for one airline at one location. This group of members is known as a "Local Council." Several carriers, for example, will have flight crew members living in the New York

[9] *29th Annual Report of the National Mediation Board,* Fiscal year ended June 30, 1963, p. 94.

City area. The members of ALPA at each of those carriers will form their own local council.[10]

Each Local Council normally elects four officers who form its Local Executive Council. They are a Council Chairman, Vice Chairman, Senior Copilot Representative, and Copilot Representative. As previously mentioned, ALPA represents the flight engineers at seven trunk lines. In the cases of Local Executive Councils at those carriers, the officers also include a Senior Flight Officer Representative and a Flight Officer Representative.

The next higher echelon in the ALPA internal structure represents all the members at one airline. It is known as the Master Executive Council. Normally it is composed of all the Local Executive Council Chairmen and Senior Copilot Representatives of that airline. For example, if a carrier had ALPA members living at ten locations, there would be ten Local Executive Councils and each one would have two members on the Master Executive Council for that carrier. Where ALPA also represents the flight engineers, each Local Executive Council is also represented on the Master Executive Council by its Senior Flight Officer Representative.

The highest governing body of ALPA is its convention which meets every two years, but its members may be polled more often if an important policy decision has to be settled in the interim. The convention delegates are the Council Chairmen, Senior Copilot Representatives, and Senior Flight Officer Representatives of every ALPA Local Executive Council. The delegates are known as the ALPA Board of Directors. In general, they set the policy by which ALPA is run during the two years between conventions.

The job of carrying out these policies rests with a nine-man Executive Committee comprised of the international officers (President, First Vice President, Secretary, and Treasurer) and five Regional Vice Presidents. All these offices are filled by election.

ALPA staffs its union in a way that is unique among trade unions. There are only two full-time offices which are permitted to be held by members of ALPA. They are the Presidency and the Executive Vice Presidency. All the other elected offices throughout the union are filled by pilots who carry on their active flying careers.

[10] Air Line Pilots Association, *Constitution and Bylaws,* November 9, 1958.

Also unique is the prohibition against members filling any of the full-time staff jobs. ALPA hires professional staff people to carry on the detailed work of the Association. For example, the ALPA negotiators are nonmembers who are hired because of their professional ability as negotiators. This stands in marked contrast to the usual union situation in which international representatives are appointed or elected from the ranks of the membership. A somewhat less uncommon aspect of ALPA's internal structure is the location of almost the entire professional staff at its home office in Chicago. ALPA has found having the staff all operate out of this city to be very efficient for its purposes.

ALPA represents an interesting combination of democracy and extremely strong centralized control. The democracy stems from the active participation of the convention in establishing the general policies of ALPA and, to a degree, from the autonomy of each Master Executive Council. The strong centralized control arises in the carrying out of those policies by the Executive Committee. The centralized power of the Association stems from the following clauses in its *Constitution and Bylaws:*

> Article XVIII, Section 1. Conferences or negotiations shall not be initiated, carried on, or concluded in the name of the Association by any member, group, or groups of members thereof to make or establish employment agreements relating to rates of pay, rules, or other conditions of employment, or any other agreements, contracts, or documents of a similar or related character, or any form of agreements, contracts, or documents without the prior approval of the Executive Committee or the President. *Any and all agreements,* contracts, documents of any and every character whatsoever *shall not become effective,* binding or operative unless and *until they bear the signature of the President* or other officer or officers duly authorized so to sign by the Board of Directors, Executive Board, or Executive Committee. (Emphasis added.)

Under this authority the President of ALPA will refuse to sign a new agreement which he believes does not meet the standards of working conditions ALPA is trying to establish. As will be detailed in Chapter 8, the authority of the President to refuse to sign an agreement of which he does not approve and, indeed, to negotiate himself in place of the negotiating team designated by a master executive council was tested in a bitter intra-ALPA struggle in 1963. It resulted in the pilots at American Airlines leaving ALPA and forming their own union, the Allied Pilots Association.

The Flight Engineers' International Association differs in its internal structure from ALPA in two essential regards. In the first place, its smallest structural unit is the FEIA "Chapter" which represents all the engineers at one airline. Second, while some local autonomy exists within ALPA, local autonomy has been one of the principal features of FEIA's organization since its founding.

The flight engineers at each airline form a Chapter and elect a President, Vice President, and Secretary-Treasurer. The Chapter is analogous to an ALPA Master Executive Council.

The convention of FEIA establishes the policies by which it is supposed to be run. Each Chapter is permitted to send one delegate for every 75 members to the convention. In addition, the international officers of the Association and the Presidents of each Chapter are delegates to the convention. The international officers (President, Executive Vice President, and Vice President—Engineering) and the Chapter Presidents also form the Master Executive Council which runs the Association between conventions.

The autonomy of the individual Chapters stems from the following clause in the *FEIA Constitution and Bylaws:*

> Section 15.b. The appearance of the signature of the President of the FEIA upon the contract or working agreement of any chapter shall constitute FEIA approval of such contracts and working agreements. Failure of his signature to appear upon a contract or working agreement shall indicate that such contract or working agreement is not in accord with the policies, aims, or objectives of the FEIA and therefore does not meet with its approval. *Any such disapproval would not in any way affect the validity of such contracts or working agreements.* (Emphasis added.)

The complete autonomy of the individual Chapter of FEIA, which has permitted it to negotiate agreements which expressed the individual desires of a group of members at one airline, has tended to dilute the power of the Association as an international union. The matter of where the focus of power lies within each union has been the most important difference between the internal structures of ALPA and FEIA.

SUMMARY COMMENTS

The characteristics described in this chapter either have significant impacts on the airline industrial relations system or raise significant questions concerning it. In an industry, for example, in which the total number of firms is as small as 51, the variation in firm size is tremendous, and four firms predominate, one is interested to see if some form of industry-wide or multi-employer bargaining exists. Furthermore, with the industry lines drawn so clearly, if multi-employer bargaining does not exist (as is the case), one is interested to know whether pattern bargaining exists, which firms set the pattern, and how strongly the pattern is transmitted throughout the industry.

The industry has undergone an interesting situation in that amid a strong over-all growth trend which would make one expect a relatively easy and expansive atmosphere to pervade the industrial relations scene, flight crew members have experienced periods of level or declining employment opportunities which would make one expect a difficult and tight industrial relations atmosphere. Given these conflicting tendencies, other aspects of the description in this chapter take on significance. The introduction of large, highly productive turbojet aircraft in large numbers could be expected to affect employment adversely and to raise issues of crew size, new job qualifications, duties, and training. Such issues might be predicted to be severe because two well-entrenched unions were involved in the cockpit. In addition the relative youth of the pilot group would indicate potential blocks to the advancement of younger men and limited attrition-created employment opportunities, both possible sources of industrial relations stress.

The description of the far-flung nature of airline operations, in addition to raising organizational problems for airline managements and unions, points to some interesting questions. Flight crews work without direct supervision most of the time. What is the significance of this fact upon the nature of supervision, discipline, and contract administration? What roles do grievance handling and arbitration play in such a work environment?

The data concerning flight crew earnings and their proportion of total operating revenues raise some significant questions. With pilot earnings roughly triple and flight engineer earnings roughly double the earnings of all airline employees, can meaningful wage comparisons be made between flight crew members and the others? With pilots averaging around $18,000 a year, can meaningful wage comparisons be made between them and other unionized groups? How, therefore, are pilot wage increases assessed? What factors explain the wide differentials among pilots? Are there occupational differences to justify them or are they personal differentials based on seniority? What pressures, if any, do they create within ALPA which represents flight engineers, copilots, and pilots? Of what significance to bargaining power is the fact that the pilot wage bill represents only about 8% of total operating revenues?

From these summary comments it is clear that the characteristics described in this chapter have raised a number of industrial relations questions. Answers to these questions will be given in the ensuing chapters.

CHAPTER 2

Historical Perspective

THIS CHAPTER describes briefly the formation and early development of unionized employee groups within the scheduled airline industry in the United States. Particular emphasis will be placed on the evolution of unionization among pilots. The chapter also presents enough of the development of scheduled aviation itself to portray the context in which the unionization of pilots took place. In presenting these developments this chapter continues to carry out the purpose of the first three chapters which is to set the stage for the analyses and conclusions to follow in Chapters 4 through 10.

This historical presentation purposely has been kept brief for two reasons. First, this is not primarily a historical study. Second, these early developments have been competently handled by other authors on whose work this chapter is largely based.[1]

The difficult question of whether to include the details of the histories of major contract areas in the broad sweep of history presented in this chapter, or to place them in the later chapters

---

[1] Paul T. David, *The Economics of Air Mail Transportation* (Washington: The Brookings Institution, 1934).

Federal Coordinator of Transportation, *Hours, Wages, and Working Conditions in Scheduled Air Transportation,* Washington, March 1936.

John H. Frederick, *Commercial Air Transportation* (Chicago: Richard D. Irwin, 1946).

Mark S. Kahn, *Industrial Relations in the Air Lines,* Unpublished Ph.D. Thesis, Harvard University, 1950.

Mark S. Kahn, "Wage Determination for Airline Pilots," *Industrial and Labor Relations Review,* April 1953.

Karl R. Weber, *Collective Bargaining Between the Air Line Pilots Association and the Airline Transportation Industry,* Unpublished M.A. Thesis, Stanford University, 1949.

which concentrate on the major aspects of the airline industrial relations system has been answered with a decision to hold as much of the detailed material as possible for the appropriate chapter later in the book. Thus detailed histories of the development of flight crew methods of compensation, scheduling procedures, and pension plans will be presented in Chapters 4 through 6. A detailed description of the unionization of flight engineers may be expected in Chapters 7 and 8. This decision has one further ramification for this chapter. Because the important developments since 1947 will be given major emphasis in the later chapters, no need exists to duplicate their history beyond that date in this chapter.

The history of scheduled aviation in this country from the first successful heavier-than-air flight of the Wright brothers in 1903, until 1927 when the air carriers first began to carry a substantial number of passengers, is the story of attempts by the Post Office Department to develop an airmail system. In 1911 it permitted U.S. mail to be carried officially by plane for the first time between two airfields on Long Island as a part of an air meet. It was followed by many similar isolated flights. The first practical steps had to wait until Congress was willing to pass an appropriations bill which included the necessary funds. Several airmail appropriations requests were turned down before the Postmaster General succeeded in obtaining $50,000 in the Post Office Appropriation Bill of 1917.

The airmail service which is in existence today began May 15, 1918, between New York City and Washington, D.C. The equipment and the pilots were provided by the Army, and the necessary funds came from an appropriation by Congress of $100,000. This arrangement continued for only three months because the department was not pleased with the apparent inability of the army cadets to carry the mails on close enough schedules. On August 12, 1918, the Post Office Department took over the airmail service with civilian pilots and six airplanes, but no immediate improvement came about in the scheduled completion of flights. The Post Office continued to fly the mail until the summer of 1927.

Under the direct operation of the department the airmail service made slow and steady progress. In the three years following 1918 the first transcontinental route was developed from New York City to San Francisco via Chicago and Cheyenne. By 1921 mail was being carried by air continuously from coast to coast.

As the transcontinental route was being completed, the department began work on the problem of night flying. Post Office officials realized that the value of the airmail service could be greatly enhanced if mail could be carried between large cities at night so that businessmen could count on a letter mailed in New York, for instance, being delivered in Chicago early the next day. Not until July 1, 1924, however, was night flying regularly scheduled over the entire transcontinental route.

No doubt the pilots were intrepid men during those years. The early planes were subject to mechanical failures, and the flight instruments were rudimentary. The pilots for the most part flew by themselves with no copilots or passengers.

Many of the early pilots were trained initially during World War I, and when the war was over a large number of them purchased surplus planes from the government. This was the group which went around the country on barnstorming tours doing stunts —an operation that increased the nation's interest in flying while perhaps decreasing the respect in which it was held.

While these men were brave, the first recorded pilot strike in 1919 among the pilots who were flying the mail for the Post Office Department indicates that they were not interested in undergoing unnecessary risk. It came about when the pilot's concern for safety came in conflict with the traditional post office attitude so well expressed by the quotation, "Neither rain, nor snow, nor gloom of night, stay these couriers from the swift completion of their appointed rounds." When two pilots were discharged for staying on the ground in poor weather, the other pilots struck in protest, demanding the right to decide when it was safe to fly. A settlement was worked out under which the airport manager was given the final word in deciding when it was safe to fly.

On February 2, 1925, the first Air Mail Act was passed by Congress. It permitted the Postmaster General to contract for the carrying of the mails by private air carriers provided the rate paid to any particular carrier for its services was not over 80% of the revenue received by the Post Office from the airmail service it rendered. In other words the Congress did not intend to subsidize the carrying of the mail by air.

Another important piece of legislation in this period was the Air Commerce Act of 1926 which gave the Department of Commerce the responsibility for the first time to foster air commerce and to encourage the development of airports, airways, and so on. On the basis of these two acts the Post Office Department was able to turn the actual flying operations over to private air carriers during the years 1926–1927.

Two years of tremendous expansion in the air transport field followed. The boom started with the carriers bidding for contracts to fly the mail and with the captivating flight of Lindbergh across the Atlantic spurring interest in aviation. In 1927 the industry flew 8,700 passengers approximately 2,000,000 miles in scheduled operations. These carriers operated largely with pilots who had flown for the Post Office and with planes purchased from the same source.

The boom reached its peak during the next two years as capital became readily available to the industry in the enthusiasm of the stock market. Under a 1928 amendment to the Air Mail Act some airmail carriers were able to make large profits. Interestingly, this amendment allowed a situation in which a carrier was paid more by the government for carrying a pound of mail than the postage costs of sending such a package. This led to the questionable practice of a carrier's sending airmail material of significant weight (like a truck axle) to itself because it made a direct profit on every pound carried.

The boom came to an end with the stock market crash in late 1929. Many airlines failed and aviation stocks fell to a fraction (about one-fourth) of their 1929 highs.

On April 29, 1930, Congress passed the Watres Act in an attempt to improve the worsening financial conditions of the airline industry. This act gave sweeping powers to the Postmaster General to control and consolidate the airline industry—powers which the incumbent utilized to the fullest. The man in question, Postmaster General Brown, accomplished many things of great value to the scheduled airline industry in the first years of the 1930's. He established two new transcontinental routes: one from New York City to Los Angeles and the other from Atlanta to Los Angeles. He brought about needed consolidation among carriers. He used the fact that mail payments to air carriers under the Watres Act were based on the space made available for mail in the aircraft rather than the amount of mail carried to subsidize new passenger routes into areas where there was not enough of a volume of airmail to support the operation. He required the airmail carriers to carry passengers as well as mail. In essence, he created the major outlines of the air transportation system we have today.

The combination of airline failures plus the consolidations under the Watres Act more than matched the number of new carriers starting business in the early 1930's. As a result, the number of air carriers dropped from 46 in 1930 to 26 in 1934. Interestingly, however, the number of pilots and copilots in air transportation did not drop proportionately. On the contrary, the number of pilots and copilots in scheduled aviation rose from 661 in 1930 to 751 in 1934. These figures are presented in Table 2.1.

The picture of total pilot employment, however, was not as satisfactory. Aeronautical activities other than air transport were failing and releasing numerous pilots. Pilots in air transportation

TABLE 2.1 THE NUMBER OF U.S. AIR CARRIERS AND THE
SIZE OF THE PILOT GROUP, DOMESTIC AND
INTERNATIONAL OPERATIONS: 1928–1940

	Air Carriers			Pilots and Copilots		
Year	Domestic	Inter-national	Total	Domestic	Inter-national	Total
1928	34	—	34	294	—	294
1929	38	—	38	509	48	557
1930	43	3	46	580	81	661
1931	39	3	42	621	72	693
1932	32	3	35	632	77	709
1933	25	3	28	674	77	751
1934	24	2	26	659	92	751
1935	26	2	28	863	121	984
1936	24	2	26	1,042	186	1,228
1937	22	2	24	1,049	291	1,340
1938	16	2	18	1,127	278	1,405
1939	18	2	20	1,385	287	1,672
1940	19	3	22	1,910	340	2,250

SOURCES: CAA, *Statistical Handbook of Civil Aviation,* 1944, p. 33.
FAA Statistical Handbook of Aviation, 1959, pp. 75, 76, 91, and 93.

were experiencing greatly increased hours and the threat of wage reductions. Hours of flying had risen from about 10 per week prior to 1927 to 15 per week in 1929, and as high as 30 hours per week in 1931 in at least one case. Thus in 1931 the entire pilot group faced either unemployment, lower wages, or longer hours.[2]

As the financial conditions in the industry grew worse in 1930, the carriers looked for ways to cut costs. Cutting the wages of their employees, particularly the relatively high-paid pilots, was one obvious way, and the carriers were not slow to move in this direction. Their threatened wage reductions, however, brought about the inevitable consequences.

The first recorded reaction of the pilots came in the form of a secret meeting in Chicago of six veteran pilots to discuss the wage cuts and their fear of unemployment. This meeting resulted in the idea of the formation of an association of air pilots on the scheduled airlines—some 661 men at that time.

In the spring of 1931 the air carriers put into effect a nationwide cut for all pilots and copilots. In response, on July 27 pilot representatives met in Chicago and formed the Air Line Pilots Association. Less than 20 pilots were in attendance at this meeting but they represented all the major air carriers at that time. These men adopted a set of bylaws for the Association and elected David L. Behncke President.

Under Behncke's dynamic and colorful leadership, ALPA immediately turned its attention to the nation's capital. Within the first year ALPA sent a full-time representative to Washington to lobby for its interests, and Behncke often appeared "on the hill" to obtain something for the pilot group. To strengthen its position ALPA immediately sought affiliation with the AF of L, and was granted a charter in August 1931. That these political efforts were not in vain will become readily apparent in this history.

Apparently the Air Line Pilots Association had very little difficulty in organizing the pilot group. *The New York Times* reported ALPA had a membership of 450 mail and passenger pilots on November 1, 1931, which would indicate that about 65% of the air transport pilots had joined.[3]

[2] David, *op. cit.*, p. 198.
[3] *The New York Times*, November 1, 1931, IX, 7:5.

David spoke of the formation of ALPA as follows:

The result [of the nationwide wage reduction] was the immediate
and almost spontaneous formation of the Air Line Pilots Association. A short period of intensive undercover work by pilots well-
known to each other brought about the formation of local
organizations for all the principal airlines. The establishment of
the association to the point of including employees of all air mail
carriers except one of the smallest seems to have been an accomplished fact before the carriers had any clear realization of what
was happening. The association soon included more than three-
quarters of the actual line pilots of the United States.[4]

The second recorded pilot strike occurred in January 1932 when
Century Air Lines announced it was going to cut wages although
the rates it was paying at the time were lower than the industry
average. At that time pilots generally were averaging $621 per
month and were flying about 86 hours per month. At the same time
copilots were earning $231 for a month's work that averaged 125
flight hours and hours spent working on the ground. The announcement by Century Air Lines coincided with its offer to fly all the
mails at one-half of the current rates. At the same time the House
Committee on the Post Office and Post Roads was meeting to consider airmail legislation, but through efforts of the pilots it became
a forum in which the conditions leading to this strike were aired.
As a result Century did not obtain its mail contract, and the Committee told the Postmaster General it desired the pilots of all airlines involved in future airmail contract negotiations to have the
privilege of collective representation.

The next crisis in the airline labor situation occurred in September 1933 when five major carriers announced they were going to
change their method of compensating pilots. The dispute this announcement caused is so important to this history that a word or
two about the change is required here. Traditionally pilots had
received a flat monthly salary plus so many cents per mile. The use
of methods of wage payment which included some type of mileage
formula was not uncommon in the transportation industry. For
decades the operating crafts of the railroads had been paid under

_____
[4] David, *op. cit.*, p. 198.

a separate formula for freight and for passenger service which contained mileage elements. The change the companies announced in 1933 was to shift from the mileage rate to an hourly rate based on the number of flight hours flown. This was a vital difference. The crucial point is that throughout the history of aviation aircraft speeds have been increasing. In such a situation the pilots stand to gain more pay under a mileage formula because the faster planes will allow them to cover more miles in any given period of time. The carriers equally stand to gain on an hourly basis because with faster equipment they can get more flying out of their pilots within any given period of time.

The reaction of ALPA to the announced change by the five carriers was to threaten a nationwide strike. When the carriers went ahead with their plans, ALPA asked the National Labor Board (NLB) to hear the case. The NLB decided to hear the dispute and established a three-man fact-finding board composed of Behncke, L. D. Seymour, President of American Airways, and Judge Bernard L. Shientag, as neutral. The appointment of this board was an excellent early example of the ability of ALPA to use both economic force and appeals to the government to obtain its goals.

The National Industrial Recovery Act had established the National Labor Board and also provided for the establishment of industry codes which, among other things, were to dictate the wages, hours, and working conditions for employees in each industry. When the Air Transport Codes had been established, ALPA successfully had had the pilots excluded on the grounds that they were professional employees because it feared the minimum conditions of the codes might become the maximum conditions. ALPA was perfectly willing, however, to have the NLB provisions of the same act apply, and under a nationwide strike threat succeeded in having its 1933 wage dispute settled by the NLB. The decision in this dispute established a new method of compensating pilots which still forms the basis for pilot pay.

The fact-finding board held meetings on October 4 and 27, 1933, during which each side argued for the method of pay (hourly or mileage) which would best suit its position. The board then made recommendations to the National Labor Board in what has since been referred to as the Shientag Report. Essentially it recommended a pay formula that embodied both mileage and hourly pay principles, and also suggested a limit of 85 hours of flying per month for a pilot or a copilot. These recommendations were promulgated in NLB Decision #83 which became the accepted standard of pay in the industry. The essential elements of the pay formula have continued to apply as have the 85 hours of flying limitation. Without doubt Decision #83 was the most far-reaching ruling ever issued in the airline labor field.

On February 9, 1934, the government annulled all airmail contracts. This action was prompted by the government's feeling that several of the contracts had been obtained in 1930 under the Watres Act through collusive arrangements between the Post Office Department and the managements of favored carriers. The government also had a direct interest in the airmail situation because it had paid an estimated $34,506,435 in direct subsidy to the airmail carriers in the period 1931–1933.[5] The army was ordered to fly all the airmail, but after several army pilots had been killed in accidents, the President ordered a sharp reduction in the amount of army flying. This situation led Congress on June 12, 1934, to pass the Air Mail Act of 1934.

The new Air Mail Act had important effects on the air carriers and the pilots' association. In the first place, it permitted the carriers to submit bids once again to obtain mail contracts provided they were not the same companies which had been accused of collusive practices in the past. This led to token changes in the names of several carriers. Many of them changed from "airways" to "air lines," or "airlines" at this time. Several management officials were purged for their supposed parts in the previous bad practices. Under their new contracts the carriers started carrying the mail again in the summer of 1934.

The act also divided the regulation of the airline industry among three governmental agencies. The Post Office Department still awarded the airmail contracts and established the postal regulations incident thereto. The Interstate Commerce Commission was given the authority to set the rates the carriers could charge for all their services, including both mail and passenger rates. The

---

[5] *Ibid.*, p. 167.

Department of Commerce retained its control over aviation safety and the maintenance of the airways.

Through the Air Mail Act of 1934 ALPA was able to accomplish an important political victory. The practical effect of Decision #83 was negligible when it was announced on May 10, 1934, because the five carriers to which it applied were changing their corporate identities, and the legality of the NLB itself was in question. ALPA was able to have the matter resolved in its favor, however, by having a clause inserted in the Air Mail Act of 1934 which required a carrier to conform to "the rate of compensation and the working conditions" of the decisions of the National Labor Board as a condition for obtaining an airmail contract. These requirements applied to all flights of an airmail carrier but did not apply to the non-mail carriers. Through this legislation ALPA obtained a minimum wage law for its membership at all the important air carriers. Perhaps part of the pilots' success in the legislative area can be explained as reaction by the Congress against the airline managements for their parts in the collusive arrangements which necessitated the new act.

The final important political effort on the part of ALPA in this period attained success on April 10, 1936, with the passage by Congress of Title II of the Railway Labor Act. In essence Title II placed the airlines under the procedures for handling labor disputes over new employment terms which had been established in 1926 to apply to the railroads. These procedures included direct negotiation, mediation by the National Mediation Board (NMB), voluntary arbitration, and finally a Presidential Emergency Fact-Finding Board. The airlines also became subject to the authority of the NMB in regard to procedures governing union representation elections. The airlines did not come under the National Railroad Adjustment Board which had been established under a 1934 amendment to the Railway Labor Act to settle grievances under existing employment conditions. Instead provision was made to set up a similar National Air Transport Adjustment Board for the airline industry if and when the NMB deemed it necessary. Such a board was not established, and grievances came to be handled on an individual carrier basis utilizing private arbitration.

After the passage of Title II, ALPA shifted its attention to the collective bargaining area. Until that time ALPA had frequently taken its disputes to the NLB and later to the NLRB. They included the following matters of contention: discrimination, coercion, labor representation, union recognition, working conditions, wage rates, methods of payment, and hours of work. In one dispute in 1936 ALPA urged that pilots be limited to a certain number of miles per month in order to stabilize employment with the approach of faster aircraft—an oft-repeated theme throughout its history.

The first recorded ALPA move toward collective bargaining with an individual carrier came in 1938 when the National Mediation Board reported mediation of a dispute in which ALPA and an air carrier formed a joint board to discuss the conditions surrounding the discharge of one of its members. The first ALPA contract was signed in May 1939[6] with American Airlines. It was followed shortly by another contract because the NMB reported having two ALPA contracts in its files as of June 30, 1939. Thus, ALPA was headed in the direction of "business unionism."[7]

In 1937 the NMB reported that airline mechanics and radio operators had begun to form unions and were holding initial collective bargaining conferences leading to labor contracts.[8] Only the mechanics must have met with much success because as late as June 30, 1941, the NMB reported that except for the pilots and mechanics, airline employees had failed to take advantage of their rights to organize under the Railway Labor Act.[9]

The Civil Aeronautics Act of 1938 for the first time brought all aviation activities under one agency, the Civil Aeronautics Authority (CAA). This act permitted the industry to have a degree of stability and cohesiveness that had been previously lacking. For ALPA the act continued the minimum wage requirements of the Air Mail Act of 1934 and, therefore, of Decision #83. In the 1938 act, however, the requirements applied to any carrier which wanted a route certificate rather than merely to those seeking a mail contract.

The Second World War brought about the same type of boost to aviation as the First World War. Thousands of planes were built

[6] *4th Annual Report of the National Mediation Board.*

[7] *5th Annual Report of the National Mediation Board.*

[8] *3rd Annual Report of the National Mediation Board.*

[9] *7th Annual Report of the National Mediation Board.*

with new designs, thousands of pilots were trained, and the knowledge of aviation was greatly enhanced. The war activities also kept the airlines operating at their maximum capacities throughout the first half of the 1940's. Although every phase of their activities was controlled by the government, the air carriers remained under private ownership.

After the war the carriers expanded their capacity rapidly in anticipation of a boom in business. They had to rehire former pilot employees and in addition they hired scores of ex-service pilots. They purchased the new, four-motored DC-4 and Lockheed Constellation equipment in order to obtain their increased speeds and load-carrying capacities. That some carriers had overestimated the market potential became painfully obvious during 1947 when several hundred pilots had to be furloughed. Total pilot and copilot employment rose sharply from 5,897 in 1945 to 7,220 in 1946 and then dropped to 6,637 in 1947.[10]

Competition of a new type began for the major carriers in the late 1940's. The Civil Aeronautics Board, a sister agency to the CAA, started certifying air carriers to give local service to small communities. While these lines had the beneficial effect of bringing passenger and freight traffic into the airports of the larger cities where this traffic could pick up a flight of a major carrier, these lines also obtained routes that some of the major carriers might have applied for and obtained. In some cases the routes of the local service lines were not actually between small communities. The encroachment of the local service lines into the routes of the major carriers has not abated since.

During the decade of the 1940's ALPA put its major emphasis on the negotiation of labor agreements. It also made clear the fact that it would not accept permanently the wage scales in the formula set forth in Decision #83. ALPA's successful attempts to obtain wage increases were highlighted by disputes with TWA when that air carrier twice obtained new types of Boeing equipment which were more productive than the aircraft then in use, and by a dispute with the industry in 1947 over the introduction of the DC-4 and the Constellation. The latter dispute stands out as the first serious attempt by ALPA to gain through collective bargaining a

[10] *FAA Statistical Handbook of Aviation,* 1959, pp. 76 and 93.

monthly limitation on the number of miles a pilot should be allowed to fly, and as the first attempt of the airline industry to employ industry-wide bargaining. These disputes will be described in Chapter 4.

SUMMARY COMMENTS

The overriding significance of the material in this chapter to the airline industrial relations system is the early and continuous interest, regulation, and support received from the government. The infant industry was brought into being by the government. The government provided the original investment, much of the early pilot training, the flight equipment, the airports, the air traffic facilities, and the source of continuing revenue. In addition, the responsibility for accidents in the early, more hazardous days was shouldered by the government. Thus, this was not a case of the government's moving in on a young industry whose patterns had not jelled. In this case the government formed the original patterns.

The continuous nature of the government's close connection with this industry will be detailed in the next chapter. Suffice it to say here that the government still provides financial support for and heavy regulation of this industry. These facts mean that many of the decisions made concerning this industrial relations system are either directly or indirectly made by the government or are tripartite in nature. The airline managements and the flight crew unions are restricted in the decisions they can make compared with similar parties in industries not directly regulated or supported by the government.

Several aspects of the early history of ALPA are of significance. First, one should not assume that the formation of a pilots' union was inevitable. In level of pay, in degree of skill, in possessing a common body of knowledge, and in feeling a sense of belonging to a high status profession, pilots, particularly in the early days of aviation, had some of the markings of a professional group. Thus, they might well have formed a professional association much like the American Medical Association or the National Education Association and have looked askance either for a number of years or permanently at trade union activities. As it was, ALPA did not indulge in negotiations until the late 1930's, in part perhaps because of professional feelings, in part because of success on the legislative front, and in part because prior to the 1936 amendments to the Railway Labor Act airline managements generally refused to recognize or to deal with it. Given these facts, the advent of the Depression and the consequent unfortunate treatment the airlines gave their pilots in terms of reduced pay, increased hours, and a shift to hourly pay are of prime importance as the impetuses to the formation of a pilots' union.

Once formed, it is significant to ALPA's growth and strength that Mr. Behncke was really very adroit in providing results, first in Washington and then at the bargaining table. The importance of winning the mileage pay component in Decision #83 and making it permanent through ensuing legislation cannot be overstressed. As will be detailed in Chapter 4, it meant that the pilots had won an automatic improvement factor based on productivity. The wisdom of seeking coverage under the Railway Labor Act rather than the Wagner Act or a bill specifically designed for pilots is less clearcut. It meant that the pilots came under the act's formal procedures for settling disputes over new or changed contract terms, and these procedures have come in recent years to be regarded by many as a quagmire. As will be seen, however, it has been a quagmire in which the pilots have prospered. At the same time, avoiding the unworkable procedures of a National Adjustment Board to handle grievances under the act as it applies to the railroads saved the pilots and the airline managements untold frustration and poor contract administration.

The information given in this chapter concerning World War II and the immediate postwar years is significant in three regards. First, one sees the government providing the training for a bountiful supply of flight crew members. Second, one sees the CAB fostering increased competition among airlines, thus increasing the likelihood of industrial relations problems. Third, the postwar period of pilot unemployment rekindled the pilots' fears regarding job security, frustrated copilots by slowing their career progressions, and made very real the fear of technological unemployment with the advent of turbo-jet aircraft around 1958.

CHAPTER 3

Factors Influencing
Airline Industrial Relations

THE AIRLINES and their unions operate in an environment subject to constraints not typical of other industries. These environmental factors could be called determinants in that they have tended to determine the nature of the airline industrial relations system. One factor, for example, affects negotiations between the parties because under the Railway Labor Act the airlines and the unions must follow a definite bargaining procedure. Weather conditions continually change airline flight operations, and these changes in turn affect wages, hours, and working conditions of the flight crews. As a result crew members have been anxious to obtain guarantees which would protect them from the vagaries of the weather. The effect of these and other environmental factors on the airline industrial relations system will be discussed below.

These factors have been divided into the following categories: (1) governmental influence over the airline industry, (2) the economics of the airline industry, and (3) the nature of airline operations. In some cases these categories overlap. This is particularly true of the influences of the government and airline economics.

Two further aspects need to be emphasized. First, not all the factors which influence the airline industrial relations scene will be presented. An attempt has been made to select those factors having a unique and/or important influence. Second, in this chapter the description of the various factors will receive more stress than the explanation of their specific influences. While their general influence will be presented, the analysis of their specific influence will have to await the presentation of detailed characteristics of the airline industrial relations system later in this book.

GOVERNMENTAL INFLUENCE OVER THE AIRLINE INDUSTRY

The influence of the government will be subdivided into four areas. These are governmental labor regulation, economic regulation, safety regulation, and financial aid to aviation.

Governmental Labor Regulation

On April 10, 1936, Congress amended the Railway Labor Act to include the airlines and their employees. This action had the strong endorsement of ALPA.

The five stated purposes of the act are as follows:

(1) To avoid any interruption to commerce or to the operation of any carrier engaged therein;
(2) To forbid any limitation upon freedom of association among employees or any denial . . . of the right of employees to join a labor organization;
(3) To provide for the complete independence of carriers and of employees in . . . self-organization . . . ;
(4) To provide for the prompt and orderly settlement of all disputes concerning rates of pay, rules, and working conditions, and
(5) To provide for the prompt and orderly settlement of all . . . grievances. . . .

Fundamentally this act gave airline employees the right to organize into unions and to bargain collectively through representatives of their own choosing. Further, it placed a duty on a carrier to treat with the representatives of its employees for the purposes of the act. Both parties had to follow the procedures of the act for handling disputes arising over new conditions of employment and for processing grievances through final and binding arbitration. In that it established these basic ground rules, the Railway Labor Act has exerted a tremendous influence on the airline industrial relations situation.

The Railway Labor Act established the National Mediation Board as an independent agency in the executive branch of the government. The two important functions of the National Mediation Board are to decide representation questions when disputes arise as to who are the proper union representatives of a group of employees, and to use its good services to mediate: (1) disputes which concern changes in rates of pay, rules, or working conditions, (2) any unadjusted dispute not referable to the grievance procedure of the act, or (3) any labor emergency at any time.

As to the function providing for decision on representation questions, there are two matters of interest. The act calls for employees to be represented by classes or crafts (the terms are used interchangeably) on a carrier-wide basis. This means that all the pilots employed by one airline will be represented as a whole. Of course, the majority of any class or craft has the right to determine who shall be its representatives. The National Mediation Board can influence collective bargaining decisively under the representation authority by deciding what types of employees make up a class or craft. As will be detailed in Chapter 8, the Board's decision on craft representation profoundly influenced airline labor relations in the cockpits in a dispute in 1959–1961.

The second important influence of the Board in representation disputes comes from its authority to decide exactly which employees are allowed representation under the act. The act permits "employees and subordinate officials" to be represented. The real question therefore becomes where in the management hierarchy does a man cease being a "subordinate official." Throughout the years the Board has liberally interpreted this term, and as a result it has permitted several echelons of management to be represented by the appropriate class or craft union. These decisions by the Board have influenced the willingness of lower echelons of management to discipline employees who are fellow union members and may have influenced the bargaining strength of some carriers by having members of the same union on both sides of the bargaining table.[1]

The mediation function of the National Mediation Board is carried out as the second step of the Railway Labor Act procedure for settling disputes over changes in rates, hours, or working conditions. The first step is direct negotiation between the parties without a mediator present. Under the act a carrier may not change any conditions of work without giving 30 days' notice, and if a

[1] See Chapter 10.

dispute ensues, it may not change any conditions of work without going through all the steps of the procedure. Similarly, a union may not legally strike until all the steps have been pursued.

The Board starts its mediation after direct negotiations have failed to produce a settlement. It will continue to mediate until a settlement is reached, or until it becomes convinced that its efforts will be unsuccessful. In the latter event the Board must offer voluntary arbitration to the parties. If one side does not agree to arbitration, as is usually the case, the Board must notify the parties that its mediatory efforts have failed. The parties must still maintain the *status quo* for another 30 days after which, with one exception, the carrier may change the conditions of work over which bargaining has transpired, and the union is free to strike.

The exception occurs when the Board believes a dispute "threatens substantially to interrupt interstate commerce to a degree such as to deprive any section of the country of essential transportation service." In that case the Board must notify the President of the emergency and he may create a Presidential Emergency Board to investigate the dispute and to make recommendations. If the President creates an Emergency Board, the parties must maintain the *status quo* until 30 days after its report has been submitted. Thereafter the parties are free to use any legal means to settle the dispute including economic force.

The government also exerts an influence over grievances or over interpretations of contracts covering existing rates, hours, and working conditions. The Railway Labor Act requires that they be processed through some type of final and binding arbitration. In the case of the railroads, disputes of these kinds are finally decided by the National Railroad Board of Adjustment on a nation-wide basis. This may be an appropriate type of arbitration in the railroad situation in which the parties traditionally have agreed to negotiate settlements that apply on a nation-wide basis. In the airlines, however, where the unions traditionally have refused to use industry-wide bargaining, as is their right under the act, both negotiations and arbitration have been conducted on an individual carrier basis. The act gives the National Mediation Board the authority to establish a National Air Transport Adjustment Board when and if it deems such action necessary, but this authority has never been exercised because the airline parties, in general, have agreed to use private grievance arbitration. In the grievance area, therefore, governmental regulation has influenced airline industrial relations by essentially requiring arbitration.

Governmental Economic Regulation

The Federal Aviation Act gives the Civil Aeronautics Board the authority to control the entrance of airlines into the industry by giving it the power to issue to them certificates of public convenience and necessity granting the right to engage in air transportation between stated cities. In order to obtain and hold a certificate each carrier must meet the economic conditions which are spelled out in the act or which the CAB believes are necessary to implement the act. Because no air carrier may operate without such a certificate the economic control of the CAB is inescapable. Carriers are, however, essentially free to change schedules, equipment, accommodations, and facilities.

The CAB has the power to approve the rates charged by each airline and to set the airmail rates under which each carrier will be compensated for carrying the mails. The CAB is required to consider in connection with rates the need of each airline under efficient management for sufficient revenue "to maintain and continue the development of air transportation to the extent and of the character and quality required for the commerce of the United States, the Postal Service, and the national defense." The airline industry traditionally has received a government subsidy under the guise of payment for mail service. Since 1953, however, the government has applied various formulas to decide what part of these payments is for airmail services rendered by the carrier and what part is government subsidy. The Postmaster General now pays the former amount to the carrier from his appropriations while the CAB pays the part labeled subsidy.

The economic control of the CAB over the air carriers includes many aspects of their ownership. Accounting procedures, economic reports, and financial reports are required. No mergers, consolidations, purchases, leases or acquisitions of any part of another carrier, or interlocking relationships between air carriers or persons controlling air carriers are permitted unless approved by the CAB.

Once a carrier has obtained CAB approval for some financial arrangement, however, it is exempt from the provisions of the anti-trust laws in carrying it out.

The Federal Aviation Act directly influences airline industrial relations by making compliance with the minimum wages, maximum hours, and working conditions of Decision #83 and the provisions of the Railway Labor Act a condition for obtaining a certificate of public convenience and necessity. Interestingly, the CAB has the power to exempt carriers from all its economic regulations except the maximum hours limitation of Decision #83. It is free to permit deviations from the minimum wage requirements of Decision #83 only in certain very limited circumstances.

Governmental Safety Regulation

The Federal Aviation Act of 1958 gives the Administrator of the Federal Aviation Agency (FAA) the authority to control the safety aspects of aviation through the issuance of various types of certificates without which it is illegal to carry on most aviation activities. He is specifically charged with the responsibility of prescribing minimum standards of design for aircraft and parts; reasonable rules and minimum standards for inspection, overhaul, and servicing of aircraft and parts; reasonable rules governing reserves of aircraft; reasonable rules governing maximum hours of airmen and other airline employees; and reasonable rules applying to civil aeronautics he finds necessary for national security and air safety.

The Administrator exerts his most direct influence over airline industrial relations through his control of airmen certificates. Each pilot, copilot, and flight engineer must possess the type of airman certificate required by his position. The requirements for these certificates are set by the Administrator, and with them he ensures that every flight officer meets his minimum standards of health, training, proficiency, etc.

The Administrator has the power to check the standards of any airman at any time and to revoke his certificate for proper cause. In 1959 he passed a regulation which in effect made pilots retire at the age of 60, a ruling which influenced airline labor relations considerably.

The Administrator issues type certificates for aircraft, aircraft engines, propellers, and appliances, and production certificates to manufacturers, both of which certificates apply to the design of the aircraft or part. He issues an air worthiness certificate which the registered owner of any particular plane must obtain before it may be flown and, finally, an operating certificate which a carrier must have to operate.

The CAB has the responsibility to investigate aircraft accidents under the Federal Aviation Act of 1958. The investigation of accidents is an area of great concern to the Air Line Pilots Association because part of the aircraft accident report has always been an assessment of the probable cause of the accident. Under the previous act the CAB and the CAA were both under the Department of Commerce. Since the Board investigated accidents and the Authority was responsible for ensuring aviation safety, ALPA did not believe that the procedures had enough inherent objectivity when the cause of accidents was being ascertained, say, between assigning the cause to pilot error or to a mistake made by a CAA traffic controller. Under the present act ALPA believes it has finally obtained an independent agency to investigate aircraft accidents. This act specifically charges the CAB to investigate aircraft accidents in accordance with the rules which the CAB itself sets up, to report the facts and the probable cause of the accident, and to make recommendations to the Administrator of the FAA of ways to prevent similar accidents in the future.

Governmental Financial Aid to Aviation

The FAA Administrator is authorized and directed to ensure safe and efficient use of the navigable air space; to acquire and improve the air navigation facilities; to see to their operation and maintenance; to authorize federal expenditures on airports; and to formulate necessary traffic rules.

Under these powers, the Administrator and his predecessors have built an immense air traffic network which the air carriers use at no cost. By 1958 the FAA reported there were a total of 182,575 miles of airways in this country. An airway is a path through the sky ten miles wide and separated by 1,000 feet of altitude. To control navigation and movement along these airways the FAA in

1963 operated 927 radio range stations, 278 nondirectional radio beacons, 210 airport towers, 32 airways centers, 68 combined station-towers, 336 flight service stations, and 237 instrument landing stations. In essence, federal funds make available a vast aerial highway system to private, military, and air transport aviation.[2]

Two broad forms of governmental financial aid from which the airlines benefit have been mentioned in this chapter: direct subsidy to the carriers and the federal airways system. The remaining broad use of federal funds for aviation comes in the form of grant agreements made with local governments to assist in the construction or improvement of airports.

There can be no doubt that the expenditure of time, money, and effort by the federal government in direct subsidy, in aiding air navigation, and in helping to finance airport construction is of great value to the air carriers. Competing transportation industries believe that too much government aid is available to the airline industry. In any event one factor seems clear. The aid the airlines receive from the federal government is accompanied by a great deal of regulation limiting the freedom of an airline in the conduct of its daily operations. Almost every step in the progress of an airplane, from the time it leaves the ramp until it stops at the ramp at its next destination, is controlled in some way by government.

THE ECONOMICS OF THE AIRLINE INDUSTRY

The purposes of this section are to point out a few of the salient aspects of airline economics and to indicate their general influence upon the industrial relations situation. No attempt will be made to discuss the complexities of airline economics because that is unnecessary for this study and certainly beyond its scope.

The government controls entry into the industry and into any particular segment of it through its power to award routes. For example, since 1955 the CAB has increased the amount of competition within the industry by awarding new competitive routes and by following a policy of increasing the route structures of the

[2] *FAA Statistical Handbook of Aviation,* 1964, p. 27.

medium-sized trunks relative to those of the Big Four.[3] The increase in competition is indicated by the number of carriers authorized to operate between various pairs of cities, known as "air travel markets." There had been no competition over 60% of the country's 400 most important air travel markets prior to 1955. By June 1958 the CAB had granted new route certificates to the point where 87% of these air travel markets had at least two air carriers competing with each other over them.[4] Another way to express this increased competition is in terms of the average number of carriers competing over the 400 best air travel markets. In the three years prior to 1958 the average number of carriers per market had risen from 1.5 to 2.2. When the 50 most heavily traveled markets are considered, the average number of competing carriers had risen over the same period from about 2.0 to about 3.0[5] This increased competition and the emphasis it gave to letting medium-sized trunks move into greater direct competition with the Big Four have meant that more of the trunks have had to move quickly into the most modern aircraft in order to capture a new market or to maintain an old one.

The government exerts an influence over the economics of this industry through its rate-setting powers and therefore through its ability to influence profits. For several years prior to 1958 the CAB "generally required the trunk line carriers to maintain the existing level of fares," but since then it has permitted domestic passenger fare increases which "raised first-class and coach fares by approximately 26% and 30%, respectively."[6] During recent years the CAB has also permitted a variety of promotional fares designed to create new business. The major domestic passenger fare changes from 1958 to 1963 are presented in Table 3.1. The net effect was that the average passenger revenue per passenger mile rose from 5.64 cents in 1958 to 6.17 cents in 1963.

In November 1960 the CAB decided that an "allowable rate of return on investment" for the Big Four was 10.25% and for the

[3] Paul W. Cherington, *The Status and Economic Significance of the Airline Equipment Investment Program,* p. 9.

[4] *Ibid.,* p. 5.

[5] *Ibid.,* p. 10.

[6] CAB, *Annual Report,* 1961 and 1963 editions.

TABLE 3.1   MAJOR PASSENGER FARE CHANGES,
DOMESTIC TRUNK LINES: 1958–1963

Date	Nature of Change
February 1958	All fares increased 4% plus $1 per ticket (about a 6.6% increase).
October 1958	Eliminated or reduced certain discounts (about a 3.5% increase).
Early 1959	Allowed jet surcharges ranging from $2 to $10 per ticket depending on the length of the flight.
Early 1960	All fares increased 2.5% plus $1 per ticket. (Other increases more limited in scope were allowed, e.g., in major transcontinental and north-south markets, jet coach fares were allowed to increase to 75% of first class jet fares.)
February 1962	All fares increased 3%.

SOURCE: CAB, *Annual Report,* 1958–1963.

other trunks 11.125%.[7] As shown in Table 3.2, over the ten-year period 1955–1964 the rate of return on investment of the domestic trunk lines approached the "allowable rates" only during the first and the last year.

Periodically throughout the years the airline industry has had to find funds with which to purchase new, more productive equipment. Relatively large amounts have been needed, particularly for the purchase of jet aircraft since 1958, as shown by the increase in the net investment in flight equipment of the domestic trunk lines from $725 million in 1957 to $1.98 billion as of September 30, 1964.[8] Since the Second World War the primary source of funds for equipment purchases has been long-term debt. As Professor John H. Frederick has written:

> Probably never before in the business history of the United States has there been an industry which has required such a huge relative capital expansion in such a short period of time as has been true of the airline industry since 1958. The intensity of need

[7] CAB, *Annual Report,* 1961, p. 27.
[8] ATA, *Facts and Figures: Air Transportation,* 1959 and 1965 editions.

TABLE 3.2.   SUMMARY OF PROFIT OR LOSS, DOMESTIC
TRUNK LINES: 1955–1964
(000,000)

Year	Total Operating Revenues	Net Operating Income	Net Profit or Loss	Rate of Return on Investment*
1955	$1,133	$123	$63	11.8%
1956	1,263	101	58	9.4
1957	1,420	42	27	4.9
1958	1,513	95	45	6.6
1959	1,799	105	62	7.1
1960	1,943	35	—	2.8
1961	2,026	−8	−35	1.5
1962	2,250	75	8	4.1
1963	2,452	144	11	4.2
1964†	2,790	296	137	10.1

* Net income before interest and after taxes as a percentage of net worth and long-term debt. Not reduced by those tax benefits resulting from the investment credit which, under provisions of the revenue law, will be excluded by the CAB in its official method of calculating the rate of return.

† Preliminary figures.

SOURCE: ATA, *Facts and Figures: Air Transportation,* 1959 and 1965.

has been the product both of the amount needed and of the short time within which the need had to be met coming at a time when there was a universal shortage of funds and a great demand for capital.[9]

He also points out that the large amount of funded debt among the airlines is dangerous because "it imposes relatively heavy fixed charges on an industry whose margin of revenue after operating expenses has fluctuated from time to time and, on the average, has been low."[10]

Because the airline managements have been concerned about what they consider inadequate profits and rates of return, they have been anxious to purchase more productive equipment in order to

[9] John H. Frederick, *Commercial Air Transportation,* p. 334.
[10] *Ibid.,* p. 332.

obtain their better operating efficiencies and lower unit costs. In addition, competition has forced them to move rapidly to purchase the latest, fastest aircraft available.[11] Purchasing new equipment has had a profound influence on airline industrial relations. It has meant that repeatedly the flight crew unions have been in a position to demand a share of the increased productivity represented by the more productive aircraft. At the same time the airline managements have been anxious to reach a labor settlement in order to be free to put the new equipment in use, and they have been aware that the new equipment would bring efficiencies out of which some increased wage rates could be met. There has been no more impor- tant characteristic of the airline industrial relations scene in recent years than the continued drive of the flight crew unions for a share in the increased productivity of new flight equipment.

When the local service lines are considered, direct federal sub- sidy becomes the important influence of airline economics on indus- trial relations. All the local service lines regularly obtain direct subsidies as a vital part of their economic survival. In 1963 these feeders received $69.2 million in direct subsidies which represented 82.2% of the total subsidy awarded ($84.2 million).[12] Including this subsidy the feeders had a total operating profit of only $5.1 million in 1963.[13] The trunks received no subsidy in 1963 and had not for several years. The industrial relations situation at the local service lines is strongly influenced by the federal subsidy because it gives them their ability to pay increased wage rates. This situa- tion tends to be accentuated by the attitude of the CAB in regard to negotiated wage rates. The CAB assumes negotiators will succeed in arriving at as fair and as economical wage rates as is possible. Such an attitude, however, on the part of the agency which also decides on the amounts of subsidy may well itself affect the attitudes of airline and union negotiators as they bargain over wage rates.

[11] Frederick W. Gill and Gilbert L. Bates, *Airline Competition* (Boston: Division of Research, Harvard Business School, 1949), pp. 91–92. These authors concluded that in the postwar period, airline competition emerged as the most important single influence on new aircraft purchase. Other reasons were anticipated lower unit costs, high public demand for space, and a desire to render specialized services.

[12] CAB, *Annual Report,* 1963, p. 16.

[13] ATA, *Facts and Figures: Air Transportation,* 1965, p. 26.

THE NATURE OF AIRLINE OPERATIONS

In this section a few of the characteristics of airline operations which influence industrial relations will be discussed. For the most part these are characteristics with which most people are familiar. They are presented here merely to highlight their effects on industrial relations in the industry.

By its very nature an airline must be a far-flung operation in which many small groups work with a minimum of supervision or with no supervision at all. Flight crew employees, for example, have no supervisors with them during flight operations except in rare instances. The first pilot (sometimes called the captain) is in absolute command of the plane during flight, and he also possesses the authority to decide whether any of his flights will take off or not. The pilots are entrusted with equipment which can cost up to $5 million and with the safety of all the passengers and crew. They can also affect the direct operating costs of their carriers by the countless decisions they make which may either shorten or lengthen a flight by a significant amount. These characteristics of airline operations influence industrial relations in the selection and training of personnel, the steps managements are willing to take to make the flight crews satisfied with their jobs, the continual importance placed on employee health, the hours that flight crews will be used consecutively, and so forth. In short, the nature of flight operations demands the employment of large numbers of highly skilled, physically fit aviators who, incidentally, are accustomed to command. Their presence exerts a strong influence on airline industrial relations.

Interestingly for this study, the job requirements for pilots differ somewhat from those for the flight engineers. Because there is no supervision on board, a pilot must be self-reliant and able to command. The flight engineer must be able to do a highly skilled job, but he does not need to have the self-reliance or the command abilities. The demands of safety require that all flight officers be in excellent health, but again the requirements for the pilots are stiffer and they are checked more frequently. All the flight officers face the very real threat of losing their jobs early in their careers through health deficiencies which normally would not affect the employment of a manufacturing worker. Shifting from one aircraft type to another affects a pilot more than it does a flight engineer because aspects of the latter's job show more consistency among aircraft types. This fact means that a pilot must spend relatively more time in training than a flight engineer when a new aircraft is put into service. Finally, because of his strategic position the pilot is in a much stronger position to shut a carrier down during a strike than is the flight engineer.

These requirements of their jobs have great effects on the industrial relations that have developed between the carriers and these two groups of employees.

The nature of the airline industry makes severe and unique demands on the lives of its flight officers. They must come to work at all hours of the day and night throughout the entire year. Although the nature of their jobs makes them highly skilled and important men to their company, their usual contact with the company is with the personnel in the airline dispatching office. Rarely do they have any contact with officers of the company, even with the officers in the operations department. This inevitably leads to frustrations and inconsistencies about their relations with their company. One writer believes that the frustrations of these very capable men, upon whom airline managements seldom call for advice, leads them to adopt militant trade unionism.[14]

Finally, in a very real sense flight operations can be seen as a continual struggle of men and aircraft against the weather. The weather is constantly changing flight schedules—either lengthening them, shortening them, or canceling them. As these events occur, they affect the wages, hours, and working conditions of the flight crew members. The influence of this one factor has led to a dominant characteristic of the airline industrial relations scene—the continual comparison of the scheduled situation with the way the flight was actually flown because of weather conditions. Much of the effort of flight officers throughout the years has been to obtain guarantees of their wages, hours, and working conditions regardless of how the weather affected their flights.

[14] Robert Sheehan, "What's Eating the Airline Pilots?" *Fortune,* April 1959, p. 122.

Summary Comments

The material in the first section of this chapter indicated once again how this industry is heavily regulated and controlled by the government. Much of this government activity affects the industrial relations situation. For example, the government can dictate the minimum training and qualifications required of flight crew members. In union-management relations generally such requirements are set unilaterally by the employer or jointly with the union. In the airline industry a third party sets them, and the management and unions are placed in the position of having to persuade the FAA to meet their desires. With hazard to crew members, passengers, and the general populace involved, the government has a legitimate interest in seeing that proper precautions are taken regarding crew members and regarding all aspects of aviation, but such precautions provide constraints within which the industrial relations system must operate. This fact gives a continuous political tone to the system.

The government makes decisions which affect the bargaining power of the airlines. For example, by controlling prices and by fostering competition the government can influence the airlines' ability to pay increased labor costs. In addition, the CAB is supposed to allow prices and to set airmail rates with a view to compensating properly efficient airline managements. Potentially, therefore, the CAB could stiffen the backs of the airline managements by not allowing airlines to pass along to consumers the cost of what the CAB might consider excessively expensive labor agreements. That the CAB does not do so at least arguably weakens the resistance of airline managements at the bargaining table.

The impacts of airline economics will be analyzed in Chapter 10. Suffice it here to say that such factors as the advent of ever more productive flight equipment, with consequent lower unit costs, the tight financial positions of carriers, the low proportion of total costs represented by flight crew wages, and the freedom of the airlines to pass labor cost increases along to the consumer in an inelastic demand situation have combined to weaken airline managements' resistence to union demands.

The nature of airline operations places a set of unusual technological constraints on this industrial relations system. The constraints are unusual in relation to the familiar manufacturing plant in which the production and maintenance employees are represented by a union. For example, flight crew members move through space as they carry out their jobs. They frequently must eat and sleep hundreds of miles from their homes. They work odd and irregular hours. Their work requires lengthy training, a high level of skill and coordination, unusually high health standards, and forced retirement at the age of 60. In addition, they are subject to some degree of hazard and are responsible for lives and property valued in millions of dollars. Each of these technological aspects of the job calls for a unique web of rules.

PART II

Wages, Hours, and Working Conditions for Pilots and Flight Engineers

In CHAPTERS 4 through 8 the material shifts from general background information to detailed descriptions and analyses of the following unique and significant characteristics of the airline industrial relations system: flight crew compensation, scheduling, pensions, and work assignment.

Answers to three basic questions about each of these characteristics will be presented. First, what are the detailed rules, regulations, and agreements which have been developed? Second, how have these characteristics evolved? What mechanisms were involved? For example, government regulation was the mechanism through which the flight crew members were limited to 85 hours of flying per month, while reductions below 85 hours have come from contract negotiations. Basically there are five interrelated mechanisms by which new characteristics are evolved. They are government regulation, contract negotiation, arbitration decisions, unilateral actions by one of the parties, and successive small changes made in the daily administration of these industrial relations areas. These chapters abound in examples of the five mechanisms. Third, why have these rules, regulations, and agreements come into being? While a partial answer to this third question will be given in Chapters 4 through 8, a more complete answer must await an analysis of the bargaining power of the airline managements *vis-à-vis* the pilots, which will be presented in Chapter 10.

CHAPTER 4

The Methods of Compensating
Flight Crew Members

THE COMPENSATION of flight crew members is an interesting
industrial relations subject because potential earnings are so high
and the formulas by which they are paid are unique. Today, a
domestic jet pilot can earn over $30,000 per year. About the only
other unionized employee groups with wages even approaching that
figure are the diamond cutters, a few Hollywood cameramen, and
during World War II some commercial fishermen. In these cases,
the unions involved have limited memberships. Never has a union
the size of the Air Line Pilots Association (reported membership
16,650)[1] succeeded in obtaining such high earnings for its
members.

This chapter is divided into three parts. The first part contains a
detailed description of the methods of wage payment used to compensate flight crew members at a domestic trunk line. The second
part is devoted to an analysis of the evolution of the methods of
compensating flight crew members. The third part analyzes the
structure and the general level of flight crew pay.

METHODS OF WAGE PAYMENT

The methods of wage payment for domestic flight crew members
may be divided into three broad categories for ease of presentation.
These categories are the basic wage formula, the guarantees, and
the supplemental forms of payment. Within each of these categories
there are the following wage payment methods:

---

[1] U.S. Bureau of Labor Statistics Bulletin No. 1395, *Directory of National
and International Labor Unions in the United States,* 1963.

The Basic Wage Formula

- (a) Longevity Pay
- (b) Hourly Pay
- (c) Mileage Pay
- (d) Gross Weight Pay

The Guarantees

- (a) On-Duty Time Ratio
- (b) Trip-Time Ratio
- (c) Minimum Monthly Guarantees
- (d) Miscellaneous Flying Guarantee
- (e) Guarantee of Schedule Integrity

The Supplemental Forms of Wage Payment

- (a) Vacation Pay
- (b) Sick Leave Pay
- (c) Training Pay
- (d) Deadheading Pay
- (e) Travel Pay
- (f) Moving Pay
- (g) Standby Pay
- (h) Offshore Pay
- (i) Transoceanic Pay
- (j) Operational Duty Pay
- (k) Severance Pay

The trunk line in question has a wage clause covering every method of wage payment with the exception of Offshore, Transoceanic, Operational Duty, and Severance. These will be described at the end of the first half of the chapter, based on wage clauses in use at other air carriers.

The Basic Wage Formula

As the name implies, the basic wage formula combines the factors which form the bulk of flight crew compensation. It is also used to determine the amount of pay under all the guarantees and many of the supplemental forms of wage payment. Under the basic formula flight crew members are paid by the month, the flight hour, the mile, and the gross weight of the aircraft.

Longevity Pay. Longevity pay is an amount of money a crew member receives each month based on his longevity as a pilot, as shown on the pilot seniority list. During a man's first year as a pilot this is the only compensation he receives and it is referred to as his salary. After his first year a pilot is compensated under the full spectrum of wage methods. For this reason the amount of longevity pay typically drops sharply between the first and second years as the pilot picks up additional pay from the other factors. Longevity pay usually rises in equal increments from the second to the ninth year and then remains constant thereafter. At the domestic trunk line under consideration pilots receive a salary of $500 per month during their first year and $230 per month during their second year. Longevity pay increases thereafter by $20 per month per year to a maximum of $370 per month during the ninth and all succeeding years.

Throughout this discussion "pilots" will refer to captains, co-pilots, and flight engineers. Perhaps this is a good place to mention that copilots and flight engineers (when they are included in the pilot agreement) receive the same amounts of longevity pay as captains but they do not receive the full amounts of captain hourly, mileage, and weight pay. The exact amounts they receive and the methods by which their pay is calculated will be presented in this chapter after the basic wage formula has been described.

Hourly Pay. Captains are paid at an hourly rate for each flight hour they accrue. The hourly rates vary with the speed of the air-craft and whether the flight hour was accrued during the day or the night. The hourly rates at this carrier are shown in Table 4.1. From this table it is apparent that the hourly day rates rise $.20 per hour for every speed bracket, while the hourly night rates increase $.30 per hour for each bracket. It is also clear that the night rates are 50% above the day rates.

The most important new concept which must be understood is the "pegged speed of an aircraft." Since the hourly rates vary with the aircraft speed brackets, it is necessary to decide the speed bracket within which an aircraft type falls in order to decide how much a pilot should be paid for a flight hour accrued in such an aircraft type. For example, a pilot may fly a DC-6B between

TABLE 4.1   HOURLY RATES OF CAPTAIN PAY BASED ON
SPEED BRACKET OF AIRCRAFT AND TIME OF DAY

Speed Bracket (mph)		Per Hour, day	Per Hour, night
Under 155		$5.80	$ 8.70
155 UTBNI* 175		6.00	9.00
175	200	6.20	9.30
200	225	6.40	9.60
225	250	6.60	9.90
250	275	6.80	10.20
275	300	7.00	10.50
300	325	7.20	10.80
325	350	7.40	11.10
350	375	7.60	11.40
375	400	7.80	11.70
400	425	8.00	12.00
425	450	8.20	12.30
450	475	8.40	12.60

* UTBNI means "up to but not including."

two cities on a schedule which calls for an average speed of 276 mph. However, because of head winds he may actually fly the flight at a speed over the ground of 250 mph, although he is moving through the air at 305 mph. The question is at what hourly rate should he be paid? The answer is that the parties have negotiated a pegged speed for the DC–6B of 280 mph. Thus an hour's flight time in a DC–6B will earn the pilot $7.00 during the day and $10.50 during the night. Emphasis must be placed on the fact that a pegged speed is a negotiated figure. While it may approximate the speed at which an aircraft will normally cruise, no direct correlation exists between the two.

The pegged speeds at this carrier were:

Aircraft Type	Pegged Speed (mph)
Douglas DC-3	175
Convair CV-240 and CV-340	250
Douglas DC-6B	280
Viscount 798	295
Convair CV-880	430
Boeing 707	450

Once the pegged speed of an aircraft has determined the proper speed bracket, the only remaining factors needed to calculate hourly pay are the number of flight hours and a way to decide if they were accrued during the day or night. Pilots are credited with the greater of the scheduled or the actual time for each leg of a trip. This is called the "greater time principle." Suppose a flight crew is scheduled to fly a sequence with two legs of 60 and 100 minutes, but they actually fly the first leg in 55 minutes because of tail winds, and fly the second leg in 110 because they had to circle the airport for 10 minutes before obtaining clearance to land. Actual flight time is measured from the moment the aircraft moves from the ramp for the purpose of flight until the moment it stops at the ramp at its destination. This is known as "block-to-block time." In this case the crew member received the scheduled flight time of 60 minutes on the first leg because it was greater than the actual flight time of 55 minutes and the actual flight time of 110 minutes on the second leg because it exceeded the scheduled flight time. Thus, he would receive credit for 170 minutes. The parties have negotiated a definition of day and night flying. By this definition day flying is all flying done between the hours of 5:45 a.m. and 5:45 p.m. standard time, while night flying is all flying done during the other twelve hours. In case a flight is scheduled to pass into an area with a different time zone, the time of the station from which the plane last took off is used to calculate day and night minutes for that leg.

Mileage Pay. The third wage payment method included in the basic formula is mileage pay. At this carrier pilots receive 2 cents per mile for the first 22,000 miles flown in a month and 3 cents per mile for all miles over 22,000 per month.

The number of miles are determined by multiplying accrued pay time in an aircraft by a pegged speed for that aircraft. The pegged speeds are the same as given above except the Viscount 798 and the Boeing 707 speeds are 320 mph and 435 mph, respectively. This is another indication of the fact that all pegged speeds are negotiated rates and do not represent some type of actual speed of which the aircraft is capable.

The fact that all miles over 22,000 a month are worth 3 cents places a premium on flight time accrued in the faster aircraft because it permits a pilot to accumulate many miles at what is considered a high rate. For example, 85 hours in a DC–6B will generate only 23,800 miles, whereas 85 hours in a Boeing 707 will generate 36,975 miles. Once a pilot accumulates 22,000 miles in a month, every additional hour he flies a Boeing 707 pays him $13.05 ($.03 × 435 mph) in mileage pay alone.

Gross Weight Pay. The last method of wage payment in the basic formula is gross weight pay. At this carrier pilots receive 2 cents per 1,000 pounds of the maximum certificated gross weight of each aircraft for each hour flown. Gross weight pay is in effect an hourly rate based on aircraft weight.

The maximum certificated gross weight is obtained from the Federal Aviation Agency which lists a weight for every model of every aircraft type. For example, a DC-6B will have one weight when it is fitted with many seats for coach service and another weight when fitted with fewer seats for first class service. Therefore different models of the same basic aircraft type will have different certificated weights. Rather than bother with a different rate for each model, however, the parties normally agree on one weight to be used for all models of each aircraft type. Thus, in a sense, gross weights are negotiated figures. The parties at this trunk line have agreed to use the following gross weights:

DC-3	25,000 lbs.
CV-240	42,000
CV-340	47,000
DC-6B	100,000
Viscount 798	64,000
CV-880	185,000
Boeing 707—331	326,000

Now that the four parts of the basic wage formula have been described, it is possible to demonstrate how they are combined to form a pilot's monthly pay:

Suppose a first pilot with eight years of longevity as a pilot accrues 60 hours of day flying and 20 hours of night flying in a month. Further assume that all his flying is done in a DC-6B. His basic pay is calculated as follows:

(1) *Longevity Pay*
    Eight-year pilot $ 350.00

(2) *Hourly Pay*
    Pegged speed of a DC-6B is 280 mph
    Hourly day rate for that speed is $ 7.00
    Hourly night rate for that speed is   10.50
    Therefore: 60 hours × $ 7.00 = $420.00
                20 hours ×   10.50 =   210.00
                    Total hourly pay = $ 630.00

(3) *Mileage Pay*
    Pegged speed of a DC-6B is 280 mph
    80 hours × 280 mph = 22,400 miles
      22,000 miles × $.02 per mile = $440.00
        400 miles × $.03 per mile =   12.00
                    Total mileage pay $ 452.00

(4) *Gross Weight Pay*
    Gross weight of a DC-6B is 100,000 lbs.
    $\dfrac{100,000 \text{ lbs.}}{1,000 \text{ lbs.}}$ × $.02 per hour = $2.00 per hour

                 80 hours × $2.00 = $ 160.00

         TOTAL MONTHLY PAY $1,592.00

Copilot and Flight Engineer Flight Pay. Copilots and flight engineers receive percentages of the first pilot hourly, mileage, and gross weight rates. At this carrier copilots receive the full amount of longevity pay plus the following percentages of captain hourly, mileage, and gross weight pay:

Year	Per Cent
2nd	46
3rd	53
4th	54
5th	55
6th	56
7th	57
8th	58
9th and thereafter	59

The same pay factors are involved in the compensation of flight engineers, but the percentages of first pilot flight pay are smaller.

They start at 39% during a flight engineer's second year of service and rise to 49% in his ninth year and thereafter.

At this carrier the flight engineers come under the pilot agreement. As will be seen in the second half of this chapter, when they are not under the pilot agreement a different form of flight engineer compensation may have been negotiated.

The Guarantees

The guarantees do not introduce new methods of wage payment. Instead they guarantee captains, copilots, and flight engineers certain amounts of "pay time" for which they will be compensated in accordance with rates set by the basic wage formula. Throughout this analysis, the term "pay time" will be used to designate any time which is credited against the 85-hour limitation. A pilot may obtain pay time in several ways. The primary source of pay time is the flight time he accrues under the greater-time principle for the flights he flies. Pay time also includes the additional time which a pilot can accrue under a number of guarantees yet to be described. By contract agreement all the flight time credited under the guarantees is counted in the 85 hours of flying a flight crew member may accrue in a month.

On-Duty Time Ratio. At this airline the parties have negotiated a provision, known as the on-duty time ratio, which guarantees a crew member one hour of flight time for every two and one-half hours he is scheduled to spend on duty. A crew member is on duty from one hour before the scheduled departure of his first flight in a sequence until the scheduled termination of the last flight in the sequence. The only way in which an on-duty period can be broken for the purposes of this ratio is for the crew member to be scheduled for an eight-hour rest period if accommodations for sleeping are provided at the airport, or a ten-hour rest period if the pilot must leave the airport to get his rest.

For example, if a pilot was scheduled to report for duty at 8:00 a.m. and to remain on duty until 8:00 p.m., he would be scheduled for a 720-minute on-duty period. Suppose he was scheduled to fly two flights during that period with a total scheduled flight time of 200 minutes. This pilot would be credited with an additional 88 minutes of flight time for this sequence because he is guaranteed one hour of flight time for every two and one-half hours he is scheduled to be on duty. Applying that ratio to a 720-minute on-duty period gives 288 guaranteed flight minutes. He would therefore be credited with the difference between the guarantee and the scheduled flight time. The 88 minutes he receives because of the guarantee counts exactly like actual flight time for pay purposes.

When a pilot is credited with additional flight time under this ratio, he is compensated for it at rates determined by the basic wage formula. For example, if a DC-6B sequence was scheduled with one hour of flight time for five hours on duty, the pilot would be credited with a second hour of flight time under the guarantee. For that hour, he would receive hourly, mileage, and gross weight pay at DC–6B rates under the wage formula.

Trip-Time Ratio. The trip-time ratio represents another negotiated guarantee. It guarantees a flight crew member one hour of flight time for every four hours he is away from his home domicile on a trip. The trip time is measured from the time a crew member is required to report, one hour before his first departure time, or the actual time he does report, whichever is later, until the time he actually arrives back at his home domicile at the end of a trip. This period of time may cover several days. This ratio applies on an actual basis. For example, if a crew member's flight was cancelled for any reason at a base which was not his home domicile, he would be guaranteed one hour of flight time for every four hours he was delayed in getting back to his home domicile. If a pilot actually reported for duty at 8:00 a.m. one day and was actually released from duty at his own domicile again at 8:00 p.m. the following day, the trip would have lasted 36 hours. Under the one for four guarantee he would be guaranteed nine hours of flight time. If his actual flight time was seven hours, he would be credited with two more flight hours for pay purposes and for flight time limitation purposes.

When a pilot is credited with additional flight time under this guarantee, he receives pay for it in accordance with the basic formula. For example, if a pilot accrued six additional flight hours in a Viscount because his return trip is delayed for 24 hours, he would be paid for six hours at hourly, mileage, and gross weight rates as they apply to the Viscount pegged speed and weight.

Minimum Monthly Guarantees. All pilots at this airline with more than one year of longevity as a pilot come under guarantees which ensure them compensation for no less than 60 flight hours each month at rates commensurate with their flight crew positions.[2] Pilots with less than one year of longevity are guaranteed their salaries regardless of the flying they do each month.

The same type of 60-hour guarantee applies to copilots and flight engineers. The only difference is that copilots are guaranteed 60 hours of flight time paid at copilot hourly, mileage, and gross weight rates; while flight engineers are guaranteed the same number of hours at flight engineer rates. Most flight crew members will normally exceed the guarantee because they will fly more than 60 hours in a month.

An interesting application of the minimum monthly guarantee comes in its application to reserve pilots. Reserve pilots (captains, copilots, and flight engineers) are assigned schedules which require them to be available on short notice on certain days of the month to fly flights that are not manned by regularly scheduled pilots. The contract calls for a reserve pilot to be paid at captain hourly, mileage, and gross weight rates for flight time that he accrues when flying as a captain, and to be paid at copilot rates for flight time he accrues when flying as a copilot. But the important fact is that a reserve pilot has to fly only once as a captain during the month to be eligible for a minimum monthly reserve guarantee of 60 hours *at captain rates.* When a reserve pilot spends a large proportion of his time flying as a copilot and only occasionally flies as a first pilot, this guarantee can increase his monthly earnings significantly.

The Miscellaneous Flying Guarantee. The purpose of this guarantee is to ensure that if a pilot stays in contact with the airline so he can be notified of cancellations and if he takes the time and

[2] During the first year after a pilot bids and completes transition training to the CV–880 or the Boeing 707, in general he must bid nothing but that type of equipment. During that period his minimum monthly guarantee is 70 hours. As will be explained in Chapter 5, the individual flights to be flown in each succeeding month are grouped into assignments with a number of flight hours appropriate for a pilot to fly in a month. Such assignments are posted, pilots bid for them, and they are awarded solely on the basis of seniority.

effort to get himself to the airport, he will at least accrue one hour of flight time. Such time is credited against a pilot's maximum of 85 hours of flying a month and is paid for in accordance with the basic wage formula.

Guarantee of Schedule Integrity. "Schedule integrity" is a fancy name for a rather simple concept. Pilots want to have as much assurance as possible that they will fly and be paid for the flights they are assigned on the basis of seniority. If a pilot actually flies the flights as assigned, he enjoys perfect schedule integrity. Similarly, if his actual flights bear little resemblance to his assigned flights, his schedule integrity will be low.

In order to improve their schedule integrity the pilots at this carrier have negotiated a provision to the effect that when a pilot is removed from his assigned flight when he is available to fly it and it is flown by another pilot, the former pilot will be paid and will receive flight time credit for it as if he had flown it.

The Supplemental Forms of Wage Payment

Of the eleven supplemental forms of wage payment to be described in this section, the first six appear in some form in almost every flight crew contract. These are pay for vacations, sick leaves, training, deadheading, and expenses for travel and moving one's household. The remaining five forms are not commonly found in flight crew contracts but are included to make this chapter a complete description of the types of clauses found in the compensation area. Three of these less frequent forms are pay for standing by at an airport, flying offshore between domestic cities, and flying between the mainland and U.S. states or territories. The last two are operational duty pay which essentially is a special hourly rate paid for time a pilot spends on duty but not accruing flight time, and severance pay.

Vacation Pay. At the trunk line being described, all pilots receive one day of vacation per month during their first year of service, two weeks per year during their second through their ninth year, three weeks per year during their tenth through nineteenth year, and four weeks per year thereafter. During his vacation a pilot is paid at the rate he has been averaging during the preceding three months.

For every day a pilot spends on vacation, he is credited with two hours and fifty minutes of flight time toward his 85-hour monthly maximum. In this way he is protected from being assigned a great amount of extra flying time during the part of the month he is not on vacation. He is also prevented from taking many extra hours from the unassigned time, which, if permitted, might lower the number of flight hours the reserve pilots could accrue during the month to the point where the company would be forced to make payments under the reserve guarantee.

Sick Leave Pay. Pilots at this trunk line accrue sick leave credit at the rate of four pay hours per month of service up to 250 hours, and thereafter at the rate of two pay hours per month up to a maximum of 350 hours.

When they are sick, reserve pilots with more than one year of longevity use up their sick leave credits at the rate of 2.8 hours for every day they are unavailable for duty. Thus they receive pay and flight time credit for 2.8 hours per day of illness. Pilots not on reserve receive pay and flight time credit for the trips they missed because they were sick until they run out of sick leave credits. In their first year pilots continue to receive their salaries while they are sick.

Training Pay. Many types of flight crew training, retraining, and checking of proficiencies are continually being carried on at every airline. In the first place, a man must demonstrate his general ability as a pilot in order to obtain and maintain the required government certificates. Then he must demonstrate proficiency in any particular type of aircraft which he is going to operate commercially. At the same time he must show that he has the general knowledge and ability to operate in a scheduled airline service. Finally he must demonstrate familiarity with each individual route over which he will fly. First pilots must be able to demonstrate general proficiency every six months, while copilots and flight engineers are examined every twelve months for general proficiency.

As a general rule air carriers expect to give a crew member

extensive periods of training which will preclude his flying on a regular schedule when he is first hired, when he trains to qualify for a higher position (when a flight engineer becomes a copilot or a copilot trains for his first pilot certificate), and when he is qualifying for the first time on another aircraft type. When a man is training for a higher position he undergoes "upgrading training." When a man trains to operate a new type of equipment he undergoes "transitional training."

In addition, in order to stay qualified in a position and on a type of aircraft a pilot must continually accumulate a given number of flight hours in that position or equipment type. If he fails to accumulate enough hours, he must requalify before operating in that capacity or on that type of equipment.

At the carrier in question, the method of calculating training pay varies with the type of training as follows. When a pilot is undergoing upgrading or transitional training he receives pay and flight time credit at the rate of 2.8 hours per day, based on flying one-half day and one-half night (the hourly rates are averaged) in the equipment for which he is training. When a pilot is requalifying, he receives the same 2.8 hour credit on days he was otherwise scheduled to be off duty and he receives credit for the scheduled time of flights actually missed on days he was scheduled to fly. When a pilot is training to take or actually is taking a proficiency check, he receives no pay time credit.

Deadheading Pay. A pilot is said to be deadheading when he is traveling as a passenger on an airplane or some other form of transportation. Not infrequently a carrier will order a pilot to deadhead to another base to fly (protect) a flight which is originating there. This might occur because the pilot's assigned flights called for him to deadhead between two bases, or because the cancellation of a flight caused a pilot not to get to the base from which his next flight was scheduled to leave. Occasionally pilots will request to be deadheaded somewhere on the line for personal reasons. When this company orders a pilot to deadhead, it credits him with one-half hour of flight time for pay and credit purposes for every hour he spends deadheading. He is paid at rates for the equipment of the flight being protected, not for the equipment in which he deadheads. For example, if a pilot was ordered to dead-head in a DC-3 to another base to protect a Viscount flight and if the deadheading flight took 180 minutes, based on the greater of scheduled or actual time, the pilot would receive pay and credit for 90 minutes of flight time and would be paid at Viscount rates.

In some cases this carrier can avoid what is known as a "double deadhead," without making any payment to the affected pilot and in other cases by making only a partial payment. To understand a double deadhead, suppose a pilot based in Chicago is scheduled to fly to Dallas and to return. Suppose further that before he leaves, his return trip is cancelled and that there happens to be a Dallas-based pilot in Chicago who is available to fly this pilot's Chicago-Dallas flight. If the company did not use the Dallas-based pilot for that flight, it would have to deadhead him home and deadhead the Chicago pilot, after he flew his flight to Dallas, back to Chicago. This would be a double deadhead.

In this type of situation, this carrier may use the Dallas-based pilot and avoid the double deadhead, but it must pay and credit the Chicago pilot as if he had flown the Chicago-Dallas flight (not, however, pay or credit him for the missed deadhead from Dallas to Chicago).

Under slightly altered circumstances the company can avoid any extra payment. Suppose the Chicago pilot's outgoing flight from Chicago to Dallas was cancelled and that another Chicago-based pilot happened to be in Dallas and was available to fly the first pilot's return flight from Dallas to Chicago. Again a double deadhead would be involved if the first pilot deadheaded to Dallas and the other pilot deadheaded home to Chicago. In this situation the carrier is free to avoid the double deadhead and to give no pay or credit to the original pilot. According to a company official, making no payment is considered appropriate in this second set of circumstances because the pilot deprived of a return flight can be notified of the changed schedule well in advance and could prob-ably have himself reassigned to some other flight. In the first set of circumstances an originating trip would be taken away. Thus, early notification and the chances of finding an alternative flight on short notice would be more remote. When a pilot dead-heads for his own convenience, he receives neither pay nor credit of any type.

Travel Pay. All pilots receive expenses for meals, lodging, and transportation when they are away from their domicile for given periods of time on their assigned flights. When the company assigns them to duty at another domicile, they receive all reasonable expenses incurred thereby.

Moving Pay. A pilot will be reimbursed for certain expenses when he moves his family to another domicile at company request. The number of such moves, however, is limited by the fact that when a pilot moves because his seniority makes him the successful bidder for an already existing assignment at another domicile, he is not considered to be moving at company request. The only situation in which expenses for such moves are reimbursed arises if the flight assignment for which the pilot moved is discontinued within eight months.

When the carrier opens *new* domiciles or *new* flight assignments, the situation is changed. In those cases the successful bidders are considered to be moving at company request and are therefore reimbursed.

Standby Pay. Standby pay is not found frequently in flight crew labor contracts. It refers to a rate paid to a pilot while standing by at an airport to fly an extra section or some other flight that opens up at the last minute. It is rarely used any more at this trunk line. Pilots receive flight time credit for 50% of the time they stand by and pay based on the type of equipment they are standing by to fly.

That is the last of the methods of wage payment to be found at the trunk line in question. The four remaining methods are found in the flight crew contracts of other large trunk lines.

Offshore Pay. A few carriers have long flights which take their crews over an ocean or the Gulf of Mexico between domestic cities. One carrier has agreed to pay first pilots and copilots an additional $1.00 and $.55 per hour, respectively, on specified flights which are at some point at least 50 miles from the nearest shore.

Transoceanic Pay. This is a type of pay for flying over water similar to offshore pay. The difference is that transoceanic flights are between bases on the U.S. mainland and bases on isolated states, territories, or possessions. Carriers pay first pilots an additional $3.00 per hour on these flights while copilots receive an extra $1.75 to $2.00 per hour.

Operational Duty Pay. Operational duty pay represents an attempt to limit the amount of time a pilot spends on duty but not earning flight pay. In this regard it is similar to an on-duty ratio. Whereas the latter typically guarantees a pilot a certain proportion of flight time to on-duty time, however, operational duty pay measures the time a pilot spends on-duty but not earning flight pay and compensates him at an hourly rate for that time directly. Usually a first pilot receives $2.00 per operational duty hour, while the rate for a copilot is $1.00 per operational duty hour. For example, suppose a first pilot reports for duty at 7:00 A.M. for an 8:00 A.M. departure. He flies a four-hour flight and lays over at a layover base from noon until 2:00 P.M., at which time he flies back to his domicile on another four-hour flight. He is finally released from duty at 6:15 P.M. His operational duty hours would be figured by subtracting the flight time (8 hours) from the total on-duty period (11 hours and 15 minutes). Thus, he would have three hours and fifteen minutes of operational duty time for which he would be paid $6.50.

Severance Pay. Since 1958 agreements providing for severance pay have been negotiated in a handful of flight crew contracts as part of the settlements of a dispute between pilot-trained and mechanically trained flight engineers over the third seat on the turbojets. This dispute and the terms of settlement will be detailed in Chapters 7 and 8.

A major carrier signed a contract in 1958 under which all the mechanically trained flight engineers in the employ of the company as of the signing date (about 251) were each offered $20,000 in severance pay if they could not qualify or did not care to qualify as a pilot—a requirement they had to meet to fly as a flight engineer on the company's new jet equipment.

Under this agreement, if a flight engineer decided not to leave the company on the date the $20,000 became available, he could continue to fly as a flight engineer on the diminishing number of piston aircraft as long as his seniority permitted him to hold a position anywhere on the system. But for every year he continued with the company his severance pay was to be reduced by $2,000 to a minimum of $10,000. As this section worked out, less than five flight engineers took the severance pay.

In 1962 two other carriers reached similar agreements with their flight engineers. In these cases, however, the maximum severance pay was $39,400.

Up to this point all the methods of wage payment for flight crew members found in some form in the airline industry have been described. To follow is an analysis of each of these methods.

ANALYSIS OF THE EVOLUTION OF
FLIGHT CREW COMPENSATION

In this section the evolution of the basic wage formula and of the guarantees will be traced and analyzed. Although the supplemental forms of compensation have evolved somewhat, their evoluations are not considered significant enough to trace and analyze.

For several reasons a number of the characteristics of compensation presented in detail based on the latest agreement between the trunk line and ALPA do not represent the latest or "most advanced" versions of such characteristics in the industry. Therefore tracing the evolution of some of these characteristics will involve not only moving back in time but also presenting more recent versions than have already been described. In this way the trends in some of these characteristics will be made evident. Knowledge of these trends in turn will enhance one's appreciation of the impact which the flight crew unions have made in the area of compensation. Such an impact will be emphasized in the last section of this chapter.

Analysis of the Basic Wage Formula

1925–1947. The genesis of today's method of compensation was the pay scale used by the Post Office Department to compensate its mail pilots during the early 1920's. It used a scale which included base pay and mileage rates. The starting base pay was

$2,000 per year for pilots flying schedules that included only day flying.The starting base pay rose incrementally for schedules calling for increasing amounts of night flying as follows: $2,400 per year when less than one-third of the mileage was to be flown at night; $2,600 per year for over one-third night flying; and $2,800 per year when only night flying was involved. These starting rates were raised $100 per year for each 500 flight hours a pilot accrued up to a maximum base pay of $3,600 per year.

The mileage rate varied according to the hazard of the route over which it was flown, and whether day or night flying was involved. The day rate was 5 cents per mile between Cleveland and Cheyenne; 6 cents per mile between Cheyenne and Reno; and 7 cents per mile between Reno and San Francisco and between New York and Cleveland. These mileage rates were doubled when the flying was done at night.[3]

Although they appear in different forms today, two of the current methods of wage payment were clearly evident in the Post Office formula—longevity pay and mileage rates. The terms "base pay" and "longevity pay" will be used interchangeably here as they are in the airline industry. A pilot's eligibility for base pay has always been measured by the number of flight hours, or more often, by the number of years he has accrued in the pilot category. It is not based on the number of years a man may have spent in the employ of the airline. Only recently, as a number of former mechanics have become eligible for this type of pay either as flight engineers or as pilots, has the term "longevity pay" appeared in the contracts. Its purpose is to make clear the fact that eligibility for base pay is based on a man's longevity as a pilot and not on his seniority with the company.

The Post Office Department probably established such a pay scale for a number of reasons. Base pay represented a guarantee of a certain amount of money to the pilot regardless of the flying he accomplished each month. In those days when aircraft were relatively unreliable, navigational aids primitive at best, and poor weather necessitated widespread flight cancellations, some type of pay guarantee was clearly needed.

[3] Federal Coordinator of Transportation, *Hours, Wages, and Working Conditions in Scheduled Air Transportation* (Washington, March 1933), p. 34.

The measurement of seniority in terms of flight hours rather than years is interesting. It is probably a reflection of the youth of the industry and the relative paucity of flight experience among the pilots. When the entire group had little flight experience, a difference of 500 flight hours was significant. At later periods of time when first pilots had accrued hundreds of hours of flying time in the copilot seat, when airlines hired copilots with hundreds of flight hours to their credit, the law of diminishing returns set in to make an additional 500 flight hours a less significant measure of experience. When those conditions came about, base pay was changed from a flight hour to a longevity basis.

In choosing an incremental pay component, the Post Office decided to use mileage rates instead of hourly rates. This is interesting because at least since 1930 airline employers have consistently tried to emphasize the importance of hourly pay. Employers have preferred hourly rates because they stand to get more productivity from pilots at the same cost as aircraft speeds increase. The Post Office Department probably chose mileage pay as a direct incentive to encourage pilots to do a lot of flying because the more miles they flew the more they would be paid. An entirely different reason may have been involved, however. The Post Office officials probably knew of the complicated pay formula used at that time by the railroads to compensate their operating personnel involving both mileage and hourly components. The Post Office officials may have chosen a mileage rate simply to avoid so complicated a formula.

The two remaining variables in the Post Office formula, night and terrain differentials, were both related to hazard. The differentials for flying at night could significantly affect a pilot's base and mileage pay, being worth up to $800 in base pay and 100% of a man's day mileage rate. The importance of this differential was justified by the fact that night flying was being pioneered in the early 1920's with the use of crude beacons and landing flares. It will be recalled that the entire transcontinental route was not flown regularly at night until July 1, 1924. In those days night flying involved real hazard and the pay differential for doing so was large. Increasingly over the years this hazard has declined and with it the proportion of the pay formula to which a night differential applies.

The terrain pay differential did not depend solely upon the ruggedness of the terrain over which a route was scheduled. Also considered was the type of weather conditions typically encountered on the route. For example, the prevalence of thunderstorm activity between New York and Cleveland was used to justify its mileage rate of 7 cents. Again the technology of the airplanes in those days made appropriate a differential for the hazards of high altitudes or poor weather. Interestingly, as will be discussed shortly, a terrain differential persisted on a few airlines until recent years.

The data which are available indicates that during the 1920's pilot earnings were unsteady and that mail pilots may have earned more than nonmail pilots. Pilots had average annual earnings of $6,760 in the fiscal year 1925. One study reported an average monthly mileage pay for December 1926 of $382, corresponding with an average flight time of 45 hours for the month. Seven months later another study reported average mileage earnings of $438 for July 1927, corresponding with 53.5 flight hours. At the time the Post Office turned the airmail service over to private hands in the summer of 1927, mail pilots were earning a total pay per month of between $600 and $650.[4]

When the commercial carriers took over the pilots and planes of the Post Office Department, they also adopted the Post Office pay scale and most of them continued to use it during the period 1927 through 1929. After the Depression arrived, some of the carriers felt a need to cut flight crew costs. Some of them cut the base and mileage rates, while still maintaining the same type of formula. Others shifted to paying their flight crew members a flat salary. The flat salary meant lower unit costs to the carriers because flight hours were rising, and pilots were competing with each other to hold their jobs in the Depression. A survey of the industry in October 1931 disclosed that one quarter of the airlines had shifted to a flat salary for all their pilots but the other 75% continued to use base pay and mileage rates. The mileage rates for night flying were no longer double the day rates. One quarter of the carriers had reduced the base pay between 33% and 50%, while the mileage rates had been reduced from 10% to 36%. These reductions are

[4] *Ibid.*, p. 35.

important to this study because they were the immediate cause of the formation of the Air Line Pilots Association in July 1931.

The next two years witnessed a basic shift in the methods of wage payment for pilots. By July 1933 nine companies (including three of the larger ones) were paying their pilots a base pay or a minimum monthly dollar guarantee plus an hourly rate. In other words they had eliminated the mileage rates entirely and were paying between $3.00 and $5.00 per flight hour for day flying and between $4.80 and $8.25 for night flying. The rates varied in accordance with the carrier, the terrain, and the type of equipment. After these changes the number of hours pilots were flying per month increased by 8% in the South Atlantic region over the comparable figure in 1931 and actual pilot earnings dropped by 7% in the same region and over the same time period. The pattern was similar in other areas of the country.

Two reasons primarily accounted for these changes in the pilot pay formula. The reductions were a reflection of the depressed economic conditions of the airline industry which manifested itself in a desire to trim wage costs. In shifting to an hourly rate the carriers were counting on the introduction of faster equipment and thus lower pilot cost per aircraft mile. In addition, the substitution of hourly for mileage pay would not lessen the pilot's incentive to do a lot of flying.

This move to base plus hourly pay culminated on October 1, 1933, when the five largest carriers announced the adoption of a new, uniform pay scale as follows:

Base Pay: Initial base pay of $1,600 per year, to be increased $200 per year for each year of service to a maximum of $3,000 per year.

Hourly Pay: The foregoing base pay to be augmented by the following amounts per flight hour:

Speed bracket (mph)	Per hour, day	Per hour, night
125 or less	$4.00	$6.00
126 to 140	4.20	6.20
141 to 155	4.40	6.40
156 to 175	4.60	6.60
176 to 200	4.80	6.80
Over 200	5.00	7.00

One of the five carriers proposed to pay in addition to the above rates a bonus of $.10 per hour, day, and $1.10 per hour, night, for flying over regular terrain, and $1.10 per hour, day, and $3.10 per hour, night, for flying over rough terrain. The four other carriers were completely abandoning terrain differentials.[5] When these carriers announced this new pay scale along with the introduction of faster equipment, they sparked the wage controversy with the Air Line Pilots Association that led to the momentous Decision #83 of the National Labor Board.

ALPA decided to fight this fundamental wage issue with a national strike if necessary. Its first move was to attempt to negotiate a mileage formula with the carriers. To accomplish this, ALPA made the following counter proposal:

Base Pay: Initial base pay of $1,800 per year, to be increased $200 per year for each year of service to a maximum of $3,000 per year.

Mileage Pay: The foregoing base pay to be augmented by the following amounts per mile flown:

	Per mile, day	*Per mile, night*
Flat terrain	4 cents	7 cents
Hazardous terrain	5 cents	9 cents

Flight Limitation: Individual flying within any month to be limited to 80 hours or 10,000 miles.

Apparently ALPA was willing to propose lower mileage rates than had applied in the 1920's because of the Depression and in recognition of increased aircraft speeds.

When negotiations proved to be fruitless in the fall of 1933, the pilots threatened a nationwide walkout. This was prevented by the last minute acceptance of the dispute by the National Labor Board which had been created the previous August under the National Industrial Recovery Act. Although the five carriers joined in submitting the dispute to the NLB, they put their proposed pay scales into effect on October 1, 1933, and agreed to make any wage settle-

[5] *Ibid.,* p. 43.

ment retroactive to that date. Submitting this dispute to the NLB represented the use of voluntary arbitration to decide basic wage and hour terms.

The NLB appointed a fact-finding board, headed by Judge Shientag, which held hearings on October 4 and December 14. The industry maintained that its wage scale should be supported by the NLB and that no limitation on the pilots' work was necessary beyond the existing 100 flight hours per month maximum (set by the Department of Commerce in 1931). ALPA argued that mileage pay was necessary in order that pilots might share in the increased productivity of the new aircraft. The following excerpt from the testimony of an ALPA official before the NLB is quoted because it is so typical of the wage arguments ALPA has been making before government boards and in negotiating sessions ever since.

> The standard rate of pay for pilots today is 4 cents per mile for day flying. This rate was established about three years ago and prior to that it was 5 cents. At that time, companies adopted the hourly rate of $4.00, which, at the speed of 100 mph, which was averaged then, was equivalent to 4 cents per mile. . . . Where the companies formerly paid $4.00 for 100 miles they now propose to pay $4.00 for 125 miles, or $3.20 for 100 miles, a 20% cut. . . . The new pay scales can result in an increase only if some of the present personnel are released and those remaining do proportionately more work. . . . Each pilot must fly more miles in a month than he does at present in order to earn (his present) pay. This . . . means that . . . pilot personnel . . . must be released in order that those remaining may be enabled to earn their present salary.[b]

That is a classic statement of ALPA's position.

Based on the Shientag report, the NLB accepted both the hourly and the mileage pay arguments and limited pilots to 85 hours of flying per month. Decision #83 read in part as follows:

> *Base Pay:* Initial base pay of $1,600 a year, increased $200 for each year of service to a maximum of $3,000.
> *Hourly Pay:* The foregoing base pay to be augmented by the following amounts per flight hour:

[b] *Ibid.,* p. 105.

At flight speed	Per hour, day	Per hour, night
Under 125 mph	$4.00	$6.00
125 to 139	4.20	6.30
140 to 154	4.40	6.60
155 to 174	4.60	6.90
175 to 199	4.80	7.20
200 or over	5.00	7.50

Mileage Pay: The foregoing elements of base and hourly pay to be augmented by the following amounts for mileage flown at speeds in excess of 100 miles per hour:

Miles flown in a month	Per mile
Under 10,000	2 cents
10,000 to 11,999	1.5 cents
12,000 and over	1 cent

Hazardous Terrain: The differentials existing on October 1, 1933, for copilots and for flying over hazardous terrain shall be maintained.

Mileage Limitation: Experience has not crystallized sufficiently to put a maximum on the monthly mileage of air pilots.

Although this ruling was supposed to apply for only one year, ALPA succeeded in making compliance with these rates a condition for holding an airmail certificate under the Air Mail Act of 1934, without regard to any expiration date. The pilots were able also to have compliance with these minima written into the Civil Aeronautics Act of 1938 and the Federal Aviation Act of 1958.

Several aspects of the Decision #83 rates should be explained because they differ from the current application of base, hourly, and mileage rates. Under Decision #83 first pilots received some compensation from all three of the factors regardless of their longevity, while copilots received flat salaries. Therefore, the base pay figure for the first year under the decision did not represent salaries. It was the base pay of any man who was fortunate enough to become a first pilot in his first year.

Under Decision #83 a first pilot's hourly pay depended on the speed of the aircraft and on the number of flight hours he could accrue. In those days pegged speeds were not used to determine the speed bracket of each aircraft type. Instead, the scheduled speed of the aircraft was used on all scheduled flights, and the actual speed was used on all nonscheduled flights. The accrual of flight hours was handled in a similar fashion. The scheduled flight time was used for all scheduled flights regardless of whether the flight actually took more or less time than was scheduled. Only on nonscheduled flights was the actual time of flight considered. ALPA had not yet won the greater time principle.

The application of the mileage formula of Decision #83 caused a great amount of controversy. In the first place, the number of miles a pilot generated on each scheduled trip was the official government map mileage between the two bases. Only when the mileage between two points was not known did the first use of a pegged speed come into play. For the nonscheduled flights actual flight time was multiplied by an agreed-upon pegged speed to calculate the mileage. The use of map miles meant that a pilot received no additional mileage pay if he had to circle an airport waiting for the weather to improve.

A severe controversy came from the unclear wording of the mileage pay clause. If a pilot's mileage totaled 9,999 miles or less, the carrier would pay 2 cents for each mile flown in excess of 100 mph. If his mileage totaled 10,000 miles or more, however, the carriers argued that the mileage rate for all pay miles should "revert" to 1.5 cents, and that is the way they compensated their pilots for years. The pilots, of course, maintained that the first 9,999 miles should never revert to 1.5 cents. The calculation of pay miles which were miles flown in excess of 100 mph required agreement on the speed of the aircraft on each trip. Where possible, the scheduled speed was used. A typical calculation went as follows:

Suppose a pilot accrued 13,000 miles in a DC–3 on schedules calling for 160 mph.
Then mph over 100 mph equals 60 mph
$$\frac{60}{160} \times 13,000 = 4,875 \text{ miles}$$
Since all miles over 12,000 "revert" to the 1 cent rate:
Mileage Pay = \$.01 × 4,875 = \$48.75

At aircraft speeds then in existence (125–160 mph), Decision #83 stressed base and hourly pay over mileage pay. For example, in the above case if the pilot had eight years of longevity he would earn $3,000 per year or $250 per month from base pay and $373.75 from hourly pay compared with only $48.75 from mileage pay. Even without reversion he would earn only $97.50 from mileage pay. These figures explain why, as will be seen, ALPA was anxious to receive mileage pay for all miles flown rather than just for miles flown over 100 miles per hour.

The impact of Decision #83 on the incentive of pilots to do a lot of flying was ambiguous. Essentially because the hourly rates were much higher than the mileage rates when translated into flight hours, pilots would have an incentive to fly as many hours as possible. But because of the reversion feature, discontinuities in earnings occurred as pilots passed the reversion points of 10,000 and 11,999 miles per month. For example, if a pilot flew at 160 mph for 74.99 hours, theoretically[7] he would cover 11,999 miles and receive $67.50 in mileage pay and $344.95 in hourly pay, a total of $412.45. If, however, he flew 75 hours at 160 mph, theoretically he would cover 12,000 miles and receive $45.00 in mileage pay and $345.00 in hourly pay, a total of $390.00. Thus, by flying a hundredth of an hour longer he would lower his pay by $22.45. He would have to fly an additional 4.3 hours to come back up to $412.45.

With hourly pay calculated according to scheduled speeds and scheduled flight times and mileage taken directly from official map mileages, pilots had only the incentive to get off duty to encourage them to bring flights in on time. On the other hand, they had no incentive to lengthen flights.

After the passage of the Air Mail Act of 1934 and some amendments a few months later, the pay scale of Decision #83 became the uniform standard for the airline industry for the balance of the 1930's. As stipulated in that Decision, the few carriers which had not dropped terrain differentials were required to continue them. This meant that for many years those carriers had higher hourly rates than their competitors. And as carriers came to compete over

[7] At that time map mileages were used. These calculations assume map mileages would be identical with the product of aircraft speed times flight time.

the same routes, situations arose in which two airlines flying over the same hazardous terrain would have to pay markedly different hourly rates. Over the years, however, terrain differentials have gradually lost any relevance. For practical purposes terrain differentials have been eliminated by the adoption of so-called composite hourly rates. These composite hourly rates combine the hourly rates for flat terrain and hazardous terrain, and all flight hours are paid for at composite rates regardless of the terrain over which they were accrued. The composite hourly rates are now comparable to the regular hourly rates of the rest of the carriers.

The first labor agreement between ALPA and an airline, signed on May 15, 1939, contained Decision #83 rates to the letter. Its only change from the description above came in the method of accruing flight hours. In this contract the pilots were able to take the first step toward today's greater time principle. When a trip was delayed by Air Traffic Control over an airport for more than 30 minutes, the first pilot received credit for the scheduled flight time of the trip plus the actual time he was delayed beyond that half hour.

The first changes in the rates outlined in Decision #83 came on July 21, 1941. On that date an arbitration board awarded increases to first pilots who were flying the new Boeing 307 equipment. When a major carrier had ordered the 307 the previous year, the company had maintained that the rates then in effect would have adequately compensated the pilots for the increased productivity of these new planes. ALPA did not agree. Both sides were willing to submit the dispute to arbitration from which came an award of an additional $.80 per hour for day flying and $1.20 per hour for night flying. These additional rates applied only to the Boeing 307 and were added onto the Decision #83 hourly rates. The second change in these rates came from an almost identical situation in 1945. At that time Boeing produced a more productive version of the 307 and again the ensuing wage dispute was submitted to arbitration. This time the award merely doubled the additional rates given in 1941. These disputes at least indicated ALPA's reluctance to continue indefinitely under the pay rates of Decision #83, although always insisting that its formula be maintained.

If any doubt of ALPA's intentions remained in 1945, it was completely eliminated in a wage dispute over the introduction of the DC–4 and the Lockheed Constellation which brewed from late in 1945 until it was settled on January 22, 1947, by arbitration. In this dispute ALPA wanted a complete upward revision of the pay scales of Decision #83, while one of the major carriers was willing to raise the existing rates by $3.00 per hour for flying the DC–4 and $4.00 per hour for flying the Constellation. The arbitration award, which came after a pilot strike, maintained the formula of Decision #83. The previous base rates, however, were raised $600 per year and the hourly rates were extended with four more speed brackets of 25 mph each. The $.20 increments between brackets for day flying and the $.30 increments for night flying were also continued. Thus, the top day hourly rate was $5.80 for aircraft speeds of 300 mph or more. The comparable night figure was $8.70.

During the dispute the carriers attempted to institute industry-wide bargaining for the first time. Their attempt failed because ALPA refused to bargain in that manner, a position amply supported by the Railway Labor Act, as amended. This aspect of the 1945–1947 dispute is of primary concern to the discussion of the negotiating process coming in a later chapter, but it also affected the evolution of the methods of wage payment. After winning its point against any joint bargaining, ALPA began to negotiate vigorously on an individual carrier basis.

Since 1947 ALPA has placed primary emphasis on winning a new wage concession from one carrier and then forcing the next carrier with which it negotiates to meet or better the last concession. The important point about this "whipsawing" technique for the evolution of the methods of wage payment is that it led to many different rates as the years passed. These years have seen the compensation area change from relative simplicity to extreme complexity. These variations have resulted in part from the attempts of individual carriers to meet the ALPA demands with new approaches that each believed would be less costly, given its operating practices, route structure, etc. Therefore, although there continued to be clauses granting some type of base, hourly, mileage, and, later, gross weight pay, they were not identical clauses. Whereas the years 1934–1947 witnessed approximately identical Decision #83 pay scales throughout the airline industry, the years since 1947 have seen all the methods of wage payment in a variety of forms. For this reason it will be necessary to discuss the predominant or the most advanced forms of wage payment as this analysis traces their evolution from 1947 to the present, with the understanding that all carriers did not negotiate each new wage form at the same time, or perhaps at all.

Base Pay Since 1947. The evolution of base pay since 1947 may be briefly summarized because its form has been changed in only three ways. In 1951 copilots started to receive the same base pay as first pilots. This was at the time when copilots were shifted from a flat salary to base pay plus flight pay. The carriers, however, wished to keep copilots on flat salaries during their two-year probationary period. Therefore, the common base pay scale was established with higher rates in the first two years. Today, base pay scales generally have a salary rate for only a one-year probationary period and copilots start to receive flight pay after one year.

In recent years the eight-year base pay scales have been extended by another year or two. This provides additional increments for a pilot's ninth and tenth years.

The third change established base rates on a flight hour basis for pilots after their first year rather than on a monthly or yearly basis. For example, the following longevity rates per flight hour were agreed to at one trunk line:

Year	Per hour
2nd	$2.79
3rd	2.99
4th	3.18
5th	3.38
6th	3.57
7th	3.77
8th	3.96
9th	4.16
10th and thereafter	4.35

According to an ALPA negotiator, the change to hourly longevity rates resulted from a compromise made in the 1958 negotiations. A major carrier proposed a simplified pay structure comprising base pay based on longevity and mileage pay based on equipment type. As will be discussed later, this proposal was part of an industry move to obtain a simplified pay structure. Although the pilots did not agree to the proposal, they were willing to shift longevity pay to an hourly basis and thereby ease the carrier's administrative burden in calculating pilot compensation because all aspects of the basic formula then could be combined into hourly rates which varied only with longevity and equipment type. At the same time hourly base rates were established so that at 77 pay hours per month they equaled the previous monthly base rates.

Over the years base pay has declined as a percentage of total pay. Whereas in the 1920's a pilot might have received 50% of his $600 per month from base pay, today a jet pilot will earn in the neighborhood of $2,000 per month, of which only about $350 or 17.5% will come from base pay. Pilots have not stressed base pay. Instead they have been interested in getting all they could in increased mileage rates, while the carriers have been trying to put any increase into the hourly rates. Base pay has been neglected.

Hourly Pay Since 1947. The general format of hourly pay has not changed since 1947. Hourly rates have continued to rise incrementally for each speed bracket and to be greater for night flying than for day flying. The changes have occurred in the number of speed brackets and in the dollar amounts for each bracket.

These changes may best be presented by quoting some hourly rates as they have risen over the past 12 years at individual carriers. For example, the trunk line described in the first half of this chapter, like most of the industry, had a top hourly day rate of $5.80 in 1947 corresponding to the 300–325 mph speed bracket. This represented a straight extension of Decision #83 rates. Its hourly rates remained unchanged until the 1956 contract when the 300–325 mph rate was raised to $6.38. Thereafter it was raised as follows: $6.60 in 1958; $6.90 in 1960; and $7.20 in 1963. The $7.20 figure amounted to a 24.2% increase over the comparable Decision #83 figure. During these years additional brackets were added such that the *top* hourly rate was $6.58 for 325–350 mph in 1956; $7.00 for 350–375 mph in 1958; $8.10 for 450–475 mph in 1960; $8.40 for 450–475 mph in 1961.

The picture of higher rates and additional speed brackets applies throughout the industry. There are, however, almost as many hourly rates for each speed bracket as there are carriers. Hourly rates have changed from being relatively uniform in 1947 to being the method of wage payment with the most divergent sets of rates. The spread may be seen in Table 4.2 which shows the hourly pay rates of the domestic trunk lines for the 400–425 mph speed bracket in contracts effective as of December 31, 1962.

TABLE 4.2.   CAPTAIN HOURLY PAY, 400–425 MPH:
AS OF DECEMBER 31, 1962

Carrier	Per Hour, Day	Per Hour, Night
American	$8.85	$11.35
Braniff	8.60	12.95
Continental	8.20	12.30
Delta	8.15	10.65
Eastern	8.282	12.423
National	7.68	11.52
Northeast	8.00	12.00
Northwest	8.50	11.00
Trans World	8.16	12.24
United	8.85	11.35
Western	8.10	12.15
Average	$8.30	$11.80

SOURCE: ALPA records.

From these data one may calculate again that hourly day rates have risen about 24% over the rate obtained by extending Decision #83 rates to a 400–425 mph bracket. The latter figure is $6.60, which divided into $8.30 gives 126%. These data indicate also that at four trunk lines (American, Delta, Northwest, and United) the night hourly rate was less than 150% of the day hourly rate.

These examples illustrate that the pilots have been able to win significant increases in their hourly rates in the last 17 years primarily by negotiating rates for faster and faster speed brackets and secondarily by negotiating higher rates within each bracket. The increases in hourly rates indicate that the carriers have been able to keep some of the wage increases out of the mileage rates and have been able to maintain the relative importance of hourly rates.

The developments in two aspects of hourly pay have had important effects on flight crew pay. These aspects are the way in which flight time is counted and the use of pegged speeds.

In 1951 a major carrier agreed for the first time to credit flight hours in accordance with the greater time principle. It agreed that a pilot should receive the greater of the scheduled time or the actual time *for an entire trip*. The parties agreed that if a trip took longer than scheduled, the pilot should be paid and credited for the longer time. Some carriers believed some pilots were actually not carrying out their flights as rapidly as possible perhaps to build pressure for winning the greater time principle. Also, as will be seen, with the calculation of mileage pay shifting from map mileages to the multiplication of pegged speeds times actual flight times, the pilots if not guaranteed scheduled times would have an incentive to make each trip actually last at least its scheduled time to increase mileage pay. Of course, under the greater time principle, pilots might tend to make each flight as long as possible to accrue maximum actual flight time. Apparently the only countervailing forces were the great pressures in the industry to accomplish flights on schedule, the pilots' pride in doing so, and the latent threat of discipline for purposely slowing down.

Pressure on a carrier to encourage its pilots to operate as close to schedule as possible stems from the costs of their operating too slow or too fast. A pilot can exert considerable control over the length of any particular flight. During 1962 the direct cost of operating a DC–3 averaged $139.10 per hour. The comparable figures for a DC–6 and a Boeing 707–120 were $349.72 per hour and $822.92 per hour, respectively.[8] If the pilots should decide to make flights as long as possible rather than as short as possible, they would have a significant effect on a carrier's operating costs. On the other hand, operating faster than the appropriate speed causes inefficient fuel utilization and tends to increase maintenance problems and costs.

[8] FAA, "Direct Operating Costs and Other Performance Characteristics of Transport Aircraft in Airline Service: Calendar Year 1962," p. 16.

The current application of the greater time principle on a leg-by-leg basis was negotiated generally throughout the industry by 1953. It should be noted that this was no small victory for ALPA because the accrual of hours affects a pilot's mileage and gross weight pay as well as his hourly pay. This is true because mileage is calculated through the use of pegged speeds and accrued flight time, and the gross weight formula yields an hourly rate for each type of aircraft.

Pegged speeds, as has been pointed out, are negotiated figures and do not necessarily represent actual aircraft speeds. Table 4.3 indicates the variations between block-to-block, cruising, and pegged speeds for domestic trunks for DC–6B and Boeing 707–120 aircraft.

TABLE 4.3. COMPARISON OF BLOCK-TO-BLOCK, CRUISING, AND PEGGED SPEEDS OF THE DC–6B AND THE 707–120

Aircraft	*Block-to-Block Speeds*		*Cruising Speed*	*Range of Pegged Speeds*
	200-Mile Trip	*1,700 Mile Trip*		
DC–6B	208 mph	270 mph	315	270–300
707–120	286 mph	507 mph	590	425–450

SOURCES: CAB, *General Characteristics of Turbine-Powered Aircraft,* February 1960, Charts 1 and 2; and ALPA records.

The most important feature of pegged speeds is the infinite flexibility they give the parties to negotiate selected pay increases for particular subgroups of the pilots at an airline. If the parties believe that the most junior pilots and copilots are entitled to a larger pay increase than the more senior pilots and copilots, they will negotiate relatively higher pegged speeds for the type of aircraft the junior groups normally fly, e.g. the Convair and the DC–6B. In recent years the parties at a number of airlines have agreed to establish one pegged speed for all the piston equipment. For example, in 1963 a major carrier agreed to use the DC–6B pegged speed of 300 mph for the DC–3, CV–340, DC–4, DC–6, DC–6A, and Viscount. This, of course, resulted in greatly increased pay, for example, for the DC–3 crew members, and a pegged speed much higher than the maximum cruising speed of the aircraft.

Taking advantage of the flexibility provided by pegged speeds in this way can be beneficial to both parties. From ALPA's viewpoint it raised the pay of the junior captains, copilots, and flight engineers and helped to keep their pay in an equitable relationship to that of the more senior captains, copilots, and flight engineers. From the carriers' viewpoint, it established a pay scale in which as a man moved from flight engineer to copilot to captain his pay would increase, regardless of the type of equipment he flew on. Prior to this change a DC–3 captain, for example, could earn less than a jet flight engineer. Such a situation, it was thought, led to decreased morale and increased movement by crew members among types of equipment and crew positions. Reducing such movement would tend to reduce a carrier's training costs. Also by having all piston rates the same a crew member would be less likely to bid on a faster type of piston equipment as soon as his seniority permitted it, and again training costs would tend to be reduced.

Throughout the industry the parties have purposefully kept the pegged speeds of the jets low relative to their potential speeds (see Table 4.3). This is the reverse side of the coin—preventing the jet crew wages from rising out of an equitable relationship with those of the piston crews. It was also a way for ALPA to allow the junior pilots to share in the pay increases won in the jet negotiations.

Mileage Pay Since 1947. Since 1947 the flight crew unions have placed major emphasis at the bargaining table on improving the mileage pay element of the basic formula. Their efforts have resulted in a variety of mileage formulas, increased mileage rates, and a larger proportion of total compensation coming from mileage pay.

The first change the pilots wanted in the Decision #83 mileage formula was the elimination of the "reverting" interpretation. The first step in this direction came in a 1944 contract. Under its terms, a pilot would be paid at the rate of 2 cents per mile for all miles flown at speeds over 100 mph up to an aggregate monthly miles of 9,999. Then he would be paid at the rate of 1.5 cents for miles flown in excess of 100 mph for the monthly mileage including

10,000 up to 11,999 miles, and so forth. The point is that all pay miles would not "revert" to the 1.5 cent rate as soon as the monthly mileage reached 10,000 miles. This contract marked the end of reverting at one carrier in 1944, but the major drive to remove this unpopular interpretation was not successfully accomplished until the 1947–1948 negotiating sessions.

The next major step in the evolution of mileage pay also came in the 1947 round of negotiations. One carrier agreed to abandon the use of official map mileages in measuring mileage over scheduled routes. Instead it agreed to calculate mileage by the use of pegged speeds, multiplying the pegged speed by the actual time of the trip. This was an important step forward for the pilots because it meant that they would receive mileage pay for the time they were delayed in the air for any reason. This change is interesting because it was in part justified by the increasingly crowded landing conditions at our major airports. Because the airports were becoming more and more crowded, the pilots found themselves increasingly stacked up, waiting for a clearance to land. In this situation it seemed reasonable to compensate them for the miles they had to fly in circles prior to landing. This justification stands in contrast to the usual reason for increasing pilot pay—the increased productivity of the equipment. One carrier shifted to the use of pegged speeds for the mileage calculation in 1947, but the rest of the major carriers did not follow suit until the 1951 round of negotiations when the matter of mileage loomed very large indeed.

For the second time in its history, ALPA made a determined effort in 1951 to limit the number of miles a pilot could fly each month. The main reason for this drive was the same one that had motivated its previous attempt in the hearings before the Shientag fact-finding board in 1933, fear of technological unemployment with the advent of more productive equipment and the desire to share in this increased productivity. ALPA proposed in the negotiations with one of the Big Four a monthly mileage limitation based on 13,600 miles (the number of miles a DC–3 could generate in an 85-hour month at a pegged speed of 160 mph). This proposal, known as Mileage Increase Determination (MID),[9] would have

9 Mark L. Kahn, "Wage Determination for Airline Pilots," pp. 330–331.

limited monthly mileage on a faster type of equipment to 13,600 miles plus one-half of the difference between 13,600 and the product obtained by multiplying the pegged speed of the faster equipment by 85 hours. For example, the pegged speed of a DC–6B is 280 mph which multiplied by 85 gives 23,800 miles. Adding one-half of the difference between 13,600 and 23,800 to 13,600 gives a monthly mileage limitation for the DC–6B of 18,700 miles. This mileage would then be divided by the pegged speed of the aircraft to yield the maximum number of flight hours a pilot would be allowed to accrue in that aircraft type. In this case that figure is 66.8 hours. Under the MID proposal the hourly rates would have been adjusted in order that no loss of earnings would have resulted from this decrease in flight hours. Also the gross weight rate would have been converted to a mileage base for the same purpose. In spite of a Presidential Emergency Board and a short strike at one major carrier, ALPA did not succeed in winning acceptance of the MID approach or a direct mileage limitation.

The first settlement that established a new mileage pay formula came at a major carrier on August 28, 1951. Until that time Decision #83 mileage rates were used except that as noted the reversion feature had been dropped. The new formula paid 1 cent per mile for monthly mileages up to 17,000 miles, 2 cents for each mile flown between 17,000 and 22,000 miles, and 3 cents for each mile over 22,000 miles. This format was adopted by several carriers. Other carriers, however, settled a few weeks later for a mileage formula that paid 1.5 cents for each mile flown. This was the middle rate of the Decision #83 formula. In both patterns the concept of paying only for miles flown in excess of 100 mph was eliminated. Crew members were paid for all miles flown. At the rate of 1.5 cents per mile, this change increased pay $1.50 per flight hour.

Over the years the pattern calling for one rate for all miles came to predominate in the pilot contracts with the trunk lines. In part it came about because the carriers preferred one rate to ease the administrative burden of calculating flight crew compensation. In addition, as Table 4.4 indicates, higher mileage rates were negotiated.

TABLE 4.4.   MILEAGE RATES, DOMESTIC
TRUNK LINES: AS OF DECEMBER 31, 1962

Carrier	Miles Accrued in a Month	
	0–22,000	Over 22,000
American	$.022	$.022
Braniff	.023	.023
Continental	.022	.022
Delta	.025	.025
Eastern	.0255	.0255
National	.02	.03
Northeast	.02	.03
Northwest	.02	.02
Trans World	.022	.022
United	.022	.022
Western	.022	.022

SOURCE: ALPA records.

From this discussion, it is clear that ALPA has made great strides in mileage pay. It went from a decreasing rate based on map mileages paid only for miles flown in excess of 100 mph to a uniform or increasing rate for all miles flown calculated by multiplying pegged speeds by actual flight times. It also increased the rates per mile significantly. These changes put the pilots in a position to obtain large wage increases from their mileage formulas as the new equipment with greatly increased speeds arrived on the scene. This is in effect an automatic improvement factor based on productivity. It also means that airline managements have the burden of trying to negotiate lower rates as faster equipment arrives.

Gross Weight Pay. Decision #83 did not contain a gross weight pay element. Obtaining some type of weight pay was a major goal of ALPA during the 1945–1947 wage dispute during which the air carriers attempted to institute industry-wide bargaining. When the arbitrator did not grant ALPA's request for a weight element, the association then sought it in negotiations with individual carriers. These efforts met with success when a major carrier agreed in April 1947 to a gross weight clause which was identical in form to the one already presented in the first half of this chapter except that the rate was 1.75 cents per 1,000 pounds per flight hour instead of 2 cents.

Gross weight pay has remained essentially unchanged since 1947. The pattern originally set in the industry has been adopted by every carrier, and since 1953 a rate of 2 cents per 1,000 pounds per flight hour has become standard for first pilots. The reason for the slight interest on the part of the pilots to improve their gross weight is that the more consistently rising aspect of the new aircraft since 1947 has been speed. This has shifted ALPA's attention even more strongly than ever to the mileage rate. Gross weights have risen dramatically in the cases of some models of the Douglas DC–8 and Boeing 707 (as high as 326,000 pounds). Most models of these planes, however, weigh around 250,000 pounds. On the other hand, the turbo-prop Electra weighs less than the DC–7 (about 122,000 pounds for the DC–7 compared with about 113,000 pounds for the Electra), and the Viscount only weighs about half as much as the DC–7. The new BAC–1–11 and DC–9 aircraft weigh only about 80,000 pounds. Thus, gross weight has not been a talking point for ALPA in its productivity argument, and the gross weight rate has been practically unchanged for twelve years.

Copilot Pay. One central fact explains the evolution of copilot pay. The average length of time a man had to serve as a copilot on the major carriers before being promoted to first pilot rose sharply following the Second World War from a prewar average of two to three years to a postwar average as high as twelve years.

In the early days of aviation copilots were thought of as "necessary evils" placed on the planes by regulations of the Department of Commerce. They were expected to do all the menial tasks including serving as cabin attendants for the passengers. They were paid flat salaries which by 1933 only averaged $231.13 per month. Their hours of work were long both in the air and on the ground, totaling about 125 hours per month in 1933.[10] In spite of these conditions

---

[10] Federal Coordinator of Transportation, *op. cit.*, p. 34.

copilots were willing to accept their lot because they expected to move into the first pilot seat in a matter of a few months.

This situation was greatly altered following the Second World War. The airlines were swamped with many returning servicemen who regained their places on the pilot seniority lists. As a result many men who had been flying as first pilots during the war were bumped back into the copilot seat. The airline industry started to re-equip with the more productive DC–4 and Constellation aircraft and in so doing generally overestimated the potential size of the market. Both of these facts led to heavy layoffs of pilots in the recession of 1948. All these factors combined to make the copilot's outlook for promotion very dim, and the continuing introduction of faster equipment did not help the situation.

The first step the copilots took in their behalf was to obtain "first class citizenship status" in their union by insisting they be given an equal vote with the first pilots in all union matters. They obtained an equal voice during the ALPA convention of 1947. Since that time the proportion of young pilots on all types of ALPA committees has been rising. This has come about because the younger men outnumber the old timers in the union. The older pilots have increasingly lost interest in union affairs, while the younger men have shown increasing interest because they want to improve their wages and working conditions. Evidences of their success may be seen in the advent of flight pay for copilots, reserve guarantees, duty-time ratios, and narrowing of the wage gap between copilots and first pilots.

Copilots remained on flat salaries until the negotiations of 1951. In that year they succeeded in obtaining a common base pay with the first pilots plus their own hourly, mileage, and gross weight formulas. These formulas were in turn replaced in the next round of negotiations with the base pay plus percentage of first pilot flight pay formulas which have been described in the first half of this chapter.

In the late 1950's the senior copilots became concerned that under a formula comprising captain's base pay plus a percentage of captain hourly, mileage, and gross weight pay, their pay on the jets was proportionately less than it was on the pistons. Mathematically this was caused by the fixed base pay element representing less and less of total pay as larger and faster planes increased the hourly, mileage, and weight pay elements. Such an erosion of the copilot percentage could be stopped by constantly adjusting copilot percentages, and at least one carrier adopted two sets of copilot percentages, one for piston and one for jet copilots. In order to avoid having to adjust copilot percentages each time a faster piece of equipment arrived, the parties at most carriers changed their copilot formula so that copilots received percentages of *total* captain pay.

Over the years copilots have been able to raise their percentage of captain pay. Table 4.5 sets forth the most advanced set of copilot percentages of total captain pay as of the end of 1962.

TABLE 4.5.   COPILOT PERCENTAGES OF TOTAL
CAPTAIN PAY: AS OF DECEMBER 31, 1962

Year	Per Cent	Year	Per Cent
1st	$525*	7th	66%
2nd	600*	8th	67
3rd	62%	9th	68
4th	63	10th	69
5th	64	15th	72
6th	65		

* Salary

SOURCE: ALPA records.

This discussion of copilot pay has indicated the improvement of the copilot over the years both in his status in his union and in his percentage of captain compensation. The reasons for this improvement were the increasing seniority of the copilot group, its increasing size as a proportion of the total pilot group, and a growing frustration regarding promotion to captain.

Second Officer Pay. Second officers are third pilots on turbojet aircraft and are represented by the pilots. In most cases they are paid percentages of total first pilot pay or the joint base rate plus a percentage of first pilot flight pay. At one airline at least they receive copilot pay.

At another carrier, where they are no longer represented by ALPA,[11] their only form of compensation is a set of hourly rates which vary with longevity, type of equipment, and time of day (i.e., day or night). This, incidentally, represents a type of simplified compensation system which a number of carriers have been seeking at least since 1958.

Typically, the second officer percentages are below those for copilots with the same longevity. The top second officer percentages approximate the lowest copilot percentage. The percentages in Table 4.6 are in effect at a major carrier.

TABLE 4.6.   COPILOT AND SECOND OFFICER
PERCENTAGES OF TOTAL CAPTAIN PAY

Year	Copilot	Second Officer
1st	$500*	$500*
2nd	51%	38%
3rd	60	42
4th	61	43
5th	62	44
6th	63	46
7th	64	48
8th	65	49
9th	66	50
10th	67	51

* Salary

SOURCE: Applicable labor contract.

Flight Engineer Pay. Prior to 1951 flight engineers received flat salaries. As the result of an arbitration award in that year, they started to receive compensation under a formula comprising base, hourly, mileage, and gross weight similar to, but at lower rates than, the first pilot formula.

In 1958 flight engineer groups represented by the Flight Engineers' International Association agreed to the first significant simplification in the Decision #83 format. They agreed to a combined base and hourly pay element which varied with longevity and

[11] They are represented by the Allied Pilots' Association; see Chapter 8.

whether day or night, but not with aircraft speed. As a result, flight engineers after their probationary period received compensation from only three parts of the basic wage formula. (See Table 4.7.)

TABLE 4.7.   FLIGHT ENGINEER HOURLY,
MILEAGE, AND GROSS WEIGHT PAY

Year	Per Hour, Day	Per Hour, Night
3rd	$3.95	$5.45
4th	4.15	5.65
5th	4.35	5.85
6th	4.55	6.05
7th	4.75	6.25
8th	4.95	6.45
9th	5.15	6.65
10th	5.35	6.86

Mileage Pay: 1.8 cents per mile for each mile flown.
Gross Weight Pay: $.01 per 1,000 pounds of gross weight up to 150,000 pounds and $.002 per 1,000 pounds thereafter.

The flight engineers were probably willing to make these changes for at least two reasons. First, the airlines had been very anxious to simplify the methods of compensating flight crew members. This being true, the flight engineers may have been willing to abandon part of the Decision #83 formula as a concession to obtain more in the way of job security. Obtaining more job security has been the primary goal of the flight engineers since their inception. Second, the flight engineers may have been willing to eliminate the use of speed brackets to determine hourly pay because varying hourly pay in accordance with seniority produced about the same result. This was because the senior flight engineers usually flew on the faster types of equipment. Regardless of the reasons, these changes were interesting as the first departures from the Decision #83 format to which a group of flight crew members agreed.

Since 1958 most flight engineer groups have come to be represented by the pilots, and as a result now receive second officer percentages as outlined in the preceding section. At the domestic trunk lines where flight engineer compensation is still negotiated by the FEIA, the flight engineers have continued to improve their wage rates in the four typical elements of wage payment.

Analysis of the Guarantees

The Duty-Time Ratios. During the last decade the duty-time ratios have become more stringent. Although the evolution shows some variations, in general the following pattern may be said to have been typical: (1) in the late 1950's the on-duty ratio guaranteed one hour of pay time for every two and one half hours of *scheduled* on-duty time, and the trip-time ratio guaranteed one hour of pay time for every four hours of scheduled or *actual* trip time; (2) by 1963 a number of the ratios had been changed from a scheduled to a scheduled or actual basis; and (3) by mid-1965 a number of the on-duty ratios guaranteed one pay hour for every two hours on duty on an actual basis and a number of trip-time ratios guaranteed one pay hour for every three and one half hours on duty.

Some important variations from this pattern should be pointed out. An increasing number of contracts called for a flat minimum number of pay hours for each on-duty period no matter how short. This minimum has increased from three to four hours. In the case of TWA, as of October 1, 1966, the minimum guarantee for trips lasting more than 12 hours will be 6 pay hours. Another important exception is the negotiation of an on-duty guarantee of one pay hour for every one and three quarters hours on duty and a trip-time ratio of one pay hour for every three trip hours. This agreement contained these stringent duty-time ratios and, as will be seen shortly, an 81-hour minimum monthly guarantee for reserves, but it maintained the 85-hour monthly flight time limitation.

Why did ALPA create the duty-time ratios in the mid-1950's and continue to negotiate aggressively for a decade to obtain and to improve them? There were really two major problems that the pilots have been trying to solve, and the beauty of the duty-time ratios was that they tended to solve both of them.

In the first place, even the carriers will admit that in the past at least 5% of the monthly lines of flying normally represented very poor working conditions. They required a pilot, for example, to work long hours, many days per month, or spend several nights away from home. The carriers will also grant that scheduling abuses occurred in the past. Airlines traditionally placed a great deal of attention on devising profitable airplane schedules, while placing relatively little attention on devising pilot schedules which would ensure good working conditions. The duty-time ratios tended to alleviate this problem in two ways. They tended to make the carriers rearrange their crew schedules to avoid the ratios, and this meant better working conditions. Second, where poor sequences could not be eliminated, the pilot at least received credit for additional pay time for flying them, and thus his maximum exposure to poor working conditions was reduced on the basis of the monthly flight time limitation.

The second major problem continually threatening the pilots was technological unemployment. As far back as the hearings which led to Decision # 83 in 1934, pilots tried to solve this problem by a direct limitation on the number of miles a pilot could fly per month. But Decision #83 contained only an hourly limitation. The pilots tried unsuccessfully again to get a direct mileage limitation through negotiation in 1951 but the neutral in that case declined to give it to them. After these two defeats the pilots decided to attack the problem of unemployment from another direction. They decided to establish limitations by negotiating minimum standards for their working conditions and then to let the carrier schedule as it wished within those limitations. Until 1963 negotiating duty-time ratios was the pilots' method of establishing the limitations.

The duty-time ratios attack the problem of technological unemployment by diminishing the amount of actual flying an airline may obtain from a group of pilots. Every time a pilot receives credit for additional pay time under a duty-time ratio, his airline is losing actual flight time for which he is available. The airline then has to get someone else to make up the lost flight time. An assessment of the impact of these ratios in this regard will be made in the last section of the next chapter.

The Minimum Monthly Guarantee. The minimum monthly guarantees generally were raised from 60 to 70 hours during the period from 1958 to 1963. Since then a number of pilot contracts have called for direct reductions in monthly flight hours and proportional reductions in the guarantees. A new development has been the increase of the reserve guarantees to 81 hours accompanied by no reduction in monthly flight time.

The impetus for the minimum monthly guarantees came from the same junior pilots who pressed for copilot flight pay in 1951. Generally they succeeded in obtaining both the flight pay and the 60-hour guarantee in that year or soon thereafter. These were the men who found themselves blocked from early promotion to first pilot status. Hence they began looking for ways to improve their positions as copilots or as reserve first pilots. A good indication that the senior pilots did not feel strongly about obtaining the 60-hour guarantee is that it means very little to a senior pilot who can bid onto the type of equipment he wants and can generally fly a full schedule.

The manner in which the reserve guarantee has been negotiated has made it particularly beneficial to the reserve pilots who have somewhat less seniority than the most junior permanent first pilots. The typical clause guarantees them 70 hours at first pilot rates, even if they fly as first pilot only once during a month. By this guarantee some copilots have been able to raise their earnings significantly.

These pilots have also pressed for high ratios of reserve pilots to regular pilots because in that way more of them could become eligible for the 70-hour guarantee at first pilot rates.

The most important aspect of the minimum monthly guarantee is its setting of a floor below which the pay of reserve captains, copilots, and flight engineers will not drop regardless of the flight hours they are actually able to accrue in a month.

The Miscellaneous Flying Guarantee and the Guarantee of Schedule Integrity. A number of the methods of wage payment for pilots can be explained in terms of a theory which will be called the "Being Made Whole" theory for lack of a better title. This theory holds that pilots realize their flying careers are limited and that just 85 hours (or less with reductions) are available to them each month. Every flight hour is valuable because, once lost, it can never be made up. For these reasons, pilots always want their activities to be covered by some type of guarantee which will ensure that they do not lose pay for one of their valuable hours. They always want to be "made whole" when they lose a flight hour.

An example of this is the guarantee of schedule integrity. Under the uncertainties that surround flight schedules, the pilot wants at least to be guaranteed that if he is removed from his schedule by the company, he will be paid for his scheduled time anyway. He wants to be "made whole."

The same theory explains in part why the pilots have negotiated aggressively in the last few years for full pay when they are taken from their schedules for any type of training. Of course another reason for this particular drive is the ever-increasing amounts of training which pilots have been required to take within the last decade.

The miscellaneous flying guarantee is only partly explained by this theory. Its principal purpose is more to prevent the company from continually calling a pilot to the field for a very short flight. An interesting problem arose at one major carrier over this guarantee. The contract guaranteed a pilot two hours of flying for a miscellaneous flight but left unclear whether the pilot got another two hours if he took a second ten-minute flight. In one case this carrier credited a pilot with six hours of flight time because he had taken three short flights, no one of which was over fifteen minutes.

IMPACTS OF THE METHOD OF COMPENSATION

The preceding description and analysis permit some summary comments on the origin and importance of the basic wage formula. In addition, they lead to some assessments of the impacts of the formula on the wage differentials among flight crew members and on the general level of their wages.

The basic formula resulted from a voluntary arbitration award by a governmental board in 1933. With the pilots arguing for mileage pay and the carriers arguing for hourly pay, the government compromised and included both forms. Then ALPA was able to persuade Congress to make compliance with Decision #83 a condition for obtaining and keeping a route certificate. Since 1933 ALPA has refused to bargain away this basic pay formula involving base, hourly, and mileage rates. In addition, it has been able to negotiate a gross weight component.

This series of events indicates the interaction of arbitration, legislation, and negotiation to produce and maintain the fundamental wage terms in this industrial relations system. It highlights again the close ties between the parties and the government and the uniqueness of the institutional setting. The five carriers probably agreed to voluntary arbitration because, aware of their public relations image, they did not want labor strife to add to the risk of more governmental legislation and regulation. Although weak as a trade union, ALPA apparently could muster ample support in Congress to obtain legislation giving Decision #83 the force of law and thus in effect perpetuating it beyond attack at least at the bargaining table.

The importance of ALPA's efforts in obtaining and maintaining the basic pay formula cannot be overestimated. First, the carriers were opposed to its mileage component in 1933 and over the years have attempted to alter it. Clearly, without the strength and determination of ALPA a different pay formula would now be used. Second, by locking earnings to hourly and mileage rates which automatically increased earnings as aircraft speeds increased, ALPA could reap increased earnings without even negotiating any higher rates.

A clear illustration of the wage increases which faster and heavier aircraft bring about can be obtained from comparing potential earnings on the most lucrative pistons just prior to the first round of negotiations concerning jet wages with potential earnings on the most lucrative jets following those negotiations. Such data are presented in Table 4.8. The first jet negotiations produced earnings for captains with nine years of seniority flying 85 hours, one-half day and one-half night, which ranged among the trunks from 30.3% to 48.0% higher on the most lucrative jets than they had been on the most lucrative pistons under the preceding contracts. On July 24, 1959, American Airlines and ALPA amended their first jet contract and the comparable percentages increased to between 51.0% and 65.4%. The reader may recall that jet pegged speeds were purposefully kept low relative to their cruising speeds in order to keep an equitable relationship between jet and piston pilots. If this had not been done, the percentage increases presumably would have been higher.

One effect of the wage formula has been wide differentials among flight crew members. As will be discussed below, such differentials

TABLE 4.8.   INCREASES IN POTENTIAL EARNINGS OF NINE-YEAR
CAPTAINS BECAUSE OF THE EARLY NEGOTIATIONS
OVER JET AIRCRAFT

(Rates based on 85 hours, one-half day, one-half night)

Carrier	Date Contract Signed	Previous Pay on Most Lucrative Equipment	New Pay on Most Lucrative Equipment	Per Cent Increase in Pay
National	1-15-58	$1,678 (DC–7B)	$2,235 (DC–8)	33.2%
Western	11-19-58	1,489 (DC–6B)	1,940 (Electra)	30.3
Eastern	8-22-58	1,752 (DC–7B)	2,335 (DC–8)	33.2
American	1-13-59	1,602 (DC–7)	2,372 (707–123)	48.0
Delta	4-10-59	1,755 (DC–7B)	2,480 (DC–8)	41.3
United	5-12-59	1,817 (DC–7)	2,482 (DC–8)	36.6
TWA	5-28-59	1,811 (L–1649A)	2,437 (707–331)	34.6
Continental	5-29-59	1,845 (V–840)	2,405 (707–123)	30.4
As of 4-1-60			2,481 (707–123)	34.5
Northeast	7-13-59	1,670 (V–798)	2,568 (707–331)	53.8
American	7-24-59	1,602 (DC–7)*	2,518 (707–123)	57.2
Braniff	10-1-59	1,828 (DC–7C)	2,468 (707–131)	35.0
National	2-3-60	1,678 (DC–7B)†	2,247 (DC–8)	33.9
As of 8-1-60			2,533 (DC–8)	51.0
Western	6-1-60	1,489 (DC–6B)‡	2,462 (707)	65.4
Northeast	7-1-60	1,670 (V–798)	2,604 (707)	55.9
As of 1-1-61			2,678 (707)	60.4

* Prior to January 13, 1959, contract.
† Prior to January 15, 1958, contract.
‡ Prior to November 19, 1958, contract.

SOURCES: *ALPA News Bulletin,* Vol. 9, Nos. 3 and 25, Vol. 10,
Nos. 2, 11, 12, 13, and 16, Vol. 11, Nos. 5, 13, and 15, and ALPA,
"Second Interim Report of the ALPA Wage and Working Condi-
tions Policy Committee."

could be the result of definite occupational differences in job content or of personal differentials based on seniority.

Large differentials in earnings resulting from the formula exist
among flight crew members at each carrier. For example, the differential between a newly hired pilot engineer at $6,000 per year
and a senior captain at over $30,000 per year has already been
mentioned. One of the most dramatic changes in flight crew pay
differentials over the last three decades has been the increase in
copilot pay as a percentage of captain pay. As Table 4.9 shows,

TABLE 4.9. AVERAGE MONTHLY PAY OF DOMESTIC
CAPTAINS AND COPILOTS: 1933–1963

Year	Captain Pay	Copilot Pay	Copilot Pay as Per Cent of Captain Pay	Year	Captain Pay	Copilot Pay	Copilot Pay as Per Cent of Captain Pay
1933	$428	$202	47.2%	1949	N.A.	N.A.	N.A.
1934	524	201	38.4	1950	N.A.	N.A.	N.A.
1935	541	206	38.1	1951	N.A.	N.A.	N.A.
1936	N.A.	N.A.	N.A.	1952	$1,132	$ 628*	55.5%
1937	646	221	34.2	1953	1,201	689	57.4
1938	678	237	35.0	1954	1,222	675	55.2
1939	N.A.	N.A.	N.A.	1955	1,281	752	58.7
1940	704	214	30.4	1956	1,294	749	57.9
1941	684	215	31.4	1957	1,360	748	55.0
1942	684	214	31.3	1958	1,447	734	50.7
1943	582	230	39.5	1959	1,587	949	59.8
1944	660	234	35.5	1960	1,630	1,017	62.4
1945	N.A.	N.A.	N.A.	1961	1,769	1,101	62.2
1946	691	290	42.0	1962	1,846	1,196	64.8
1947	N.A.	N.A.	N.A.	1963	1,932	1,247	64.5
1948	N.A.	N.A.	N.A.				

* The copilot pay data for 1952–1963 include ALPA-represented second officers, flight engineers, and navigators.

SOURCES: 1933–1935 and 1938, *Air Commerce Bulletin,* Vol. 11, No. 4, October 15, 1939, p. 101; 1937, Air Transport Association of America records; 1940–1959, U.S. Government, "Report of the Presidential Railroad Commission," *Pay Practices for Flight Employees on U.S. Airlines* by Mark L. Kahn, Appendix Vol. IV, February 1962, p. 26; and 1960–1963, ALPA, *The Airline Pilot,* October 1964, p. 6.

this percentage declined during the period 1933 to 1940 when it reached a low of 30.4%. Since 1940 it has risen more or less steadily to a high of 64.5% in 1963. This reduced differential resulted from pressure of senior copilots within ALPA being exerted at the bargaining table, plus recognition by the carriers of the basic equity of their cause.

The wage formula has resulted also in substantial differentials among flight crew members of the same rank (captains, copilots, and flight engineers). For example, based on the rates described in the first part of this chapter, a captain with nine or more years of longevity flying 85 hours, one-half day, one-half night, in a DC-3 would earn $1,369 per month; whereas a similar captain flying an identical month in a Boeing 707 would earn $2,705.95. Thus the Boeing 707 captain would earn almost exactly twice as much as the DC-3 captain. ALPA has insisted on the use of straight seniority in the assignment of work. Thus, the senior captains bid the faster and heavier equipment and receive markedly higher earnings (and rates) than the junior captains at their airline. Similar differentials exist among copilots and flight engineers.

Another set of differentials brought about by the wage formula comes among earnings of pilot groups at different carriers. Table 4.10 which contains average monthly earnings of trunk line and local service line pilots carrier by carrier for 1952 and 1962 demonstrates this point. For example, in 1962 average monthly earnings of Central Airlines' pilots were $844, whereas the comparable figure at Braniff was $1,756. In 1962 the weighted average of all trunk line pilots was $1,587, while the local service line pilots

TABLE 4.10.   AVERAGE PILOT MONTHLY EARNINGS ON TRUNK LINES
AND LOCAL SERVICE LINES—1952 AND 1962

Trunk Lines	1952	1962	Local Service Lines	1952	1962
American	$892	$1,569	Allegheny	$629	$1,154
Braniff	824	1,756	Bonanza	620	1,160
Capital	771	—	Central	526	844
Continental	740	1,521	Frontier	688	1,064
Delta	770	1,432	Lake Central	563	951
Eastern	850	1,623	Mohawk	629	983
National	782	1,737	North Central	539	1,068
Northeast	692	1,361	Ozark	574	959
Northwest	954	1,646	Pacific	613	1,047
Trans World	890	1,712	Piedmont	667	1,100
United	813	1,562	Southern	598	857
Western	791	1,417	Trans-Texas	665	1,025
			West Coast	670	1,017
Weighted Ave. $843		$1,587	Weighted Ave.	$623	$1,018

SOURCE: Calculated from Appendices 2 and 3.

averaged $1,018. Over the period 1952–1962 the differential increased primarily because of the introduction of the large jets by the trunk lines. In 1952 average monthly earnings of local service line pilots were 73.9% of those for trunk line pilots. In 1962 the comparable percentage was 64.1%. So, the flight crew pay formula creates wide and increasing differentials among pilot groups.

These differentials represent in part valid occupational differences and in part personal differentials based on seniority. Differentials in base pay vary with straight seniority. On the other hand, hourly pay rate differentials based on aircraft speed, which were first initiated by the airline managements, probably represent valid occupational differences. They could probably be justified by such job evaluation factors as skill and responsibility. Similarly, some differentials between flight engineers, copilots, and captains could probably be so justified. Mileage pay, however, as a very minimum greatly exaggerates any earnings differentials which could be justified as meaningful occupational differentials. The same probably can be said of gross weight pay. To the extent that these differentials cannot be justified as occupational differences, they become personal differentials based on seniority. On balance one may say that the earning differentials of flight crew members are in large measure the accidental consequences of the wage formula being applied to the characteristics of new types of aircraft as they come along. In some measure these accidental consequences have been modified through the negotiation of guarantees and artificial pegged speeds. In general, however, the result has been a set of unplanned occupational and personal differentials of considerable magnitude.

An important question, of course, is whether ALPA was able to raise the general level of pilot pay above the level it would have obtained had the pilots been unorganized. Although no absolute answer can be given to this question, the combination of ALPA's success in maintaining and improving the Decision #83 pay formula and some analyses of increases in the general levels of pilot and nonpilot earnings strongly suggest that ALPA exerted a significant independent effect on the general level of pilot earnings.

As an example of one pertinent analysis, Professor H. Gregg Lewis estimates that "the relative wage effect of the Air Line Pilots Association on the relative wages of commercial airline pilots in 1956" was "24 percent if private training costs are applicable and 30 percent if Air Force training is applicable.[12] His estimates are based on refinements he made in an earlier study by Stephen Sobotka.[13] These studies are based on 1956 data and use chemical engineers as a nonunion bench mark group.

Another way to assess the impact of ALPA on the general level of pilot pay is to compare the earnings of pilots with other employee groups.

One such comparison can be made between pilot earnings and earnings of all production workers. Over the past 35 years a pervasive characteristic of wage patterns in this country has been a narrowing of the differentials between the skilled, the semiskilled, and the unskilled. Particularly marked has been the decrease in the differentials between the skilled as a group and the semiskilled and unskilled as a group.[14] Against this background, one would expect that over these years the differential in earnings between the pilots (a skilled group) and all production workers (on the average a much less skilled group) would have narrowed sharply. As shown in Table 4.11, such has not been the case. Indices based on average weekly earnings of captains and production workers for the period 1929–1931 show that by 1963 captains had risen to 402.5% of their earnings in the base years compared with a 437.0% for all production workers. By adding to this analysis a similar index for journeymen in the building trades which is a skilled union group generally recognized as exerting a strong influence on its earnings, one can gain a better appreciation for the role ALPA played in raising the general level of pilot pay. In 1963 such an index for journeymen stood at 317.5 (see column 6 of Table 4.11), thus indicating that the journeymen were significantly less successful than the pilots in preventing the narrowing of differentials with the less skilled employee groups.

[12] H. Gregg Lewis, *Unionism and Relative Wages in the United States* (Chicago: University of Chicago Press, 1963), pp. 99 and ff.

[13] Stephen Sobotka *et al.*, "Analysis of Airline Pilot Earnings," Unpublished and Classified Mimeograph MS, Transportation Center, Northwestern University, 1958.

[14] W. S. Woytinsky and Associates, *Employment and Wages in the United States,* Chapter 40 "Occupational Wage Differentials in Industry," by Harry Ober (New York: The Twentieth Century Fund, 1953), pp. 466–474.

TABLE 4.11. COMPARISONS OF THE AVERAGE WEEKLY EARNINGS
OF CAPTAINS AND PRODUCTION WORKERS ON MANUFACTURING
PAYROLLS: 1929–1963

Year (1)	Ave. Weekly Captain Pay (2)	Ave. Weekly Earnings of Production Workers (3)	Index of Captain Pay: 1929–1931 Base (4)	Index of Production Worker Pay: 1929–1931 Base (5)	Index of Ave. Union Hourly Rates of Journeymen in the Bldg. Trades: 1929–1931 Base* (6)
1929	$126.44	$24.76	114.6	108.6	97.1
1930	105.75	23.00	95.8	100.9	101.3
1931	98.85	20.64	89.6	90.5	101.6
1932	94.94	16.89	96.0	74.1	86.9
1933	98.39	16.65	89.2	73.0	84.6
1938	155.86	22.07	141.3	96.8	103.4
1943	133.79	43.07	121.3	188.9	116.0
1948	—	53.12	—	—	—
1953	276.09	70.47	250.2	310.3	212.8
1958	332.64	82.71	301.5	362.8	261.5
1963	444.14	99.63	402.5	437.0	317.5

* Journeymen worked approximately 10% more hours per week during the base period than in 1963.

SOURCES: Captain pay calculated from data given in the following sources: 1933 and 1938, *Air Commerce Bulletin*, Vol. 11, No. 4, October 15, 1939, p. 101; 1943–1958, U.S. Government, "Report of the Presidential Railroad Commission," *Pay Practices for Flight Employees on U.S. Airlines*, by Mark L. Kahn, Appendix Vol. IV, February 1962, p. 26; 1963, ALPA, *The Airline Pilot*, October 1964, p. 6.

Pay for production workers on manufacturing payrolls from U.S. Bureau of Labor Statistics Bulletin No. 1312–2, *Employment and Earning Statistics of the United States: 1909–1964*, December 1964, p. XVI; and U.S. Bureau of Labor Statistics Bulletin No. 1432, *Union Wages and Hours: Building Trades*, February 1965, p. 6.

On balance, it would appear that ALPA by holding to and improving the basic wage formula has raised the general level of pilot pay significantly above the level the pilots could have achieved bargaining as individuals. During these years the pilots had the opportunity to take advantage of an expanding industry undergoing important technological changes which increased productivity. Although a detailed look at the bargaining power of the parties will be taken in Chapter 10, it might be pointed out that in such a situation a union group's relative bargaining power to win wage demands is enhanced. To use Chamberlain's terms, "the cost to management of disagreeing with the union" is relatively low.[15]

This analysis is not intended to pass judgment on the absolute level of pilot earnings or on their earnings relative to other employee groups. No set of rules exists to indicate how much pilots should be paid. One may point out, however, that the pilots as a group have essentially held their differential with all production workers and have widened their differential with journeymen in the building trades during 30 years when the skill, responsibility, and hazards of their job have probably declined.

[15] Neil W. Chamberlain, *Collective Bargaining* (New York: McGraw-Hill Book Company, 1951), p. 221.

CHAPTER 5

The Characteristics of Airline Scheduling

SCHEDULING is one of the most important subjects in the working life of an airline flight crew member. It is important because an individual's flight schedule largely determines his wages, hours, and working conditions. If a flight crew member has one schedule, he could conceivably miss his son's graduation from high school or his daughter's wedding. One schedule will mean that he will leave his home at 3:00 A.M. every Friday morning and will not return until 11:45 P.M., Sunday evening. One schedule will call for him to fly only ten days during a month and be home every night, while another will require him to fly twenty days in a month and to be in a hotel hundreds of miles from home for ten nights. Since the average pilot can be assumed to enjoy being home every night, to enjoy having weekends and holidays free to share with his family, and to wish to work relatively few days rather than many, scheduling is a subject in which he is normally very much interested.

Scheduling is also of the greatest importance to an air carrier. This statement applies to the scheduling both of the airplanes and of the flight crews. Airplane scheduling determines in large measure how much revenue a carrier will receive because it is so directly related to load factors. One airplane schedule will enable a carrier to fill a plane to capacity in the early morning rush of businessmen between two cities, while a schedule that calls for a little later departure from the same city may mean an almost empty airplane because most of the businessmen will have left on a competitor's flight.[1] One airplane schedule will enable passengers to connect

[1] Paul W. Cherington, *Airline Price Policy* (Boston: Division of Research, Harvard Business School, 1958), p. 35. The author pointed out that in 1955 travel for business reasons accounted for about 55% of all air trips. The percentage is higher for first class flights (up to 65%) and lower for coach flights (down to 22% for the irregular carriers).

conveniently with another flight and therefore be popular. A slightly altered schedule may miss that connection and lose some passengers thereby. One way of scheduling a carrier's planes results in flight crew schedules which permit it to get a full month's work from every flight crew member, while another will result in relatively poor crew utilization. Because the management of an airline normally may be assumed to be attempting to maximize profits, it too is vitally interested in the scheduling process.

This chapter is divided into three parts. The first part contains a description of the scheduling process at the same domestic trunk line used as an example in Chapter 4. Scheduling is subdivided into the following four steps: (1) airplane scheduling; (2) building sequences of flights which represent a day's work for a crew member; (3) combining sequences into monthly lines of flying which represent a month's work for a crew member; and (4) the daily administration of flight crew scheduling. The second part contains an analysis of the impacts which the flight crew unions have made throughout the industry on the same four steps in the scheduling process. The third part analyzes a resulting decline in flight crew utilization.

A DESCRIPTION OF THE SCHEDULING PROCESS

Airplane Scheduling

The first step in the scheduling process is airplane scheduling. At this small trunk line airplane scheduling is the primary responsibility of the General Traffic Manager and the Manager of Schedules. Working two months in advance of the date on which a new schedule will become effective, these men decide the times, the stops, and the equipment of every flight the airline will offer to the public. They produce two documents—the general schedule and the ship routing chart. The general schedule is a detailed version of the familiar airline passenger schedule. It portrays the arrival and departure times of all the flights to be offered to the public. The ship routing chart shows exactly which particular airplane will be used to fly which particular flights. Thus, the general schedule refers to the scheduling of traffic while the ship routing chart applies to the scheduling of the individual aircraft.

In general, an airline offers the same flights to the public every day. The exceptions come on weekends and holidays when several flights are usually dropped and a few are added. This daily repetition means that basically the airplane schedulers have to figure out a schedule for the entire airline system for only one day. The schedule for one day will apply to every day for which there are not weekend or holiday exceptions. However, devising proper schedules for one day is a complex art.

The process of scheduling airplanes has been described correctly by one airline executive as the making of countless compromises in an attempt to maximize profits. The primary consideration is having the type of service available at the proper times and places in order to generate full loads. But even this consideration involves compromises. For example, 5:00 P.M. is the "magic hour"—the most popular time of the day for departing as far as passengers are concerned.[2] This tends to mean that if a carrier could have aircraft depart from most of the cities it serves at 5:00 P.M., it could probably obtain good pay loads. A carrier, however, does not have enough aircraft to give every city on its route complete late afternoon service. The carrier could not afford to have that many planes because the volume of traffic throughout the day would not support them. Compromises, therefore, must be made to obtain the best load factors from the available equipment. The airplane schedulers will spread their aircraft around the system as much as possible to give good late afternoon service, but some cities will not have an attractive late afternoon flight offered by this carrier. So some of the travelers will take a competitor's flight, take a train, or drive.

The compromises required to get the best load factors are not the only ones the airplane schedulers must make. In the first place, they must schedule any airplane with enough time in between flights to enable the operations department to gas and provision it, and to permit the flight crews to give it a pre-flight inspection. Also, if they expect to maintain schedules, they must allow some time between the arrival of one flight and the departure of the next flight using the same plane. Otherwise a delay in the first flight will cause a delay in the second flight.

The maintenance department is required to carry out periodic

[2] Air Transport Association of America, *Airline Scheduling,* (Washington: By the Association, 1961), p. 58.

aircraft inspections and overhauls. Although their frequency and duration vary among airlines and types of equipment, this carrier operates as follows: an aircraft engine is given a terminal check every 40 flight hours, an equalized check every 175 flight hours, and a block overhaul every 2,500 flight hours. On the average these checks keep an aircraft out of service for 5 hours, 12 hours, and 10 days, respectively. Thus, the head of the maintenance department is very much interested in seeing that the airplane schedulers have scheduled the planes into a base where maintenance is performed often enough and long enough to get the maintenance done. At the carrier in question, he checks the ship routing chart in its provisional form, and requires changes in it when maintenance cannot be accomplished properly.

Another set of compromises in the area of airplane scheduling occasionally is required by the men who do the flight crew scheduling. They also check the provisional ship routing chart to make sure that the airplane schedules do not contain situations which will inevitably cause impossible or extremely poor flight crew schedules. Because such schedules occur infrequently, the impact of flight crew scheduling on airplane scheduling is minimal. The crew schedulers try to eliminate flight crew schedules which would not be permitted by government regulation. For example, Civil Aeronautics Regulation 40.320(b) reads as follows:

> An air carrier shall not schedule any flight crew member for duty aloft for more than 8 hours during any 24 consecutive hours, unless he is given an intervening rest period at or before the termination of 8 scheduled hours of duty aloft. Such rest period shall equal twice the number of hours of duty aloft since the last preceding rest period, and in no case shall the rest period be less than 8 hours.

What this regulation means can best be explained with examples. In the first place, the airplane schedulers could not schedule an airplane on a nonstop flight which was scheduled to last longer than eight hours because there would only be one way to give the crew "an intervening rest period at or before the termination of 8 scheduled hours."[3] The one way would be to have two crews on

[3] Exceptions have been granted by the government in the case of westerly coast-to-coast DC–7 nonstop flights.

the flight, a procedure which is never followed in domestic service because of cost considerations.[4] The airplane scheduler must schedule an aircraft in such a way that the flight crew can get the proper amount of rest. For example, a plane could be scheduled to leave at 1:00 a.m. with crew members who have been off duty for 24 hours. The first flight could be scheduled to last for five hours which would mean that it would be scheduled to arrive at 6.00 a.m. At that point the crew would have to be given a rest of "twice the number of hours of duty aloft since the last preceding rest period" before taking a flight that would give them more than three more flight hours. So they would need a ten-hour rest. Throughout the airline industry flight crews are required to report one hour before the departure of their next flight.[5] Because that is the time at which the rest period terminates, this flight crew could not be scheduled for another flight which would give it a total of 8 hours aloft with a departure time earlier than 5:00 p.m., which is eleven hours after its 6:00 a.m. arrival. An earlier flight of that length would be illegal for this crew to fly. Usually there will be a way to have another crew available to take the second flight if it is illegal for the first crew to take it. If the crew schedulers find an airplane schedule which inevitably would lead to a flight crew's being illegal, however, they will ask the airplane schedulers to change their schedule.

Another unusual situation which the crew schedulers wish to eliminate from the ship routing chart is any proposed airplane schedule which will require grossly inefficient use of the flight crews. In such a case the crew schedulers will suggest that changes be made in the airplane schedules, and the airplane schedulers will decide whether a profit can be made from the anticipated load on that schedule even though the flight crew utilization will be inefficient and costly. Perhaps a slightly different schedule can be devised which will get the load and allow good crew utilization.

After the Manager of Schedules and the General Traffic Manager have revised the airplane schedules to eliminate impossible maintenance or flight crew problems, they review their work with the

---

[4] Multiple crews are used on international flights.

[5] Also throughout the industry flight crews are allowed either 15 or 30 minutes at the end of their last flight to check in and to fill out the necessary reports. This debriefing time has been omitted from the scheduling calculations in this chapter in the interest of simplicity.

President and Vice President-Sales of the airline. The primary purpose of this review is to ensure that the airplane schedules have been arranged to obtain as high load factors as possible while still giving adequate service to all parts of the routes over which the carrier is required to operate. Flight crew scheduling, which is of greatest concern to this analysis, only enters the picture when impossible or illegal situations occur. This carrier does not and economically cannot start by devising flight crew schedules which would result in excellent hours, wages, and working conditions, and then work out airplane schedules to fit. Therefore, the basic conditions under which the crew schedulers work out the flight crew schedules have been given to them. Then their job is to devise flight crew schedules which will ensure as good manpower utilization and working conditions as the airplane schedules permit.

Before discussing the manner in which flight crew scheduling is carried out at this small trunk line, some definitions will be helpful. An airline flight may make several stops between its points of origin and termination. The segments of the flight between each stop are known as "legs" of the flight. The airports at which an airline stops are generally called "bases." A carrier will have flight crew members living at only a few of its bases, and those bases are known as "domiciles." The carrier being described here maintains three domiciles.

Building Flight Crew Sequences

The two men who carry out the first two steps in the flight crew scheduling process at the airline in question are known as Chief Crew Schedule Planners. Working from the ship routing chart and the general schedule, they first write down the scheduled flight times and the type of equipment for each leg of every flight which appears on those documents. The reason for obtaining all these individual times is to get themselves in a position where they can group a number of legs together to make a good day's work for a crew member. Each of these groupings is known as a "sequence." A sequence may consist of any number of legs. In the case of long, nonstop flights, an entire sequence may consist of only one leg. Usually several legs will be combined to form a sequence which will result in a good day's work for a crew member.

TABLE 5.1. SAMPLE LIST OF SEQUENCES

Sequences	Time of Each Leg	Total Time	Origin City Time	Termination City Time
{710–711, 611–611*	40 + 40 + 63 + 265	408 } 718	"A" 0700	"D" 1525
{618–622	250 + 50	310 }	"D" 1430	"A" 2200
{607*	340	340 } 660	"A" 0800	"D" 1410
{630	320	320 }	"D" 1545	"A" 2130
{609–609*	63 + 265	328 } 638	"A" 0830	"C" 1425
{624–624	250 + 60	310 }	"C" 1600	"A" 2140
{863–863*	63 + 270	333 } 653	"A" 2230	"E" 0450
{864–864	260 + 60	320 }	"E" 2300	"A" 0505
{869*	310	310 } 605	"A" 2359	"D" 0509
{880	295	295 }	"D" 0100	"A" 0555

* Remains overnight away from domicile. Bracketed sequences are flown by the same crew.

One way to make this clearer is to present some sequences actually scheduled by the crew schedule planners. Table 5.1 presents ten of the DC–6 sequences which were scheduled to be flown from one domicile of this airline. Other sequences covered the other types of equipment and domiciles. Table 5.2 presents some excerpts from the passenger schedule which was effective during the same month. These tables should be read together. For example, the fifth line in the list of sequences contains a sequence that consists of two legs of Flight #609. The first leg is scheduled to have 63 minutes of flight time and the second leg is scheduled to have 265 minutes for a total of 328 minutes. The sequence starts in City "A" at 8:30 a.m. and ends in City "C" at 2:25 p.m. The excerpt from the passenger schedule gives the missing information which is that Flight #609 stops at City "B" for 27 minutes at 9:33 a.m.

TABLE 5.2   EXCERPT FROM THE PASSENGER SCHEDULE

East to West *Flt. # 609*	*West to East* *Flt. # 624*
City "A" leave 8:30 A.M.	City "C" leave 4:00 P.M.
City "B" arrive 9:33	City "B" arrive 8:10
leave 10:00	leave 8:40
City "C" arrive 2:25 P.M.	City "A" arrive 9:40

The list of sequences would also inform a flight crew member that he could expect to fly the sequence on line five in conjunction with the sequence on line six. The bracket around the two sequences means they are flown together, and the asterisk signifies that the flight crew spends the night away from its domicile. Sequences are referred to by the flight number of the first leg of the sequence. Therefore, these are the 609 and the 624 sequences.

By using the information on the list of sequences and the other excerpt from the passenger schedule, the nature of the 624 sequence may be determined. It starts in City "C" at 4:00 p.m. and arrives in City "A" at 9:40 p.m. after having stopped for 30 minutes in City "B". If the pilot flew these sequences as scheduled, he would accrue 638 minutes of flight time—328 minutes on the trip west and 310 minutes in the other direction. He would be gone from 8:30 a.m. one day until 9:40 p.m. the next day.

There are several important rules, regulations, and agreements which the crew schedule planners must adhere to when they are making up the sequences each month. One of them has already been mentioned in the description of airplane scheduling. To comply with that government regulation they must allow a certain amount of time for an intervening rest period between flights when they schedule a flight crew for more than eight hours of flight time within any 24-hour period.

In the late 1950's the job of the crew schedule planners was made more difficult by the negotiation of the on-duty and trip-time ratios because they impinge on the crew schedule planners' freedom to schedule the flight crews.

Although no additional flight time is involved, the 609 sequence in Table 5.1 provides an example of the way the on-duty ratio is calculated. The first departure of the 609 sequence is scheduled for 8:30 a.m. which means that the crew member's on-duty period is scheduled to start at 7:30 a.m. The last leg of the sequence is scheduled to terminate at City "C" at 2:25 p.m.; therefore, the crew member is scheduled to be on duty for 6 hours and 55 minutes, or 415 minutes. The on-duty ratio guarantees him at least one hour of flight time for every two and one-half hours on duty. Another way to say this is that he is guaranteed flight time equal to 40% of the time he is scheduled to spend on duty. In this case, 40% of 415 minutes is 166 minutes. The 609 sequence is scheduled to provide the crew member with 328 minutes of flight time. Therefore, since the scheduled number of minutes of the sequence is greater than the number of minutes guaranteed under the on-duty ratio, the flight crew member would be receiving no additional flight time in this case. Interestingly, in no instance in the schedule given in Table 5.1 did a flight crew pick up additional flight time under the on-duty time ratio. And since that ratio only applies *on a scheduled basis,* the crew schedule planners could be certain before any flights took place that no additional flight time would be guaranteed under the on-duty time ratio.

The way the trip-time ratio is calculated may be demonstrated by the 609 sequence of Table 5.1. In that case the crew member's trip time will start at 7:30 a.m. one day, or at the time he actually reports if it is later than 7:30 a.m. The trip time will end at 9:40 p.m. the following day if he arrives on schedule, or at the actual time he does arrive if it differs from 9:40 p.m. If he flies the 609 and 624 sequences exactly as scheduled, his trip time will be 38 hours and 10 minutes, or 2,290 minutes. In this case he would be guaranteed 573 minutes. Because these two sequences are scheduled to have 638 minutes of flight time, again the crew member would be guaranteed no additional flight time under the guarantee. But if his 624 sequence should be cancelled for any reason and he should be rescheduled to take the 624 sequence 24 hours later, he would be guaranteed an additional 6 hours of flight time for the extra time away from his home domicile. In that case, if he flew the 624 sequence the following day exactly as scheduled, his trip would be from 7:30 a.m. one day until 9:40 p.m. two days later —a total of 3,730 minutes. Therefore, he would be guaranteed 933 flight time minutes. Thus he would pick up 295 minutes of flight time which is the difference between his actual flight time and his guarantee.

Table 5.3 shows some sequences which were paired in the schedule for the same month in such a way that if the flight crew members flew them as scheduled, they would pick up additional flight time under the trip-time guarantee. Of course any sequence could result in additional flight time under this guarantee if it was delayed long enough when it was actually flown.

The crew schedule planners are anxious to build sequences which are not likely to give the flight crew members credit for any flight time under the guarantees of the duty-time ratios. This is important because every minute which is credited to a flight crew member under the guarantees is deducted from the 85 hours of flying he may perform in a month. As was mentioned in Chapter 2, the National Labor Board's Decision #83 set a limitation of 85 hours of flying per month on every flight crew member. This limitation was meant to apply to hours actually spent in the air flying an aircraft. By contract agreement, however, the time which is credited under the duty-time ratios is now included as "hours of flying" and therefore is deducted from the 85 hours. Such deductions directly reduce the amount of actual flying an airline can get from its flight crew members each month. For example, a crew member flying sequences 241 and 194, shown in the first two rows of Table 5.3, would accrue 45 minutes of flight time if they were flown on

TABLE 5.3. LIST OF SEQUENCES INVOLVING TRIP TIME

Sequences	Time of Each Leg	Total Time	Extra Trip Time Minutes	Origin City Time	Termination City Time
{Sat. 241*	110	110}		"A" 1745	"F" 1935
{Sun. 194–194–255–818	65 + 55 + 110 + 95	325} 435	45	"F" 1645	"A" 0035
(300–303)–320–321*	27 + 100 + 84 + 84	295}		"A" 0615	"G" 1314
358–359–[478–483]–[378–379]	64 + 64 + 84 + 27 + 46 + 46	331} 626	28	"G" 1530	"A" 0045
Sat. 127–127–240–255*	60 + 75 + 95 + 110	340}		"A" 1300	"F" 2150
Sun. 258	95	95} 435	75	"F" 2030	"A" 2205
{332–333–350–351–366*	52 + 52 + 74 + 74 + 97	349}		"A" 1050	"H" 2257
{355	99	99} 448	112	"H" 2125	"A" 2310
{Sat. 403–320–321*	99 + 84 + 84	267}		"A" 0625	"G" 1314
{Sun. 384–387–492	100 + 100 + 107	307} 574	71	"G" 1640	"A" 0004
[Sat. 342–343–361*	46 + 46 + 161	253]		"A" 1255	"G" 1900
{Sun. 320–321–358–359*	84 + 84 + 64 + 64	296} 856	44	"G" 0950	"G" 1819
[Mon. 384–387–492	100 + 100 + 107	307]		"G" 1640	"A" 0004

* Remains overnight away from domicile.

schedule. The crew member would receive pay for that 45 minutes and would be limited to 84 hours and 15 minutes of time actually flying an aircraft during that month. Sequences 332 and 355 on the same table credit the flight crew member with 112 minutes if flown on schedule. Since those sequences are flown every day of the month, there are 3,360 minutes of time actually available for flying an aircraft which must be deducted from both the captain group and the copilot group. Putting this another way, the airline loses 56 hours of pilot and copilot time which would be available for actually flying an aircraft if the trip-time ratio were not in effect. Therefore, the airline must have an extra pilot and copilot on its payroll to cover these hours lost on only these two sequences. Needless to say, the crew schedule planners attempt to devise sequences which will avoid any flight time accruals under the on-duty or the trip-time ratios.

Apart from the government regulations and the contract terms which the crew schedule planners must watch, at this airline some pertinent scheduling rules have been mutually worked out and signed by representatives of the operations department and of the pilots' local scheduling committee. One rule reads as follows:

> The daily on-duty time will not normally exceed twice the flight time and will be as near as possible to the flight time.

The practical meaning of this rule is that the crew schedule planners should normally set up the sequences in such a way that flight time will equal at least 50% of the on-duty time. This is 25% more rigorous than the 40% established in the on-duty ratio. The rule also means that both parties would like to see crew members spend as little time on duty as possible when not actually flying. For example, an ideal sequence would consist of one eight-hour leg. That would give the crew member eight hours of flight time for nine hours on duty, considering the one hour reporting time.

A second scheduling rule reads that it is desirable for any sequence or group of sequences not to involve more than one type of aircraft. For example, a sequence with three legs could conceivably require a crew to fly a DC–3, a DC–6, and a Boeing 707, all in the same day. At that extreme, the demands on the flight crew to adjust to the variations among the different aircraft types and to stay qualified on all three would be too great. Such a sequence would not be put together. Also pistons and jets would not be put in the same sequence. A sequence mixing DC–6 and DC–7 equipment might be made, but it would still be counter to this scheduling rule. The basic reason why the airline might wish to mix equipment is to obtain more flexibility in putting the sequences together. This is simply a question of a greater number of alternatives giving a better chance for the planners to work out satisfactory schedules. The basic reason that the crew members might be opposed to mixing equipment is that it negates seniority. In general, the larger and faster aircraft are used on the long flights with few stops. This type of flight is desirable because it has a high ratio of flight time to on-duty time, and does not involve the work of landing and taking off very frequently. The senior crew members normally want as many of these flights as they can get and believe that their seniority affords them this privilege. But if the sequences are constructed with mixed equipment which implies some long and some short legs, the senior crew members must fly that mixture. So to give seniority its due, this scheduling rule was adopted.

With these rules, regulations, and agreements in mind, the crew schedule planners put the sequences together. They start by making sequences out of the legs of the most desirable equipment which they think will involve a crew's remaining overnight (RON) away from its domicile. They start with RON's because they are likely to involve on-duty or trip-time ratios, or to be in conflict with one of the other rules or regulations. After they have the RON's satisfactorily put into sequences, the planners then work out the rest of the sequences for that type of equipment, almost as one would do a jigsaw puzzle. Then they repeat the process for each type of equipment, in decreasing order of speed and desirability. Their work is definitely an art rather than a science. One factor which saves them a great deal of effort is that relatively few airplane schedules are changed from one month to another so that many of the sequences may be used again. Because this is a matter of adjusting many interrelated factors, however, occasionally just one change in the airplane schedule will necessitate an almost complete revision of the flight crew sequences.

When all the sequences have been built, the planners must calculate the total amounts of flight time which will be required in each type of equipment at each domicile. Such calculations are necessary to ensure that enough flight crew members will be found at each domicile with the requisite qualifications to handle the flying assigned to that domicile. The planners must know how many flight crew members at each domicile will not be flying during the month because of time spent on vacation, leaves of absence, or training. They will usually deduct some flight time also from each domicile to cover unexpected exigencies. Fortunately leeway is available to the planners in assigning flight time among the three domiciles. For example, on Table 5.1 the first two sequences (710 and 618) have been combined in such a way that they would be flown by a flight crew domiciled at City "A." This is true because the crews flying these sequences start and terminate at City "A." However, if the planners found they were assigning more flight time to the City "A" domicile than could be flown by the available number of City "A" flight crews, they could reverse the 710 and the 618 sequences. In that case they would be flown by a crew from the City "D" domicile because then the sequences would start and terminate at City "D." If such switching of sequences does not completely match the total flight time assigned to a domicile with the flight crews available to handle it, the company has the right to assign a crew from another domicile to handle the excess.

When the crew schedule planners have set up all the sequences, they review their work with the Chief Pilot and the Manager of Crew Schedules. Then these four men together proceed to combine the sequences into groups which can be flown as a month's work by a flight crew member. These groups of sequences are known as "monthly lines of flying." Their formulation is the next step in the crew scheduling process.

Building Monthly Lines of Flying

The crew schedulers try to put sequences together in such a way that the flight crew member will actually fly just under 85 hours each month. They want the crew members to be close to that amount because it represents the maximum utilization the carrier can obtain from its crew members under Decision #83. The crew members themselves want to be credited with close to 85 hours because that produces maximum earnings for them. Both parties have agreed in their scheduling rules that each line of flying will contain as close to 85 hours as possible.

Four of the DC–6 monthly lines of flying which were offered to the flight crews at the City "A" domicile are presented in Table 5.4. Similar lines of flying existed for the rest of the equipment types offered to this domicile and the other two domiciles. The first column in Table 5.4 lists simply the days of the month with weekends in boldface. The second column lists the sequences which were combined to form a monthly line of flying known as A 11. This line of flying consists of seven pairs of sequences 609 and 624, and one sequence 730.

These four monthly lines of flying contained the following scheduled amounts of flight time in minutes: A 11, 4,929; A 12, 4,794; A 13, 5,104; A 14, 4,776. There are 5,100 minutes in 85 hours. So line of flying A 11 comes within 171 minutes of being scheduled up to the maximum. Line A 13 with 5,104 minutes contains just over 85 hours. This is not an infrequent occurrence. The planners have found that on some types of flights, and at certain times of the year, they can schedule flight crews slightly over 85 hours, and be relatively certain that a cancellation will actually bring them under that limit during the month.

The planners must of course follow the rules, regulations, and agreements which have already been mentioned. In addition there are several others to be heeded. Civil Aeronautics Regulation 40.320(a) does not permit them to schedule a flight crew member over the following flight time limitations:

(1) 1,000 hours in any year
(2)   100 hours in any month
(3)   30 hours in any seven consecutive days

As a practical matter, only the third limitation must be heeded because the 85-hour limitation of Decision #83 is more stringent than either the first or second of these FAA limitations. By contract agreement the 85 hours of flying has come to mean 85 hours of accrued pay time. Therefore, a crew member could not reach the 100-hour flight time limitations because by its construction pay time will always be greater than actual flight time. Also, the 1,000 hour yearly limitation would seldom be reached because 1,020 hours per year is the maximum permissible under the 85-hour monthly limitation. Very few flight crew members will be over 83 hours in any given month.

TABLE 5.4. SAMPLE MONTHLY LINES OF FLYING
Sequence Numbers

Days of the Month	A 11	A 12	A 13	A 14
1			609	624
2	609		624	
3	624	609		
4		624	609	
5			624	609
6		609		624
7	609	624		
8	624			609
9			609	624
10	609		624	
11	624	609		
12		624	609	
13			624	609
14		609		624
15	609	624		
16	624			609
17			609	624
18	609		624	
19	624	609		
20		624	609	
21			624	609
22		609		624
23	609	624		
24	624			609
25			609	624
26	609		624	
27	624	609		
28		624	609	
29	730		624	609
30		609		624

Note: Days of the month with weekends in bold face.

The 30-hour limitation does impinge on the planners as they are building the sequences. The regulation applies on a scheduled basis which means that no violation of the law occurs if the crew member is scheduled for less than 30 hours but actually goes over that amount in a seven-day period. Again by contract agreement, the 30 hours are calculated on the basis of pay hours rather than on actual flight time.

The final government regulation which they must watch requires each crew member actually to be relieved from all duty for at least 24 consecutive hours in any seven consecutive days. It should be noted that this does not refer to a calendar day free from all duty. The regulation would be satisfied if a crew member terminated one sequence at any location at noon on one day and reported for duty the following day at 12:01 p.m. The parties on their own, however, have agreed to a scheduling rule under which an attempt will be made to give a crew member at least 48 consecutive hours free of all duty in any seven consecutive days. An example of a monthly line of flying in which the planners failed in this attempt can be seen in the A 11 line of flying in Table 5.4. In the seven-day period from November 23 through 29, the crew member was not scheduled to be off for 48 consecutive hours.

Agreement has also been reached in the scheduling rules that successive overnights will be avoided whenever possible. The reason, of course, is to have the crew member home at least every other night. An instance in which the planners failed to meet this agreement can be seen in the last group of sequences in Table 5.3. In that case, a flight crew leaves City "A" at 12:55 p.m. on Saturday and does not return to City "A" for a night until 0:04 a.m. Tuesday morning.

A description of the scheduling process would not be complete without mentioning the scheduling of reserve crew members. As the name implies, reserve crew members are kept in reserve to fly any flights which are not included in the monthly lines of flying, or which are not covered for some reason as the month progresses. Two good reasons might be the illness of a crew member who was scheduled to take a flight, or the addition of another flight during the month to handle an unexpected volume of traffic. Reserve first pilots are men who are qualified in every way to fly as a first pilot but do not have the seniority to get one of the monthly lines of flying. If the most senior pilot on the airline, however, chose to fly in a reserve capacity for a month, he would be a reserve first pilot for that month. The less senior pilot who moved up to a monthly line of flying because of the vacancy would become a regular first pilot for that month.

In accordance with the scheduling rules at this carrier, the crew schedulers must establish one reserve schedule for every six monthly lines of flying at each domicile. The reserve schedules merely list the days of the month on which the reserve first pilot holding that schedule can be certain of being off duty. Each reserve schedule must contain at least three 48 consecutive hour periods off during the month. An example of four reserve schedules is shown in Table 5.5. On the days marked with an "R," the reserve first pilot holding that schedule must keep himself available to depart on two hours' notice. On the blank days, he will be completely off duty.

The last step in building the lines of flying is to establish what is known as "pool time." This time consists of flights which are not included in the monthly lines of flying. Having such a pool is advantageous to the crew members for use in building up their flight time close to 85 hours as the month progresses. For example, a crew member originally may be scheduled with a line of flying with 84 hours but flight cancellations during the month could bring that figure down to 75 hours. In that event, he could use some of the flights in the pool to get his total flight hours for the month back up to around 85. The word "projection" is used in this regard to mean the pay time a crew member has accrued in a month plus the flight time which he is still scheduled to obtain later in the month. Thus, in the above example, the man's original projection was 84 hours, then his projection dropped to 75 hours, and by using pool flights he brought his projection back up near 85. Since pool time is advantageous to have, the parties have agreed that about 10% of the total scheduled time will be placed in the pool when the lines of flying are made up each month. An example of DC–3 pool sequences is shown in Table 5.6.

After all the monthly lines of flying, reserve schedules, and pool times have been constructed, copies of them are distributed to every crew member. The crew members submit bids on a system-wide basis for the monthly lines of flying and reserve schedules. Since both the pilots and the flight engineers at this airline are represented by the Air Line Pilots Association, all the flight crew members come under the same labor agreement and scheduling rules. This leads to practically identical schedules for the two groups. The differences come from the fact that no flight engineers are carried on the DC–3 planes. Flight engineers, therefore, do not submit

TABLE 5.5. SAMPLE OF A RESERVE FIRST PILOT
SCHEDULE OF DAYS ON RESERVE

Days of the Month	A 70	A 71	A 72	A 73
		DC-3 Reserves		
1		R		R
2				R
3	R		R	R
4	R	R	R	
5	R	R	R	
6		R	R	R
7		R		R
8				R
9	R		R	R
10	R	R	R	
11	R	R	R	
12	R	R	R	R
13	R	R		R
14				R
15			R	R
16	R	R	R	
17	R	R	R	
18	R	R	R	
19	R	R		R
20	R			R
21			R	R
22		R	R	R
23	R	R	R	
24	R	R	R	
25	R	R		R
26	R	R		R
27	R		R	R
28			R	
29		R	R	
30	R	R	R	R

Note: Days of the month with weekends in bold face.

bids for DC–3 lines of flying. Also, in the few sequences in which DC–3 equipment is mixed with larger equipment which does require a flight engineer, there will be separate lines of flying for flight engineers.

TABLE 5.6.   DC-3 POOL TIME

Days of the Month	A 70	A 71	A 72	A 73
1				306
2				306
3			342	306
4				306
5				
6		300		
7		318		306
8				
9				
10			342	306
11			342	306
12				306
13		300		306
14		318		
15				
16				
17				306
18				
19				306
20	300			
21	318			
22				
23				306
24	403			306
25	384			
26				306
27				306
28				
29				
30				

Note: Days of the month with weekends in bold face.

After the crew members have submitted their bids, they are awarded lines of flying strictly in accordance with system-wide seniority, provided they are qualified in all respects.

The Daily Administration of Scheduling

The nature of the airline industry makes the daily administration of crew scheduling important. When actually carrying out the flight schedule, the carriers can expect deviations from the planned situation literally as often as the winds change. Countless events can cause a shift in the crew schedules. Something no more unusual than a head wind may make a plane 30 minutes late. An ice storm may ground all the planes at a major base for 24 hours. A mechanical defect, discovered in a plane, may cause a flight to be cancelled. Or the pilot may not be able to take his scheduled flight because of illness, or, more often, because some earlier deviation from his scheduled line of flying has caused him to exceed one of the time limitations. These events are constantly occurring. Incidentally, each one may cause a crew member to have different wages, hours, and working conditions from those which he anticipated when he was awarded his monthly line of flying.

The daily administration of flight schedules is handled by a group of men at each domicile known as crew schedulers. Their job is to ensure that every flight is manned with a full crew regardless of the scheduling changes that might arise. Of course, the great majority of the flights are covered by the crews who are scheduled to take them. For flights which depart between 9:00 a.m. to midnight, the crew schedulers assume that every crew member will take the flight for which he is scheduled. On flights which depart between midnight and 9:00 a.m., the crew members are required to notify the crew schedulers by phone two hours before their departure that they are going to cover the flight as scheduled. Any crew member who cannot take his next scheduled flight must notify the schedulers as soon as possible.

The crew schedulers normally try to discover and to fill any vacancies a day in advance of their departure. Sequences which were scheduled as pool time would represent flights to which no crews had been assigned. These sequences are known as soon as the monthly lines of flying are distributed. As crew members notify the schedulers that they are not legal to take their next flights, they create vacancies. An example of a possible way in which a crew member may become illegal stems from a government regulation which has not been mentioned as yet. The regulation makes mandatory a 16-hour rest period for any crew member who actually has been on duty aloft for more than eight hours in any 24-hour period. If a crew member had been scheduled for seven and one-half flight hours to be followed by a ten-hour rest period before his next flight, he would be illegal to take that flight whenever the seven and one-half hour flight time was actually extended over eight hours because of weather or some other cause. When this happens to a crew member, he will notify the crew schedulers when he arrives that they are going to have to get someone else to cover his next flight. Finally, vacancies occur because the airline decides to add additional flights to the schedule during the month. A typical addition might come from a charter flight to carry a football team to a postseason bowl game. The crew schedulers record all the pilot, copilot, and flight engineer vacancies a day in advance, and then start filling them.

An important source of crew members for filling these vacancies has already been mentioned. They are the crew members who were awarded reserve schedules. An equally important source of crew members is those people who are low on flight time during the month and who desire to do some extra flying to increase their pay. These people make themselves available for extra flying by signing up in a notebook provided for that purpose. Each crew member must indicate the days on which he is free to fly, and he may state the types of equipment and/or flights on which he will be willing to pick up more flight time. Crew members may not make themselves available for extra flights if their projection is running over 85 hours, and they may not take any extra flight, of course, if they are not legal to fly it, or if it would prevent them from carrying out their own monthly line of flying.

Definite priorities exist which the schedulers must follow in filling any vacancy. These priorities have been written down in the scheduling rules and another document known as the "pool rules." Essentially, the schedulers must offer any vacancy to the most senior qualified crew member who is on reserve *or* who has made himself available. Seniority, therefore, receives the primary consideration.

The daily administration works as follows: Crew members may make themselves available for extra flying up to 6:00 P.M. the day before they wish to fly. At that time the pool closes and in the next two hours the crew schedulers fill all the known vacancies for the following day. They start with the first pilot vacancies and offer them to the most senior first pilot on reserve or available.

That pilot can choose one of them, or he can tell the crew scheduler that he does not want to fly any of them and to offer them to some less senior first pilot. Then the crew scheduler will go down the seniority list of first pilots, offering them vacancies which they may accept or reject. Suppose, however, the crew scheduler has five first pilot vacancies unfilled when he has completed calling all the first pilots on reserve or available, and has three reserve first pilots who did not wish to fill any of the vacancies. In that case, the scheduler would recall the three reserves in the order of seniority and each one would have to take one of the five vacancies. To fill the remaining two vacancies, the crew scheduler would assign them to a first pilot who has the necessary amount of free time the following day. These assignments are made in the reverse order of seniority . . . a process known as "junior manning." The crew scheduler would contact the most junior qualified first pilot whose line of flying would permit him to cover the vacancy. Unless this man pleaded illness or some other convincing excuse, he would be assigned to the vacancy. Then the scheduler would call the next most junior qualified first pilot to fill the last remaining vacancy. After the first pilot vacancies were filled for the following day, the scheduler would repeat the process for copilot and flight engineer vacancies.

This is the process used to fill vacancies known by 6:00 P.M. the day before the flights are scheduled to depart. As vacancies open up closer and closer to scheduled departure time, the administration of flight schedules becomes less and less formal. For example, if a crew lands with a plane full of passengers at a domicile for a short stop before continuing on another leg of its flight in ten minutes and if the pilot is so ill that he cannot continue to fly, the crew scheduler is not going to look down the seniority list to find the most senior reserve first pilot who is sitting by the phone in his home an hour away from the airport. The crew scheduler is going to run into the crew lounge to grab the first pilot he sees and hope he is legal to take the flight.

Filling vacancies the preceding day or at the last minute represents the extremes in the daily administration of flight scheduling. In between the extremes the crew schedulers offer flights as time permits to reserves and crew members who make themselves available. When they cannot find any crew member desirous of taking a flight, the schedulers assign it to the reserves in reverse order of seniority. And, as a last resort, they use junior manning.

The crew schedulers must watch the projections of all the crew members as the month progresses. The obvious reason is that if many of them accrue 85 flight hours before the end of the month, the airline is going to be hard-pressed to find crew members who are legal to cover all the flights on the last days of the month. Two steps are available to this airline when flight time starts to get tight. First, the airplane schedule contains some flights which may be combined to conserve flight time. Second, the carrier can remove trips from a crew member's line of flying after the tenth day of the month in order to give that man enough time to fly any flights for which he is scheduled on the last two days of the month. If the carrier does take time away from a crew member for this reason, it must credit and pay him for any flight time he might later miss during the last two days of the month. For example, if a crew member has a projection of 87 hours on the twelfth of the month, the company could take a 3-hour trip from him so that he would have the time to fly perhaps a 7-hour sequence on the last day of the month. If that 7-hour sequence was cancelled for some reason, however, the crew member would still receive pay and credit for seven hours of flight time.

Although the daily administration of flight scheduling at this airline has an important effect on the working life of the crew members, for several reasons it is not as contentious an area as might be supposed. Both parties have agreed to priorities which recognize seniority. The crew members realize that when vacancies open up suddenly, the schedulers must move rapidly to keep the airline on schedule. Another saving factor is that most of the time a crew member who has been overlooked never learns that his seniority has been violated. Most important perhaps is the fact that at this airline whenever a crew member brings up a situation in which he probably should have been offered a vacancy, he will almost invariably receive credit for the scheduled flight time of that trip.

In summary, this carrier goes through four steps in scheduling its flight crews. At each step the airline must abide by many rules, regulations, and agreements which impinge on its freedom to schedule both airplanes and crews. This situation is typical of the scheduling process throughout the airline industry. Because it is typical, the scheduling process just described can serve as a background for the following analysis of the scheduling arrangements of a larger segment of the airline industry.

UNION IMPACTS ON THE SCHEDULING PROCESS

The ensuing analysis concentrates on the impact flight crews have exerted on the four aspects of airline scheduling already described.

Throughout the years crew members have been attempting to gain an ever-increasing control over the methods by which they are scheduled. They have been making this attempt fundamentally as a way to cure the irregular aspects of their working conditions. In recent years they have also been seeking control over scheduling in order to reduce the amount of technological unemployment. They have been making progress primarily in three directions. Through their labor organizations they have been instrumental in having governmental regulations established which prohibit their gross misuse. The prime example in this direction is the 85-hour limitation of Decision #83. Second, they have succeeded in negotiating scheduling rules into their labor agreements with individual carriers. For example, many carriers have agreed not to schedule any crew member for more than 14 consecutive hours on duty. Another example, of course, is the negotiated direct reductions in flight hours. Finally, in several instances carriers have permitted their crew members to take over certain scheduling functions. As the following analysis will show, the pilots themselves build the monthly lines of flying at some carriers. As the flight crew members make progress in any of these directions, they limit management's scheduling freedom.

The Impact of Flight Crews on Airplane Scheduling

The process of airplane scheduling is carried on and reviewed by top ranking management officials in each air carrier studied. Typically an airplane scheduling committee exists with either vice presidents or their immediate assistants representing sales, operations, maintenance, customer service, and financial control. Since airplane scheduling determines the "final product" a carrier will offer the public and in large measure the amount of revenue it will obtain, it is not surprising to find some of a carrier's best talent working on the problem. At the local service carrier, for example, the president was an active member of the scheduling committee to the point that when a major revision of the airplane schedules was needed, he occasionally took the scheduling committee into seclusion at his home for several days to give the matter undivided attention.

The flight crews do not exert an important influence on airplane scheduling throughout the country. In general, airplane scheduling is mainly determined by revenue factors, and with few exceptions crew scheduling has no effect. Because the exceptions are increasing in number and importance, however, airplane schedulers are being forced to take some note of crew scheduling.

The crew members have gained some control over the scheduled time of each leg of a flight. Most contracts have a clause which reads as follows:

> When the scheduled block-to-block time is found in actual operation to be insufficient, hearings shall be granted at the request of the pilots for the purpose of determining whether or not adjustment should be made.

If the pilots should not receive satisfaction in such a hearing, they can appeal this matter to the CAB which has ruled that scheduled times must be realistic. One reason that crew members want to have some control over the scheduled time of the leg of the flight stems from the fact that they accrue flight time on the greater of scheduled or actual time for each leg. In this way they are guaranteed at least the scheduled time of any leg they fly, and this guarantee becomes meaningless if the scheduled time is unrealistically short. Another important reason is that crew members normally take pride in completing their flights on schedule. If the scheduled time is too low, they cannot come in on time without jeopardizing safety or, in most cases, regardless of the way they fly the flight. Also the crew members are constantly dealing with the public which wants to get to its destinations on schedule. The working day of the crew member is much more pleasant if the scheduled times are ample and the passengers are happy. The airlines also want happy passengers so they are inclined to make scheduled times realistic. When some of them do not do so, they are attempting to take passengers from competitors by offering apparently faster service between two cities. In general this control of the crew members on scheduled times is seldom employed and must be considered to have a negligible effect on airplane scheduling.

The on-duty and trip-time ratios are the most important factors in forcing airplane schedulers to give some consideration to crew scheduling. This is true because these ratios create flight crew scheduling problems of such importance that in isolated cases the crew schedulers tell airplane schedulers a particular schedule must be changed. In some cases the crews would accrue so much extra flight time for which they are paid under the ratios as to make a flight unprofitable. In almost all cases, however, the airlines do not change their airplane schedules to avoid the extra crew flight time. Instead they maintain their schedules and let the ratios apply as they may. Most crew schedulers can point to a case in which they cannot avoid giving the crews an extraordinary amount of flight time under the ratios. For example, Mr. Melvin A. Brenner, Vice President—Schedules and Equipment Utilization, American Airlines, made the following statement to the CAB:

> Another type of limitation on scheduling stems from "pay and credit" provisions of our pilot contracts. Our flight crews are guaranteed a minimum amount of pay for time spent away from base. This will sometimes make a particular schedule highly inefficient to operate. Example: we recently had a schedule in which a crew flew a few hours in the evening from Los Angeles to Phoenix, remained in Phoenix a day and a half, and then flew a few hours back to Los Angeles. At one point it was estimated that the inefficiencies of this crew routing would cost about $11,000 per month, or over $130,000 a year.[6]

This is indicative of the situation throughout the airline industry. Airplane schedulers are forced to consider flight scheduling, but

[6] ATA, *Airline Scheduling,* p. 65.

their primary considerations must remain adequate service to the routes and airplane schedules which will result in good loads.

The Impact of Flight Crews on Building Sequences

A different situation applies at the second step in the scheduling process. The crew members have been able to exert a significant amount of control over the way sequences are put together and the way total flying time is apportioned among the domiciles. They have exerted their influence primarily through obtaining government flight time limitations and by negotiating scheduling rules in their contracts. In only one instance in the study had they actually done the work of the second step in the scheduling process. In that case, the pilots at one time made up the sequences at the local service carrier, and had decided how many flight hours should have been assigned to each domicile. The company retained the final authority to change their work, however, and it later reassumed the entire work of the second step.

Even at the large trunk lines the second step in the scheduling process is usually associated with one man. He will have a few assistants, but essentially he alone sits down when the necessary information about all the legs of all the flights has been gathered, and he puzzles through the countless ways they can be arranged until he has every flight included in a sequence. Interestingly, companies that produce electronic data processing equipment have tried to mechanize this operation but have not succeeded. While much of the information can be readied by machine and reports can be made by a machine listing the sequences for distribution, the job of building sequences as yet requires a man's judgment and experience.

The man doing the job at any airline must, of course, abide by the government regulations which have already been discussed. In addition, the labor agreement will usually put further restrictions on his work. For example, one carrier has agreed to a philosophy of "assigning equipment to seniority." This means that to the extent possible the carrier will assign premium flying among the domiciles in proportion to the mix of crew member seniority at the domiciles. One domicile has a very high proportion of senior crew members who have chosen to live there while another has a relatively low proportion. The crew schedule planner would attempt to assign to the first domicile a high proportion of premium flying, which means fast equipment and long hauls. He would do the reverse for the other domicile. The reason for this philosophy is that neither party wants the crew members to have to move to get a type of flying commensurate with their seniority. This philosophy cannot be adhered to completely because some domiciles do not have much premium flying scheduled into them, yet they happen to have a high proportion of senior crew members.

In some cases the freedom of a scheduler to make up sequences is curtailed by traditional scheduling rules which preceded any organized employee groups. For years one airline employed "directional scheduling." This meant that the first pilots were not only divided among eight domiciles but were further divided into groups within each domicile. At any particular domicile a group of pilots could only be scheduled on flights to the west of that domicile, while another group would only go to the east. Directional groups existed at all eight domiciles, the number depending on the number of cardinal compass directions in which flights were scheduled from the domicile. The origin of directional flying went back to the days when the Post Office Department was flying the mail. At that time the aircraft had short ranges and the crews had to know the route well because only poor navigational aids existed. Thus, it made sense to have pilots fly out of a domicile in only one direction. Another historical factor was that this carrier was formed by mergers of several small carriers with essentially different routes. When the mergers took place, the crew members did not want to move their homes or to fly strange routes. Directional flying suited their purposes and gave seniority protection to the crew members on their premerger routes because they remained the only first pilots who could leave the domicile in a certain direction. With the advent of faster equipment and coast-to-coast nonstops, the directional flying system became increasingly complex and valueless so during negotiations the pilots agreed to drop it. Interestingly, the job of the crew schedule planner became more complicated after directional flying was dropped because he was then free to fly any first pilot in any direction from a domicile, and this fact gave him more alternatives to choose from when he was building sequences.

The advent of on-duty ratios added another important consideration with which the crew schedule planners must wrestle. They must try to build sequences which will not give the crew members extra flight hours because each flight hour must be paid for and must be deducted from the 85 hours of flight time any crew member can cover for an airline in a month. The deduction of flight time means, therefore, that the airline must have additional crew members on the payroll to cover any flight time lost to the on-duty ratio.

The impact of a particular on-duty ratio depends on its nature and on many characteristics of the airline to which it applies. For example, one local service line agreed to an on-duty ratio years ago under which a crew member was guaranteed one hour of flight time for every two and one half hours of *actual* on-duty time. Under that ratio crew members seldom picked up any additional flight time. The same situation applied at the small trunk line. It usually gave no additional flight hours under the on-duty ratio.

Because the on-duty ratios were seldom applied at these airlines it did not mean that they had no effect on the way the sequences were put together. It meant that the characteristics of these carriers were such that they were able to devise sequences which consistently provided the crew members with more than one hour of flight time for every two and one half hours on duty. But the point is that the ratios may have forced the schedule planners to alter the way they had previously been scheduling, and to give the crew members a better ratio of flight time to on-duty time. At least at the small trunk line, the crew members and the schedule planners said that this was precisely what had happened.

In summary, government regulations, scheduling rules, and contract agreements which have been discussed in connection with the second step in the scheduling process, when considered together, indicate that the crew members have gained a significant measure of control over this area. As far as maintaining final authority over the scheduling freedom which remains, the carriers take the consistent position that they still have it. Many contracts permit the unions to make suggestions and recommendations concerning the way sequences should be put together and over the way flight time should be distributed among domiciles, but management is always given the last word. In the last few years, however, it has been a last word over an increasingly restricted area of the scheduling process.

The Impact of Flight Crews on the Monthly Lines of Flying

Two interesting differences are noticeable in the third step of the scheduling process. First, the crew members have actually taken over the work of building the lines of flying at one major carrier at least. Second, crew members have been close enough to the people carrying out this step to exert steady, unplanned pressure for small changes in methods by which lines of flying are constructed at local domiciles and in the bidding procedure. Apart from these two differences, the limitations prescribed by government regulations, scheduling rules, and contract agreements which have been discussed in the first half of this chapter impinge on the schedulers' freedom.

As early as 1934 the pilots started making suggestions on the way lines of flying should be built at one major carrier. Since that time, with the company's blessing, they have continually done more and more of the work involved in building the lines of flying. The pilot group at each domicile is sent copies of the list of sequences each month, and the pilots' scheduling committee actually combines the sequences into the monthly lines of flying.

This system has worked well at this carrier. The pilots have become very adept at handling this phase of scheduling and have consistently built lines of flying which the carrier has seldom altered, although retaining the right to do so in the pilot agreement. The advent of the duty-time ratios, however, raised a serious problem at this carrier.

Essentially, the pilots built lines of flying which satisfied both parties because their goals in this phase of the scheduling process were similar. Both wanted lines of flying which gave the pilots close to 85 hours of flight time per month because this meant high pay for the men and good utilization for the carrier. The only disagreement came over the degree to which all the best sequences were given to the senior men, thereby leaving the less senior pilots with some less desirable working conditions, particularly long hours on duty coupled with few hours of flight time. The carrier in general had accepted the principle of seniority, however, and the pilots had agreed on some mixing (homogenization) of good and bad flights within each line of flying. But then the duty-time ratios were negotiated into the pilot agreement and the situation changed significantly.

The ratios were specifically designed to reduce the number of lines of flying with a large proportion of on-duty time to flight time by making them expensive for the carrier. Therefore, from the union's point of view the most advantageous thing to do was to build excellent lines of flying for the senior pilots and let the duty-time ratios take care of the less senior pilots, who would then have to fly the resulting poor schedules. This was precisely what the pilots started to do; they began to build the lines of flying with less homogenization. After several years, the company agreed during contract negotiations to do away with homogenization except to the degree necessary to obtain monthly lines of flying close to 85 hours.

The duty-time ratio at this carrier was unusual because it applied primarily on a monthly basis rather than on a daily basis. First, by contract agreement all the monthly lines of flying at this carrier had to be scheduled to give each pilot 10 calendar days free from all duty each month. Under the duty-time ratio, additional free days had to be added to the scheduled monthly line of flying when it contained an excessive number of long on-duty periods. After each monthly line of flying was made up, it was reviewed to find all the on-duty periods which were scheduled to be longer than 10 hours. Within a monthly line of flying, the numbers of hours by which any of its on-duty periods exceeded 10 hours were added together. If that total was 8.5 hours or more (up to 17 hours), that particular monthly line of flying had to then be scheduled with 11 days free from all duty. If that total had been between 17 hours and 25.5 hours, that monthly line of flying would have had to be scheduled for 12 days free from all duty, and so forth.

When the duty-time ratio called for 11 days off and the monthly line of flying was originally scheduled to have 11 days off, nothing had to be changed because the minimum conditions of the ratio had been met. If it had been scheduled to have had only 10 days off, however, then enough flights had to be dropped in order to free another complete calendar day. The important effect of this particular duty-time ratio came in the following way. When flights had to be dropped from a monthly line of flying to free an additional day, the flight crew members had to receive flight time credit for them just as though they had flown them. Of course this involved a double payment for the carrier because it had to pay the flight crew members who actually did fly the dropped trips. The carrier did maintain one freedom in this situation. It was free to decide which flights would be dropped from any particular monthly line of flying. The carrier used this freedom to spread the dropped trips evenly throughout the month.

An indication of the impact of this ratio on this carrier can be obtained from counting the number of trips the company had to drop. For example, at one major domicile for one month this carrier had to drop a total of 142 trips from 118 lines of flying. One executive of the firm estimated that one out of every 17 pilots was needed to fly the flights dropped under the duty-time ratio.

The impact of this particular duty-time ratio could have become very great if the carrier had not maintained the right in the contract to redesign flight sequences after the pilots had put together the monthly lines of flying. The pilots, in building the lines of flying, began not to go out of their way to minimize the number of trips which would have to be dropped. For example, suppose in putting together sequences to make monthly lines of flying, the pilot committeeman was trying to fit in a sequence which ended at 12:30 A.M. Suppose he had the choice of making it the last sequence of a three-day series of sequences in one monthly line of flying, or the first sequence of a three-day series of sequences in another line of flying. If he chose to put it at the end of the series, he eliminated the next day as a calendar day free of all duty. If he put it in as the first day of the three-day series, he did not eliminate the day following the series as a day free of all duty. Not all the sequences could be worked around so as to avoid having to drop flights, but there were hundreds of cases every month in which they could be scheduled to invoke the duty-time ratio or not. When the carrier changed a list of monthly lines of flying submitted by the pilots, they filed a grievance stating that it was not free to reshuffle the sequences in order to avoid giving extra calendar days off. An arbitrators' decision was necessary to preserve the management's right to change the monthly lines of flying.

Flight crew scheduling at the third step is normally done at each local domicile so that the crew members are in an immediate position to discuss their problems with the crew scheduler. This becomes an area in which the carriers are vulnerable for loss of freedom in scheduling through day-by-day concessions to the crew members. The fact that many of the men responsible for crew scheduling at this stage are themselves pilots does not tend to slow up this process.

This is the type of thing that happens. A pilot learns that one of the more senior pilots is going to take a two-week vacation during the next month. Since this vacationer has more seniority, he probably has a line of flying month after month which is better than the first pilot, and the latter would like to have a chance to fly it during the two weeks of vacation. He therefore goes to the crew scheduler to ask if a way exists by which he can bid for that vacation time rather than have it go into the pool time. The scheduler tells him to make a note of it on his bid and he will see what can be done. At that moment another scheduling procedure has been started. It is known as "moving up" at the carrier in question. Pilots now not only submit regular bids for lines of flying that they think their seniority may get them, but they also have the right to bid on lines of flying which they could get only if someone more senior fails to bid, or vacates the lines for part of a month for some reason. Thus the crew schedulers not only have to award regular bids, but whenever a line of flying is vacated for a number of days they must go down the list of "move up" bids to find the most senior pilot who had asked for a line of that type in case part of one should open up. This starts a chain reaction because less senior pilots have asked to move up to a line similar to the one the second pilot will vacate when he fills the original vacancy. The point is not that seniority should not be recognized in this way. The point is that this whole process did not come out of the scheduling rules or the contract negotiations. It came from day-to-day concessions by the crew schedulers.

The Impact of Flight Crews on the Daily Administration of Scheduling

The impact of the flight crews on the daily administration of scheduling is deceiving. Actually they probably have had more influence on this step of the scheduling procedure than on any of the other three. This is not an area in which the flight crews are aggressively striving to gain more control, however, nor do many grievances grow out of disputes over the daily administration of scheduling. The main reason for the calm is that the carriers have agreed to apply seniority in filling vacancies whenever time permits. Having agreed on that principle, the parties have then formulated various sets of priorities which detail the specific manner in which seniority will be applied in each scheduling situation. The procedures for filling vacancies are similar to those described in the first half of this chapter. The procedures tend to be very complex at the large trunks while a rather simple application of strict seniority usually applies at the smaller carriers. The point is that the parties have agreed upon procedures to follow to fill vacancies, and thus this area has tended not to be contentious.

The daily administration of crew scheduling becomes more complicated and important from a cost standpoint whenever a duty-time ratio has been established on an actual basis. When that happens, the decisions of the daily crew schedulers affect the amount of on-duty time and trip time crew members accrue. For example, suppose a pilot's return trip to his domicile is cancelled for mechanical reasons. Under the trip-time ratio he accrues one hour of pay time for every four hours he remains away from his domicile. The crew scheduler could inform him to deadhead home. The pilot would receive credit for one-half of the flight time of the deadheading flight, but the trip time would stop accruing when he arrived home. The other alternative would be to have the pilot remain at that base until he could fill a vacancy on a flight coming toward his own domicile. In that case the trip time would continue to accrue for a longer time. Weighing alternatives of this type under the duty-time ratios requires a degree of judgment not previously required of the crew schedulers. Perhaps this fact will have to be reflected in new training requirements for the men who fill these jobs.

THE DECLINE IN FLIGHT CREW UTILIZATION

Assessing the impact of the scheduling rules on flight crew utilization is made difficult because, with some exceptions, the airlines do not release such data. Over the last decade, however, enough data have been made public so that a fairly clear description of the situation can be pieced together.

Two additional problems, which existed until recent years, have been at least partially solved. First, the airlines have come to keep enough records so that they are aware of what is happening to flight crew utilization. Second, they have made progress in defining what they mean by flight crew utilization so they are at least partially using the same measuring devices. Active pilot utilization refers to the flight time of pilots who are actively flying during a given period. Gross pilot utilization refers to the flight time of all pilots in the employ of a carrier during a given period, and thus would include those who were engaged in such nonflying pursuits as leaves of absences, training, and vacations. One problem is that carriers tend to include in data for active pilot utilization some time spent not actually operating an aircraft such as scheduled time when it happens to be longer than actual time. As will be seen, however, such nonflying time is not always included in active pilot utilization data. In general the airlines in 1965 had a more accurate picture of the utilization they were obtaining from their crew members than they did, for example, in 1958.

The impact of a given set of scheduling rules will vary carrier by carrier. The impact of the duty-time ratios, for example, varies with a number of the characteristics of a carrier. Perhaps the most important characteristic involved is the route structure of the airline. This can be demonstrated by setting up hypothetical extremes. Suppose a carrier had a route structure made up of cities which were all just eight hours of flying time away from each other. In that case the pilot could be scheduled to get eight hours of flight time for every nine hours on duty, and the on-duty ratios would not apply. Also the pilot could return home the next day and have 16 flight hours for about every 36 hours away from home. Thus, the trip-time ratios would not apply. At the other extreme, suppose an airline had only two bases which were one-half hour's flight time apart, and that the only times of day any passengers would travel between these two cities were at 8:00 A.M. and 5:00 P.M. In that case the crews might be scheduled out in the morning and back in the evening with the crew picking up one hour of flight time for about ten and one-half hours on duty. In this case both the on-duty and the trip-time ratios would apply. In actuality airlines will have route structures and passengers who are selective as to time of travel somewhere within some such extremes. The capability of a carrier to schedule around the ratios depends on the proportion of each type of situation with which it has to contend.

A second consideration that needs to be mentioned for its effect on the trip-time ratios is domicile policy. Since the trip-time ratios are based on the time a crew member spends away from home, the fewer the domiciles, the more likely a carrier is to have crew members spending nights away from home. This is not true for every sequence but it is generally true. A carrier runs into other problems, however, if it has too many domiciles. If a carrier keeps adding domiciles to avoid the trip-time ratio, it also keeps getting smaller and smaller groups of crew members based at any one location. This may lead to poorer and poorer crew utilization because a proper match of pool time and reserve pilots will not be possible. Also crews will have to move their families more often as flight time shifts from one domicile to another to handle ever-changing passenger demands. A carrier therefore must balance these factors in deciding on the number of domiciles to maintain, and this decision is affected by and affects the impact of the trip-time ratio.

Over the last decade the scheduling rules have been renegotiated so that they tend to apply in an increasing number of situations. This trend has already been pointed out in regard to the duty-time ratios. As the ratios become tighter and apply on an actual basis, the ability of a carrier to schedule around them diminishes. In addition, the arrival of jet aircraft with their higher speeds and shorter flight times has tended to decrease the ratios of flight time to on-duty time and thus in general has made the impact of the duty-time ratios more severe. These trends in the wording of the ratios and in the equipment to which they have been applied have been responsible in large part for the deteriorating flight crew utilization to be outlined in the next few paragraphs.

In 1956 and 1957, when the duty-time ratios were in their original forms, active pilot hourly utilization per month among the trunk lines was running in the high seventies or low eighties and gross pilot utilization was ranging from the high sixties to the mid-seventies. This pattern is indicated by Table 5.7.

TABLE 5.7. COMPARISON OF PILOT UTILIZATION ON
SELECTED TRUNK LINES ABOUT 1957

Carrier	Average Utilization per Pilot Available for Duty		Average Utilization per Pilot on Payroll	
	Hours	Minutes	Hours	Minutes
American	76	32	70	47
Braniff*	81	42	76	50
Delta	76	25	71	5
Eastern	77	27	70	56
National†	81	12	75	12
Northwest‡	82	14	71	8
Trans World§		NA	72	43
United	76	30	67	12

* Based on first 7 months of 1957.
† Based on first 7 months of 1956.
‡ Based on first 9 months of 1957.
§ Based on first 10 months of 1957.

SOURCE: NMB, Presidential Emergency Board No. 120, Eastern Exhibit No. 37B.

A similar pattern existed in 1958. One carrier reported active pilot utilization ranging between 79 and 82 hours per month, while the range for gross utilization was between 65 and 70 hours per month. Another carrier reported an active pilot utilization of 77 hours per month. The management of a local service line estimated that the duty-time ratios caused it to increase its pilot employment by 2.4%; a major trunk line estimated the comparable impact at 5.9%. Data obtained from a trunk line indicated that in its 1958 form the duty-time ratios were adding 7,902 pay minutes to 29 lines of flying chosen at random.

In 1958 the impact of the scheduling rules varied carrier by carrier. For example, one carrier reported that it always succeeded in scheduling around its on-duty ratio, whereas another carrier reported having to credit several pilots with additional pay time each month from its ratio. Just because the former carrier avoided the application of the duty ratios does not mean they had no impact. Instead it meant they had forced the carrier to improve its schedules. For a second example, one carrier reported it seldom had to deadhead a flight crew member while at another carrier deadheading, particularly around the end of the month, ran to hundreds of hours.

Pan American made a presentation comparing the impacts of some of the important scheduling rules in 1958 and 1960. This presentation was made public during the hearings conducted by Presidential Emergency Board No. 143. As indicated in Table 5.8, Pan American estimated that collateral (nonproductive) hours had risen as a percentage of productive hours from about 3% in 1958 to a range of 14.4% to 19.1% on pistons and a range of 26.6%

TABLE 5.8. COMPARISON OF PAN AMERICAN PRODUCTIVE AND TOTAL PILOT HOURS BY STATUS AND EQUIPMENT: 1958 AND 1960

Type of Flight Crew Member	Total Productive Hours in 1958	Total Collateral* Hours in 1958	Collateral Hours as Per Cent of Productive Hours
1958			
All equipment			
Captain	245,629	8,339	3.4%
Copilot	249,158	7,806	3.1
2nd & 3rd officer	314,141	12,038	3.8
1960			
Piston equipment			
Captain	88,944	12,815	14.4
Copilot	80,857	12,789	15.8
2nd & 3rd officer	113,969	21,767	19.1
1960			
Jet equipment			
Captain	100,831	26,768	26.6
Copilot	83,472	23,777	28.5
2nd & 3rd officer	107,153	30,776	28.7

* Collateral hours included deadheading, greater time principle, simulator credit, miscellaneous flying guarantee, and the trip-time ratio guarantee.

SOURCE: NMB, Presidential Emergency Board No.143, Pan American Exhibit No. 100.

TABLE 5.9. PAN AMERICAN: BREAKDOWN OF FLIGHT CREW TOTAL HOURS FOR
SELECTED DIVISIONS COMPARING 1958 AND 1960

	Captains		Copilots		2nd & 3rd Officers	
	1958	1960	1958	1960	1958	1960
Productive hours	245,629	189,768	249,158	164,329	314,141	221,122
Deadhead hours	8,339	16,730	7,806	16,581	12,038	29,827
Greater time principle*	—	3,775	—	3,349	—	4,401
Simulator credit*	—	271	—	277	—	357
Misc. flying guarantee*	—	133	—	133	—	149
Trip-time ratio*	—	18,674	—	16,226	—	17,809
Total collateral hours	8,339	39,583	7,806	36,566	12,038	52,543
Total hours	253,968	229,351	256,964	200,895	326,179	273,665

* No contract provision in effect in 1958.

SOURCE: NMB, Presidential Emergency Board No. 143, Pan American Exhibit No. 100.

to 28.7% on jets in 1960. The important new sources of collateral time in 1960, as indicated in Table 5.9, were the greater time principle and the trip-time ratios. Pan American reported that during 1960 gross pilot utilization was 53.7 hours per month while average pay hours were 79.8 per month (see Table 5.10).

TABLE 5.10. SELECTED DATA ON PAN AMERICAN
PILOT UTILIZATION: 1960

Type of Hour	No. of Hours
Total productive hours	896,642
Pay hours	1,241,430
Vacation hours	90,580
Total pay hours	1,332,010
Total man months	16,700.2
Average productive hours per month	53.7
Average pay hours per month	79.8

SOURCE: NMB, Presidential Emergency Board No. 143, Pan American Exhibit No. 74.

Trans World Airlines made similar presentations on pilot and flight engineer utilization before Presidential Emergency Boards 142 and 146, respectively. In Table 5.11, TWA presented the pay hours under ten types of scheduling rules apart from actual flight hours. Some question exists whether hours accrued under the minimum monthly guarantee should be considered nonproductive pay hours in the same sense as hours accrued, for example, under the duty-time ratios. An airline needs reserves to cover contingencies; however, it may not need as many as the scheduling rules require.

As part of the same presentation TWA reported pilot flight and pay hours for July 1961 (supposedly a high utilization month). As seen in Table 5.12, flight hours ranged from 47.3 to 72.9, while pay hours ranged from 77.2 to 85.6. Clearly, by 1961 TWA was not obtaining anywhere near 85 hours of actual flying per month from its pilots.

TWA's presentation concerning flight engineers indicated that their utilization was below that of the pilots. As seen in Table 5.13,

TABLE 5.11.   TWA PILOT PAY HOURS ANALYSIS:
SEPTEMBER 1960–AUGUST 1961

	No. of Hours	*Per Cent*
Pay Hours	873,004	67.0%
Greater time principle hours	23,362	1.8
On-duty ratio hours	13,336	1.0
Trip-time hours	31,297	2.4
Pay assignment hours*	18,627	1.4
Deadhead hours	12,630	1.0
Standby hours	7,191	0.6
Vacation hours	65,545	5.0
Training hours	97,519	7.5
Sick leave hours	28,248	2.2
Minimum monthly guarantee hours	125,903	9.7
Other	5,839	0.5
Total pay hours†	1,302,501	100.1%

* Hours credited when a pilot is removed from a flight by the company.
† In addition, 444,331 hours of operational duty pay were paid.

SOURCE: NMB, Presidential Emergency Board No. 142, TWA
Exhibit No. 93.

flight hours for flight engineers in July 1961 ranged from 47.7 to
58.0. Again TWA broke down the types of productive and nonproductive hours (see Table 5.14). The report to the President
of Presidential Emergency Board No. 146 summarized its findings
on flight engineer utilization with the following statement:

> The evidence shows that, with a maximum of 85 paid hours per
> month . . . actual flight time realized averages 57.2 to 64.7 hours
> per month on the various classes of service.[7]

The general decline in flight crew utilization indicated by such
data was supported by numerous statements made by industry
officials. A few people stated that in part the decline was caused
by the removal of flight crew members from the line for jet transitional training and by initial jet scheduling inefficiencies. In their

[7] NMB, Presidential Emergency Board No. 146, p. 20.

TABLE 5.12. TWA FLIGHT CREW UTILIZATION:
JULY 1961

Type of Flight Crew Member	Flight Hours	Pay Hours
Domestic		
Jet captain	65.0	82.0
Piston captain	61.2	83.1
Regular reserve captain	48.4	77.2
Jet copilot	62.7	81.6
Piston copilot	60.8	82.8
Regular reserve jet copilot	47.3	77.2
Regular reserve piston copilot	61.1	79.2
Second officer	72.9	83.2
International		
Jet captain	68.6	84.4
Jet copilot	67.1	85.6
Second officer	66.3	82.3

SOURCE: NMB, Presidential Emergency Board No. 142, TWA Exhibits Nos. 55–59.

TABLE 5.13. TWA FLIGHT ENGINEER UTILIZATION: 1961

Flight Engineer by Type of Equipment and Division	Flight Hours	Additional "Earned" Hours	Minimum Monthly Guarantee	Pay Hours
Domestic jet	58.0	13.5	7.3	78.8
Domestic piston	54.3	16.3	7.2	77.8
International jet	52.2	16.2	10.9	79.3
International piston	47.7	19.9	12.8	80.5

SOURCE: NMB, Presidential Emergency Board No. 146, TWA Exhibit No. 96.

view utilization would climb once these problems had been solved. According to the data in Tables 5.9, 5.11, and 5.14, however, training time was not that important by 1960–1961, and yet utilization was low. Assessing the impact of initial jet scheduling inefficiencies is not possible from these data. The question of whether

TABLE 5.14. PERCENTAGE BREAKDOWN OF TWA JET FLIGHT
ENGINEER PRODUCTIVE AND NONPRODUCTIVE PAY AND
CREDITS DURING 1961

Pay and Credits	Per Cent
Productive Pay	
Flight pay	68.28%
Operational duty pay	2.06
Nonproductive Pay	
Greater time principle	1.35
On-duty ratio	.57
Trip-time ratio	2.48
Pay assignment*	1.77
Deadhead pay	.89
Standby pay	.47
Vacation pay	5.43
Training pay	2.93
Sick leave pay	1.87
Minimum monthly guarantee	10.57
Other	1.34
Total	100.01%

* Pay received when removed from a flight by the company.

SOURCE: NMB, Presidential Emergency Board No. 146, TWA
Exhibit No. 52.

utilization would have risen again probably became academic with
the new scheduling rules of the 1963–1965 period, including the
negotiation of a direct reduction in the monthly flight time limitation of 85 hours.

For many years a goal of ALPA had been a direct reduction in
the 85-hour monthly flight time maximum with no reduction in
pay. In the early 1950's the leadership of ALPA shifted from that
goal to the indirect reduction in flight time represented by the
duty-time ratios. Individual pilot groups, however, continued to
desire a direct reduction and by 1963 two of them had succeeded
in obtaining it. Both of these reductions resulted from negotiations
which brought solutions to a major crew complement problem on
the jet aircraft. Those negotiations will be detailed in Chapter 8.
The reductions are mentioned here because, of course, they caused

an important impact on flight crew scheduling and utilization. On May 6, 1962, TWA and ALPA signed a contract to the effect that when pilots operated jets domestically as part of three-man crews they would receive 64 minutes of flight time credit for every 60 minutes of scheduled or actual flight time, whichever was greater. Under certain circumstances TWA pilots in international service would receive 66 minutes of flight time credit for every 60 minutes of scheduled or actual flight time, whichever was greater. Hours of flight time so credited came to be known in the industry as "rubber hours" since the normal 60-minute hour had been stretched a little.

A more dramatic reduction came in a contract between American Airlines and its pilot group on July 9, 1963. They agreed that 75 and 80 pay hours, respectively, would be the monthly maximums for jet and piston pilots.

Since 1963 ALPA has negotiated agreements with a number of other carriers calling for a direct reduction in hours. Specifically, two of the latest contracts call for reduced hours for crew members flying the BAC–1–11 jets (a two-pilot plane). In the latest negotiations between ALPA and the small trunk line discussed in detail in this chapter, the pilots are seeking a reduction to 80 hours per month on all types of equipment.

In recent contracts of these types stringent scheduling rules, particularly duty-time ratios, and direct reductions in monthly flight hours have combined to affect flight crew utilization. One major carrier reports having to increase its flight engineer employment from about 600 to about 720 (20%) because it agreed to apply the pilot scheduling rules and direct reduction in hours to the engineers for the first time.

The other side of flight crew utilization must be clearly stated. The evolution of scheduling rules has brought about improved working conditions for junior flight crew members. In many instances both industry and pilot officials will agree that such improvements were needed. The question is whether in making them the parties have not gone "too far" in reducing flight crew utilization. When the current agreements are fully implemented, the scheduling rules, including direct reductions in hours, will have so limited the airlines as to how they can use flight crew members that an unreasonable reduction in flight crew utilization will have taken place. In this regard the Civil Aeronautics Board in its interest in maintaining an efficient, economical airline industry should consider requiring the airlines to submit to it on a regular basis reports of flight crew utilization.

CHAPTER 6

Pilot Pensions

IN THIS CHAPTER the evolution of pilot pension plans will be traced. As will be seen, they are unusual in form as well as in levels of benefits and costs. The analysis will be divided into six sections as follows: (1) early pilot pension plans; (2) the pension philosophy of ALPA; (3) negotiating the first set of ALPA pension plans; (4) amending the ALPA pension plans; (5) a quantitative evaluation of the ALPA pension plans; and (6) a qualitative evaluation of the ALPA pension plans.

EARLY PILOT PENSION PLANS

By 1954 the managements of ten domestic trunk lines had established unilaterally ordinary fixed benefit pension plans for which pilots, among others, were eligible.[1] Most of them were contributory, group deferred annuity plans. They were defined benefit plans containing formulas which established the levels of benefits.[2] The typical formula provided for a monthly benefit amounting to 1% of a participant's first $250 of monthly earnings and 2% of the excess. Pilot contributions were based on formulas calling for about 4% to 7% of earnings, whereas employer contributions were the additional amounts necessary to provide the defined benefits. Usually these plans contained a unit benefit formula which required that "a discrete unit of benefit [be] credited for each year of recognized service with the employer."[3] The benefits were of the

---

[1] Three other pilot groups were covered by pension plans. ALPA estimated that by 1954 some 80% of its membership was eligible for a pension plan.

[2] Dan M. McGill, *Fundamentals of Private Pensions* (Homewood, Ill.: Richard D. Irwin, 1964), p. 62 and ff.

[3] *Ibid.*

career average type in that "the unit of benefit credited during any particular year of employment [was] based upon the employee's compensation during that year."[4] Generally their past service benefit formulas provided for annual benefits of 1% of each participant's earnings during the 12 months prior to the plan's inception times his years of service over age 25 less his first year. Pilots generally were eligible after one year of service provided they were between 25 and 60. Most plans had a normal retirement date for pilots at age 60, and provided for early retirement with company consent between 50 and 60 with actuarially reduced benefits. They did not ordinarily include any disability benefits. The most typical provisions under which a pilot would be eligible for retirement benefits even if he withdrew from the plan prior to retirement were age 45 and ten years of service. As a rule such provisions are known as vesting provisions. The so-called "normal form of benefits" called for a monthly payment from retirement until death and at the time of death for a beneficiary to receive a benefit equal to the pilot's contributions, usually with 2% interest, less the amount of benefits paid prior to death. Most plans provided for some optional forms of benefits.

These plans were administered by the companies, whose determinations were conclusive as to such matters as eligibility, dates of employment, employee earnings, and questions involving interpretation or application. The companies retained the rights to amend, suspend, or terminate these plans.

While most of these plans included groups other than pilots, they did recognize the relatively shorter working career of pilots by reducing the normal retirement date for them from age 65 to age 60. Another probable result of the age 60 normal retirement date was the relatively high ratio of pilot contributions to future service benefits. In some of the plans that ratio was 4 to 1, even almost 5 to 1; whereas more normal ratios would be between 2 to 1 and 3 to 1.

The benefit levels embodied in these plans could be considered to have produced low benefits to pilots retiring soon after their inceptions, particularly when judged by more recent pilot retirement plans. For most of these pilots much of their benefits were

[4] *Ibid.*

based on past service benefit formulas utilizing percentages of levels
of annual earnings of the 1940's. As annual earnings have risen
sharply, benefits based on earnings prior to the last decade have
been dwarfed by comparison with future service benefits for which
those pilots retiring in the early years, of course, have not been
eligible.

The benefits (all in addition to social security) even in those
early days, however, were certainly adequate when compared with
the pensions for most American workers, who were fortunate if
they had only social security benefits. For example, Eastern Air
Lines submitted to Presidential Emergency Board No. 121 the data
in Table 6.1 regarding pension benefits for eight Eastern pilots who
had retired.

TABLE 6.1. LIST OF CAPTAINS RETIRED TO JULY 1, 1955,
UNDER EASTERN AIR LINES' RETIREMENT PLAN, THEIR
DATE OF RETIREMENT AND ANNUAL RETIREMENT PAY

Date of Retirement	Annual Retirement Pay	Remarks
7-31-50	$2,071.44	Elected early retirement (55)
3-1-52	2,081.28	Normal retirement (60)
7-1-52	992.88	Early retirement (50)
3-1-56	1,184.28	Early retirement (50)
6-1-56	4,015.44	Normal retirement (60)
9-1-56	2,608.80	Early retirement (55)
6-1-56	4,075.08	Social security level payment method*
7-1-55	3,737.88	" " " "

* Amounts shown were payable at age 60 when these two captains retired. At age 65, the company paid these same amounts, reduced by the
amount of social security payments due, so that a constant amount was
received through the entire period of retirement.

These plans, as originally written, could have produced relatively high pensions. For example, if a pilot averaged $18,000 per
year over a 30-year career as ALPA is now projecting, a benefit
formula of 1% of the first $250 of monthly earnings and 2% of
the excess would provide a pension of $825 per month, not includ-
ing any social security benefit.

In assessing these early fixed benefit plans in 1953, one writer for ALPA stated that in the then existing plans flexibility and benefit accrual had been unnecessarily sacrificed to attain soundness. He said that they were characterized by high pilot contributions, correspondingly high benefits, rather weak recognition of the problem of forced pilot retirement, and meager vesting and disability provisions. In addition, he believed that they did not meet the problem of the superannuated pilot, nor did they provide a hedge against inflation.

ALPA PENSION POLICIES

In 1954 the membership of ALPA endorsed for the first time the negotiation of pension plans. According to a top ALPA official, pensions had been previously opposed because pilots preferred to stress wage increases. Probable other causes had been the relative youthfulness of the pilot group and hence an antipathy toward pensions, their strivings to improve working conditions, and their appreciation of the likely resistance of airline managements to bargaining about pensions.

ALPA's pension policies did not change overnight. In May 1947 ALPA formed a committee to investigate pensions. Working with an eminent retirement authority this committee drafted an "Air Line Pilot Retirement Bill" which proposed that the government provide commercial pilots with pensions comparable to those received by railroad workers under the Railroad Retirement Act. The question of whether to submit this bill to Congress was put to a vote of the ALPA membership. On May 19, 1949, it was voted down 1,657 to 1,113 because, according to President Sayen, the Railroad Retirement Act did not allow enough "flexibility for estate planning." Another ALPA official reflected a probable viewpoint for the negative vote when he said belittlingly, "Railroad workers, after working 100 years, only get a pension of about $100 when they retire."

In 1952 the Board of Directors of ALPA passed a resolution directing the President of the Association "to investigate and produce a retirement pension plan including disability benefit provisions as they pertained to the peculiar characteristics of the

airline piloting profession and the insecurity presently existent."
In response to this resolution the President formed an Advisory
Committee to the President on Retirement Problems, the recommendations of which were the immediate cause for the 1954 change
in the ALPA policies on pensions.

The report of the Advisory Committee is important to this analysis because it recommended that ALPA start to negotiate concerning pensions and particularly because it endorsed the negotiation
of variable annuity pension plans. The adoption of its report represented a major turning point in the history of ALPA.

The committee decided for a number of reasons that the time
had come for ALPA to negotiate over pensions. Pensions had
become an increasingly important aspect of collective bargaining
generally.[5] The courts had upheld the National Labor Relations
Board in a ruling that employers were required to bargain on pension demands, and a Presidential Emergency Board by returning
pensions to be bargained by the parties in a railroad dispute had
indicated the extension of the NLRB philosophy to the Railway
Labor Act. The Committee considered 1954 a propitious time for
ALPA to consider a deferred wage increase because "pilot salaries
[were] at a point where a 5% increase in salary [would] be meaningless after income tax [had] taken its toll."

The committee made some general pension recommendations.
Because the combination of high income taxes and low interest
rates would preclude a pilot's building his own retirement fund, because the membership had voted down a government pension
proposal, and because social security benefits were "pitifully inadequate," ALPA should negotiate pensions with the airlines. Although the financial burden of old age was not unique to pilots,
their short working careers in general and the ever-present risk of
a pilot's career being shortened even further by a medical disability

[5] One survey estimated that the number of workers covered by pension
plans under collective bargaining had increased from a negligible amount
in 1945 to 5.1 million in 1950 and 7.1 million in 1954. It also estimated that
the percentage of employees under collective bargaining agreements who
were covered by pension plans increased from a negligible percentage in
1945 to 34% in 1950 and to 38% in 1954. U.S. Bureau of Labor Statistics
Report No. 228, *Health and Insurance and Pension Plan Coverage in Union
Contracts,"* 1960.

which might not affect the career of a nonpilot called for pilot pensions of greater magnitude and duration than those of other employee groups. More specifically, pensions were to be fully funded in advance; to be obtained "by reason of the work performed," not because of old age or long and faithful service; to be thought of as deferred wages which could be negotiated in lieu of a wage increase; and to be tailor-made to conform to the requirements of the peculiar position of pilots.

The committee set ALPA's ultimate goal as a "realistic income at a realistic age" and its fundamenal aim as making possible voluntary retirement at age 55. To enable the pilots to meet this goal, the committee recommended contributory plans to be used solely for retirement purposes and not as a tool for obtaining severance, furlough, or disability pay. The committee said that a long-term aim of ALPA, if the future experience of the industry permitted, was voluntary retirement prior to age 55.

The report spelled out "a realistic income." As of 1954 the minimum basic attainable benefit level was considered to be 40% of a pilot's average annual salary for the five years preceding his retirement at age 55. At that time benefits were to be set at 1% of annual earnings for past service and 2.1% of annual earnings for future service. The committee set a goal of $300 as a monthly minimum on newly established plans for pilots between the ages of 45 and 55 who had completed 10 years of service. As soon as a pilot was assured of receiving 50% of his salary at retirement, both company and pilot contributions in his behalf were to cease.

The committee made some recommendations as to the principal features of the plan. Probationary copilots were to be excluded, but no minimum age limit was to be set. Deferred vesting and vesting for retirement purposes only were recommended. Full vesting for retirement purposes was to come after five years or age 40, whichever occurred sooner. The committee recommended against disability provisions, except for immediate vesting [for retirement purposes only] in the case of disability regardless of age. Disability provisions would reduce the chances of obtaining a realistic income at a realistic age and in effect were partially available through ALPA's Mutual Aid and Loss of License Insurance programs. The committee recommended that pilots, at their own option, be permitted to retire between 45 and 55 with actuarially reduced benefits. The committee did not favor the providing of death benefits unless such a feature was necessary to sell pensions to pilots. The typical contingent annuitant option to the effect that the option had to be opted at least five years before retirement was recommended. The committee also accepted the feature of the contingent annuitant options in those days that if the pilot died before retirement the only benefit would be the return of his contributions plus interest. The committee recommended, however, that if the contingent annuitant died before the pilot retired, the benefit scale for the pilot should revert to the amount which he was entitled to prior to the selection of the option.

The committee set as a goal an equal voice for ALPA in the administration of any pension plan, on any board of trustees, and in the selection of third parties to invest the pension funds and of actuaries. The committee stated, however, that ALPA should not become involved in determining the nature and type of investments to be made.

The committee set the fundamental aim for modifying the then current plans as "the same retirement income at the age of 55 as is now received at the age of 60." The committee concluded that the cost of reducing retirement to age 55 would be so high that the plans would have to continue to be contributory. The committee recommended that pilot contributions should not exceed 8% to 9% of salary and that all further increases in benefits should be made available by increased employer contributions.

As previously indicated, the recommendation of the variable annuity type pension plan was of prime importance. During its study the committee learned from people at the Teachers Insurance and Annuity Association of America (TIAA) of the development of such plans. They were developed to provide "retirement income through periodic investments in common stocks and the payment of a variable, or unit, annuity in combination with a traditional fixed dollar annuity."[6] At that time TIAA was offering a variable annuity pension in combination with a fixed benefit plan to college

[6] For further details, see Teachers Insurance and Annuity Association of America, *A New Approach to Retirement Income* (New York: By the Association, 1951).

professors under the College Retirement Equities Fund. Similar plans were then in effect at the Long Island Lighting Company and the Chemstrand Corporation.[7]

Under such a plan, one half of the contribution was to be used to purchase fixed dollar benefits guaranteed by "insurance type" of investments and the other half was to be used to purchase common and/or preferred stocks. Upon retirement the benefit payable would be determined by the market value of a participant's share in the equity fund plus the guaranteed benefit from his insurance type of pension. The committee stressed that the variable annuity plan as devised by TIAA incorporated the "dollar averaging" principle under which a given dollar amount was used at regular intervals to purchase stocks regardless of their then market value. This means that more shares are bought when prices are low than when prices are high. The committee explained that the variable annuity plan was based on historical records which indicated that the cost of living and stock prices moved together. The committee saw the fixed plans as furnishing a base upon which the retired pilot could always rely regardless of cost of living fluctuations and the variable annuity plan as furnishing a hedge against inflation.

The ALPA Advisory Committee on Retirement "heartily" endorsed this type of insurance as a hedge against inflation, "the deadly enemy of all pension plans." Although the committee did not state so explicitly, the variable annuity type of pension by taking advantage of capital appreciation of common stocks would potentially permit a pilot to build retirement income for an age 60 or age 55 retirement faster than he could do so by using fixed benefit plans. The variable annuity pension amounts to an investment program.

In surveying the negotiating task ahead of the Association, the committee predicted that the negotiators would encounter a great deal of resistance from the airlines which already had plans in existence and which would resent efforts to modify or improve them. The committee predicted that employers would not cooperate in providing data on which to estimate pension costs. To answer this problem the committee suggested that ALPA negotiators rely

[7] In addition, National Airlines announced in July 1954 that it had adopted a pension plan in which participant retirement benefits were adjusted to reflect changes in the cost of living.

on actuarial experts for the technical work involving pension costs and financing. The committee also proposed that ALPA bargain for fixed employer contributions to avoid having to delve into the details of a pension plan at the bargaining table (thus simplifying the bargaining process and allowing the negotiations to be conducted "in the traditional manner just as though a straight wage increase was under consideration"); to eliminate the need for advanced, expensive actuarial studies; and to allow ALPA to adopt a conservative benefit approach because favorable actuarial experiences would accrue to the fund. The committee also recognized, however, that this approach would place great responsibility on ALPA to ensure the adequacy of the funds relative to the benefits they were designed to provide.

The committee recommended the negotiation of a complete withdrawal of the pilot group from the then current fixed benefit plans with immediate vesting of rights and with the surrender of no superior benefits. It recommended the negotiation of a new self-insured pension plan combining fixed and variable annuity pensions. It recommended that ALPA negotiators employ actuaries to tell them how the then current plans could best be modified to meet ALPA's needs.

In effect the committee foresaw negotiations in which a fixed employer contribution would be obtained along with a very general set of benefits and a rough outline of the type of plan structure. Later on, the details of the benefit schedule and the method of funding would be drawn up by actuarial experts. The committee believed that after the amount of the employer contribution had been established, a definite benefit schedule could be set up to meet the needs of the membership. Setting up such a schedule, it believed, would be facilitated because the airline's cost would not be further affected. Thus, the details of the benefit schedule would not be of as extreme concern to the airlines as if the pensions were of the defined benefit type.

In November 1954 the ALPA Board of Directors adopted the retirement program as recommended by the committee, accepted the principles embodied in its report as the guide for negotiating pensions, and made the negotiation of pensions according to the committee's general format a proper element of pilot compensation and a valid objective of negotiations.

NEGOTIATING THE FIRST SET OF ALPA PENSION PLANS

In 1954 ALPA proceeded to negotiate pensions and by October 1960 reported that fixed and variable annuity plans had been negotiated with 34 carriers. At first ALPA met resistance from several airline managements which maintained that pensions were not a bargainable issue under the Railway Labor Act. ALPA was able to overcome this resistance because of its bargaining power and because of the rulings, previously mentioned, that pensions were bargainable issues under the Taft-Hartley Act and apparently under the Railway Labor Act as well. According to one airline executive, given the nature of the times in the pension area, maintaining that pensions were not a bargainable issue was untenable. So carriers which had maintained that pensions were not bargainable in effect went ahead and bargained on them, stating "while pensions are not a bargainable issue, what do you want, a wage increase or pension." One carrier, for example, agreed to "change" pensions but not "negotiate" on them.

Negotiators for both sides reported the difficulty of preparing for and mastering the complex aspects of pension negotiations. Both made extensive use of legal and actuarial talent. ALPA staff economists became deeply involved in the negotiations of pensions, and ALPA hired a firm of actuaries on a consulting basis.

The carriers made wide use of a number of types of experts. For example, one negotiator said that during negotiations he was "almost sure" of what he was saying because he could call on actuaries from the airline's insurance department, from an insurance company, and from an actuarial firm. He said that during negotiations he never made a move without checking beforehand with the actuaries.

Typically, during pension negotiations the pension experts from the finance department of carriers were called in sporadically or continuously to give advice. At some carriers the insurance and pension experts did some of the actual negotiating. Interestingly, the experience of coming into negotiations has been an eye opener for some of these experts. For men who are used to precise language and the niceties of actuarial calculations, the agreeing to an important contract term with ALPA while both sets of negotiators were crossing an avenue on the way to lunch has been an education for them in the art of negotiation. It has also required the insurance and pension people to cooperate more with the personnel people, and vice versa. At a number of carriers, however, one still senses a feeling of mutual suspicion.

As the negotiators have negotiated pensions over a number of contract talks, they have themselves become somewhat more expert on the subject and, as a result have had to call less and less on experts.

The consistent bargaining pattern in the period 1954–1958 was to reach a "skeleton agreement" confirming that there would be a variable annuity plan as well as the fixed benefit plan; that the pilot and company contributions would be a certain percentage of pilot earnings; and that representatives of both sides would get together later to draft definitive pension documents.

Company and union negotiators viewed differently the later discussions over the details of the pensions. From the companies' point of view they were just a continuation of negotiations in which ALPA tried to get more for its members than had really been agreed to in the "skeleton agreement." From the union's point of view, of course, taking an active role in the drafting of definitive documents was of vital concern to the protection of the pension rights of its members. Unlike most unions which have a tendency to leave the drafting of the document to the company's experts, ALPA and its experts watched and argued every step. Often the discussions leading to the definitive documents took a year or two to complete.

Modifying Fixed Plans

Fundamentally, ALPA in this period was attempting to negotiate its "standard ALPA pension program" which consisted of a fixed benefit and a variable benefit plan with certain more or less standard major provisions. As to the fixed benefit plans, ALPA attempted either to have them amended so that they applied only to pilots or to have them cancelled and replaced with new fixed benefit plans similarly limited in coverage. As of 1958 about half of the fixed benefit plans were considered by the parties to apply to pilots only.

In these negotiations ALPA desired to modify the fixed benefit plans in specific areas. A good summary statement of their desired modifications was made by Mr. Clarence N. Sayen, the President of ALPA from 1951 to 1962:

> *Question:* Mr. Sayen, leaving aside from consideration the [absence of a variable benefit plan], what is wrong with the present . . . Airlines' plan as a fixed benefit plan?
>
> *Answer:* Well, most of the things that we have proposed to change. The first thing . . . the eligibility is too long. We propose one year versus three years. We propose to change the vesting to five years instead of ten years. We propose to include disability vesting, which is not currently included. We propose to remove the company required approval for retirement, early retirement. The contribution of the pilot in terms of the benefits accumulated is too high. There is no provision for review. The participant has no knowledge, really, of the plan. . . . It is completely a plan that has been put in unilaterally by the company, could be altered or changed or amended at any time—or terminated.[8]

ALPA desired to increase the retirement benefits of pilots who were about to retire or had retired immediately prior to the negotiations. Generally ALPA succeeded in establishing flat monthly minimum benefits.

ALPA was concerned with the relationship between the pilots' contributions to the fixed benefit plans and the corresponding future service benefits. ALPA employed a standard format which called for a pilot contribution of 2% of his first $250 of monthly earnings and 4% of the excess and a monthly retirement income based on career earnings and amounting to 0.75% of the first $250 of monthly earnings and 1.5% of the excess (a ratio of 2.67 to 1). To achieve a balance between the fixed and variable plans, ALPA strove to combine a fixed benefit plan with that ratio with a variable plan requiring a total contribution of 7% to 8% of participating pilot payroll. These goals resulted in the negotiation of several changes in the pilot contributions and the future service benefit formulas of the then existing fixed benefit plans. For example, the standard format replaced a formula for one fixed benefit plan

[8] NMB, Presidential Emergency Board No. 121, transcript, pp. 575–576.

which had previously required a pilot contribution of 4% of the first $250 of monthly earnings and 8% of the excess and had yielded 1% of the first $250 of monthly earnings and 2% of the excess. In a number of cases, however, ALPA did not succeed in reaching its standard as such.

Generally in the first round of negotiations the early retirement provision was changed so that pilots could retire between the ages of 50 and 60 with actuarially reduced benefits without the consent of the company. In addition, in at least four of the negotiated plans pilots could, if they had company approval, retire with actuarially reduced benefits between the ages of 45 and 50.

During the first round of negotiations ALPA was able to improve vesting rights under the fixed benefit plans, but with a variety of vesting provisions. The ALPA goal was to have pensions vest after 10 years of service. By 1958 most plans provided for vesting after 10 years of continuous service and some plans further stipulated a minimum age. ALPA made additional progress by having furloughs, sick leaves, leaves of absence, military leaves, or in some cases the "aggregate period of employment as pilots" included in the years of service for vesting purposes.

In most instances ALPA succeeded in having pensions fully vested for retirement purposes at the time a pilot became disabled. In addition, the time at which a pilot could start receiving retirement benefits after he was disabled was lowered. For example, five plans were modified so that a disabled pilot could start receiving a retirement benefit at any time following the incident of the disability, four other plans called for the pilot to receive benefits any time after age 50, and one plan after age 45. In one plan a pilot was vested immediately after he failed a proficiency test as a pilot and could receive disability benefits any time thereafter.

As to the amount of disability benefits pilots would receive, normally they were to receive the benefits they had accrued in the fixed benefit plan actuarially reduced from age 60 to the age at which they actually started receiving those benefits. Actuarial reduction amounts to between 5% and 6% per year. By 1958 ALPA had succeeded at four companies in negotiating what it termed "jacked-up actuarial reduction." For example, in two of these contracts, if the pilot deferred receiving benefits for 48 months after his disability, he would receive as disability benefits the amount of benefits his contribution and the company's contributions would have accrued as of age 60 reduced only 3% per year.

In those plans in which the number of options did not include at least contingent annuitant and social security options, ALPA negotiated those options into the fixed benefit plans.

Initial Variable Annuity Plans

The variable annuity plans negotiated by the airline parties had many of the same types of provisions as the fixed benefit plans. They will be described shortly. First, however, a brief description might be helpful concerning the unique aspect of these plans—the variable benefit—and how it is made possible.

Over a number of years each participant in a variable plan contributes on his own behalf a portion of his earnings into a fund. Over the same period the company contributes an amount (usually equal to the participant's contributions) on his behalf into the same fund. The fund is invested in common stocks which over the years change in value, and hence, act to change the value of the fund. The value of the fund and the demands made upon it are also affected by such occurrences as the withdrawal or death of participants. At the time a participant retires, his share of the fund at that time is calculated in dollar terms, say $40,000. Then depending on the option he chose, the actuaries calculate the amount of pension $40,000 would produce, say $200 per month. The participant receives $200 per month for the balance of the then current 12-month accounting period of the fund. At the end of the accounting period (and each succeeding accounting period) the actuaries recalculate the value of the fund relative to the demands outstanding against it. For example, suppose its relative value increases by 5% largely because the value of the common stocks in its portfolio has risen. Then the amount of pension of the retired participant will be changed during the next accounting period to reflect directly the change in the relative value of the fund. In this case the 5% increase will raise his pension to $210 per month.

The important provisions of these plans were as follows. As to eligibility, these plans followed the pattern of the fixed benefit plans already described. Without exception, however, a man must have been on the pilot's seniority list. In the great majority of cases, they provided for both pilot and company contributions. The standard form was for the company to contribute annually 4% of participating pilot payroll and for the pilot to contribute 2% of his first $3,000 and 4% of the remainder of his annual income. In a number of plans the pilots could, in addition to their required contribution, voluntarily contribute an additional percentage of their annual earnings, usually up to 5% more.

Typically, the normal retirement date was age 60.

In every plan a pilot could retire early at his own option between the ages of 50 and 60, and in four plans as of age 45 with company approval, in either case with actuarially reduced benefits.

The vesting provisions varied widely and were identical with those of the fixed benefit plans.

In case of disability, a participant's rights to pension benefits would be vested based on his contributions and those made by the company in his behalf. Disability was defined as "the permanent inability of a member for medical reasons to pass a periodic physical examination required for all pilots."

The various types of options under the variable annuity plans paralleled those in the fixed benefit plans.

The death benefits a participant in the variable annuity plan provided for his beneficiary varied depending on whether he died before or after retirement and upon the option he had selected, if any. If a pilot died before retirement, his beneficiary received the amount of his share of the fund based on his contributions.

Under these plans, generally speaking, if at the time a pilot retired his income from the fixed plan, from the variable annuity plan, and from the normal form of social security did not provide him a dollar minimum such as $400 a month, the company would make up the difference. Thus the fixed benefit plan became liable for increased costs in the event the variable annuity plan suffered stock market reverses.

Modifications Applying to Fixed and Variable Plans

In general the administration of the pension plan remained in the hands of the airlines. According to President Sayen, at least two airlines offered to let ALPA administer at least the variable annuity plan in its entirety but ALPA refused. In testifying before Presidential Emergency Board No. 121, President Sayen discussed plan administration as follows:

> We made the decision quite a few years ago, after studying this whole subject, that the best method of handling the pension program was to have the program administered by the company but with the employees—the pilots—having a right to review the administration periodically through a constituted board having authority and to have a dispute-settling procedure for settling disputes out of interpretation or application.

By and large the picture that President Sayen painted did in fact take place. The companies administered the plans and in that sense the plans were not jointly administered. To one degree or another, however, ALPA was given the right to review the administration of the plan and to be a part of the dispute settling machinery as to interpretation or application of the pension plan document. The degree of ALPA participation varied significantly. In the case of trusteed plans, the pattern called for the Association to approve the trust agreement between the airline and the trustees, and any amendments thereto.

Concerning the selection of the trustee, in some cases the company could select the trustee with no restriction; in other cases the company had to select a trustee from among the banks in a large metropolitan city with at least a stated minimum amount of assets. In still other cases ALPA's approval of the selection of the trustee was necessary. Frequently, ALPA had the power to negotiate a change in the trustee if it did not approve of his investment philosophy. In no case, however, did ALPA have the authority, nor apparently did it want the authority, to instruct the trustee to buy particular stocks.

Joint committees provided the mechanism through which ALPA took part in the administration of these plans. The scope of such committees varied widely. In some cases one committee reviewed the work of the trustee and the administration of the plan, and handled disputes which arose as to interpretation or application of the pension plan documents. In other cases one committee was established for the fixed benefit plan and another for the variable benefit plan. Almost without exception there was a joint committee with the power to handle disputes arising over application or interpretation of the pension documents, with binding arbitration as the final step. Less frequently, the retirement committee or joint board could make binding recommendations as to the work of the trustee. The trustee generally was instructed to consider 100% investment in common stocks reasonable, to employ "dollar averaging," and to refrain from buying the stock of the airline involved.

Both the procedures and the will of the parties for a joint administration varied. In general, procedures were established but were not used, or were used very infrequently. The typical pattern saw an occasional dispute concerning the rights of a participant arising and being settled without much controversy. Practice also varied in the administration of the pension plans by the companies. Most typically the pension plan came under an insurance and pension section of the finance department.

In most cases a pension dispute-settling board was established. President Sayen stated that the reason for not having such disputes handled through the regular grievance procedure was that by establishing a permanent dispute board for pensions, one could get continuity and thereby some general expertise in the pension area. He also said that handling both regular grievances and pension board cases would be too much of a job for one group of active line pilots. In addition, he said that in most cases the airlines themselves wanted a separate board for pension disputes. In setting up a separate dispute board, however, ALPA made clear that questions or disputes which arose concerning an employee's employment rights as established by the basic collective bargaining contract would be resolved through the regular grievance procedures (see Chapter 9).

In general the companies maintained the right to the extent permitted by law to amend, suspend, or terminate the pension plans as the dictates of the business required. Also, ALPA generally succeeded in reaching agreement with the companies that the pension plans would run concurrently with the basic agreements. This form of protection for the pension plan was of more than academic interest because since 1954 at least two airlines have terminated or suspended parts of their pension plans.

Amending the ALPA Pension Plans

For a number of reasons once an airline and ALPA had nego-tiated the initial pension program, typically several years elapsed before it was amended. This led to a relative hiatus in pension activity on the domestic trunk lines during the period 1958–1960. Some of the reasons for the hiatus were: (1) interest in working conditions and wage rates on the newly acquired jet air-craft; (2) an attitude that pension documents should be stable; (3) the spending of up to two years to work out the original, definitive pension documents; and (4) long periods during which pensions were not reopenable.

ALPA showed renewed and continuing interest in the pension area beginning in 1961. Company negotiators believed that the increased pressure to improve pension plans was the most important element in the negotiations of these latter years. The only other major topics discussed as far as some airlines were concerned were the pay and working conditions of the copilots and second officers.

The most marked change in the pension plans as a result of the amendments in the years 1961–1963 was the picking up by the companies of part or all of the contributions previously made by pilots to both the fixed and variable annuity plans. The pilots were more successful in having the companies take over some of the contributions to the variable annuity plans than in having the com-panies assume more of the costs of the fixed plans. As of March 1, 1964, however, three airlines had agreed to amend their fixed plans so that pilots were to contribute nothing to the fixed plans. In addition, one plan was, from its inception, noncontributory. Also as of March 1, 1964, pilots were making no required contributions to the variable annuity plans at five of the domestic trunk lines and greatly reduced contributions at most of the others. In the majority of the cases in which companies picked up pilot contributions, the increased company costs were matched either by wage reductions, by no increased wages, or by wage increases decreased by the amount of the company's additional pension costs. Of course, with pilot earnings generally placing them in high tax brackets such amendments represented a tax gain.

Normally under a noncontributory pension plan, if a participant terminates or dies, he receives no benefits. Under the normal contributory plan, when a pilot terminates or dies, he receives back as a minimum his contribution plus a guaranteed amount of interest. The unique feature of the pilot plans as the companies picked up the pilot contributions was that upon termination or death a pilot was to receive not only his own contribution plus interest but also an amount equal to the increased contributions made by the company in his behalf. Thus the increased company contribution was to be treated as if the pilot had made it.

This feature was in line with ALPA's thinking that pensions were merely deferred wages. That was true to the extent that companies picked up pilot contributions in lieu of increasing pilots' wages. Therefore, the pilots believed with some justification that the company's increased contributions were really pilots' money that they would otherwise have had in wages. This feature, however, was not strictly in line with ALPA's desire for pure retirement plans because guaranteeing the increased company contributions to the pilot upon death necessarily resulted in lower general pension benefits. This is because the company loses the opportunity to increase pensions or decrease pension costs by having available money which participants do not receive back upon withdrawal or termination. Having such money available is known as reversion.

As of March 1, 1964, ALPA had negotiated three fixed benefit plans in which company contributions in the range of about 3.5% to 4.0% were to be treated as pilot contributions in case of termination or death. Seven variable annuity plans treated similarly company contributions ranging from 2.5% to 4.0%.

In the period 1961–1963 pilot pension plans were amended to create or to improve already existing levels of normal benefits and minimum guarantees for an age 60 retirement, for early retirement, and for retirement in the case of disability. The levels of minimum guarantees for retirement at age 60 were raised to a range of $500 to $650 per month. Generally benefits accruing from the fixed and variable plans as well as from social security were included. To qualify, a pilot generally had to have participated continuously in the fixed and/or the variable plans from stated dates and in some cases to have accrued a stated number of years of service.

By 1963 a pilot retiring early for reasons other than disability typically would receive either his normal pension or the minimum guarantee, both actuarially reduced, whichever was larger. In two plans the minimum guarantee would be reduced only 3% per year below age 60. Frequently to be eligible for voluntary early retirement a pilot had to have reached age 50.

Pilots retiring early because of a disability would again receive either the normal benefit or the minimum guarantee, whichever was larger. In disability retirements, however, the normal benefit would in some plans be reduced only 3% per year (rather than actuarially); and the minimum guarantee typically would not be reduced if the pilot was retiring between the ages of 50 and 60 and would reduce 3% per year for pilots retiring under age 50. Again to be eligible generally a pilot would have to have participated regularly from a stated date and to have accrued a stated number of years of service. Of course, a pilot would have to be disabled, usually in the sense that he was "medically unable to continue as a pilot."

During these years the plans were amended also to improve or extend to additional plans such provisions as those covering eligibility requirements, interest guarantees, and the right to make optional contributions. A significant change was negotiated in the contingent annuitant option at one carrier to the effect that if a pilot died between the ages of 50 and 60, regardless of what option he had taken and even if he had taken no option, his designated beneficiary was to receive a monthly pension equal to the monthly pension the pilot employee would have received if he had retired early under a two-thirds joint annuitant option. In addition, this benefit was to be a cost to the company because the actuarial tables for the contingent annuitant option were not actuarially adjusted to take into account this new provision.

A Quantitative Evaluation of the
ALPA Pension Plans

Over the years statistical data concerning the pension plans in the airline industry have been closely guarded. This is because they are by and large controlled by financial people who inherently have no desire to pass out financial data of this nature, because they are an element of competitive costs, and because through reversions carriers' costs actually can be less than the unions might think they are. In addition, managements have some freedom under the laws to vary pension costs reported in any one year. For example, past service principal can be charged off at the rate of 10% a year or at an amount equal to the interest on the principal.

With the passage of the Welfare and Pension Plans Disclosure Act of 1959 this secrecy changed somewhat. Now administrators of pension plans are required to submit financial data annually to the government. These data are made available to the public. In Appendix 1, selected data available pertaining to pilot pension plans as of June 1963 are presented.

Another source of information related to pension costs are the reports issued by the CAB concerning numbers of pilot and co-pilot personnel and employee payrolls. Appendices 2 and 3 contain the employment and salary information submitted to the federal government by the domestic trunk and local service lines for the years 1940–1962.

Pilot Participation in Pension Plans

As of 1962 pilot participation in pension plans was relatively high. Comparisons of employment data in Appendices 2 and 3 with participants in Appendix 1 indicate that for the trunks, participation in the fixed benefit plans was over 90% and in the variable plans generally over 80%. Comparable figures for the local service line pilots ranged from 58% to 90% and from 42% to 95%.

Estimating the Cost to the Carriers
of the ALPA Pensions

Unfortunately only two trunk lines reported contributions to the pilots' fixed benefit plans separately from those to the general company plans. A number of local service lines, however, did file such separate reports.

Approximations regarding pension costs can be made using straightforward calculations with the data in Appendices 1, 2, and 3. For example, for the years 1959–1962 percentages which the carriers' total contributions to both the fixed and the variable plans were of their total reported pilot payrolls ranged from about 7% to 17 % for the trunks and from about 1% to 12% for the local service lines. Similarly for the years 1959–1962 the *total* employer and employee contributions to just the fixed benefit plans as percentages of total reported pilot payroll were around 9% for the trunks and around 6% (range from 0.7% to 12.9%) for the local service lines. During these years comparisons of employer with employee contributions to the fixed benefit plans indicated that employers had made from 30% to 150% larger contributions than had employees. Pilots contributed typically 2% of their first $250 of monthly earnings and 4% of the excess. Contributions at those rates average out to about 3.5%. This being so, it would appear as though employer contributions of the domestic trunk lines to the fixed benefit plans were as high as 10% of participating pilot payroll.

An important measure of pension costs is the employer's contribution as a percentage of participating payroll. It is generally recognized in the industry that as far as pilot pension plans are concerned, this figure for the most advanced plans is approaching 22% of participating payroll. This is an unusually high percentage for anybody. A comparable figure for the average employee group is probably about 4% to 5% of participating payroll.

Pension costs as a percentage of participating payroll rose rapidly in the four years preceding 1963. In 1959 it was averaging for advanced pension plans about 12% of the payroll. Using data in Appendices 1, 2, and 3, approximations can be made of the employer contributions as a percentage of participating payroll. It should be emphasized that these are rough approximations merely to indicate that costs ranging upwards to 18% to 22% of pilot payroll are not out of the question under the current plans. The total contributions to the fixed benefit plans and the company contributions to the variable plans as percentages of average reported 1962 pilot earnings were 15.8% and 19.3% for two trunk lines and ranged from 8.3% to 20.9% among the local service lines. Total contributions to the fixed benefit plans were used because as these plans become noncontributory, such contributions presumably would have to be made entirely by the companies. These percentages are presented in Table 6.2.

The reasons that contributions have reached such relatively high percentages of pilot payroll are found in the terms of the contracts, a number of which are costly. A normal retirement date of 60 instead of 65 is estimated to raise the cost of providing a pension by 50%. Plans are becoming completely noncontributory while still promising high retirement incomes. In addition, these plans contain a number of features which could possibly prove costly, such as having some company contributions returned to pilots in case of termination or withdrawal, liberal vesting provisions, and and potentially expensive early and disability retirement provisions. In actual practice voluntary early retirements by pilots are essentially unheard of.

TABLE 6.2. TOTAL CONTRIBUTIONS TO FIXED BENEFIT PLANS
AND COMPANY CONTRIBUTIONS TO VARIABLE ANNUITY
PLANS AS A PERCENTAGE OF AVERAGE EARNINGS

Carrier	Total Contributions to Fixed Plans Per Active Employee as Per Cent of Average Earnings*	Company Contributions to Variable Plans as Per Cent of Average Earnings	Total Contributions to Fixed and Company Contributions to Variable Plans as Per Cent of Average Earnings
Continental	8.6%	7.2%	15.8%
United	10.7	8.6	19.3
Allegheny	12.0	7.0	19.0
Frontier	5.9	5.7	11.6
Lake Central	13.5†	7.4	20.9
Mohawk	3.5	7.3	10.8
North Central	7.7	7.5	15.2
Ozark	10.4	7.0	17.4
Pacific	13.2	5.0	18.2
Piedmont	9.4	7.0	16.4
Trans Texas	7.3	1.0	8.3

* 1962 data.　　† 1961 data.

SOURCES: ALPA records and calculations from data in Appendices 1, 2, and 3.

Because of the cost of pension plans both ALPA and the airlines have realized that in negotiations they could not discuss wage increases without becoming involved in a discussion of pension proposals, and vice versa. In a number of cases a pension improvement has been tied directly to the amount of the wage settlement. In some cases in order to get a variable annuity plan pilots have agreed to a contract with no wage increase whatsoever. In another case they took a 7% reduction in wages in order to get an improvement in the pensions. In still another a company agreed to negotiate concerning the fixed benefit plan so long as its costs were not increased. The resulting agreement called for the pilots to contribute less to the fixed plan and to receive less benefits. The actuaries calculated these changes so that the carrier's costs remained the same.

ALPA has been ready to tie pensions and wage increases together. This coincided with its philosophy that pensions were merely deferred wages. In reporting the results of negotiations, ALPA has begun to adjust wage rates by the amount of the increase in pension costs. Quite frequently carriers have picked up an additional percentage of the pilot's compensation as a company contribution to the pension plan. Where that has been done, ALPA has announced the wage increase as including the amount picked up by the company under the pension plan. ALPA has also recognized the cost of pension plans, particularly on the local service lines, by negotiating "stage agreements" under which the company would agree to contribute in increasing stages to the variable annuity plan. For example, a carrier would agree to pick up as of the effective date of the contract 1% of participating pilot payroll and each year thereafter to pick up an additional 1% until it was picking up 4%.

Typical Benefit Levels

From 1954 to 1964 the expected average retirement income for a commercial airline pilot increased from roughly $100 to $1,000 per month, exclusive of social security.

According to President Sayen, when ALPA started negotiating pensions, it originally was shooting for an average retirement income exclusive of social security which would approximate 40% to 50% of a pilot's pay in his final five years. By 1958 he reported that ALPA had reached that goal. At that time, projected annual retirement incomes, including social security, were 100% of average career earnings. Mr. Sayen pointed out, however, that a pilot retiring at age 55 was getting 30% or less of his level of pay for his last five years.

Under relatively constant pension formulas the projected benefits for pilots, of course, increased with increases in their average career earnings. From 1959 to 1964 none of the past service benefit formulas of the trunk lines and only three of their future service benefit formulas were changed. As shown in Table 6.3, however, projected retirement incomes on the trunk lines as of 1958 based on an average annual salary of $12,000 and 30 years of participation would amount to about $10,000 per year. Table 6.3 also shows that the expected retirement incomes of pilots on the domestic trunk lines as of 1964 based on an average annual salary of $18,000 per year over a 30-year period would result in retirement incomes of about $15,000 to $16,000 per year. These benefits are in addition to social security benefits. They are, however, based on the assumption that the benefits accruing from the variable annuity plans will compound at the rate of 5% per year.

TABLE 6.3. ESTIMATED TOTAL FUTURE SERVICE BENEFITS
BASED ON AVERAGE SALARIES OF $12,000 FOR 1958 AND
$18,000 FOR 1964; 30 YEARS OF PARTICIPATION; PLUS
RETIREMENT AT AGE 60

Carrier	*As of 4/58*	*As of 3/1/64*
American	10,142	17,220
Braniff	10,083	15,570
Continental	10,183	15,675
Delta	8,659	11,610
Eastern	5,670	16,890
National	10,158	16,080
Northeast	8,417	12,750
Northwest	10,044	15,900
Trans World	10,667	16,005
United	10,820	16,635
Western	10,487	17,790

SOURCE: ALPA records.

The actual benefits pilots will receive, of course, depend in part on what happens to the funds invested in the variable annuity plans. By 1964 at one major carrier an original contribution of $10 to the variable plan was worth $18. At another carrier the value of a $10 investment had risen to $14. In addition, a pilot could raise his retirement income by making optional contributions to the variable annuity plans.

Airline executives knowledgeable in the field of pensions reported that as of 1963, and really throughout the period of years prior to that, the benefits paid by the major trunk lines were very similar. The important difference was who picked up what proportion of the contributions necessary to buy the similar benefits. He said that the benefits were very similar among the large trunk lines because of the pressure from ALPA and because of the industry's efforts to "level" itself.

The average pension levels of pilots well surpass those of most employee groups. For the bulk of American workers, retirement income is based entirely or in large part on social security benefits. Since the individual maximum primary social security benefit is $135.90 per month, or something over $1,500 per year, the progress that airline pilots have made in the pension area is clear.

QUALITATIVE EVALUATION

Generally speaking, actuaries and pension experts approve of the ALPA pension program. They see it as sound because of its balance between the variable annuity and the fixed benefit plans. Because of this balance, pilots are guaranteed a fixed benefit and have a hedge against inflation with the variable annuity benefit. Pilots are sophisticated enough to understand the risks of the variable annuity plan. In addition their earnings and their fixed benefits are deemed to be high enough so that they can afford the risks of the variable annuity plan. Also their risk is somewhat reduced through the use of "dollar averaging." Pilots thus are betting that the economy will continue to be inflationary and erosion of fixed benefits will be offset by growth of variable benefits.

Actuaries state that similar combinations of fixed and variable benefit plans are becoming more generally used by employee groups. In 1954 the adoption of a variable annuity plan by an employee group was rare. By 1963 these plans were less unusual as other employee groups had gained similar pension coverage.

When ALPA decided to negotiate pensions, it sought group rather than individual plans. It also sought essentially pure retirement plans rather than mixed plans involving severance pay and other types of benefits. To a certain extent some features of the pilots' plans, such as disability, have diluted the pure retirement aspect of their pensions. Pilots also made a decision not to seek a government pension. They did so presumably because government pensions in the transportation industry (i.e., in the railroads) were far below the benefit levels that pilots were after and because they saw government pension plans as not allowing flexible estate planning. Pilots fashioned their pension plans quite realistically on their high standards of living and their real fears of shortened working careers.

The only disclaimers made by experts in the industry concerned the potential costs of the minimum guarantees and the disability provisions. As to the former, if when a pilot retired the benefits he had accrued under the fixed and variable plans and under social security did not come up to the level of his minimum guarantee, the fixed benefit plan would have to be increased to make up the difference. Thus the cost of the fixed plan might have to be increased over anticipated costs if the variable annuity plans suffered stock market reverses. The actuaries are worried also about the potential cost of the minimum guarantees in cases of early retirement in which the guarantees are reduced less than actuarially. They are concerned also about the costs of flat dollar minimum guarantees in the event normal retirement dates are lowered.

As to the disability minimum guarantees, when they were first negotiated the actuaries were uneasy because the qualifications for disability have been loosely written. They would have preferred to have disability defined in the stricter social security terminology under which a person had to be incapable of gainful employment because it would have been potentially less costly and because they would have had adequate historical data on which to make reasonable actuarially assumptions. Some actuaries would have preferred the negotiation of long-term disability insurance rather than the disability minimums because of its low costs which are known in advance. By 1966, however, the actuaries are somewhat less concerned. The first two years of experience under these loosely worded definitions of disability have been reassuring because pilots have not been claiming disability with questionable ailments and the numbers with legitimate ailments have been very small. Right after one plan had been installed in 1963, out of a participating pilot group of about 1,600, 10 pilots who had been on medical leaves of absence immediately qualified and went on disability retirement. During the ensuing seven months only two more pilots had satisfied the company's medical director that they qualified for disability. By early 1966 another 10 pilots had qualified out of the pilot group which had grown to 2,000. An actuary at this airline stated that the clause was not being abused. He said, however, that potential costs were still unknown. He worried that when a large group of the pilots who are presently in their mid-40's reach their early 50's, more of them might claim disability with questionable ailments. He thought possibly the arrival of the supersonic transports might cause a similar reaction.

An actuary at another airline reported in early 1966 that after two years of experience only two pilots out of a pilot group of 1,500 had retired under the disability clause. He said this experience was less than the company had anticipated.

The cost of the disability provisions, therefore, appears to be less than anticipated and to date more potential than real.

Variable annuity plans for pilots are most appropriate because pilots have reached earning levels at which increased dollars of income are highly taxed. In this situation pilots have turned to pensions in lieu of more current income. The tax implications are also great regarding the difference between the company or the individual providing pensions. Given the pilots' tax bracket, a pilot would have to earn about $1.40 to $1.50 to be able to pay for a dollar's worth of company-bought pension benefits. Before a pilot could pay any money into a pension plan on his own, he must pay income tax. Additionally the yield on money invested in pension plans accrues on a tax-free basis. Also of importance, a pilot will receive retirement income at a time when his earnings are lower than they were during his active life. Thus, he will pay less taxes on pension money than he would have on additional wages. For these reasons obtaining pensions was an appropriate goal for pilots.

Perhaps the two most unusual aspects of these variable annuity pensions are the amounts of retirement income they stand to provide pilots and the high company contributions they have come to require. Interestingly, the general movement toward pensions by pilots has in many respects paralleled the general pension movement of the employee groups throughout the United States. Also the type of amendments pilots have sought have been more or less in line with some of the general trends in the pension area. For example, the benefit formulas and other provisions of pension plans in general have also been liberalized. Other provisions showing parallel movements are early retirement and disability retirement benefits, increased death benefits, survivor options, and increased vesting rights. The types of improvements made by pilots have coincided with those made generally.

On balance, one can say that the pilots have used the variable annuity appropriately to build up benefit levels toward age 60 or age 55 retirements more quickly than they could have using just fixed benefit plans. The variable annuity type of pension fitted the pilots' goal of a "realistic pension at a realistic age." The variable annuity plans, the variety of early retirement features, and the benefit levels are unique. Very recently some other negotiated pension plans (e.g., in automobile and steel) have begun to approach the early retirement features which the pilots have had for some years. It is probable that the fear of the pilots regarding forced early retirement was a strong motivating factor leading them to strive for their early retirement benefits. As of 1966 the known costs of the pilot pension plans are uniquely high. Enough experience has not been accrued to state definitely how costly some of the potentially costly items, such as the early retirement features, are going to be. Preliminary experience indicates such potential costs may have been overestimated.

CHAPTER 7

Work Assignment: 1933-1957

CHAPTERS 7 AND 8 contain an analysis of adjustment to technological change over a 30-year period. This technological change involved the advance in the design of commercial airplanes from the Fokkers and China Clippers of the mid-1930's to the large piston aircraft of the late 1940's, such as the Lockheed Constellation and Douglas DC–6 and DC–7 series, to the use, beginning in the late 1950's, of the large turbojets, such as the Boeing 707 and the Douglas DC–8.

The analysis in Chapters 7 and 8 will have a narrow focus. It will investigate the changes in the amount and character of the work to be performed by the flight crew as technology advanced aircraft design from 1933 to 1964. Even within that narrow focus, this analysis will concentrate specifically on the changes in the amount and in the character of the work of a flight engineering nature[1] to be performed by flight crew members over and above the work performed by the pilot and copilot.

The analysis, of course, will include the reactions of interested parties to this technological change. It will continue to highlight the interplay of the airline managements, the leaders of the unions, and the officials of the government on decision making in this industrial relations system.

---

[1] As will be seen, merely selecting a phrase to label this work without introducing an unintentional bias is difficult because whether the work is of a "mechanical," "piloting," or "flight engineering" nature is one of the issues in this analysis. The phrases "flight engineering nature" or "flight engineer's work" will be used for convenience but should not be taken as indicating bias.

THE WORK NEEDED ON LONG-RANGE AIRCRAFT:
1933–1946

The first use of a crew member in addition to the pilot and co-pilot occurred in 1933 when Pan American started to carry a "copilot-flight mechanic" on international flights of its Fokker equipment. Two years later Pan American included a mechanic, designated a "flight engineer," as a member of the flight crew on its China Clippers.

The technology of these aircraft and the technical aspects of Pan American's operations determined the principal duties of these early flight engineers. Because the range of these aircraft permitted them to be flown to outlying air stations around the world where it was not feasible to maintain full-scale maintenance staffs, a need arose to have on board a mechanic who could make or supervise the handling of repairs at such outlying air stations and who possessed the governmental ratings required to certify an airplane as airworthy once it had undergone repairs. This type of work was the primary duty of these flight engineers. In addition, they made in-flight repairs and assisted the crew in whatever duties were assigned to them. They often helped the flight attendants with the passengers.

During World War II some four-engine piston aircraft were put into operation by the military and by commercial air carriers which were operating under contract to the military. Examples of such aircraft types were the Boeing Stratoliner and Douglas C–54 (the military version of the DC–4). The military and the carriers voluntarily assigned a mechanic as part of the flight crew, although one was not required,[2] primarily to handle repairs at outlying air stations as, for example, on the islands of the Pacific. In addition, they assigned a navigator and a radio operator on international C–54 flights.[3]

Evidence exists that when the pressurized Boeing Stratoliners were introduced into service, the management of TWA initially desired to add a third pilot to the flight crew at the third cockpit position. ALPA protested that the nature of the work did not fall

[2] NMB, Presidential Emergency Board No. 121, Pilot Exhibit 224.
[3] NMB, Presidential Emergency Board No. 121, Pilot Exhibit 233.

within the definition of the work of a pilot as found in the Civil
Air Regulations and that therefore a mechanic should do the work.
The management is said to have acceded to the pilots' thinking and
to have continued to assign mechanics to aid the pilots and copilots.[4] Thus, even at this early stage, an airline management was
yielding its right to man an aircraft type as it desired.

Immediately after the war the airlines converted their C–54's
for civilian use as DC–4's with the cockpit arranged for a two-pilot
crew. When they started operating DC–4's without a third crew
member, the pilots protested that their instrumentation was too
complex for two pilots to handle. The domestic airlines held firm.
The international carriers, on the other hand, believed a need
existed for a flight engineer on long international DC–4 flights and
included one in the crew.[5] For short international flights, however,
at least one carrier used only a two-pilot DC–4 crew[6]. TWA, which
operated both internationally and domestically, continued to use
a flight engineer on all flights of its Boeing 307 equipment.[7]

Thus during these years the managements of some airlines, particularly those operating internationally, saw a need to add another
member to the crew of certain aircraft on certain routes. They
realized the need was for a person with mechanical qualifications
and exercised their management initiative to assign mechanics to
the job. The pressure by pilots for a three-man domestic DC–4
crew indicated a continuing interest by pilots in matters of crew
complements. As this analysis proceeds, the relative freedom and
flexibility in making manning decisions possessed by airline management during this early period will stand in marked contrast to
the situation after 1946.

THE ARRIVAL OF THE POSTWAR PISTONS

During the period 1946–1948 technological developments occurred in the form of three new, large, four-engine piston airplanes.
Their size, the number of their engines, and their cockpit com-

[4] D. Kuhn, "The Thrust Lever," *Flying,* November 1960.
[5] NMB, Presidential Emergency Board No. 120, FEIA Exhibit 107.
[6] NMB, Presidential Emergency Board No. 121, ALPA Exhibit 225.
[7] NMB, Case C-2946, transcript, p. 217.

plexity kept very much alive the issue of whether the pilot and copilot needed additional help of a flight engineering nature.

Although these planes were similar to each other in the sense of being large piston aircraft, they were not carbon copies. The first to be introduced into commercial service was the Lockheed Constellation (L–049), which arrived in January 1946.[8] The Constellation, which weighed about 107,000 pounds, was designed and built with a third cockpit position for a flight engineer. The second new plane to appear, the Douglas DC–6, arrived early in 1947.[9] The DC–6, which weighed about 92,000 pounds, was designed and built for a two-pilot crew and had no station for a flight engineer. The last of these new planes to appear was the Boeing Stratocruiser, designated the B–377. It was introduced into service in 1949.[10] Like the DC–6, the B–377 had originally been designed as a two-pilot plane without a flight engineer station.[11] It weighed about 146,000 pounds. All three of these planes were considerably more productive than their predecessors. For example, the Constellations and the DC–6's were estimated to have eight times the capacity of a Douglas DC–3.[12]

When the Constellations arrived in 1946, they were used first by the international carriers and were manned with a flight engineer. Later in 1946 a domestic carrier received its first "Connie" and also included a flight engineer.[13] These carriers really had no choice because the plane had been designed for a three-man crew.

When the Douglas DC–6 arrived, it became the center of the flight engineer controversy. Although similar to the DC–4, it was some 20,000 pounds heavier and some 50 miles per hour faster. Even so, it was the smallest of the three new airplane types and had been designed for two-pilot use. Generally speaking, the airlines manned the DC–6 with two pilots for domestic flights and added a flight engineer for overseas flights. Thus, American Airlines carried no flight engineer domestically, but added one for American

---

[8] NMB, Presidential Emergency Board No. 146, TWA Exhibit 23.
[9] CAA, *Statistical Handbook of Civil Aviation,* 1948, pp. 62 and 82.
[10] *Ibid.*
[11] NMB, Presidential Emergency Board No. 120, FEIA Exhibit 98.
[12] Kuhn, *op. cit.*
[13] NMB, Case C-2946, transcript, p. 207.

Overseas Airlines flights to Europe "principally for the purpose of keeping the meticulous records to assure that adequate fuel [would] be available for the flight."[14] Similarly, United Air Lines carried a "maintenance technician" only on its San Francisco-Honolulu flights.[15]

The Boeing 377 was not put into service before government regulations were promulgated which, as will be discussed in the next section, required a flight engineer as part of its crew.

The different technical aspects of these planes created diverse pressures which are not difficult to picture. The manufacturer of a plane designed for two crew members could be expected to view the need for a flight engineer differently from the manufacturer of a similar plane designed for a three-man crew. Domestic airlines with DC–6 equipment would view the problem, perhaps, differently from an international carrier with either DC–6 or Constellation equipment. Regardless of the type of equipment, the international carrier would be likely to view the need to carry a flight engineer with less alarm than his domestic counterpart both because a flight engineer could be put to use on fuel management on long international flights and because the carrying of extra crew members to relieve the regular crew on long flights is advantageous and sometimes essential to stay within governmental flight time limitations. Domestic airlines which were operating DC–4 equipment with two-man crews and which were planning to buy DC–6 aircraft could be expected to desire a two-man rather than a three-man DC–6 crew, both for the operating savings on the DC–6 and, equally important, for the added assurance it would give that a third crew member would not have to be added to the DC–4 crews. As for the crew members themselves, if they were pressing to have a flight engineer on the DC–4, the arrival of the larger piston aircraft types was certain to increase such pressure.

GOVERNMENTAL REGULATIONS

Under the Civil Aeronautics Act of 1938 and legislation which preceded it, the federal government had the general authority to

---

[14] NMB, Presidential Emergency Board No. 120, ALPA Exhibit 224.
[15] NMB, Presidential Emergency Board No. 120, FEIA Exhibit 107.

allow or not allow aircraft with particular design characteristics, such as the layout of the cockpit, to be used in scheduled air service. It had similar general powers to regulate the minimum number and qualifications of crew members who had to be carried on particular types of aircraft in all its uses or just in specific types of operations. Prior to 1945, however, it had not used them to issue specific regulations concerning work of a flight engineering nature.

During the four-year period 1945–1948 the CAB issued a number of regulations which affected work of a flight engineering nature. Some of these regulations clarified the powers of the CAB and of the Administrator of the CAA over crew complement issues in general. Others established a government certificate which flight engineers had to possess and which began to spell out the experience, knowledge, and skills required of flight engineers. Still others regulated the types of aircraft and operations on which flight engineers were to be required. With these new regulations by the end of 1948, the government had exercised much of its statutory power over the flight engineer and his work.

In 1945 for the first time the CAB made explicit its authority to establish the minimum flight crew on each type of aircraft. Also in 1945 the CAB for the first time stated explicitly for international operations only: (1) when a flight engineer would be required; (2) that he would have to possess a flight engineer certificate; and (3) what his operating qualifications would be.

On February 15, 1946, the CAB gave formal notice that it was proposing to establish a flight engineer certificate. The experience requirements one had to meet to be eligible for such a certificate are important for this analysis. They were:

(1) Four years of practical experience in the repair and maintenance of aircraft and aircraft engines. *Or*
(2) An engineering degree plus one year of experience in the repair and maintenance of aircraft and aircraft engines. *Or*
(3) Two hundred hours of flight experience in the duties of flight engineer. *Or*
(4) An adequate course in flight and ground instruction concerning flight engineering duties. *Or*
(5) Two hundred hours of flight time as a pilot in command of an aircraft having four engines or more.

The next steps taken by the CAB were to require a person who was operating as a flight engineer in domestic service to have a flight engineer certificate, to require all flight crew members to meet appropriate qualifications and requirements, and to establish qualifications for domestic flight engineers.

In 1947 President Truman appointed a Special Board of Inquiry to investigate and make recommendations concerning air safety. He acted after a number of fatal airplane crashes and amid continuing pressure for flight engineers on the large pistons. As a result of this inquiry, the board recommended, *inter alia,* that the CAB conduct hearings to ascertain if additional help was needed among the flight crews of commercial aircraft.

On September 5, 1947, the CAB responded by giving notice that it would hold hearings on whether and under what circumstances and conditions it would be reasonable and would promote safety to require a full-time certificated flight engineer on four-engine aircraft. At the hearings the airline managements generally opposed any regulation requiring a flight engineer, while the pilots' representatives testified to the need for a flight engineer.

On April 14, 1948, the CAB added to the Civil Air Regulations as follows:

> After December 1, 1948, an airman holding a flight engineer certificate shall be required [on all domestic and international flights] solely as a flight engineer on all aircraft certificated for more than 80,000 pounds maximum take-off weight, and on all other aircraft certificated for more than 30,000 pounds maximum take-off weight where the Administrator has found that the design of the aircraft used or the type of operation is such as to require engineer personnel for the safe operation of the aircraft.[16]

In promulgating these regulations, the CAB stated that "the multiplicity of instrumentations and complexity of operational controls" on certain aircraft limited "the pilots' ability to focus attention on all the critical instruments and controls." The CAB "believed that a competent flight engineer by assuming certain mechanical duties" would "enable pilots to concentrate on actual flight of the aircraft, radio operation, and receipt of traffic control

[16] 12FR2160.

clearances, particularly during instrument conditions." The CAB considered "that the flight engineer was required on aircraft of the size and complexity of the Douglas DC–6 and the Boeing 377."

The Air Transport Association (ATA), representing the airlines, and a number of individual airlines protested the new regulations. They pointed out that the estimated annual cost to the airlines of the regulations would start at $20 million and would increase over the years. They noted, for example, that the notice of the hearing had spoken only of four-engine aircraft, and yet the regulations would authorize the Administrator to require flight engineers on some two-engine planes; that during the hearings the weight of the aircraft had not been considered as a distinguishing criterion; and that the language of the regulation which required a flight engineer *solely* as a flight engineer would aggravate "an already difficult jurisdictional union problem" as neutrals would interpret the word differently, and would cause "constant bickering between airlines and between the unions as to which class of airman [was] to handle what duties."

After considering the protests, the CAB on June 9, 1948, gave notice that it was considering the following amendments "designed to clarify" the April regulations and invited interested parties to comment:

> Where the provisions of this part require for a particular route or route segment the performance of two or more functions for which an airman certificate is necessary, such requirement shall not be satisfied by the performance of multiple functions by any airman over such route or route segment.
>
> After December 1, 1948, an airman holding a flight engineer certificate shall be required on all *four-engine* aircraft certificated for more than 80,000 pound maximum take-off weight, and on all other *four-engine* aircraft certificated for more than 30,000 pounds maximum take-off weight where the Administrator finds that the design of the aircraft used or the type of operation are such as to require a flight engineer for safe operation of the aircraft. (*Emphasis added.*)

By these amendments the CAB meant to clarify its intention that one airman with, for example, both a flight engineer certificate and a flight navigator certificate could operate for part of a flight as a flight engineer and for another part as a flight navigator, but could not fulfill requirements for both functions at the same time. In addition the CAB, agreeing with the airlines, removed the words "solely as a flight engineer" from the flight engineer requirements and limited the regulation to four-engine aircraft.[17]

In response to the CAB's request for comments, American Airlines filed a petition for relief of these regulations, particularly as they applied to the DC–6.[18] American wanted the CAB to study the problem scientifically before ruling. Similar petitions were submitted by the Air Transport Association and three other airlines. The petitions were supported by four other airlines. Primary among the objections raised in these additional letters was the requirement of a flight engineer on board the DC–6. The airlines pointed out that the DC–6 had been designed by Douglas and tested and approved by the Administrator of the CAA for operation with a two-pilot crew. They pointed out that the plane had no flight engineer station and that placing a flight engineer on a "jump seat" between the pilot and copilot might decrease safety as three crew members interfered with each other in reaching for the various controls.[19] In addition, the airlines argued that the regulations represented a dangerous and unnecessary assumption of managerial responsibility by the Board that would tend to restrict technological development and increase operating costs. The petitions stated that in a period in which no one had enough experience with four-engine equipment to specify whether or not a flight engineer was necessary, these regulations would establish inflexible practices which would tend to prevent the airlines from attaining future efficiency and optimum safety. They argued that the industry was in a period in which airline managements should be allowed to determine through experience and daily consultation with pilots if flight engineers were needed on particular types of aircraft.[20]

By the latter half of 1948, however, the airlines were not unanimous in their opposition to carrying a flight engineer on the DC–6.

[17] 14CFR, Parts 41 and 61.
[18] CAB, Civil Air Regulations Amendment 41-I.
[19] NMB, Presidential Emergency Board No. 121, ALPA Exhibit 223.
[20] *Ibid.*, ALPA Exhibit 232.

The management of one of the Big Four had become convinced that a flight engineer was needed on the plane and was training men to fill its needs.[21]

The pilots presented counter-arguments to the CAB. They maintained that the DC–6 cockpit contained "so many instruments, levers, buttons, and switches that . . . two men can and do exceed the saturation point of being able to watch and manipulate [them]. . . ." They pointed out that except for weight the DC–6 was similar to the Boeing 377, which they said the ATA agreed should have a flight engineer. They contended that the DC–6 cockpit had been improperly designed because it did not have a separate flight engineer station and that pilots had not been consulted while it was being designed. They pointed out that flight engineers had been carried for years without creating interference among the crew members. They stated that the board which the Administrator had created to evaluate and issue a type certificate for the DC–6 had operated before the Civil Air Regulations required a flight engineer and that the board, in approving the DC–6 for two-pilot operation, had only been applying the regulations as they then had been written. They contended that in any case the accident record of the DC–6 did not tend to support the finding of the board. They stated, "The Lockheed Aircraft Company and purchasers of the Lockheed aircraft [the Constellations] had the air safety foresight to realize that it was too much airplane with too many gadgets and controls in the cockpit for a two-man crew to monitor and operate and, therefore, they wisely provided for a flight engineer and a flight engineer station." They stated that the Boeing 377 had had a two-man cockpit when originally ordered but that after the October 1947 CAB hearing, "The Administrator reversed himself and caused the Boeing Aircraft Company to add a station for the flight engineer. . . ." They stated that the DC–6 should be handled similarly.

On October 5, 1948, the CAB reaffirmed its amended regulations, but delayed the effective date of the flight engineer requirement to March 31, 1949.

Thus, over a four-year period the government moved in to regulate an area of airline operations. In one sense the result could be

[21] NMB, Presidential Emergency Board No. 120, FEIA Exhibit 98, p. 3.

viewed as heavy regulation. The government made clear its authority to determine and regulate minimum flight crews and implemented its authority by requiring flight engineers on three specific
planes of the period and on future similar aircraft. From a practical
standpoint the CAB compromised by allowing the airlines to use
the DC–4, on which they were heavily committed, as a two-crew
airplane, and by requiring a third crew member on the DC–6,
which was new to the fleet and on the Boeing 377, which had not
arrived.

In another sense these regulations could be considered broad
and relatively mild. The CAB did not, for example, specify the
duties flight engineers were to perform, leaving that decision to
airline managements.[22] In addition the CAB set only minimum requirements regarding training and it created so many alternate ways
in which an applicant for a flight engineer certificate could meet
the experience requirement that both mechanics and pilots could
qualify without difficulty.

The analysis to this point indicates also that technological change
can produce an unexpected result. Perhaps, because the words
"technological change" themselves sound so monolithic, they create
an impression of unambiguous, predetermined processes and manning patterns. This is in the image of the man falling prey to the
machine. In fact, however, technological change can produce very
fuzzy manning requirements. As was seen with the development
of the large, postwar piston aircraft, an obvious manning pattern
did not result. Excellent arguments could be made that the DC–6,
for example, required or did not require a third crew member.
While most of the large carriers were opposed to carrying the flight
engineer, one large carrier decided he was necessary for safety on
the DC–6. On the other hand, Trans-Canada Air Lines operated
the DC–6 for years with a two-man crew with no apparent sacrifice
of safety.[23] As another example, although pilots called for a third
man on the DC–4, it was flown apparently safely in great numbers
over the years with a two-man crew.

Another aspect of this ambiguity is that the machines themselves
which are produced by technological change can be modified and

[22] 13FR5909.
[23] NMB, Case L-2946, ALPA Exhibit 285.

can vary one from the other even within ostensibly the same type. Thus the Boeing 377 cockpit was modified to include a flight engineer station.

THE LARGE PISTON MANNING PATTERN

With the advent of the DC–6, the Boeing 377, and the Constellation aircraft, a shift occurred in the nature of the flight engineer job. Whereas prior to their arrival his primary duty had been handling repairs on the ground along the routes and a secondary duty had been assisting the flight crew in operating the aircraft, on these larger pistons the latter job became primary and the former one all but disappeared. The shift became even more pronounced during the 1950's as the DC–7 and the Super Constellation series appeared.

In essence, technological development had made the cockpits more complex and more mechanically oriented than the cockpits of the preceding planes. These new four-engine planes had many more cockpit displays of switches, dials, and gauges, the great majority of which concerned the mechanical functioning of the aircraft and its engines, as opposed to the relatively few flight instruments and controls in the older planes. In such a cockpit the former flying mechanic became a flight engineer who was actively participating during flight in the proper functioning of the aircraft. Under the captain's direct authority, he was responsible for inspecting, operating, monitoring, and, where possible, repairing the aircraft engines and accessory systems.

The flight engineer had a complicated job in starting, running, and monitoring four piston engines. He had to ensure that each one got the proper amount of fuel, oil, and air. He had to see that each cylinder ran at the proper temperature and that the spark plugs were firing properly. He had to open panels in the cowling around each engine when the plane was on the ground or in the process of landing to ensure that the engines would not overheat. He adjusted the pitch of the propellers so that they were delivering the proper amount of thrust for any given maneuver of the aircraft. He controlled the power settings of the engines so that the aircraft would move through the air at the speed the captain demanded. During turbulent weather conditions this required constant adjustment of the power controls. The flight engineer was also continuously syncronizing the four engines so that they were turning all the propellers at the same number of revolutions per minute. Although the later models of the piston aircraft made synchronization somewhat automatic, the flight engineer still had several adjustments to make in this regard. In essence, the flight engineer monitored the engines by watching inputs such as fuel and air, by learning how the engine was functioning internally through the use of the analyzer, and by watching the output of the engine in terms of revolutions per minute and the horsepower developed.

The flight engineer had some additional duties. He was responsible for the operation of several auxiliary mechanical systems such as the electrical and air-conditioning systems. Another part of his job was the rapid switching to alternate systems when something failed. For example, when an engine failure occurred, the flight engineer took most of the steps to get the engine working again or to get it completely out of action. He also had the controls to fight all fires aboard the airplane.

When the flight engineer requirement went into effect in late 1948, the airlines had to find at least 322 additional flight engineers.[24] To meet this need, the airlines drew on individuals from every one of the five experience categories. The result was a very mixed manning pattern.

For the interest of this analysis the focus is on those flight engineers who had backgrounds as pilots and those who had nonpilot backgrounds. Roughly speaking, of the twelve domestic trunk lines plus Pan American during the large piston era, five airlines drew essentially all their flight engineers from nonpilot backgrounds, three used pilots, and five drew from both types.

Several reasons help to explain why the mixed pattern resulted. In 1948 some airline managements did not believe any flight engineer was needed and therefore had not given much thought to or were indifferent as to what type of background was possessed by a person they viewed as unneeded. Other airline managements had

---

[24] Calculated conservatively by multiplying the net increase in aircraft requiring a flight engineer at the end of 1948 compared with the end of 1947 times 3.5, which is a rough estimate scheduling experts use as the minimum ratio of crews to aircraft.

been experimenting with the use of flight engineers and had not concluded definitely which background was preferable. The international carriers had been using experienced mechanics as flight engineers for years and continued to use men with mechanics' backgrounds. Some carriers happened to have pilots on furlough when they first had to use flight engineers so that matters of equity and a ready supply tended to cause them to use pilots. Some carriers used pilots because they believed a three-pilot crew to be safer than a two pilot and one mechanic crew. In 1948 at least two carriers tried to hire pilots with flight engineer certificates, and being unable to meet their needs, started in-company flight engineer training programs in which they trained newly hired or formerly furloughed pilots.[25] Finally, some carriers got their first large pistons late enough to see that a bitter jurisdictional fight was brewing between pilots and nonpilot engineers, as will be described in detail later, and were thus in a position to use pilots as flight engineers to avoid the controversy.

Because the airlines drew on both pilot and mechanic backgrounds, the flight engineers, as a group, included men with other government certificates or ratings in addition to their flight engineer certificates. For at least two reason some knowledge of these other ratings is important to this analysis. In the first place, arguments over the need for certificates in addition to the flight engineer certificate became important in the jurisdictional fight which ensued over work of a flight engineering nature. Second, from an administrator's viewpoint pertinent questions arose concerning the airline managements' ability to match the qualifications needed by the work with the qualifications implied by the ratings of the job occupants and the managements' ability to retain freedom to man their aircraft appropriately in the face of technological change.

In addition to the flight engineer certificate, the pertinent certificates were the general mechanics certificates with aircraft and aircraft engine ratings (A&E) and the commercial pilot license with instrument rating (C&I).

In order to obtain a general mechanic's certificate with aircraft and aircraft engine ratings a person had to be 18 years of age. Obtained individually, each rating required 18 months of practical

[25] NMB, Presidential Emergency Board No. 121, ALPA Exhibit 237.

experience with the applicable procedures, practices, materials, tools, machine tools, and equipment used in the construction, inspection, maintenance, repair, and alteration of aircraft *or* aircraft engines, depending on the rating being obtained. If the applicant wished to obtain both ratings from concurrent experience on both aircraft *and* aircraft engines, he had to have 30 months of such experience. Another way to have received credit for the necessary experience was to have graduated from a certificated mechanic school, most of which took a minimum of two years. The applicant had to show skill in maintaining, repairing, inspecting, and altering any part of an aircraft for which a rating was sought.

In order to obtain a commercial pilot license, a person had to be 18 years of age and must have been in good enough physical condition to obtain the government's second class medical certificate. The applicant must have had 160 hours of flight time to his credit if obtained from an FAA approved school; otherwise he had to have logged 200 flight hours. He had to pass a written examination on meteorology, navigation, the principles of safe flight operation, and the pertinent Civil Aeronautics Regulations. He had to demonstrate an ability to execute landings, spirals, turns, and other maneuvers.

Each of these airman certificates implied that its holder possessed certain skills and capabilities. The general mechanics certificate with A&E ratings implied that its holder was competent to repair aircraft and aircraft engines. It also carried with it the authority to certify as airworthy aircraft and engines. The flight engineer certificate implied that its holder could give aircraft flight checks, could monitor and adjust in flight the mechanical aspects of an airplane, and could recognize incipient malfunctions. It did not, however, imply that he could repair aircraft or engines, nor was he authorized to certify such work. Holding a commercial pilot license and instrument rating implied a person had certain piloting skills. Also, because of the knowledge of a mechanical nature required to obtain it and as indicated by the fact that two pilots handled all mechanic work on aircraft under 80,000 pounds, holding a C&I implied certain capabilities of a flight engineering nature even if the person in question did not have a flight engineer certificate. The holder of a C&I was authorized to fly as copilot in commercial aviation.

The amount of time necessary to obtain each of these certificates varied. Persons with either piloting or with mechanical backgrounds could obtain a flight engineer certificate with a few weeks of study. Obtaining a C&I in one's spare time took about two years. The A&E ratings took about two years of full-time work directly in the field or in a course of that duration.

The practical results of these facts were that pilots were essentially precluded from obtaining a mechanic's certificate with A&E ratings, that mechanics had to spend a couple of years of fairly extensive spare-time activities to obtain a C&I, and that both pilots and mechanics could have qualified with relative ease for the flight engineer certificate. This analysis permits an evaluation of the fit between needs for work of a mechanical nature and the qualifications of the job holders during the 1933–1948 and the 1949–1957 periods. In the former period the airlines flying internationally needed a mechanic on board the planes to be on hand during stops to handle repairs. They assigned mechanics with A&E ratings to the job. Because the A&E rating implied the capability to handle repairs and carried the authority to certify aircraft to be airworthy after being repaired, the match between the job and the qualifications of the job holders appears to have been good. In the second period, granting that a flight engineer was needed on the large pistons, again a good fit apparently was made. Regardless of the type of background a flight engineer possessed, if he had been able to obtain a flight engineer certificate, he was apparently capable enough to handle the demands of a flight engineering nature on the large pistons.

THE PATTERN OF UNION REPRESENTATION: 1943–1958

Over the period 1943–1958 a variety of unions represented the men who carried on the flight engineer function in the airline industry. The pattern of representation is displayed in Table 7.1. The first group of flight engineers to be represented by a union was at American Airlines. In 1943 it became represented by the Airlines Mechanics Association.

A few aspects of this pattern are of interest to this analysis. The Airline Flight Engineer Association (ALFEA) groups at Eastern, Trans World Airways, and American Overseas and the Flight

TABLE 7.1. FLIGHT ENGINEER REPRESENTATION: AS OF JUNE 30, 1943–1958

Carrier	1943	1944	1945	1946	1947	1948	1949	1950
American	ALMA	ALMA	ALMA	ALMD	ALMD	ALMD	ACFEA	ACFEA
Braniff							ALPA	ALPA
Capital							ALPA	ALPA
Continental								
Delta							ALPA	ALPA
Eastern						ALFEA	ALFEA	ALFEA
National								
Northeast								
Northwest								
Trans World				ALFEA	ALFEA	ALFEA	FEIA	FEIA
United		FEA	FEA	FEA	FEA	FEA	FEIA	ACFEA
Western								
Pan American			SA	SA	FEOA	FEOA	FEOA	FEIA
American Overseas				ALFEA	ALFEA	ALFEA	ALFEA	ALFEA

Carrier	1951	1952	1953	1954	1955	1956	1957	1958
American	ACFEA	ACFEA	ACFEA	ACFEA	FEIA	FEIA	FEIA	FEIA
Braniff	ALPA	ALPA	ALPA	ALPA	ALPA	ALPA	ALPA	ALPA
Capital	ALPA	ALPA	ALPA	ALPA	ALPA	ALPA	ALPA	ALPA
Continental				FES	FES	FEIA	FEIA	FEIA
Delta	ALPA	ALPA	ALPA	ALPA	ALPA	ALPA	ALPA	ALPA
Eastern	ALFEA	ALFEA	FEIA	FEIA	FEIA	FEIA	FEIA	FEIA
National	FEIA	FEIA	FEIA	FEIA	FEIA	FEIA	FEIA	FEIA
Northeast						ALPA	ALPA	ALPA
Northwest			IAM	IAM	IAM	IAM	IAM	IAM
Trans World	FEIA	FEIA	FEIA	FEIA	FEIA	FEIA	FEIA	FEIA
United	ACFEA	FEIA	FEIA	FEIA	FEIA	FEIA	FEIA	FEIA
Western				ACFEA	ACFEA	ACFEA	ACFEA	FEIA
Pan American	FEIA	FEIA	FEIA	FEIA	FEIA	FEIA	FEIA	FEIA
American Overseas	ALFEA	ALFEA						

NOTE: *Symbols:* (1) International Unions: Airline Pilots Association (ALPA), Flight Engineers' International Association (FEIA), and International Association of Machinists (IAM); (2) "International unions" subchartered by ALPA: Air Carrier Flight Engineers Association (ACFEA) and Airlines Mechanics Association (ALMA); (3) Federal Labor Unions (directly affiliated with the AF of L): Air Line Flight Engineers Association (ALFEA) and Flight Engineering Officers Association (FEOA); (4) Independent Unions: Flight Engineers Society (FES), Flight Engineers Association (FEA) and "System Association" (SA); and (5) a department of the United Auto Workers: Air Line Mechanics Department (ALMD).

SOURCES: Annual Reports of NMB; NMB, Case C-2946, FEIA Exhibits 41 and 58 and ALPA Exhibit 287A; FEIA, *Constitution and Bylaws,* as amended March 5, 1958.

Engineering Officers Association group at Pan American were federal labor unions directly affiliated with the AF of L. At their request, on December 7, 1948, the AF of L issued an international charter to the Flight Engineers' International Association (FEIA). By 1958 FEIA had gained representation rights at eight major airlines. At airlines at which pilots were used as flight engineers ALPA represented them. By 1958 four such groups existed. At one time or another during the period a so-called international union subchartered by ALPA, the Air Carrier Flight Engineers Association (ACFEA), represented groups at American, United, and Western. By 1958 it had lost all representation rights. Over the period 1943–1958 all the major carriers had groups of flight engineers represented by unions.

The representation pattern over the years 1943–1958 leads to some conclusions as to the stability of the representation pattern. It can be seen that representation rights changed hands seven times (not including changes where an independent group joined an international group for the first time). These seven changes, however, occurred at only three airlines: American, United, and Western. The pattern at the other airlines was for an independent group to form and later to affiliate with a national union, or for a group to form and immediately affiliate with an international union. Thus it can be said that although changes in representation took place during this period, there was also stability of a sort. At five of the major airlines an independent group or a group initially forming became represented by FEIA and continued to be represented by that international union throughout the balance of the period. Similarly, groups of engineers at four airlines became affiliated with ALPA and remained affiliated with ALPA throughout the balance of the period. Thus, three patterns emerged: stable groups represented by FEIA, stable groups represented by ALPA, and unstable groups represented by both FEIA and ALPA, or its affiliate, ACFEA.

EFFECT OF MANAGEMENT DECISIONS

Fundamental to the evolution of the ensuing jurisdictional fight were the decisions made by individual airline managements as to whether they would use men in the flight engineer job who had pilot backgrounds, nonpilot backgrounds, or some men from each category.

The airlines which used pilots to fill their flight engineering jobs avoided the jurisdictional fight. Four carriers were in this category: Panagra, Capital, Delta, and, with some exceptions, Northeast. Because on these airlines the entire flight crews were composed of pilots, they were represented by ALPA.

At one time Northeast had some flight engineers with mechanical backgrounds. When Northeast bought its first large piston aircraft in 1956, it took about 20 mechanics from its shop as its first flight engineer group. Its management soon saw, however, that a jurisdictional dispute might ensue and thereafter utilized pilot engineers. By agreement with ALPA, the original group of mechanic engineers was placed on the ALPA seniority list and became represented by ALPA. In later years, all the mechanic engineers at Northeast Airlines were offered pilot training at company expense and all but a couple of them became pilots.

Six carriers decided that they would fill their flight engineer jobs for the most part with nonpilots. They were Continental, Eastern, National, Northwest, Trans World, and Pan American. In this way during the period 1943–1958 these carriers were able to gain stability in terms of which union would represent their flight engineer employees. The unions were either FEIA or IAM.

Saying that these carriers had stability as to the bargaining agents for engineers is not to say that these carriers did not have individual instances of bitterness between the pilots and mechanic flight engineers, nor is it to say that they were not putting themselves in a position to have trouble from the jurisdictional dispute in the post-1958 period. Some of these carriers that used nonpilot engineers had individual instances of bitterness within the cockpit where pilots and nonpilot engineers had disagreements. Commenting on such disagreements Captain David Kuhn wrote in the November 1960 issue of *Flying* as follows: "On occasion there was open dissension in the cockpit. At times, a pilot would order a flight engineer off the plane. On one airline the feeling became so bitter that chalk marks were made on the cockpit floor to show the areas of responsibility."

EFFECT OF NEGOTIATIONS ON THE JURISDICTIONAL DISPUTE

During this period some of the carriers which used nonpilot engineers and some of the carriers which used both pilot and nonpilot engineers were getting themselves into difficulties which would come to light in the post-1958 period over the matter of qualifications for the flight engineering job over and above the flight engineer certificate. Specifically, during this period six carriers agreed with flight engineer groups during contract negotiations or decided on their own to require flight engineers to possess the A&E rating in addition to the flight engineer certificate. Thus American Airlines agreed with its mechanic engineers in 1956 that flight engineers would have to have an A&E rating. Similar agreements were reached during this period by Continental, Eastern, TWA, Western, and Pan American. United Air Lines, although having an A&E requirement for its early groups of mechanic flight engineers during the Second World War, would not agree to that requirement in the postwar period.

The matter of ratings required by a flight engineer in addition to the flight engineer's certificate became one of the principal issues of the jurisdictional dispute. Wherever possible the flight engineers negotiated contracts requiring the A&E ratings; and, as has been pointed out, on four airlines flight engineers were required to have a commercial pilot's license in addition to the flight engineer's certificate. Both of those ratings were in addition to a flight engineer's certificate. In the case of the A&E requirement, however, the companies generally came to the agreement under bargaining pressure from FEIA; whereas in the case of the pilot engineers, the managements were more likely to decide unilaterally that they would require a pilot's license of their flight engineers.

The major carriers which used both pilot and nonpilot engineers later found themselves in the very center of the jurisdictional fight. The carriers in this group were American, United, and Western. The experience of United in this matter is illustrative of the way in which these carriers came to employ both pilots and nonpilots as engineers.

United Air Lines started using traveling mechanics on its military contract flights during World War II. These traveling mechanics were required to possess the A&E ratings because the significant part of their jobs was the handling of repairs at outlying stations. During this period these mechanics formed an independent union and in 1944 signed a contract with United. Three years later the parties renewed their contract and included a clause which guaranteed these employees job-bidding rights on any future commercial (and nonmilitary) flight engineering jobs which the company might have.

Immediately after the war United used a handful of these men in the capacity of observers and technicians for the engineering department. They were also used by United immediately after the war on flights to Honolulu. These engineers were assigned to occasional domestic flights of United's new DC–6 equipment to report on its mechanical functioning. This was the situation at United when the government required the carrying of flight engineers on the large pistons as of December 1, 1948.

The management decided that the flight engineering job on the large pistons could best be filled by adding to the crew a fully qualified copilot who also possessed the flight engineer certificate. In accordance with this policy, its first class of flight engineers was composed of copilots who had recently been furloughed and some newly hired pilots. The former traveling mechanics were not given bidding rights on the job on the grounds that, not being pilots, they did not qualify for the new positions. In response, these mechanics took the matter to court and affiliated with FEIA to strengthen their position. In the meantime the company had signed an agreement with ALPA covering all aspects of the employment of the pilot engineers except the matter of seniority. ALPA insisted on one seniority list, while the carrier wanted a separate list for the pilot engineers. The trouble was that the carrier was about to lay off 88 more copilots. With one seniority list the company would have had to have furloughed 88 pilot engineers it had already trained for their flight engineer certificates, and would have had to train another group of 88 pilot engineers. The management believed that the carrier's weak financial position could not stand the added training expense. This fact, plus the court case of the traveling mechanics, caused the company to change its position and to drop the pilot qualification for the flight engineer job. Because the former flying mechanics were thus again eligible, United began to negotiate a contract with FEIA for all flight engineers and signed one on June 6, 1949. Under this contract the 19 former mechanics headed the flight engineer seniority list.

The pilots were not slow to counter this move. They petitioned the National Mediation Board for an election to determine whether the Air Carrier Flight Engineers Association, the ALPA affiliate, or FEIA should represent the engineers. On July 5, 1949, ACFEA became the bargaining representative, and after many months of delay over the seniority list it signed an agreement with the carrier in August 1950. The agreement called for sandwiching at the head of the seniority list the top 19 former mechanics and the top 19 pilot engineers.

The representation picture, however, was to change once more. In the fall of 1951 FEIA asked for another election, and on the basis of that election it again became the representative of the flight engineers and remained so through this period.

In 1952 the FEIA negotiations with United were deadlocked on the matter of qualifications for the flight engineer. The union was worried lest the company once again change the qualifications for the job, namely, that it require all flight engineers to be pilots. Therefore it demanded a clause which would have required the company to supply flight engineers with facilities for any necessary pilot training and with a reasonable time to complete such training if the company should change the qualifications. Under the old contract the carrier had only to provide the incumbents with a reasonable opportunity to meet any new qualification. For almost a year negotiations proved futile. Finally, after a short strike and a report by a Presidential Emergency Board, a new contract was signed on January 30, 1953. The qualifications question was settled by the company's agreeing not to change the qualifications for the incumbents during the life of the agreement without mutual consent. FEIA agreed that the carrier had the right to set qualifications for *new* engineers.

In February 1954 the carrier again changed its position on qualifications for new flight engineers. It announced that all future engineers would be required to have pilot licenses. It planned to assign new pilots to the line as copilots for one day to establish their pilot seniority and then use them as pilot engineers.

Needless to say, FEIA was not happy with this new turn of events and made it the major issue of the 1955 negotiations. FEIA proposed that all new engineers be required to possess the A&E ratings. The company was determined to retain the right to set qualifications for new job applicants. When no progress was made, the flight engineers struck.

The strike lasted from October 24 until December 14, 1955. During that time the carrier completed 90% of its scheduled flights in large measure because the pilot engineers continued to fly. The new contract provided that the company would not establish a pilot qualification for engineer jobs on any equipment then in use, and that it would offer pilot training at company expense to any engineer who could pass the physical examination and the company's pilot pre-employment test. The contract also provided that if engineers had to be pilot-qualified on future aircraft types, they would continue to fly on the current equipment as long as it lasted, take the training to become pilots, or leave the company with severance pay.

As a result of the pilots' actions in replacing flight engineers and at the request of FEIA, when the AF of L met in convention in December 1955 it passed a resolution to the effect that unless within 10 days a satisfactory understanding and arrangement had been reached between ALPA and FEIA and an adjustment had been made regarding the organizing of people outside ALPA's jurisdiction satisfactory to the AF of L, ALPA would be suspended.

The outcome of this resolution was not suspension for ALPA. According to President Sayen's testimony at a later date, the AF of L established a super mediation committee composed of Messrs. Meany, Schnitzler, Beck, Harrison, and Hayes. This committee, according to Mr. Sayen, primarily through the work of Mr. Schnitzler, mediated a settlement between FEIA and United Air Lines. Once that settlement had been reached, the convention resolution to suspend ALPA was a dead issue.[26]

The representation situation at United Air Lines, therefore, depended on one's point of view. From the point of view of FEIA any attempt by ALPA to have pilots get flight engineer certificates or to attempt to enlist their interest in joining ALPA was a raid on the FEIA jurisdiction and membership. From the point of view of

[26] NMB, Case C-2946, transcript, pp. 471, 5244, and 5395.

ALPA the jurisdiction was an open question and ALPA believed it was certainly within its rights to try to organize pilots into its union. ALPA also believed that it should not sit idly by or support any attempt by FEIA in negotiations to win the A&E qualifications which would preclude a pilot for all practical purposes from an engineer job.

Flight engineer duties were also in dispute during this period. Right after the flight engineers were required on the large pistons in 1948, Mr. Behncke, then President of ALPA, complained to the CAB that some airlines were not assigning duties to the flight engineers.[27] In response the CAB notified ALPA that the duties of the flight engineers were in the hands of the airlines themselves. In 1960 President Sayen, who had succeeded Mr. Behncke, made the following comment about the training and duties of flight engineers during this period.

> . . . but when the third member requirement came about, . . . there was considerable confusion in the industry. I don't think all of it is gone yet, as to just what was this individual. What was he going to be? What was his job? What were his responsibilities going to be? What kind of background should he have? This whole subject was very indefinite. The regulations . . . don't help you too much, they leave it very wide open. And so there were different patterns followed, and I think the Association, like everyone else, was feeling its way somewhat on the various airlines."[28]

Effect of the AF of L and the AFL–CIO

In the immediate postwar years the groups of mechanically trained flight engineers and mixed groups of mechanical flight engineers and pilot-trained flight engineers began to seek union representation. They were inclined to look to ALPA as the natural flight crew union for them to join. They were supported in this inclination by the AF of L, which urged the pilots' association to accept mechanically trained flight engineers as members as well as such other flight groups as the stewards and stewardesses. Under the constitution and by-laws of ALPA at that time, however, non-pilots were not eligible for membership. The constitution and by-laws read as follows:

[27] NMB, Case C-2946, transcript, p. 243.
[28] *Ibid.*, p. 5440.

Any male of the white race, of lawful age and of good moral character, who is legally qualified to serve as pilot or copilot on aircraft in interstate or foreign commerce, shall be eligible for membership. . . ."[29]

The ALPA leadership at that time refused to change the wording of this section. In addition, during this period ALPA would not clearly state that a flight engineer should be required to have an extensive mechanical background. Instead of taking nonpilot flight engineers into full ALPA membership, ALPA subchartered ACFEA groups. ALPA issued a provisional charter to the ACFEA on November 24, 1947.[30] Under the provisional charter of affiliation ALPA appointed the officers of ACFEA, gave approval for any of its expenditures, and approved ACFEA's constitution and bylaws and any changes thereto. The provisional charter could be revoked by ALPA at any time. On February 17, 1953, ALPA issued a permanent charter of affiliation to the ACFEA. Under the terms of the permanent charter it could be revoked at any time for cause by the executive committee of ALPA and any changes in the ACFEA constitution and bylaws had to have ALPA approval.[31]

When ALPA persisted in its stand of not taking nonpilot engineers directly into its organization, the AF of L on December 7, 1948, chartered the Flight Engineers' International Association.

As soon as ALPA learned of the new charter, President Behncke wrote to President Green of the AF of L protesting. Mr. Behncke's protest read in part as follows:

The charter was prematurely granted without even giving ALPA, for eighteen years a good standing affiliate of the AF of L, a hearing. By this action, the Executive Board has invaded the cockpits of the airline pilots, their workshop, and given jurisdiction to another group, even to the extent of taking the cockpit controls out of the hands of the pilots and giving another group jurisdiction thereof. . . ."[32]

[29] ALPA, *Constitution and Bylaws,* as revised October 23, 1936, p. 12.
[30] NMB, Case C-2946, FEIA Exhibit 241.
[31] *Ibid.*
[32] NMB, Presidential Emergency Board No. 121, Eastern Air Lines Exhibit 183

As indicated in Mr. Behncke's letter, one of the primary issues in this jurisdictional dispute was the matter of actual jurisdiction granted to the two organizations by the AF of L. The original jurisdiction granted to ALPA in 1931 was as follows, "piloting and navigating all aircraft, including both lighter than air and heavier than air, and/or mixed (members to be licensed).[33] The jurisdiction granted to FEIA in 1948 was over "licensed flight engineers."[34]

Behind the actual words of the jurisdiction, however, was the fundamental issue of how narrow or how broad job assignments traditionally had been in the airline industry in this country. Over the ensuing years both ALPA and FEIA had arguments to make on this issue. For its part, ALPA argued that the tradition had been one of broad job confines. ALPA continually pointed to the fact that at first there was one pilot in the cockpit who did all the work both of a piloting and mechanical nature. Then, starting in the early 1930's, an additional pilot was added in the cockpit and was "created in the image" of the first pilot. ALPA pointed out that prior to 1948 and even after 1948 on aircraft under 80,000 pounds, or on aircraft with less than four engines, work of both a piloting and mechanical nature was done by just two pilots. Thus ALPA argued that its jurisdiction corresponded to the generalist concept of work assignment in the industry.

On the other hand, FEIA argued that a tradition of a specialist in the flight crew area had evolved from an early date; that pilots had been augmented by flying mechanics, by radio operators, and by navigators. For instance, it pointed to the five-man international crews of the DC–4 aircraft during World War II.

These arguments were extended to their effect on safety. ALPA argued that for safety purposes a crew should be interchangeable so that each man knew what the other was thinking and could react quickly. ALPA also argued over the years that one union in the cockpit was essential for crew harmony. For its part, FEIA argued that the complexity of the aircraft and systems were of such a nature that only a man who specialized in the mechanical aspects of the planes could hope to keep up with these complexities

[33] NMB, Case C-2946, FEIA Exhibit 218.
[34] *Ibid,* FEIA Exhibit 192.

and to be able to be in a position properly to trouble shoot and to maintain the aircraft in proper running order during flight. In addition FEIA argued along the line that mechanical specialists who were making a career as a flight engineer would be the only group motivated enough to keep up with the complexities of the mechanical aspects of the plane; whereas the pilot engineers, looking forward to careers as pilots, would find that keeping up on the mechanical aspects of the plane was mere drudgery and would not do it as eagerly and therefore as efficiently as career mechanical engineers. These arguments which started early in the jurisdictional dispute gained momentum as the jet era approached.

Because of the basic principle of labor in this country that each international union is autonomous, the AF of L was not in a strong position to get either ALPA or FEIA to do its bidding. The AF of L in this dispute took its traditional role of mediating, cajoling, and attempting to get the parties to work out their problems together.

In its early years FEIA frequently charged ALPA with not recognizing its jurisdiction. The response of the AF of L was to remind ALPA that it had chartered FEIA because ALPA had refused to take mechanical flight engineers directly into its membership, and to insist that ALPA recognize the FEIA jurisdiction. In addition the AF of L called upon ALPA to disassociate the ACFEA. Thus the President of the AF of L, Mr. Green, in 1951 wrote Mr. Behncke, ALPA's President:

> The Air Line Pilots Association lacked authority to issue an international charter to any group of workers; it is clothed with authority to charter local unions of airline pilots when and wherever the officers of said organization may decide to do so.
>
> You will recall that years ago you were requested by the officers of the American Federation of Labor to organize the flight engineers and other groups connected with air transportation. You at that time deemed it unwise and inadvisable to do so. Largely for that reason a charter was issued when the flight engineers applied for said charter.

The most drastic action of the AFL-CIO during the period prior to 1958 was its threat, already mentioned, to suspend ALPA because pilots replaced striking flight engineers at United in 1955.

Toward the end of the period leading up to 1958, and increasingly thereafter, the attempts of the AFL-CIO were directed at getting FEIA and ALPA to merge. The clearest call of this sort during the period under consideration came as a result of charges brought by FEIA that ALPA was "again cooperating with the employer by encouraging its members to obtain flight engineers licenses in order to weaken the bargaining position of FEIA on airlines all over the country; and ALPA is informing its members that this program has the support of the AFL-CIO leadership." In response to these charges on February 2, 1958, Mr. Meany appointed a subcommittee made up of Messrs. Lee W. Minton, President of the Glass Bottle Blowers Association, Joseph A. Beirne, President of the Communications Workers of America, and Richard F. Walsh, President of the International Allegiance of Theatrical Stage Employees and Moving Picture Machine Operators. On February 11, 1958, this subcommittee reported as follows:

> This committee feels that the close relationship of the flight crew, which is now faced with the introduction of an entire new series of larger and faster aircraft, powered with turbine engines, makes it imperative that the flight crew must belong only to one organization. The committee recognizes that the captain or pilot in command of an airline aircraft has the full responsibility for its safe operation and that this responsibility is placed directly on him by virtue of his being licensed by the federal government and which he cannot delegate to his employer or anyone else also makes it necessary that the flight crew be coordinated into one organization.
>
> The committee, after hearing the arguments of both FEIA and ALPA, can find no trade union reasons why the merger of these two organizations should not become a reality. The subcommittee feels that both organizations, FEIA and ALPA, should take full advantage of Meany's offer in his letter of March 14, 1957, in which he stated to President Sayen of ALPA:
>
> "Your officers and officers of Flight Engineers International union have been told on numerous occasions, this office stands ready to assist in helping bring about an amicable solution to the problems which exist in this portion of the airline industry—this offer still stands—but the solution, I must say quite frankly, will not be found by arbitrary action on anyone's part."[35]

[35] NMB, Case C-2946, ALPA Exhibit 150.

Over the years under consideration, the reaction of FEIA and ALPA to merger suggestions varied. In the early years, particularly right after FEIA was chartered, FEIA expressed a willingness at least to have a bilateral federation of ALPA and FEIA. During those early years ALPA was not particularly disposed toward merger. In the latter years toward 1958, the roles were reversed. ALPA had a committee of its Executive Committee formed to consider merger attempts and to talk merger with FEIA; whereas FEIA resolved on June 4, 1957, that "exploration or discussion leading toward a merger of FEIA and ALPA does not serve the best interests of the entire membership of the FEIA. The officers of FEIA are hereby directed and ordered not to participate in such discussions."

Underlying the flight engineers' thoughts on merger in the latter years of this period were resolutions adopted by ALPA. In 1954 ALPA resolved that the primary requirement of any newly hired aircraft operating member be the possession of a commercial pilot's certificate. In 1956 with commercial jets looming, ALPA strengthened this resolution by adopting as mandatory ALPA policy "that no turboprop or jet turbine powered aircraft will be operated unless and until it is manned at all flight stations by a qualified pilot in the employ of the company as a pilot." Current nonpilot crew members were to get job protection. ALPA also passed a resolution changing the eligibility rules for membership directly into the Association. Whereas prior to 1956 a man had to have been a pilot in order to qualify for membership, after the 1956 convention any person who served "as a flight deck operating crew member" could be eligible.

Further, ALPA resolved in 1956 that while maintaining ALPA's affiliation with the AFL-CIO was desirable, the ALPA Executive Committee was empowered to sever it if necessary to pursue its crew complement resolutions.

With these resolutions as the official ALPA policy in the post-1956 period, FEIA believed there was an irreconcilable obstacle to a merger of the two unions.

Toward the end of this period ALPA tried to take the initiative in appealing to the AFL-CIO. On March 6, 1957, President Sayen wrote to President Meany stating, "The Executive Council of the AF of L made a very serious mistake in chartering another international union on the flight deck of the commercial air carriers in 1948." President Sayen reported that after studying the problem seriously for several years ALPA had changed its constitution and bylaws "so that any flight deck operating crew member may now become a member of the Air Line Pilots Association International with all of the rights and privileges of any member." President Sayen went on, "In view of the foregoing, we request that the only other outstanding charter to flight deck crew members which has been issued by the AFL-CIO—that of the Flight Engineers' International Association—be revoked and that the jurisdiction of the Air Line Pilots Association be clarified so as to encompass all individuals who go off the ground with an aircraft for the purpose of performing duties in flight." In response, on March 14, 1957, President Meany wrote President Sayen that he agreed it would be "well for the individual employees working in this field and so affected if this problem could be solved—but solved in a democratic fashion." President Meany went on to say that *the* contributing factor in the Council's decision to charter FEIA in 1948 had been ALPA's then policy of not admitting nonpilots to full membership. President Meany said that if the AFL-CIO should revoke FEIA's charter, it would "not only be undemocratic but an autocratic abridgement of the rights and privileges of an affiliate under the provisions of the AFL-CIO constitution." President Meany continued, "It is a very easy solution on the part of ALPA in settling this question to amend its constitution and bylaws and state that from now on our policy will be thus and so because our policy has changed with the times. But may I make a simple observation —there are individuals who will be affected by your solution and I am democratic enough to believe individuals have a right to assist in the solving of their problems." Mr. Meany closed by assuring President Sayen that the officers of the AFL-CIO stood ready to help bring about an amicable solution to the problem.

Thus it can be seen that once the AF of L had chartered FEIA, the labor federation was in effect powerless to solve the problem.

EFFECT OF THE GOVERNMENT

At various times during the period from 1949 to 1958, ALPA and FEIA each petitioned the CAB to change the Civil Air Regulations in ways which would favor its side in the jurisdictional fight. Most of these recommended changes would have affected, and those that were implemented by the CAB did affect, the ease or difficulty with which a pilot or nonpilot could obtain the flight engineer certificate and maintain his qualifications to fly as a flight engineer.

ALPA and FEIA had divergent views as to changes in the types of experiences which could qualify a person to apply for a flight engineer's certificate. Frequently throughout this period ALPA suggested to the CAB that a person holding either a flight engineer's certificate or a commercial pilot's license be permitted to serve as a flight engineer.[36] For its part, FEIA not only did not believe that a man could operate as a flight engineer with just a pilot's certificate but in fact asserted that "a peculiar deficiency" inhered in the assignment to flight engineer jobs of men who possessed both the flight engineer's certificate and the commercial pilot's license.[37] Toward the end of the period ALPA supported a recommendation that a man who had 400 hours of flight time as a copilot of aircraft having four or more engines rated at at least 800 horsepower each, or the equivalent thereof in the case of turbine-powered aircraft, had enough experience to apply for the flight engineer's certificate.[38] FEIA argued that flight time as a pilot did not necessarily or automatically qualify an individual to be a flight engineer. It maintained that 400 hours of copilot time were insufficient as experience to become a flight engineer, and, indeed, that 200 hours as a pilot in command time should only be considered sufficient experience if it was bolstered by a minimum of six months' practical experience in the maintenance and repair of four-engine aircraft.[39] In early 1958, with the advent of jets not far off, ALPA recommended to the CAB that in order to be a third crew member in the future a man be required to have a commercial pilot's license.[40] Needless to say, as will be brought out in greater detail in the next chapter, FEIA did not concur. Throughout this period the CAB continued the experience requirements essentially as they were promulgated originally in 1947.

[36] NMB, Case C-2946, FEIA Exhibit 59.

[37] *Ibid.*, FEIA Exhibit 60.

[38] NMB, Presidential Emergency Board No. 121, Pilot Exhibit 245.

[39] *Ibid.*, Pilot Exhibit 246.   [40] *Ibid.*, Pilot Exhibit 247.

Another issue over which FEIA and ALPA appealed to the CAB and in one case made recommendations to the Senate was the matter of command relationships within the cockpit. Disputes arose in this period concerning such questions as whether the pilot would continue to be, as he traditionally had been, in absolute control of the aircraft and its crew during flight, whether the pilot could handle flight engineer duties during routine times and/or during emergencies, and whether a pilot without a flight engineer's certificate could give the periodic flight checks to the entire crew including the flight engineer. In 1954 the CAB proposed to add several sections to the Civil Air Regulations. From the standpoint of the pilots the net result of several of these sections taken together would have meant that the pilot would no longer be in absolute command of the aircraft. Particularly contentious was a new section which read as follows:

> On flights requiring a flight engineer, at least one other flight crew member shall be sufficiently qualified so that in the event of illness or other incapacity, emergency coverage can be provided for that function for the safe completion of the flight. A pilot need not hold a flight engineer's certificate to function in the capacity of a flight engineer for emergency conditions only.

From the pilot's standpoint that proposed section was in conflict with two other sections, one of which stated that the pilot in command is responsible for the operation and safety of the airplane during "flight time," and another section which read that no individual could serve as a flight engineer unless he had a valid flight engineer's certificate. From the pilot's point of view the combination of these sections meant on the one hand that a pilot was responsible for the operation and safety of the airplane, while on the other hand, except in emergency conditions, it was illegal for him to operate some of the devices and equipment of the aircraft, namely those that had to do with the flight engineer's job. This issue became so important in the minds of the pilot group at one major carrier that they were considering declaring each and every flight as being operated in its entirety under the emergency authority of the pilot in command and requiring the airline to provide an opportunity for pilots to get the flight engineer's certificate as a condition of continuing the operation of the large piston aircraft.

In answer to a petition by ALPA in regard to these issues, the CAB issued the following interpretation:

> The Board interprets and construes Section 40.351(c) [which said that during flight the pilot in command was in command of the airplane and the crew and was responsible for the safety of the passengers, crew members, cargo, and airplane] as conferring on the pilot in command, with respect to matters concerning the operation of the airplane, full control and authority without limitation over all other crew members and their duties during flight time, whether or not he holds a valid certificate authorizing him to perform the duties and functions of such other crew members.

In addition, the CAB reiterated its intention regarding the emergency authorities of the pilot in command to the effect that in emergency conditions a pilot could function as a flight engineer but in order to function as a flight engineer regularly a pilot had to have a flight engineer's certificate.

For the most part FEIA agreed with the CAB that the pilot in command was in absolute command of the aircraft. However, on a couple of occasions FEIA took stands which at least raised doubts about its position. For example, the President of FEIA issued a statement before the Senate Committee on Interstate and Foreign Commerce in 1954 in regard to pending legislation. His statement recommended that a flight engineer be defined as an airman who was responsible while in flight or en route for the safe and efficient mechanical functioning in airworthy condition of the aircraft and its components.[41] Had in fact the flight engineers been made *responsible* for the mechanical functioning of the aircraft during flight, then the absolute responsibility of the pilot for the safety of the aircraft and responsibility for the crew would have been diluted.

In 1958 FEIA raised with the CAB the question of whether the authority of the pilot extended to the point that he could order a flight engineer not to record a mechanical deficiency pertaining to the aircraft on the appropriate reporting form. In response the CAB upheld the authority of the pilot to issue such an order during flight, while at the same time the CAB hedged by not relieving the flight engineer of the responsibility of making the deficiency known to the proper people once the flight was over.

[41] *Ibid.,* Pilot Exhibit 244.

As to training, early in the period ALPA took the position that pilots, or other airmen for that matter, who were seeking additional governmental certificates should not be required to repeat training and examinations on material which they had mastered in order to obtain earlier certificates. For example, ALPA did not believe that a pilot who had been tested on meteorology in order to get his commercial pilot's license should be retested on that subject in order to obtain a flight engineer's certificate. ALPA's position in fact was that pilots had always done the flight engineer job on aircraft prior to 1949 and even after 1949 pilots did all the flight engineer jobs on aircraft weighing less than 80,000 pounds, and therefore pilots could be assumed to have had essentially all the training necessary to qualify for the flight engineer's certificate.

Although ALPA did not want to duplicate training in getting the flight engineer's certificate, neither did it wish to have flight engineers receive a great deal more training concerning the mechanical aspects of the aircraft than pilots received. Of course, at the end of the period when pilots were maintaining that the flight engineer had to have a commercial pilot's license in addition to a flight engineer's certificate, ALPA was advocating a great deal more training for flight engineers. For its part, FEIA took the position that the amount of mechanical training required of flight engineers should be increased. In addition FEIA took the position that for applicants who were applying for flight engineers' certificates who had not had an actual flight experience as a pilot or a flight engineer, a requirement should be established under which they would have to get at least 100 hours of flight time before being certificated. Actually during this period the CAB did add five hours of actual flight training for such applicants. Also FEIA took the position that flight engineers should not be required to learn a great deal about subject matter which pertained only to pilots.

During this period an argument raged over the amount of current experience a flight engineer had to have on a particular aircraft type in order to be scheduled as a flight engineer on that aircraft and, in addition, over the question of who could flight check a flight engineer. FEIA was able to have the CAB require a person to have had at least 50 hours of experience as a flight engineer on a particular aircraft type within the preceding six months in order to be eligible to be scheduled as a flight engineer on that equipment; before, the comparable requirement had been within the preceding twelve months. A change of this nature was of interest to the flight engineers in that if the recent experience requirement became more stringent, as in fact it did, pilots would be less likely to qualify for the flight engineer job and less likely to be able to replace a non-pilot engineer. As a part of the requirement for current experience, if a person had not met the current experience requirement he had to be checked either by a check airman of the carrier or by an authorized representative or administrator of the CAA. During this period this requirement was made more stringent by the addition of a requirement that the check had in most instances to include a check in flight, which as originally promulgated it had not required.

A related issue over which the parties argued during the period was whether a pilot could check the work of a flight engineer although the pilot did not himself have a flight engineer's certificate. Naturally, the two unions took opposing views on this subject. On this issue FEIA came out ahead because the CAB finally required flight checks to be given by check airmen who held the same airman certificates and ratings as were required of the airman being checked. In effect, this meant that a flight engineer had to be checked by a man who had a flight engineer's certificate.

One other issue arose during this period which was later to be of importance. It was whether the manufacturer of an airplane had to supply a flight engineer station under certain circumstances. The CAB passed the following regulations during this period:

> Where the work load on the flight crew is such as to require a flight engineer, a flight engineer station will be provided.
>
> Stations shall be so located and arranged that the flight crew members can perform their functions efficiently without interfering with each other.

Such a requirement by the CAB could be interpreted as strengthening the position of FEIA.

SUMMARY

Based on this analysis one can begin to see the multiplicity of people, institutions, and issues which a jurisdictional dispute in a government-regulated industry can involve. A unique aspect of this jurisdictional fight, which will become clearer in the next chapter, is this very multiplicity.

Concerning the role of the carriers in this situation, this evaluation has shown that at least initially a management could affect the outcome on its carrier by the fundamental decision it made as to the qualifications of its flight engineers. If it decided to use pilot engineers, it was able to avoid the jurisdictional fight. Even if it used nonpilot engineers, at least during the period under discussion, an airline was able to gain some stability in terms of union representation. Those carriers which wavered back and forth between pilot and nonpilot engineers ran the greatest risk of becoming embroiled in the jurisdictional dispute. Interestingly, however, carriers which adopted a mixed pattern as to qualifications had by the end of 1958 been able to extricate themselves from the difficulties of the jurisdictional fight. In one case the carrier was able to get its mechanic engineers into ALPA. The other carrier was able to fight a successful fight, involving strikes in 1952 and 1955, to maintain its freedom to set qualifications on the flight engineering job. Thus we may postulate that the easiest way to avoid a jurisdictional dispute is to see it coming, and by setting appropriate job qualifications, to avoid hiring a competing employee group. If a management does get embroiled in a jurisdictional dispute, it need not stand idly by; it can, by taking timely action, extricate itself.

This analysis has also indicated that managements can be asking for trouble by agreeing to unneeded job qualifications. Several airlines during this period agreed to require their engineers to have the A&E ratings. These ratings were established to ensure that a man repairing and certifying an aircraft to be airworthy had the proper knowledge and experience to do so; they were not created to indicate that a man could necessarily monitor the mechanical functioning of an aircraft in flight. Therefore, carriers which agreed to the A&E rating were in effect giving up flexibility in setting qualifications for future flight engineering jobs. The problem that this brought about in later years will be covered in the next chapter.

This analysis has also indicated how management lost its unilateral right to set the training and duties of flight engineers. The training of flight engineers was limited both by government regulations and by agreements made during contract negotiations with the flight crew unions. The government did not establish the duties which a carrier had to assign to flight engineers, leaving that to the individual carriers. However, some carriers gave up rights to determine those duties by yielding to pressure at the bargaining table.

As to the role of the AFL-CIO, this analysis has shown how relatively powerless the federation is *vis-à-vis* the international union. In spite of mediation attempts, orders to cease and desist, and a raft of subcommittee recommendations, the Executive Council of the AFL-CIO was unable to have either FEIA or ALPA do its bidding.

As to the role played by the government, one can state that apparently in 1948 the CAB acted hastily to create the flight engineer requirement. This will become clearer in Chapter 8 in which one sees the FAA in effect following the recommendations made in 1948 by American Airlines to study the need for a flight engineer aircraft by aircraft in a more or less scientific manner. In 1948 the CAB issued the flight engineer requirement without such studies. After creating the requirement for a flight engineer, the CAB maintained more or less strict neutrality between the contending parties. Thus it may be said that the CAB in a sense created the problem, and by taking half measures in its regulations and by not setting the training, qualifications, and duties for the flight engineers, it permitted conditions to exist in which a jurisdictional dispute could fester. On the other hand one should be slow to criticize the CAB, particularly if one believes that the more that can be left to the individual carriers and unions to work out the better.

RECOMMENDATIONS AND SUGGESTIONS

In reviewing the actions of the airlines, the unions, and the government in the period 1943 to 1958, it is difficult to find a person or an institution to praise. One must keep in mind, however, that the vantage point of hindsight is high ground indeed. The decisions made throughout this period were made by honest, intelligent men who were sincerely trying to do what seemed best for the public interest or for the interests of their individual groups. What stands out are the pressures that were placed on these people and institutions individually. Because the set of pressures on any one airline, group of employees, or government agency varied from the pressures on any other group of participants, the participants carried on divergent and conflicting actions. It is easy to criticize but one must remember the pressures the participants were under.

As to the AF of L, and after 1955 the AFL-CIO, one can recommend that the Federation would do well to move slowly in issuing international charters where there is any question as to jurisdictional conflict with another union. Specifically, the AFL-CIO should not only ask the union already in the jurisdiction to organize a new type of employees created by technological change, but should make it absolutely clear to that union that if it does not act, a rival international charter will definitely be established. The AF of L apparently did not make that point as clearly as it might have in 1948. Had it made the point more clearly to Mr. Behncke and the officers of ALPA in 1948, reason exists to speculate that ALPA might have changed its constitution and bylaws so as to admit nonpilot members directly into the Association. The importance for the AFL-CIO to act as strongly and affirmatively as possible prior to creating a new international union is that with the history of autonomy which pervades the American labor movement, the AFL-CIO is essentially powerless to eliminate a jurisdictional dispute once a rival international has been chartered.

As to recommendations for the management, this analysis would indicate that the crux of the situation is not agreeing to qualifications for future applicants of jobs of a certain variety if such qualifications are not needed or reasonable. Although it is too much to have expected airline managements to have been able to predict that the jurisdictional fight would take place, it is not too much to suggest that managements keep ever in mind that such an eventuality might occur and with that in mind temper their decisions as to the type of people they hire and the qualifications they set. This is not to say in this instance that managements necessarily should have used pilot engineers; it is to say that an airline management might have seen the jurisdictional dispute between ALPA and FEIA looming in the future and might have made its decisions based on that thought. Thus if a management wanted to minimize the chances of a jurisdictional dispute, it could have hired pilots and dealt just with ALPA. If it desired for good and sufficient reasons to use nonpilots as flight engineers, it should have realized that it would probably have to resist the policies of ALPA and would have geared up its bargaining power to be able to do so successfully.

As to ALPA, its policy of admitting only pilots to membership and its policy of subchartering international unions into which non-pilot employees would become affiliated with ALPA might have appeared in the pre-1948 period to have been a successful one. With the events of the 1948–1949 period, however, ALPA might well have reviewed that policy objectively and might have con-cluded that to change the constitution and bylaws to admit nonpilot members would have been the wisest course.

CHAPTER 8

Work Assignment: 1958-1964

THE LARGE TURBOJET aircraft which were introduced into commercial service late in 1958 represented a technological change of major importance to the airline industry. The fundamental change, of course, was the substitution of the jet engine for the reciprocating piston engine. In broad terms the extent of the change can be indicated by comparisons of general aircraft characteristics of the large pistons and the large jets. Examples of such comparisons are as follows: (1) the large pistons had average airborne speeds ranging from 250 to 300 miles per hour, whereas the comparable jet speeds were 400 to 488 miles per hour; (2) the large pistons flew at altitudes ranging from 16,000 to 18,000 feet, whereas the jets cruised at altitudes ranging from 25,000 to 37,000 feet; (3) the large pistons weighed about 122,000 pounds, whereas the comparable jet weight was about 250,000 pounds; (4) the payload of the large pistons was about 9 to 10 tons, whereas the comparable jet figures ranged from 16 to 18 tons; (5) in terms of productivity, the large pistons could generate between 2,300 and 2,700 ton-miles per hour, whereas the large jets could generate between 7,700 and 8,500 ton-miles per hour.[1]

This chapter will analyze the adjustment of the airline managements, the flight crew unions, and the government to the technological change represented by the jets. Primarily, it is an analysis of an initially unsuccessful attempt by seven airline managements to man their jet aircraft as they saw fit in the midst of the jurisdictional dispute between ALPA and FEIA over the work of a flight engineering nature. The analysis is divided into four parts: (1) the initial position of the parties concerning the appropriate jet flight

[1] CAB, *General Characteristics of Turbine-Powered Aircraft,* February 1960.

crews; (2) the first round of jet negotiations in which seven carriers agreed to a four-man crew; (3) the second round of jet negotiations in which the fourth crew member was eliminated; and (4) an analysis of the jet crew complement evolution.

THE POSITIONS OF THE PARTIES
RE APPROPRIATE JET CREWS

Prior to the introduction of jet equipment, three principal issues faced the parties: the qualifications of jet flight engineers, the structure of flight crew pay, and the level of jet wages. ALPA, FEIA, and the various airline managements took positions on these issues. In addition, various branches of the government took positions on the flight engineer qualification question.

ALPA's Position

During the period 1954–1958 ALPA developed a forceful policy in regard to the qualifications of flight crew members. In addition to the arguments it had been using over the years in regard to piston aircraft, ALPA mustered a number of other arguments, all of which it tied to air safety. ALPA argued that because the jet equipment would fly higher and faster than the piston aircraft, it would have operating problems which would call for a degree of crew coordination which would not be possible if a nonpilot-oriented crew member were present. ALPA built a case that because of the technical nature of the aircraft the piloting functions would be increased and the mechanical functions would be decreased relative to the pistons. Fundamental to this argument was the relative simplicity of operating jet engines as compared with piston engines. Also fundamental to this argument was the speed of the aircraft, requiring increased attention of a piloting nature during operations because planes would pass through various check points and types of weather more rapidly than would piston aircraft. Again fundamental to this argument were the changes made by the designers of the large jets, for example, the DC–8 and the 707. Such changes placed the power controls at the pilot and copilot stations but not at the flight engineer stations. ALPA argued that if all three flight crew members could fly the aircraft tension would be reduced and

safety increased. The pilots argued that they had created the flight
engineer job in 1948 to provide themselves a general assistant to
handle work which had previously been done by pilots and, therefore, they objected to attempts by the nonpilot engineers to extend
to the jet equipment a specialist concept of the flight engineer job.
ALPA argued that the specialist concept challenged the legal and
traditional authority of the pilot in command, thus impairing safety
and efficiency.[2]

Part of the ALPA safety argument was that three-pilot jet crews
would facilitate crew members swapping jobs within the cockpit.
This was supposed to enhance training and coordination. Some
airline managements also used this interchangeability argument.
Although it appears to be sound, in actual practice government
regulations are such that interchangeability is illegal and imprac-
tical of attainment in most cases.

A number of reasons probably brought about ALPA's position.
In the first place, to some real extent individual members of ALPA
were concerned with safety on jet equipment and conscientiously
believed that safety would be enhanced with the harmony, the training, and the interchangeability represented by an all-pilot flight
crew. In the second place, probably a desire existed on the part
of ALPA members and of some of its leadership to end the bitter
jurisdictional fight which had been brewing since 1949 with FEIA.
As will be recalled from the last chapter, ALPA and FEIA had
been making charges and countercharges of raiding and improper
activities to the AF of L and later the AFL-CIO. These types of
charges and countercharges continued during the period 1958
to 1961. In the third place, no doubt fear existed among some
members of ALPA that the jets would bring about technological
unemployment. In the past pilots on individual airlines had suffered
from large-scale layoffs because of technological unemployment.
Whether these dire predictions of technological unemployment ever
would come about was not as important as the genuine fear they
engendered within the ALPA membership.

On the question of technological unemployment, the position of
an ALPA jet study committee was that employment on some airlines would increase, on others it would remain stable, and on

[2] NMB, Report of Presidential Emergency Board No. 120.

others it would be temporarily reduced. The committee foresaw a period of transition in which problems of relocation would exist "with attendant economic and social disruptions." On an airline where it was projected that a number of turboprop aircraft would be purchased which would require a third member at a time when junior pilots were on furlough, the jet study committee took the position that "it does not make sense that new employees should be hired for these jobs while pilots are on furlough. Arrangements must be made to prevent this happening."[3] The over-all stated conclusion of the jet study committee was that the Association should negotiate better wages and working conditions for those pilots then employed rather than going all out for job security.[4] In fact, for a number of reasons the jets did not produce significant pilot unemployment and by 1964 airlines were advertising pilot openings in the newspapers.

Concerning the two other primary issues at the time of the jet introduction—the structure of pilot wages and the size of the increase on jet equipment—ALPA formed a definite policy. Since the days of Decision #83, ALPA had been insisting on negotiating a wage structure based on the Decision #83 type of formula. In 1958 in support of this approach ALPA passed the following resolution:

> The increment method of pay shall be retained and be developed and improved upon as necessary so as to enhance and improve the position of the piloting profession.
>
> Decision #83 shall be used as a foundation on which to build, extending the pay scale to allow for increases in speed, weight, and mileage flown and further that negotiated contracts be used as models and precedents wherever possible. No one formula should be used in projecting these concepts, but rather should be left to the pilot representatives in each case. Though absolute uniformity is not necessary, the identity of Decision #83 should not be lost.[5]

This policy of ALPA became important during the negotiations of 1958 because, as will be seen, a number of carriers took a strong

[3] *Ibid.*, transcript, p. 5387.
[4] *Ibid.*, transcript, p. 5267.
[5] ALPA, *ALPA Policy Manual*, p. 40.

stand that the wage structure should be simplified. With regard to the size of the wage increase on jet equipment, ALPA took the position that a "sizable increase" should be negotiated commensurate with the increased productivity of the jet equipment.

FEIA's Position

During the period 1954–1958 FEIA placed almost all its emphasis on the issue of flight engineer qualifications. It was relatively less interested in the wage structure and the amount of the jet increase.

Concerning the qualifications, FEIA refuted the pilots' argument that the jets would require increased piloting and decreased mechanical skills. FEIA argued that jets were complex machines and, indeed, complex systems of machines. FEIA argued that only an engineer with a mechanical background could do in a proper way the necessary diagnosis of jet equipment and only with that background would a man have the capability to be ingenious in making repairs to jet equipment and in keeping them functioning properly. One of the arguments made most strongly by FEIA was that only mechanic engineers would be properly motivated to do the studying and refreshing which would be required to keep up with the myriad of technical details regarding jets and their systems. FEIA argued that the average pilot engineer would be more interested in his piloting career and would never become involved in the details of jet technology. In addition FEIA argued that the CAB required a separate certificate for a flight engineer, which FEIA took as an indication that the government supported a mechanically oriented flight engineer. FEIA also pointed out that the AF of L had chartered FEIA over licensed flight engineers and had indicated thereby that it recognized the flight engineers as a separate craft. FEIA pointed out that the National Mediation Board had certified the Flight Engineers' International Association as the bargaining representative on several airlines, and thus had recognized the craft of flight engineer. FEIA also argued that contrary to the opinions of industry experts some inflight repairs and maintenance could be accomplished on jet aircraft.

The primary bargaining goal of FEIA during this period became the retention of A&E ratings as necessary prerequisites to becoming or maintaining one's position as a flight engineer.

As to the wage structure and the size of the wage increase, FEIA was not as concerned as was ALPA. For example, in 1958 FEIA negotiated contracts which eliminated from the traditional flight crew wage structure the hourly pay directly related to the pegged speed of the aircraft. In its place FEIA was willing to negotiate a wage structure under which flight engineers, starting with their third year, would get day and night hourly rates based on their years of service, not on the speed of the equipment.[6]

The Position of the Airlines

The position of the airline managements as the dates approached for the introduction of jet equipment contained elements of concerted action amid devisive forces. Discussing the latter elements first, the most fundamental difference of opinion among the airline managements was whether the jet flight engineer should be pilot-qualified. At the four carriers at which ALPA represented both the pilots and the flight engineers prior to 1958, the managements' choice was pretty clear. They were planning when they got their first jets to use pilot engineers in part because they may have felt that pilot engineers would do the better job for them but primarily to avoid running the risks of having a jurisdictional fight develop on their airlines. Although their flight engineers were represented by FEIA, United and Continental decided that they would use pilot engineers on their jet equipment. The six other major carriers had groups of mechanic engineers represented by FEIA and were, for the most part, inclined to continue to use nonpilot engineers when they received their jet equipment. Thus on the fundamental question of qualifications of jet flight engineers, the airline managements were sharply divided.

On the issue of the method of flight crew pay, for a period at least some of the major airline managements appeared to have acted with some degree of cohesiveness. According to the statement of one airline management, five of the major airlines agreed to make a serious attempt in the first round of jet negotiations to simplify the flight crew wage structure. For example, Eastern Air Lines recommended in its negotiations with ALPA a wage structure consisting solely of an hourly rate for each aircraft type plus

[6] Agreement between American Airlines, Inc. and the Flight Engineers' International Association, May 1, 1958.

a minimum guarantee.[7] As another example, American Airlines developed what it termed "The New Positive Pay Plan." Under American's plan, the pilot wage structure would have been changed to a monthly salary based on seniority plus a mileage rate of $.02 a mile. Whether an actual agreement existed among five carriers to stand together on a simpler wage structure and a moderate increase or whether there was merely an expression of hope by a number of carriers that each would be strong enough to put across its position on these issues is disputed within the industry. The management of one major airline believes that a number of major carriers had a moral obligation to stand firm on these issues; the management of another major carrier supposedly involved did not agree that a moral commitment had been involved.

As to the size of the wage increase on jet equipment, in general the airline managements recognized that some increase would be appropriate but hoped to keep it within reason.

Another concerted action by the airline managements came late in 1958 when six of them agreed to become members of a mutual aid pact under which, if a carrier was struck under certain circumstances, the other five carriers agreed in advance to turn over to it any net windfall profits that they might receive by carrying the struck carrier's business during the strike.

The most devisive force operating on the carriers as they faced the introduction of jets, of course, was that they were competing, as they always had, against each other for business. Importantly, a number of them were competing to be the first airline with jet service of one type or another.

The Government's Position

During the controversy over the qualifications of jet flight engineers, the position of the government was one of neutrality. The government agency involved until the beginning of 1959 was the CAB; thereafter, it was the FAA. The consistent position of both of these agencies was that in 1948 the government had required a flight engineer on equipment weighing over 80,000 pounds and having four or more engines. Its position was that the flight engineer's certificate as originally promulgated was all that was required

[7] NMB, Report of Presidential Emergency Board No. 121.

in the way of qualifications for the third crew member on the jets. Thus, a nonpilot engineer or a pilot engineer satisfied the government requirements which remained unchanged so long as the engineer possessed a flight engineer's certificate. On December 18, 1958, the chairman of the CAB issued copies of a letter he had sent to the Governor of Florida concerning a strike then in progress on Eastern Air Lines. The chairman of the CAB wrote in part as follows:

> It is your feeling that recognition of the problem in the Eastern strike and the decision by the Board should be an effective step in the settlement of the strike. Under the Civil Aeronautics Act, however, CAB may act in such matters only where necessary to ensure public safety. No demonstration has been made of the need for immediate emergency action by the Board to ensure public safety, beyond present requirements.

The stand of the CAB, therefore, denied both the ALPA position that a pilot's license was necessary as an additional engineer qualification and the FEIA position that an engineer had to have the A&E ratings. Throughout this period the CAB and the FAA made essentially no public statements in regard to flight engineer qualifications. By 1962, however, the then head of the FAA held a press conference in which he stated in so many words that as far as the FAA was concerned jets could be operated just as safely whether the flight engineer was a mechanic or not.[8]

The government did not have a clear-cut position on the wage structure or on the size of the increase. In general the government's position on wage increases was that any agreement reached by the two parties was acceptable.

THE FIRST ROUND OF JET NEGOTIATIONS

Unlike the situation in 1948 when the flight engineer dispute was settled essentially by regulation, the flight engineer controversy in 1958 and early 1959 was resolved at the various collective bargaining tables within the airline industry.

[8] *The New York Times,* June 26, 1962.

Of the three important issues in the first round of negotiations, the level of the wage increase and the method of compensation were settled first. The first contract which covered jet flight crews was between Pan American and FEIA. This contract, which became effective November 1, 1957, produced a 20% differential for jet flight engineers over piston flight engineers. That contract was followed on January 15, 1958, by a contract between National Airlines and ALPA which increased the size of the jet increment and continued on jet equipment the basic formula under which pilots had been paid on piston equipment. Under this contract a DC–8 captain flying one-half of his time at night and one-half of his time during the day for an 85-hour month would earn $2,234.62. A comparable Electra captain flying the same type of month would receive $1,881.87. A senior captain on National Airlines under the preceding contract for a comparable month had earned $1,678.18 on the DC–7B equipment. Thus when he shifted to the new contract and to DC–8 equipment his pay was potentially increased $556.44 per month, or an increase of 33.2%.

With the two contracts signed, both FEIA and ALPA had established patterns which called for good-sized increases for jet equipment and a continuation of the traditional wage structure. Having won these contracts, the flight unions were then able to proceed through the jet series of negotiations increasing the size of the jet increment while maintaining the traditional wage structure.

During 1958 five carriers either were continuing negotiations begun in the preceding year or commencing negotiations with ALPA over the crew complement issue. These five carriers were American, Eastern, National, Trans World, and Pan American. As the year progressed the negotiations at National, American, and Eastern took the forefront, while the other two sets of negotiations receded in importance.

Typically the 1958 negotiations between the carriers and their flight crew employees as represented by FEIA and ALPA became deadlocked because the major carriers were faced with conflicting and exactly opposite proposals from the two unions as to the qualifications for jet flight engineers. FEIA insisted that flight engineers be required to have the A&E ratings, while ALPA insisted that jet flight engineers be required to have commercial pilots' licenses and instrument cards. This situation led to a series of Presidential Emergency Boards created to investigate these disputes. The most intensive study was made by Presidential Boards No. 120 and No. 121, both with the same three neutrals, of the dispute between Eastern Air Lines and its flight crew unions.

Boards No. 120 and No. 121 issued their reports as of July 21, 1958. They recommended that turbojet flight engineers be required to have a commercial pilot license and instrument rating card and "the ability to fly and land the airplane in case of emergency." Such flight engineers would be protected while getting the pilot qualification by being maintained on the flight engineers' seniority list. Those who did not wish to become pilot-qualified could fly on the carrier's piston and turboprop equipment as long as the carrier had any. Thus the Presidential Emergency Boards did not accept the flight engineers' arguments regarding crew complement that the jets could be maintained better by career mechanics. The Boards placed greater emphasis on the pilots' argument that work of a mechanical nature in the jets would be reduced relative to the pistons, while work of a piloting nature would be increased relatively. These recommendations were rejected immediately by FEIA and accepted by Eastern and ALPA.

In order to understand how the jet flight engineer qualifications question was resolved in this period, it is necessary to trace the chronology of the negotiations during the late summer and fall of 1958 at Eastern, American, and National. On August 22, 1958, Eastern and ALPA signed an agreement on all outstanding issues but crew complement. The new pay scales were higher than those previously agreed to for jets by National and ALPA.

After Eastern signed this agreement with ALPA in August, a strike by its flight engineers appeared very likely. On September 3, 1958, the locals at Eastern Air Lines of FEIA, IAM, and ALSSA (stewardesses) formed a council for joint action and mutual support under which they agreed to honor each other's picket lines. FEIA also formed a mutual assistance pact with the Teamsters. Negotiations between Eastern and FEIA continued to be deadlocked and completely broke down on November 24, 1958, when the flight engineers struck. On the same day the machinists who had also been negotiating with Eastern struck.

These strikes at Eastern came some ten days after ALPA and Eastern had agreed that the jet equipment would carry three pilots. As these strikes progressed at Eastern with the carrier closed down, other factors started to build up pressure on Eastern to seek a settlement. This was the time when three of the major domestic carriers were about to introduce turboprop or turbojet service. Eastern planned to start running Electras on its major routes as of December 1, 1958. American was planning to be the first domestic carrier with turbojets starting in January 1959. But most importantly, on September 9, 1958, National and Pan American announced that National was planning to lease at least two Pan American DC–8's and to start turbojet service in December 1958. On November 1, 1958, the CAB gave conditional approval of the lease. Thus National was able to start turbojet service between New York and Florida on December 10, 1958. The winter season was the most important for both National and Eastern and the most important route of Eastern was this same New York-Miami route. So Eastern was under considerable pressure to settle.

Additional pressure was brought to bear on Eastern by announcements of National, ALPA, and the FEIA local union at National to the effect that the crew complement problem had been solved. National was able to get the local FEIA Chapter to agree to the use on the turbojets of a handful of its members who happened to have both A&E ratings and commercial pilot licenses. Because these engineers had pilot licenses, ALPA was willing to agree to the use of FEIA members flying as the third crew member on turbojets.

While the strike by the machinists and the engineers was in progress against Eastern Air Lines, the pilots struck American Airlines on December 19, 1958.

On December 14, 1958, one of Eastern's problems was solved when it reached an agreement with IAM. It was not able, however, to operate the airline because the machinists would not cross the FEIA picket line, in view of their mutual assistance pact. The strikes at American and Eastern continued through the balance of December 1958. During this time American's management became convinced that the 707 equipment would require three pilots *and* a mechanical flight engineer for safe operations. Such a position had been considered for quite a while as one possibility by both American and Eastern managements. It was on this basis that American had agreed with its pilot group prior to the December 19th strike that three pilots would be carried.

Eastern also decided to follow that route. On December 31, 1958, Eastern agreed with the flight engineers that it would carry a mechanic flight engineer with A&E ratings on its jet equipment and reached an agreement which ended the flight engineers' strike. The next day Eastern also reached an agreement on the pay and crew complement issues with its pilot group. Negotiations continued at American until January 10 when American and ALPA agreed that a four-man crew would be carried on its jet equipment.

Throughout the succeeding weeks of 1959 two crew manning patterns emerged. On February 4 Pan American reached agreement with ALPA that a four-man crew would be carried. On May 22 TWA and ALPA reached agreement on a four-man crew. In due course Western Air Lines and for a brief period Northwest Airlines flew their jet equipment with three pilots and a nonpilot engineer. On the other hand, the remaining major carriers were able to reach agreements under which they were able to operate their large jet equipment with a crew consisting of three pilots, one of whom possessed the flight engineer certificate. These were Braniff, Capital, Continental, Delta, National, Northeast, and United.

Thus the negotiations for the introduction of jet equipment resulted in a competitive advantage to half of the major airlines, and, conversely, a competitive disadvantage to the other half.

Early in 1959 when the jet manning patterns were being established, the airlines had had very little practical experience in operating the large turbojets. In this atmosphere an argument could at least be made that the nature of the cockpit duties on the large jets required three pilots and a flight engineer. In the ensuing years experience showed that a three-man crew could handle these aircraft safely and efficiently. Even in the early stages in early 1959 most of the experts in the airline unions, in the airline managements, and in the government agencies expressed the firm belief that a fourth man in the jet cockpit was unnecessary. Only one group of people was sincerely convinced that the fourth man was necessary. This group comprised the management of one of the major airlines. These men had concluded, based on the proving runs of the large jet equipment, that because events happened so quickly during jet flights and because the machinery was so complex, a fourth man was needed and would indeed be added by all the carriers. Such did not become the case, and the management of this carrier joined with the others who had agreed to carry four men in the cockpit in the effort to get down to the three-man crew.

THE SECOND ROUND OF JET NEGOTIATIONS

Continental Air Lines

During a two-year period which started in the fall of 1958 and ended in the fall of 1960 the management of Continental Air Lines took a number of steps which culminated in the permanent reduction of its turbojet crews from four to three men.

In September 1958 the management of Continental announced that every jet flight crew member would be pilot-qualified. On October 13, 1958, Continental and FEIA reached an agreement which allowed the company to establish such a qualification provided flight engineers could train to meet it at company expense but on the individual's time. On May 29, 1959, Continental and ALPA reached agreement that after the Continental-FEIA agreement expired the jet crews would consist of a minimum of three men who had the C&I and were on the pilots' seniority list. The following month Continental initiated turbojet operations with three pilots and a flight engineer with the C&I and covered by the FEIA agreement. On September 11, 1959, Continental notified its flight engineers that upon the expiration of their contract its jet crews would consist solely of three fully qualified pilots.

On May 29, 1960, having failed to reach an agreement with its flight engineers, Continental ceased assigning flight engineers as such to its jet crews and reassigned their duties to the third pilot. On the same date the flight engineers struck. The strike continued until an agreement was reached on October 10, 1960. During that time the pilots replaced the striking flight engineers. The agreement came as a result of tripartite discussions among the management,

ALPA, and a faction within the flight engineer group which desired settlement. Under the terms of the agreement, a majority of the flight engineers voted to dissolve the FEIA Continental Chapter. The agreement called for one seniority list and for the pilots and the flight engineers to be represented by ALPA. The flight engineers who signed the agreement were given protective re-employment options as follows: they could return to work on four-engine piston equipment on the pilots' seniority list with no pilot bid rights but with prior bid rights to all second officer positions on four-engine piston equipment; or they could return to work and indicate their preference to get qualifications as a third pilot on the jet equipment with the guarantee that if they failed to qualify they would have either the option of an immediate $20,000 severance payment or they could revert to being covered by the first option; or they could elect not to return to work with an immediate $10,000 severance payment. Those flight engineers who desired to return to work would be placed on the pilots' seniority list above the probationary employees, and thereafter all bid positions on the system held by pilots below the last regular member on the seniority list would be rebid.

Following this agreement FEIA tried without success to get an injunction to invalidate the agreement between Continental and ALPA. FEIA refused to recognize the dissolution of the Chapter at Continental and attempted to place it in trusteeship. FEIA tried to seek an injunction as representative of the Continental engineers. The court, however, dismissed FEIA's case as "moot," concluding that the trusteeship was invalid and that FEIA was left with no standing to question the dissolution which had removed FEIA as the representative of the Continental engineers and therefore as a plaintiff and appellant.

Northwest Airlines

The industrial relations system at Northwest Airlines, the next carrier to solve its jet crew complement problem, differed from the systems at the other airlines. The flight engineers on Northwest were represented by the International Association of Machinists (IAM) rather than by FEIA. Because the ground mechanics were also represented by IAM, the flight engineers were drawn from the ranks of the ground mechanics and were permitted to bump back as business declined.

A number of Northwest-IAM contracts with interrelated seniority provisions had been in effect concurrently. Thus a flight engineer on Northwest might have been accruing seniority under more than one IAM contract. Another difference which was a corollary to IAM flight engineer representation came as a result of the existence of a national accord between ALPA and the IAM reached in 1957 which called for no raiding and for ALPA jurisdiction over all crew members who flew off the ground. This national agreement put the IAM and its flight engineers on Northwest in an anomalous situation because the flight engineers in effect were fighting ALPA locally while being under a national no-raiding agreement.

Some similarities existed between the industrial relations system at Northwest and other airlines. For example, at Northwest, as elsewhere, ALPA was demanding a minimum three-pilot jet crew. For their part the flight engineers were demanding the continuation of the A&E ratings for flight engineers.

Interestingly, however, the flight engineers were willing to accept a C&I requirement to fly as jet flight engineers. Because of the IAM background, Northwest could maintain that its flight engineers were really mechanics and a part of the airline mechanic class or craft rather than a separate flight engineer class or craft.

On May 13, 1959, the management announced that it had decided that its jet flight engineers were to be trained other than as mechanical specialists. Turboprop and turbojet equipment was to be put into operation in 1959 and 1960.

On August 20, 1959, Northwest and ALPA agreed that pilots would not be asked to fly turbojets unless they were manned by a minimum crew of three members all of whom possessed the commercial license and the instrument rating, met minimum qualifications as Northwest copilots, and were accruing seniority on the pilots' seniority list.

Also on August 20 the company announced that the third flight crew member on straight jet aircraft would have to have the commercial license, the instrument rating card, and other minimum requirements as imposed by the company.

On August 24, 1959, IAM and Northwest concluded an agreement covering the assignment of flight engineers on Electra equipment. With the Electras on the property Northwest started to try to train flight engineers to be a part of the "operationally oriented" crew but they refused. As a result, Northwest obtained a court injunction requiring them not to refuse.

Northwest attempted to work out a settlement under which the flight engineers would agree to take pilot training and to be placed voluntarily on the bottom of the pilots' seniority list. The flight engineers held out for a requirement that the third man on the jet had to possess the A&E ratings. The flight engineers did not agree to go to the bottom of the pilots' seniority list.

During June and July 1960, after Northwest had tried to put the DC–8 into operation, according to the company, ALPA and the flight engineers both struck. The pilots refused to fly the jets; the flight engineers refused to train for the commercial pilot's license and instrument rating card.

On July 23, 1960, Northwest and ALPA signed a supplementary agreement covering the turbojet crew. This new contract called eventually for a minimum three-pilot crew with the third pilot to be fully trained as a copilot and to receive training for and be fully rated as a flight engineer. Training of pilots for the flight engineer's certificate was to begin immediately and to be fully implemented by January 1961. The new agreement was to run until February 1, 1962, until which date a four-man crew made up of three pilots and a mechanical flight engineer was called for. Under the terms of this contract, Northwest began operating its jet equipment on July 24, 1960, and operated the jets with four people until October 11, 1960. The flight engineers flew as part of the four-man jet crews until October 11, 1960, when the engineers, unable to get an agreement, walked off the DC–8 operations. They continued to operate on the pistons.

Following this withdrawal from jet operations, Northwest took the position that the flight engineers had renounced all claims to a seat on the company's turbojets, had no contract requiring an assignment thereon, and had no right to complain. On or about November 18, 1960, Northwest began to train pilots to obtain their flight engineers' certificates. During this period Northwest offered its flight engineers an opportunity to be placed on the pilots' seniority list while still keeping their names on all IAM seniority lists on which they had previously been placed. This possibility, however, was precluded by an IAM policy to the effect that if a member allowed his name to be placed on a non-IAM seniority list, he would lose all seniority on any IAM list.

On December 22, 1960, Northwest offered a package to its flight engineers. It proposed a tripartite agreement with cross seniority provisions and job protection. The flight engineers rejected it.

On December 24, 1960, the company announced that on December 31, 1960, it would resume jet operations with three pilots all of whom would be from the pilot seniority list. Shortly after Northwest reinstituted jet service on that basis, the flight engineers on January 9, 1961, withdrew from all service on the airline and essentially closed down all operations.

On January 10 Northwest resumed partial operations using pilots in all three seats of the jet cockpit and over the ensuing weeks returned to full operations.

When continued talks and efforts by the National Mediation Board including a proffer of arbitration failed, the President on February 24, 1961, created a Presidential Emergency Board between Northwest and its flight engineers as represented by IAM. On May 24, 1961, the Presidential Emergency Board reported. The Board did not believe that the A&E rating for the third crew member on the jet was necessary for safety or efficiency. It recommended that flight engineers be given training on company time and at company expense to obtain the commercial pilot's license and instrument rating card and minimum copilot qualifications. Since a Presidential Commission was investigating the crew complement dispute at several major carriers by this date, the Board between Northwest and IAM refrained from making specific contract language recommendations as the parties had asked because the Board felt it was inadvisable for fear of jeopardizing the work of the Commission. The Board's recommendations did not produce a settlement.

In March 1961 Northwest and IAM reached an agreement to the effect that mechanic flight engineers could resume flying on the piston and turboprop equipment without the C&I but could not fly as jet flight engineers. They would continue to be represented by IAM. On this basis by July 1961 Northwest recalled about 125 of the former flight engineers and placed the names of the remainder of them (some 125 men) on a recall list.

In July 1963 Northwest, ALPA, and IAM reached a tripartite agreement to the effect that former flight engineers who obtained the C&I on their own could transfer to and work their way up the pilot seniority list and be represented by ALPA. By early 1966 some 200 of the former flight engineers had been recalled. About 130 of them had transferred to the pilot seniority list and were flying as jet flight engineers or piston copilots. About 70 of them had elected not to get the C&I and were flying as piston flight engineers. Most of them were expecting to retire before the last pistons were withdrawn from service or to use their seniority to bump back into the ground mechanic forces at that time.

United Air Lines

Although United Air Lines had been able to work out agreements with ALPA and FEIA which allowed it to operate jets with three man crews, some events which transpired between these parties are important to this analysis because they held implications regarding the continued existence of the FEIA.

Under Section 2 Ninth of the Railway Labor Act, the National Mediation Board is authorized to determine the appropriate class or craft for representation purposes of airline and railroad employees.

On August 28, 1959, ALPA filed an application with the National Mediation Board alleging the existence of a representation dispute among the employees of United Air Lines performing the duties of the "flight deck crew members." The flight deck crew members, according to the application, were to involve the job classes of pilot, copilot, reserve pilot, third pilot, or flight engineer. Because such a class or craft would encompass both pilots and flight engineers and because pilots outnumbered flight engineers approximately three to one, the strong presumption was that if the National Mediation Board found that the flight deck crew member was an appropriate class or craft, ALPA would in an ensuing secret ballot come to represent both the pilots and the flight engineers.

United had over the years alternated between the use of mechanical specialists and pilots as their flight engineers. As a result, its flight engineer forces contained significant groups of pilot engineers and mechanical engineers. United had successfully required flight engineers on its jets to have a pilot's license and was successfully pursuing a training program to allow mechanic flight engineers to obtain a pilot's license.

For the first time in the history of the Railway Labor Act, the National Mediation Board availed itself of its right under the act to hand over to a committee of neutrals its responsibility to decide a representation question. The neutral committee stated that it could rule there was only one class or craft among the total group of flight deck crew members if the general characteristics and conditions of the work were similar. Surveying the work of the flight engineers in the airline industry in general, the neutral committee found that over the years flight engineers' work had changed in concept more than that of any other flight crew member. It found that through selection, training, and use, flight engineers, particularly at United, had come to resemble pilots more than mechanics.

More specifically, the neutral committee found that United had, to a unique degree, cross-trained and cross-utilized its flight deck crew members. It found that the employment standards for flight engineers and copilots had for a number of years been identical on United. It stated, "This cross training and cross utilization . . . has destroyed any distinguishing features between members of the crew upon which a class or craft determination would have any real basis." The neutral committee found that the crew on United was a single operating unit with the flight engineer an integrated member whose functions could not be considered separate from those of the other crew members. The neutral committee ruled that all flight deck crew members on United in the job classes of pilot, reserve pilot, copilot, and third pilot or flight engineer constituted one class or craft and should therefore vote together on one ballot for representation purposes.

The neutral committee issued its report to the National Mediation

Board on January 17, 1961. On February 6, 1961, the NMB issued its decision on the United Air Lines craft or class case and in line with the neutral committee's report classified all flight deck crew members on United as being in one class or craft. The NMB assigned a mediator to investigate and he found a representation dispute did exist. Hence the NMB ordered an election among the class or craft of flight deck crew members to determine who would be the employees' representative. The Board held such an election, and ALPA received 1,682 votes to 58 for FEIA out of 2,143 eligible votes. On May 31, 1961, therefore, the National Mediation Board certified ALPA as the representative of all the flight deck crew members at United Air Lines. FEIA made a number of unsuccessful attempts to have the ruling overturned and to prevent the NMB from holding an election.

To summarize briefly, the manner by which two carriers worked their ways out of the four-man crew has been described. The steps taken by five carriers are yet to be described. Because the government and the FEIA took some actions involving more than one carrier, the ensuing descriptions will overlap to some extent. A general picture of the state of the negotiations at the five remaining carriers as of early 1961 will help set the stage for the ensuing analysis. At Pan American the engineer contract had expired on June 1, 1960, and negotiations had failed to produce a settlement. At Western Air Lines the FEIA contract had been effective until January 1, 1961, and negotiations had started on December 28, 1960, but no settlement had been reached. At American Airlines, except for the pay and jet working conditions section, the FEIA agreement was effective until April 30, 1963. The general pay clauses and a supplementary agreement on jet working conditions had expired as of April 30, 1960. At Eastern Air Lines the engineer contract had been effective until April 1, 1960, and negotiations had failed to produce a second jet settlement. At TWA the FEIA contract had been effective until January 1, 1961. At National Airlines a second jet contract had not been worked out, and National was proceeding to operate under its special agreement which called for two pilots and a flight engineer who qualified both as a pilot and as an aircraft mechanic. At Flying Tiger, a cargo airline, the flight engineer contract with the FEIA had not been renewed.

Of the above sets of negotiations, those between FEIA and Pan American had progressed closest to a crisis. On February 16, 1961, FEIA announced that it would strike Pan American at a date not then set but clearly threatened for the weekend of February 18–19, 1961.

At about 5:00 p.m. on Friday, February 17, President Kennedy created a Presidential Emergency Board between Pan American and FEIA, which, as has been discussed, required a 60-day *status quo* period. Early that evening, however, FEIA withdrew its services at Pan American. This walkout by the Pan American engineers was bolstered shortly thereafter by the flight engineers at TWA, Eastern, American, Western, National, and Flying Tiger. Importantly, in none of these situations had the Railway Labor Act procedures been exhausted!

Four carriers quickly obtained temporary restraining orders against the illegal stoppages. With six major carriers shut down and in spite of the readiness of the federal courts to issue restraining orders against the flight engineers, the newly installed Kennedy Administration, through its Secretary of Labor, Arthur Goldberg, began a series of steps which over the ensuing months were to get the federal government heavily involved in the jet crew complement dispute.

According to *The New York Times,* FEIA members were vowing not to return to work until the National Mediation Board class or craft decision was overturned, presumably by the Labor Department.

By Tuesday, February 21, Secretary Goldberg announced that President Kennedy under an executive order was creating a Presidential Commission to consider the differences that had arisen regarding the performance of flight engineers' functions, the job security of employees performing such functions, and related representation rights of FEIA and ALPA on six of the seven struck carriers.

Six of the carriers agreed to take no disciplinary action against returning strikers and ALPA pledged not to press for collective bargaining on any carrier until the Presidential Commission had reported. Western Air Lines was not included in the original order because the management of Western had fired its 130 flight engineers almost as soon as they had engaged in the illegal strike. Western had immediately begun to hire replacements and refused to agree to no reprisals for returning strikers.

After having kept all sides in mediation sessions until 3:00 a.m. on February 23, the Secretary of Labor was able to obtain a settlement. FEIA reluctantly agreed to return to work although it could not obtain a guarantee of no reprisals against the strikers at Western Air Lines. It was agreed, however, that the President would add Western to the list of carriers covered by the Presidential Commission and the executive order was so amended. Thus, the flight engineers on six of the seven carriers agreed to return to work and the strike virtually ended. President Kennedy pointed out that Western Air Lines had again turned down strong pleas by the Secretary of Labor and other cabinet officials.

From February to May 1961 the Presidential Commission held exploratory talks with the various parties and sought through mediatory efforts to have the parties reach voluntary accord; on May 24, 1961, it issued its first report; during the summer and early fall of 1961 it made intensive efforts to effectuate mergers of the ALPA and FEIA groups at Pan American and TWA; on October 17, 1961, it issued its second report; and thereafter its chairman continued to mediate various aspects of the dispute.

In the first report the Commission established some guide lines which it believed would help the parties negotiate settlements of the crew complement dispute. The Presidential Commission recognized that the representation issue arose from FEIA's fear that ALPA would seek and would win additional class or craft elections and, as a result, FEIA would lose representation rights, the flight engineer craft would be diluted, and pilots would replace flight engineers. Throughout its work and in this report in particular the Commission emphasized the benefits that would accrue from a merger of the two unions. The Presidential Commission, as a public agency, felt an obligation to assist in achieving a reduction from four to three flight crew members on turbojets "as a means of promoting economical, yet safe, air transportation."

The Commission endorsed the principle of the reduction with reasonably adequate protection "for the job equities of those employees who may be adversely affected by such transition."

The Commission said that in moving to the three-man crews the airlines had an obligation to provide reasonable job or pay protection because, after all, the carriers had established the four-man crews. The Presidential Commission foresaw a gradual reduction to three-man crews with a start made by initiating three-man crews on all *new* turbojet equipment. The Presidential Commission recommended that the transition be made in such a manner as not to displace present incumbent flight engineers on turbojet equipment and, importantly, that such incumbents would not be required to obtain pilot qualifications.

During the summer of 1961 the Presidential Commission worked hard to get voluntary mergers of pilot and flight engineer groups. It concentrated its efforts on those groups at TWA and Pan American. Although a greater mutual understanding was said to have been achieved, the talks did not succeed in either case in producing mergers.

On October 17, 1961, the Presidential Commission, having been unable to induce the parties to reach agreement or to induce the two unions to merge, issued a second and final report. Essentially, the second report contained detailed recommendations as to the precise way in which carriers could reduce their jet crews from four to three men.

Because the qualifications that the third crew member on the jet would have to possess had been the core of the controversy for so many years, the recommendations of the Presidential Commission in this matter took on some importance. These qualifications were:

A flight engineer in the active employ of the carrier on October 15, 1961, who is to serve on a three-man turbojet, shall receive training that will enable him, in the event of an emergency created by the incapacity or unavailability of one of the two pilots, to provide appropriate assistance to the pilot then in command by possessing the following qualifications in addition to a valid flight engineer's certificate:

  (1) a commercial pilot's certificate and instrument rating;
  (2) qualifications in the type aircraft to which assigned as follows:
      (a) ability to execute enroute, approach, and landing copilot duties in the emergency situation specified

           above, including checklist functions, as would be performed by the second in command at the direction of the pilot in command, *other than manipulation of the primary flight controls;* (emphasis added)

   (b) ability to manipulate the flight controls of the turbojet airplane by reference to flight instruments to the following extent: straight and level flight, normal turns, climbs and descents at the various normal operating speeds, *but not including takeoffs and landings;* (emphasis added)

   (c) the training for and demonstration of the ability required by paragraphs (a) and (b) immediately above may be accomplished in a turbojet simulator;

(3) ability to operate radio communications and navigation equipment and weather radar;

(4) ability to read and interpret all route, terminal area, and approach charts;

(5) ability to copy and interpret air traffic control clearances and give position reports when required; and

(6) ability to maintain appropriate flight logs.

The Presidential Commission recommended that all flight engineers have prior rights to bid the flight engineer's seat on all equipment and that all flight engineers in the employ of a carrier as of October 15, 1961, be entitled to receive the training necessary to get all the qualifications they needed to fly as a jet flight engineer. This training would be at company expense but on the employee's own time.

The Commission recommended a priority list by which the carrier would have to offer this training to flight engineers. Severance pay was also recommended and again the Commission made a strong plea for a voluntary merger of FEIA and ALPA. Thus the Commission recommended reduction in the amount of qualifications that jet flight engineers should possess in addition to the pilot's license and instrument rating card. Of primary importance, it did not recommend that flight engineers should have to be able to fly and land the jets.

The carriers accepted these recommendations. FEIA accepted them on the condition that they were recommendations and not a final and binding arbitration award. ALPA never formally accepted the Presidential Commission's second report.

From this point on the work of the Presidential Commission was formally over. Its chairman, Mr. Nathan Feinsinger, however, continued to play a very active role.

Western Air Lines

When the FEIA struck on February 17, 1961, the management of Western Air Lines was in the process of instituting all-pilot, three-man jet crews.

On January 20, 1961, Western's management announced that by July 1, 1961, its jet flight engineers would have to have the commercial pilot's license and instrument rating card. The announcement stated further that management was making arrangements for the training of flight engineers to meet the new requirements on company time and at company expense.

After the strike, on Saturday, February 18, 1961, the management of Western filed a complaint in the District Court of the United States, Southern District of California, and obtained a temporary restraining order against the walkout of its flight engineers. In spite of the restraining order the great majority of Western's flight engineers continued to strike .

During the next few days Western notified each flight engineer individually that if he did not perform his duties his services would be terminated. Those flight engineers who did report for work were put back on the job. On February 21 the management furloughed 2,350 of its 2,730 employees. These employees were notified by the company that the flight engineers who refused to return to work would be removed from the payroll and that the company was employing and training replacements for them. On February 21, 1961, the management wired the Civil Aeronautics Board, the National Mediation Board, and the Secretary of Labor of its plans to employ replacements. According to the management of Western, it did not accept the opportunity to become a party to the Presidential Commission because by that date it had hired many replacements.

On March 2, 1961, Western started restoring flight service and by March 30 had restored service to all but five of the 34 cities it normally served. The replacements hired by the company were all pilots.

The replacement pilot engineers on Western Air Lines formed an association termed the Second Officers' Association. This Association petitioned the National Mediation Board to represent the flight engineers on Western. FEIA charged that Western had assisted the Second Officers' Association and had solicited authorization cards for it. The National Mediation Board, however, found no basis for the FEIA complaint. The National Mediation Board held an election and, as a result, FEIA lost its representation rights at Western.

Trans World Airlines

Following the second report of the Presidential Commission in October 1961, the parties at TWA negotiated under the mediation of such representatives of the government as the Secretary of Labor, the Under Secretary of Labor, a mediator of the National Mediation Board, and the Chairman of the Presidential Commission.

ALPA had set a strike deadline for October 18, 1961, but two days before it was scheduled to occur the pilots agreed to defer the strike in favor of further talks. ALPA later rescheduled the strike for November 12. On November 11, however, President Kennedy created Presidential Emergency Board No. 142 between TWA and ALPA. In its report on December 15, 1961, the Board recommended that jet crews be reduced from four to three in accordance with the recommendations of the Presidential Commission. The Board refused to make recommendations on other issues, declaring that in its opinion no effective bargaining could take place on them until the issues of crew complement and hours of flight time had been disposed of.

In January 1962 tripartite merger talks were held under the auspices of Mr. Feinsinger between TWA, FEIA, and ALPA. These were continuations of merger and contract talks which had taken place among the three parties during the previous summer. Both ALPA and FEIA submitted proposals to be the basis for working out the crew complement problem but neither side found the proposals of the other acceptable.

FEIA threatened to strike TWA on March 21, 1962. In order

to prevent the strike President Kennedy created Presidential Emergency Board No. 146 on March 20, 1962. In its report of May 1, 1962, this Board recommended that the Presidential Commission proposals on crew complement be accepted by both parties.

On April 27, 1962, ALPA set a strike deadline for May 5, 1962. In the negotiations that preceded that strike deadline TWA continued to insist, as it had all along, that the crew complement problem had to be disposed of before the rest of the contract issues were to be taken up.

On May 7, 1962, at 1:20 a.m., TWA and ALPA reached agreement without an interruption of service. This agreement incorporated a May 22, 1959, agreement which had called for assigning second officers to jets. However, the May 7 agreement called for further negotiations on the question of flight engineering training for second officers. That represented a step forward for TWA's management. Although TWA did not obtain a clear assurance of the elimination of the fourth man, it did obtain from ALPA a letter stating the intent of both parties to move in that direction.

As of early June 1962 FEIA was free to strike three carriers—Pan American, TWA, and Eastern—and was threatening to do so. Early in June President Kennedy recommended that the disputes on TWA, Pan American, and Eastern be submitted to binding arbitration. The three airlines accepted his recommendation, but FEIA did not.

During the first three weeks of June 1962 the crew complement dispute received the most intense pressure for settlement from the Kennedy Administration that it had had since the Presidential Commission had been established.

In the face of a threatened flight engineer strike against Pan American, Eastern, and TWA, President Kennedy entered a news conference on June 14, 1962, with a strongly worded statement regarding the flight engineers.

FEIA set a strike date of 2:00 p.m. on Tuesday, June 19, against TWA, but delayed its strike hour by hour after this deadline was passed.

During 55 of the 72 hours just prior to June 21, 1962, Secretary of Labor Goldberg, according to *The New York Times,* kept the

TWA management, the FEIA chapter representatives at TWA, and the TWA pilot representatives in separate or joint negotiations.

This intensive pressure resulted in a memorandum of agreement between TWA and the FEIA chapter at TWA, not with FEIA International. It was gained by persuading the local FEIA leaders to yield on the A&E rating and by gaining assurances from ALPA that the flight engineers would have prior rights to the third seat on the jets and that TWA could stop training pilots to obtain their flight engineer certificates. The memorandum provided for the recall of and prior rights for 67 furloughed TWA flight engineers. It provided that those flight engineers who were in active service as of January 1, 1962, would be given training for the flight engineer position on three-man jet crews at company expense and on company time. In order to fly as the third man on a three-man jet crew a flight engineer had to have the commercial pilot's license and instrument rating card, the other qualifications called for in the second report of the Presidential Commission (enumerated earlier in this chapter), "plus two hours of flight training on jet aircraft, to include instructions in three landings of the aircraft." The agreement allowed TWA to reduce from four to three men any jet crew which contained a flight engineer holding those qualifications. These flight engineers were to be entitled to prior rights at all future times and until retirement or discharge for cause. Recalled engineers were to take the training for the commercial pilot's license on their own time but at company expense; whereas the training leading to the instrument rating card and for other qualifications would be offered on company time and expense. If flight engineer vacancies occurred and flight engineers were unavailable to fill them, then the company could fill them with others *who would not have to have the A&E rating.*

The memorandum of agreement was to remain in effect without change unless a majority of the former flight engineers voluntarily voted to reopen it. The Secretary of Labor and the Chairman of the National Mediation Board stated that it was the position of the government without qualification that the FEIA chapter at TWA would not suffer "an increased risk of loss of its representational rights" through the adoption of these memoranda. No craft or class proceedings would be considered appropriate regarding TWA flight crew personnel during the period a joint flight engineer/pilot committee functioned. In spite of FEIA opposition the TWA engineers voted better than four to one in favor of ratification. On September 25, 1962, TWA and ALPA accommodated both the pilots' basic working agreement and the memorandum of understanding between them dated May 22, 1959, to the terms of the TWA-FEIA agreement.

ALPA yielded on having a third pilot from the pilots' seniority list on the turbojets as third in command and as minimum qualifications the *ability to fly the aircraft.* The pilots gained a no-furlough clause and pay protection provisions for those pilots who would in any way be hurt by the reduction from four to three man crews.

Eastern Air Lines

The pilot and flight engineer groups at Eastern were at odds with each other and maintained relatively intransigent positions. Their intransigence can be explained by the following background factors at Eastern. Eastern was planning to dispose of the last of its Martin aircraft and to furlough over 100 junior pilots. In contrast, no flight engineers were on furlough. In 1961 and 1962 Eastern Air Lines had suffered operating losses of $7 million and $20 million, respectively. During the 1958 strike Eastern pilots stood ready to replace the striking flight engineers. In June 1962 the FEIA chapters at Eastern and Pan American closed ranks with the international officers of FEIA in strongly opposing the TWA settlement.

The flight engineers at Eastern and Pan American struck on June 23, 1962. Pan American obtained a temporary restraining order. Eastern shut down. The Eastern engineers stood alone.

During July the Kennedy Administration continued to try to get the flight engineers at Eastern and Pan American to accept a TWA-type settlement. By mid-July the Administration as well as Eastern's management came to realize that, in view of the threatened lay-offs of junior pilots because of Eastern's planned disposal of Martin aircraft, Eastern pilots were not likely to agree readily to a tripartite settlement. With this realization, the Secretary of Labor started talking to the Eastern pilots regarding what they would accept.[9]

[9] *The New York Times,* July 11, 1962.

By mid-July the resistance of the Eastern flight engineers to a TWA-type settlement had reportedly weakened. By July 1962, however, Eastern was reported to believe that any retro-activity was unreasonable, a position that was unacceptable to FEIA.

During the third week of July Eastern sent a letter to each flight engineer telling him to return to work by July 24 and to agree to meet the qualifications of the Presidential Commission for jet flight engineers or he would be fired. About 100 flight engineers returned. At the same time Eastern started an intensive program to qualify its junior copilots as flight engineers.

On July 23, 1962, Secretary of Labor Goldberg suggested the following settlement terms: (1) the parties would arbitrate rates of pay; (2) the crew complement issue would be solved by a TWA-type settlement; (3) the union would immediately end its strike; (4) Eastern would immediately resume operations; and (5) if the crew complement issue was not settled, the parties would agree that it should be settled by procedures recommended by a board con-sisting of Under Secretary of Labor Willard Wirtz, Mr. Feinsinger, National Mediation Board Chairman Leverett Edwards, and Mr. Goldberg.

FEIA accepted Mr. Goldberg's proposal but the President of Eastern, Mr. MacIntyre, rejected it because, according to him, the company's economic position had changed and because the assent of the company's pilots was needed before the crew complement matter could be "buttoned up."

At this time Eastern started to resume partial service. It or-ganized what it termed the "industry's largest commercial aviation training program" to qualify new flight personnel. In addition, it petitioned the Federal Aviation Agency to reduce the type and amount of training Eastern copilots would need to qualify for the flight engineer's certificate. Although not agreeing to the course Eastern proposed, the FAA did sanction a somewhat abbreviated course.

In August Eastern began to return its jets to service and by September 13, 1962, had inaugurated its complete winter schedule.

As the strike proceeded, the FEIA instigated two unsuccessful court suits and petitioned the CAB in regard to this dispute. In response to a motion filed by Eastern on August 19, 1962, the CAB dismissed the complaint.

On October 4, 1963, ALPA invoked the services of the National Mediation Board, alleging the existence of a representational dispute among certain Eastern employees designated "pilot-engineers-third crew members."

The petition by ALPA to represent the entire flight engineer group on all types of equipment on Eastern formed the basis of a charge by the FEIA to the AFL-CIO that ALPA had violated Sections 2 and 3 of Article XXI of the AFL-CIO Constitution (the internal disputes plan). On December 16, 1963, the impartial umpire under that plan, Mr. David L. Cole, ruled that the application constituted a violation but the AFL-CIO took no further action.

On June 4, 1964, the National Mediation Board certified ALPA as representative of the flight engineers on Eastern Air Lines.

Pan American Airways

During the crucial period in 1962 Pan American had some 127 flight engineers and some 224 pilots on furlough. Being entirely an international carrier, Pan American required multiple crews on about three-quarters of its flights as of July 1962. Thus, on three-quarters of Pan American's flights the third pilot could, to the extent that he was qualified, relieve the other crew members. In addition, by agreement with ALPA, the third pilot on the Pan American jets could serve as the navigator.

Negotiations in early 1962 between Pan American and its flight engineers did not prove successful. The engineers at Pan American, like those at Eastern, were holding out very strongly for retention of the mechanic's license as a flight engineer qualification.

Two days after the agreement on TWA which eliminated the mechanic's license qualification (June 21, 1962) the flight engineers on Eastern and Pan American struck. As will be discussed in greater detail, Pan American went to court and succeeded in obtaining a temporary restraining order.

In an earlier threatened strike by ALPA against Pan American, a private, voluntarily agreed upon fact-finder had started to find the facts in February 1961. During the spring, summer, and early fall of 1961, the management, the flight engineers, and the pilots negotiated both separately and jointly with and without the fact-finder, Mr. Cole, and with and without the Presidential Commission, and thus came to understand one another's problems.

With the second Presidential Commission report pending on October 24, 1961, and with pilot negotiations not providing an agreement, Mr. Cole indefinitely recessed fact-finding procedures as of that date. Pan American was among the carriers accepting the terms of the second report.

On November 2, 1961, ALPA set a strike date at Pan American for November 10. On the latter date President Kennedy established Presidential Emergency Board No. 143 between Pan American and ALPA in spite of a protest by ALPA that its February 1961 agreement to have Mr. Cole fact-find had been accepted by the pilots in lieu of emergency board procedures. ALPA maintained that such fact-finding had met all the requirements of Section 10 of the Railway Labor Act regarding emergency disputes.

On December 10, 1961, Presidential Emergency Board No. 143 submitted its report. The Board recommended that the parties seriously consider resuming fact-finding under Mr. Cole. Following the report of Presidential Emergency Board No. 143, Mr. Cole continued his fact-finding role between the pilots and Pan American. In February 1962 Mr. Cole was joined in discussions at Pan American by Mr. Willard Wirtz, the Under Secretary of Labor.

At the suggestion of Mr. Wirtz, negotiations were carried on bilaterally between the company and the pilot representatives and not immediately with the flight engineer representatives. ALPA and Pan American agreed that: (1) ALPA did not object to a reduction from a four- to a three-man jet crew provided that the third crew member possessed the pilot qualifications which ALPA considered necessary for proper performance of the job and provided that the employment rights of all Pan American pilots were protected; and (2) that the flight engineers had a preferred right to the third seat of a three-man jet crew provided that they possessed the necessary qualifications.

On April 16, 1962, President Kennedy requested and the two parties accepted binding arbitration of the three really crucial remaining issues: the rate of transition to the three-man crew, the number of daily flight and duty hours when operating with the smaller crew, and the qualifications which would be required of the third man.

The resulting Board of Arbitration wrote to FEIA to inform the union that the Board would receive any testimony or statement FEIA desired to make as to the qualifications issue. FEIA declined since it had not been involved in the arbitration agreement.

The Board ruled that jet flight engineer qualifications be: (1) a commercial pilot's certificate and instrument rating, (2) the qualifications called for in the second report of the Presidential Commission, and (3) unique to this Board, two hours of flight training on any four-engine piston aircraft of Pan American and one hour of flight training on a jet aircraft.

The Board noted that approximately 224 pilots were on furlough from Pan American and that current and nearby manning needs would require the company to reemploy about 100 of them. The Board judged that a proper amount of protection would be attained by requiring the reemployment of 50 pilots from the furloughed list in addition to the 100 mentioned above. Thus, the Board ruled that the reemployment of 150 pilots or the exhaustion of the furlough list, whichever occurred first, had to occur before any three-man jet crews could be operated.

The Board ruled that when the flight deck crew on a jet aircraft was reduced from four to three, the maximum scheduled flight deck time for pilots would be eight hours except on flights where the third crew member position was occupied by a man holding a flight engineer's certificate and the qualifications needed to be a third pilot. On such flights the maximum scheduled flight deck duty time for pilots would be ten hours. The Board also ruled that the maximum scheduled daily duty time would be 16 hours for pilots on three-man jet crews.

FEIA was adversely affected because 147 flight engineers then on furlough were given no recall rights.

The temporary restraining order against the flight engineers' strike in 1962 lasted several weeks.

On October 18, 1962, Pan American and the flight engineers agreed to submit the unresolved crew complement issues to arbitration. The award provided that flight engineers then on furlough would have no recall rights, but would have severance pay. The award allowed 35 engineers to sever voluntarily with up to $39,400 each in severance pay.

American Airlines

In order to understand the manner in which the crew complement dispute was settled at American Airlines, one must know a little about the relationships among the management, the pilot group, and the flight engineer group as well as the relationships between each of those employee groups and their respective international union.

American and its pilots entered the negotiations in the 1961–1962 period with an unusual degree of mutual trust and confidence. The relationship between the pilot group and the flight engineer group at American Airlines was a friendly one.

During the years 1960–1962 the relationship between the American pilot group and the leadership of ALPA was not a strong, positive one. It had never been very good. Throughout the 1950's and 1960's the American pilots pressed for a direct reduction in the 85-hour monthly flight time limitation, whereas the leadership of ALPA sought to have flight time reduced obliquely through such devices as duty-time rigs. The relationship between FEIA and its chapter at American Airlines was such that the American flight engineers were willing to follow other chapters within FEIA and make a separate deal when the opportunity arose. Basically then, this relationship between American and its engineers was also a positive one.

A description of the series of events at American which led to a settlement may well begin at the time of the TWA settlement. At that time the negotiations between American and its pilots were stalemated. The pilots at American were holding out for a reduction in monthly flight hours and increases in pensions, while American was maintaining that it could not afford a reduction in hours, pensions, and the costs involved in training flight engineers to get their commercial pilot's license and instrument rating card.

American's position on the TWA settlement was that it would agree to it in theory, but in practice it knew that the American pilot group would not accept it, primarily because it provided no reasonable answer as to what should be done with some 277 third pilots American had in its employ.

In the period July 21–August 2, 1962, the head of the pilot

negotiating committee, Mr. O'Connell, asked that if the pilots were to relinquish their demands that the third crew member on the jet have the commercial pilot's license and instrument rating, if they were to give up retroactivity in the contract, and if they were to accept a merger with the mechanic flight engineers, would American Airlines reduce flight hours? Having been reassured that ALPA would agree, American in effect said yes.

In late September 1962 American and its pilots suspended talks while the pilot group sought to bring the American flight engineer group in on the agreement. These talks resulted in an almost complete merger agreement between the employee groups at American by the end of October 1962.

During November 1962 the pilots, flight engineers, and management of American Airlines carried on joint negotiations. The pilots and management thought that the flight engineers had agreed to have themselves considered as pilots, to have the pilot negotiating committee negotiate for them, and to have yielded their separate representation rights. The flight engineers thought that they had been in the tripartite negotiations, with the pilots speaking for them on most issues and with the understanding that a merger agreement was close but that all merger agreements and the yielding of their representation rights were dependent on complete agreement on all matters.

On December 1, 1962, the three parties initialed an agreement which in essence said:

(a) the company could convert to a three-man crew on jet planes;

(b) the then present American flight engineers were "pilots" under the agreement; when serving as flight engineers in a three-man crew they were to be called flight officers; they might qualify by having "any type of pilot certificate"; that is, less than the commercial pilot's license and instrument rating (for example, a student's certificate); and by taking certain prescribed training;

(c) the then present American flight engineers were to be consolidated with the pilots "into one unit for the purpose of collective bargaining representation"; and it was represented that a majority had chosen ALPA as their exclusive bargaining representative"; and

(d) the Chapter "irrevocably relinquished any right it might have had to represent employees of the Company" and acknowledged that the Company might treat ALPA as the "exclusive bargaining representative" of the then present American flight engineers.

ALPA and the American pilots disagreed as to what exactly was the bare minimum requirement to meet the crew complement policy. ALPA leadership consistently held that the C&I were minimum requirements for the third crew member in jet equipment. The American pilot group, on the other hand, argued that the crew complement policy was fuzzy and that in fact on a number of the major trunk lines the ALPA leadership had agreed to and had signed contracts which presented a variety of minima.

On January 11, 1963, O'Connell asked American that if at least three-quarters of the pilots on American indicated that they supported the pilot negotiating committee, would American Airlines recognize the group and bargain with it. Again American said yes.

On January 24, 1963, American prepared substitute pages of the December 1, 1962, tripartite agreement deleting ALPA and substituting a statement to the effect that the pilots and the flight engineers were to be consolidated into one class or craft and in effect that in the future the pilots would represent the engineers. The engineers objected strongly. The company took the position that the engineers were part of the joint bargaining group and would not negotiate with the engineers separately.

On March 1, 1963, ALPA sought an injunction requesting that American Airlines be enjoined from negotiating or making an agreement with anyone but ALPA and from refusing to bargain with ALPA.

The District Court and later an Appeals Court upheld the company and denied the injunctive relief sought by ALPA. At the request of American engineers the judge also restrained the American Master Executive Council and negotiating committee from presenting to any council meeting of the flight engineers the proposed basic agreement (the December 1, 1962, initialed agreement) and any related documents. He also ruled that American had to deal with the flight engineers separately from the pilots.

Negotiations continued between the company and the pilots and by March 15, 1963, resulted in an agreement on the basic contract and on a supplemental agreement. The basic contract covered the engineers. The crew complement part of these agreements was the same as the document initialed in December 1962 with ALPA as a party. The reaction of the American flight engineers to the March 15 agreements was negative. They maintained that the agreements did not apply to them.

Earlier in March the top leadership of ALPA had preferred charges against the MEC and the pilot negotiating committee of American Airlines for willful violation of ALPA's constitution and bylaws, and on April 24, 1963, ALPA expelled five of the leaders of the American pilot group.

At meetings from March 19 to 22 the American MEC authorized the formation of a union apart from ALPA, that union to be known as the Allied Pilots' Association (APA).

On July 9 the company recognized APA and signed an agreement with it. This agreement covered the pilots and copilots at American Airlines but did not cover the engineers. American Airlines was to be allowed to reduce the crew of its jets from four to three men by May 1964. The most important provision called for the maximum monthly flight hours to be reduced from 85 hours to 75 hours on jets and 80 hours on pistons. The contract also called for a 7% reduction in wage rates and for the company to pay the entire cost of the pilot pension plan. The net effect of these two changes was to maintain the level of pilot take-home pay. Unlike ALPA contracts, this contract provided for no retroactivity and for a two-year duration. In addition, it called for a two to one duty-time and a three and one-half to one trip-time ratio. No pilots were to be furloughed as a result of the reduction in crew from four to three. The third crew member on the jets did not have to have the C&I ratings.

On November 13, 1963, the National Mediation Board, having held an election, certified the Allied Pilots' Association as the bargaining representative of the pilots on American Airlines.

Late in 1964 the tempo of negotiations between American and FEIA picked up and resulted in tripartite agreements on December 11, 1964. The salient points of these agreements were as follows: (1) the company and APA recognized the American chapter of FEIA as the duly designated exclusive bargaining representative of the third crew members listed on the flight engineers' seniority list; (2) the flight engineers would be covered by the basic working agreement between FEIA and the company; (3) the company and the American chapter of FEIA recognized the Allied Pilots' Association as the duly designated exclusive bargaining representative of all third crew members, not on the flight engineers' seniority list, who were assigned to and served at the third crew member position; (4) the flight officers (the so-called third pilots) would be covered by the basic agreement between the Allied Pilots' Association and the company; (5) all new hires would be pilots, would be represented by APA, and would be covered by the contract between APA and the company; (6) each flight engineer would be deemed qualified for the third crew member position as long as he satisfied the minimum government requirements for such position; (7) the rights of the flight engineer to the third position on American aircraft would continue until retirement, resignation, severance, or discharge for cause; (8) on or after January 1, 1966, the flight engineers would receive the rates of pay of the flight officers, or 90% of copilot pay, whichever was higher; (9) future changes in the rules and working conditions applicable to the third pilots would also be applicable to the flight engineers; and (10) the flight engineers would not have to obtain the C&I ratings in order to fly on jet equipment. All the crew members were to have their hours reduced to 75 per month on the jet equipment and to 80 per month on piston equipment.

COMMENTS AND RECOMMENDATIONS

By 1964 every carrier had obtained the right to eliminate the fourth crew member. In broad terms three avenues of approach had produced this result: breaking a flight engineer strike through the use of pilot replacements, obtaining compromises on jet flight engineer qualifications, and arbitrating. In less broad terms one can see that unique features of each industrial relations system produced their own tailor-made solutions.

A few aspects of each industrial relations system determined the nature of the outcome. In most cases in which management took a strong position that jet engineers would have to be fully qualified as pilots and were willing to back this position with replacement pilots during the strike, FEIA did not have the power to withstand the combined strengths of the company and ALPA. In those cases in which management did not take that tack, the economics of the situation and/or the relationship between the local pilot and flight engineer group determined the outcome.

In one sense these settlements by displaying a great variety of factors support the notion that collective bargaining even under arduous conditions if imaginatively pursued can come up with a meaningful tailor-made settlement. This variety included degrees of flight engineer qualifications, whether the company or the individual was to pay for obtaining qualifications, who would have prior rights to the third seat, what would be the qualifications of future new hires, whether guarantees against furlough would be given, whether furloughed employees would be rehired, whether representation rights would be guaranteed, whether the settlement would be accompanied by better wages and working conditions, and a variety of options available to flight engineers returning to work. When the characteristics of the industrial relations system produced the proper pressures, no shortage of imaginative settlement terms was apparent.

Despite the variety of settlements, each carrier was able to reduce its crew. The over-all competitive pressure in this regard was compelling.

Comments about Airline Managements

The crucial time for the airline managements which had used mechanic engineers to stand together was during the first round of jet negotiations in 1958–1959. Once that opportunity was missed and the fourth crew member was added, costly and/or inequitable settlements were inevitable. The carriers were unable to put forth a united front because of the fiercely competitive nature of the industry and because of their divided posture in the industrial relations area.

Two generalizations emerge from the description of the carriers' attempts to reduce their crew size. If a management in the midst of a bitter jurisdictional dispute is willing to align its policies with those of the stronger of the disputants and to use replacements in a strike situation, it can obtain a relatively quick and inexpensive settlement. If, on the other hand, a management for technical and/or ethical reasons decides not to abandon the weaker of the two disputants, it can expect a costly settlement. The story in the airline industry would indicate that if a management takes this latter route, the longer a compromise settlement is delayed, the more costly it becomes.

Since the 1930's the airline managements have lost a great deal of freedom in manning their aircraft as they might desire. They have lost freedom, for example, in setting flight engineer training, qualifications, and duties. This decline was brought about by government regulations as well as by managements' yielding important rights at the bargaining table. This analysis would indicate that both striving to maintain as much manning flexibility as possible and evolving early policies to work one's way out of jurisdictional disputes are worth whatever management time and effort they may demand.

Comments about the Unions

The analysis in Chapters 7 and 8 leads to the conclusion that ALPA was the stronger organization in this jurisdictional dispute with FEIA. Primarily ALPA's strength arose from the technical nature of the job done by pilots. When a pilot group struck, the carrier was forced to shut down. When a flight engineer group struck, if it desired, the carrier could continue to operate using replacement pilots. As a corollary to the technical nature of the job, the time it takes a person to get a flight engineer certificate as contrasted with the various pilot licenses came to the fore. With a few weeks of intensive training a pilot could obtain a flight engineer's certificate whereas the reverse was certainly not true.

The internal strength of ALPA as an organization was also greater than that of FEIA. With the exception of the American Airlines group, the various pilot groups at the airlines adhered to the ALPA crew complement policy and supported one another in their various attempts to put it across in the industry. On the other hand, various flight engineer groups under varying degrees of pressure were willing to work out some type of deal in contradiction to FEIA's policy of insisting on the general mechanic's license as a qualification. An added facet of this situation was the appeal of a pilot career to a mechanic flight engineer. If the flight engineer looked forward to a growing industry and a continuing need for ever-increasing numbers of pilots, the opportunity to get pilot training essentially free and to get on the pilot seniority list was no doubt very attractive to many an individual flight engineer. The upshot of these factors was that when both FEIA and ALPA were facing the airline industry and the individual airlines, ALPA held the balance of power. One other feature of this situation was the relatively more autonomous nature of the flight engineer organization than the ALPA organization although ALPA also had some autonomous aspects. The weakness of FEIA showed up in a number of instances where back-to-work movements among the engineers proved very damaging to FEIA strikes.

The manner in which FEIA pursued the jurisdictional fight raises questions as to the soundness of its judgment. In spite of the fact that flight operations by American Airlines, by several international carriers, and by the U.S. Air Force have indicated the lack of need for a third pilot on jet equipment and have therefore undercut ALPA's crew complement policy position, the flight engineers were unable to convince neutrals of this fact. On the other hand, the operation by many carriers of three pilot crews also discredited FEIA's position that the third man had to be a general mechanic. One can argue that FEIA's effort to win general mechanic qualifications for jet engineers was a time-and energy-wasting tactic.

The leadership of FEIA may well have made its poorest decisions in the days immediately following the class or craft determination at United Air Lines. In the first place, the leadership tried to have that determination overthrown by the Congress or by the Department of Labor, at best a futile effort. Of more damaging consequence was the strike by FEIA in February 1961. In its struggle with ALPA, FEIA needed to rely heavily on the role of an underdog, the small, weak organization in need of sympathy because it was being pushed around by the strong organization. In short, FEIA needed all the moral and ethical support it could muster. Although it was fighting a losing battle, particularly in the light of the class or craft determination, the flight engineers at least initially had the sympathy and support of a number of airline managements and of government agencies. Once FEIA called its general strike which was clearly illegal, its moral position was never again as strong as it had been. It is perhaps ironical that in striking, really as a crusade over the principle of the democratic choice of collective bargaining representative, FEIA lost its role as a simon-pure underdog by engaging in a dramatic illegal activity.

The split between the FEIA groups at Eastern and Pan American from those at TWA over the question of the general mechanic's license in the summer of 1962 represented miscalculation of the strength or lack of strength that FEIA possessed. It simply did not have the power within the industry to force the general mechanic's license on those carriers. In retrospect the groups at Eastern and Pan American probably should have agreed to the TWA-type settlement at once. Had the Eastern FEIA done so, the pressure of the government probably would have been enough to force the pilot group and the management of Eastern Air Lines to go along. Also the power of the government probably would have forced Pan American to accept the TWA settlement and to have rehired the furloughed flight engineers. By not standing together and by forcing the issue of the general mechanic's license, FEIA found itself in a position where the Eastern group stood alone after Pan American obtained an injunction which was carried on several weeks by the courts and the American flight engineer group became very much interested in merger with the American pilot group. The four FEIA groups standing together probably did not have enough power to dictate terms of settlement; the Eastern group standing alone certainly did not have such power.

FEIA had valid reasons for being apprehensive about a TWA-type settlement. At Eastern they were afraid that the company would no longer feel a need for their services. They viewed the training called for by the TWA settlement as "token" and insufficient even to qualify them as a copilot and for movement up the pilot ladder. They did not trust the TWA-type guarantees of priority to the third seat or of the continuation of representational rights because they believed such guarantees could later be negotiated away. They were probably, on balance, overly frightened as to this point. Later on the American flight engineers were worried about their future representation rights when the pilot group broke away from ALPA. In addition, the flight engineer groups in general probably wished to maintain the organizational identity of FEIA primarily to provide protection throughout the future but also perhaps for personal reasons. That these fears had some basis can be seen from the fact that a number of flight engineer groups had in this controversy agreed to obtain the commercial pilot's license and instrument rating card; they had proceeded in that direction only to be forced off the carrier's jet equipment through the combination of a forceful company policy to the effect that the third crew member would be fully qualified as a copilot plus the insistence on such qualifications by the pilot group.

Over-all, one might say, when FEIA discovered that the neutrals would not buy its argument as to crew qualifications and when it saw that various of its groups would split off to make tailor-made agreements for their own benefit and to the detriment of FEIA International, perhaps FEIA should have sought a government determination of the job assignments. Failing to get that, as would probably have been the case, it might well have sued for peace with ALPA through some sort of a merger. Following the tactics that FEIA did follow, out of the seven carriers that originally went to the four-man crew, FEIA lost representation rights at four of them along with most of the flight engineer jobs. At a fifth it lost future bargaining rights and at a sixth it failed to have former flight engineers recalled. Given this record, the TWA-type settlement for many of the flight engineer groups would have represented a distinct improvement over what actually did ensue.

This analysis leads one to question the judgment of the ALPA leadership over the period 1954 to 1964. In 1954 and again in 1956 ALPA endorsed a policy to the effect that the third crew member on jet aircraft would have to be pilot-qualified. As originally conceived, the third crew member would have to be on the pilots' seniority list and a fully qualified pilot able to fly the aircraft. ALPA created this policy presumably based on safety but in fact such a policy was unneeded from a safety standpoint. As has been pointed out, American Airlines, several international airlines, and the U.S. Air Force have flown these planes successfully with no compromise to safety without a third pilot. The FAA consistently maintained that a pilot's qualifications for the third crew member was unnecessary. In spite of the unnecessary qualifications which ALPA created, it was able to force at least a good measure of its policy on the domestic airlines. ALPA was unable, however, to obtain full compliance with its 1956 policy. At four carriers ALPA was able to get rid of FEIA or IAM and to obtain most of the third crew member jobs for pilots. In these cases, however, it certainly did not follow that aspect of its policy which would provide protection for incumbent flight crew members. At two additional carriers ALPA was able to have the third crew member required to possess the C&I but not to be on the pilot seniority list and in no sense be a fully qualified pilot. Then at American Airlines, of course, ALPA lost representation rights and in that case the commercial pilot's license and instrument rating were not made part of the qualifications. Mention should also be made of the fact that at National Airlines the qualifications of the third crew member were very scant in terms of ALPA's original policy. Thus, even if ALPA was out to increase safety on jet aircraft, it ended up agreeing to settlements which on its own original terms would have been unsafe.

In another sense, however, by taking a strong policy stand with perhaps extreme qualifications ALPA could appear to yield gracefully to the recommendations of presidential emergency boards and to other pressure from the government. Thus, at Pan American ALPA yielded prior rights to the third seat to the flight engineers and also agreed to a reduction from four to three men before agreeing to arbitrate the crucial differences. At TWA the settlement represented a major concession from ALPA policies. For example, ALPA had had at TWA an agreement that the third pilot would be from the pilot's seniority list and third in command. In addition, his qualifications were to have been the minimum TWA copilot qualifications including the C&I and *the ability to fly the aircraft*. In addition, ALPA gave up the opportunity for second officers to secure the flight engineer's certificate. Earlier in this over-all dispute ALPA had agreed to the recommendations of Presidential Emergency Boards No. 120 and No. 121 which gave first rights to the jets to former flight engineers as long as they had the C&I. Also ALPA was willing to change its policy on turboprops and to let flight engineers fly on that type of equipment without the C&I. Again ALPA agreed to a third pilot qualification greatly watered down from its original policy. Flight engineers were to be represented by FEIA rather than by ALPA. Thus, by taking a very strong position early ALPA throughout this decade was able to back off from aspects of its policy and to appear to be yielding to demands of the situation. One must keep in mind, however, that no real need existed for the policy in the first instance.

In considering the policy adopted by ALPA, it is perhaps constructive to consider what alternative policies it might have adopted in 1956. It could have pursued the course that it had taken at various times throughout its history—that of going to the government for what it wanted. For example, when ALPA wanted a third crew member on the large pistons in the postwar period, it used the CAB to force such a requirement on the industry. Presumably ALPA could have attempted to force pilot qualifications for jet flight engineers through the medium of the CAB and FAA safety regulations. This would have meant, however, that ALPA would have had to persuade a governmental agency in effect to eliminate a craft of employees, that of the professional flight engineer. ALPA probably properly assessed the fact that it would be difficult to get a politically oriented agency to eliminate a craft directly. As will be discussed below, by 1964 ALPA had succeeded in getting various departments and agencies of the government indirectly to decimate the flight engineer craft.

Alternately, in 1956 ALPA could have decided that the time had come to push for a reduction in hours for all flight crew members and to have cooperated with FEIA to work out such a reduction. This would have been a difficult policy for ALPA to have countenanced during the period because of the bitter jurisdictional fight. In addition, ALPA had attempted at an earlier period to reduce flight hours without success. In spite of the fact that the American Airlines pilots were interested in a direct reduction in hours, ALPA membership in general and the ALPA leadership decided against that route. As was seen in the chapter on scheduling, the attainment of a reduction in hours was not as difficult as ALPA might have expected it to have been in 1956.

It was at American that the major problem from ALPA's point of view with its policy came to the fore. By insisting on the C&I at the various airlines and forcing these airlines to go to the expense of training flight engineers up to the level of the C&I, ALPA by 1962 was locked into its crew complement policy to the point where it could not permit the American group to deviate from that principle. The leaders of the pilot groups on the other trunk lines, particularly those where strikes had ensued and pilots had lost pay over the crew complement issue, were very reluctant—not to say downright unwilling—to have the American pilot group agree with American Airlines that the latter could avoid the several million dollar training costs involved in the C&I in spite of the attractive notion of a reduction in hours. Had they permitted the American pilots to do this without protest, the managements of their carriers could, with some reason, have asked why they had had to spend millions of dollars to train their mechanic engineers up to the level of the C&I while ALPA let American Airlines avoid similar costs.

With the advantage of hindsight one can say that the policy adopted by ALPA in 1956 which required it to build the myth that for safety reasons the jet engineer had to be pilot-qualified did not represent the height of statesmanship. It led to the elimination of jobs for mechanic flight engineers in large numbers; it brought about the break-up of ALPA; and when the industry was viewed across the board as of 1964 the policy had been watered down to the point of almost being meaningless even in terms of the C&I. Furthermore, in view of the change in the employment picture from one of technological unemployment to one of a shortage of pilots as of 1965, one can say that ALPA's policy was shortsighted.

Had ALPA joined with FEIA to work out a reduction in hours in 1956, it might have provided from the over-all union point of view a more equitable settlement. From the management point of view a reduction in hours at that time would have been an anathema but it has come about anyway as of 1965. As has been said, getting together with FEIA would have been difficult for ALPA because of the jurisdictional fight. Nevertheless, it would have been a more straightforward and honorable path for ALPA to have followed.

Comments Regarding the Government's Role

This analysis has shown how for the first time in the history of the Railway Labor Act the National Mediation Board availed itself of the right to hand over to a committee of neutrals its responsibility to decide a representation question. The scope of each craft must be determined in some way. Prior to government legislation in this area, the AF of L and the organizing strength of the individual unions made such determinations. Under the Railway Labor Act the National Mediation Board has been granted that power. The act also authorizes the Board to establish a neutral committee to decide such questions. The courts in this country have been slow and perhaps properly so to review or even to consider that they have the power to review decisions by boards such as the National Mediation Board. This is all perfectly appropriate. In addition, because of the cross-training and cross-utilization which had been going on at United Air Lines, the merits of the case probably justified the Board's finding one class or craft. This is all according to the way laws are written and carried out. Two questions, however, may be raised about this situation. First, the National Mediation Board turned the question over to neutrals in part because it was tied up with the major dispute of the firemen on the railroads and in part because it thought if it decided the craft determination in this rather bitter controversy it could no longer function effectively in its other role, that of a mediator. If the National Mediation Board cannot handle effectively important decisions determining craft or class and the mediation function, Congress should create a new agency to take over one of those functions. The second point is that the procedures of the National Mediation Board in determining proper classes or crafts when placed in the hands of an administration which is willing and anxious to intervene in labor controversies are not so clear cut as they appeared in this craft determination in 1960 and early 1961. If the Administration and the Chairman of the National Mediation Board in 1962 had the power to deem that decisions over appropriate crafts would be considered untimely, and if the Administration in 1962 could stress the human rights of the flight engineer group and the need to take their human rights into special consideration, then presumably the National Mediation Board could have done the same thing in 1959 and have denied the petition of ALPA in the United case. A more preferable turn of events would have had the powers of the National Mediation Board and the Administration more clearly spelled out so that they would be consistently applied in all cases.

When the flight engineers struck in February 1961, the Kennedy Administration acted too quickly to intervene in the dispute. The strike was clearly illegal; the Federal courts were consistently issuing injunctions and levying fines against FEIA. The Railway Labor Act, the primary piece of legislation in this area, had not been exhausted as to any of these disputes. An emergency requiring federal intervention had not transpired by the time the government intervened. This was a time for the laws and for the courts to handle a clearly illegal strike by FEIA.

Once the Kennedy Administration had entered the dispute, the primary initial action it took, that of creating a Presidential Commission to investigate the facts, was an inappropriate step. The efficiency of Presidential Commissions established to investigate facts and make recommendations concerning a dispute which involves the industrial relations system at more than one carrier is very limited. Such a broad study cannot deal effectively with the unique aspects of each dispute on each carrier. Each industrial relations system has its own characteristics and appropriate solutions are shaped by them. Presidential Commissions, in addition, interfere with the efforts of the parties and of Presidential Emergency Boards to work out tailor-made solutions to fit each unique situation. As soon as the Presidential Commission was formed, the Secretary of Labor had to tell the Presidential Emergency Board at Pan American to act in "a limited sphere." Time and again thereafter during the dispute Presidential Emergency Boards were hampered in their work and in the recommendations they could make because they felt constrained to be consistent with the work and the reports of the Presidential Commission. Presidential Emergency Boards themselves are not terribly effective if one or both parties do not care or do not feel constrained to make a settlement. They are, however, created at one carrier in one situation and stand a better chance than a Presidential Commission to work through the unique characteristics and pressures of that industrial relations system to come up with a meaningful tailor-made set of recommendations. It is not impossible to conjecture that a number of the Presidential Emergency Boards, had they not been hampered by the work of the Presidential Commission, might have solved some of these disputes carrier by carrier.

The work of the Presidential Commission was not completely without value. Apparently it did help to improve the relationship between the pilot and flight engineer groups at Pan American and at TWA.

On balance one might say that the Presidential Commission both helped and hurt the cause of the flight engineers. It hurt that cause by insisting on the C&I ratings; it helped the cause by not insisting that the flight engineers should be able to fly and land the jets; it carried forward the recommendations of Presidential Emergency Boards No. 120 and No. 121 that flight engineers should have prior rights to the third seat if they were properly qualified. Most important from the flight engineers' point of view was the fact that the Presidential Commission, by providing them with an extended sympathetic forum comprised of highly respected administration endorsed individuals, somewhat salvaged the flight engineers' cause from the severe damage it had suffered as a result of the general wildcat strike in February 1961.

The early entrance into this dispute by the Kennedy Administration and the creation of the Presidential Commission led it inevitably to take some additional unfortunate steps. In the TWA settlement the Secretary of Labor and the Chairman of the National Mediation Board stated that it was the position of the government without qualification that the FEIA chapter at TWA would suffer no "increased risk of loss of its representational rights" through the adoption of the agreement. The Secretary of Labor and the Chairman of the National Mediation Board were to undertake to establish a joint committee of TWA pilots and flight engineers along with a member to be appointed by the Secretary of Labor to review the possibilities of merger of the representational functions of ALPA and FEIA at TWA. It was "the position of the Government that in view of the joint committee's consideration of the representational matter and also in view of the circumstances of transition from four- to three-man jet crews, no craft or class proceedings would be considered appropriate regarding TWA flight crew personnel during the period of the joint committee's functioning." The government's having taken such a role regarding representational rights and particularly regarding withholding class or craft petitions represented authority not provided under the Railway Labor Act. Also it put the government in an anomalous situation because at a later date the pilots filed a petition for one class or craft at Eastern Air Lines and the government went ahead and processed it. This meant that the government made these decisions *ad hoc* depending on how it was disposed to the individual flight engineer group at the moment.

The other unfortunate step by the government was to be a party to the arbitration between Pan American and the pilot group at Pan American. This was unfortunate because FEIA was not a party to this arbitration but was affected by it since 147 flight engineers then on furlough were given no recall rights in contrast to the flight engineers on furlough at TWA. FEIA believed that the arbitration was illegal and as a minimum one could say that FEIA had a legitimate complaint. This would indicate another instance in which equity was not done to the flight engineers. That the highest ranking labor officials of the government were directly involved is an indication of how desperate they apparently were to get a solution to the problem.

This whole dispute was the Administration's first move into the transportation labor field. For this reason it was widely reported in the press that Administration prestige was riding heavily on the outcome of the disputes, particularly the one at TWA. In addition, the Administration apparently hoped to work out a settlement of this issue which would provide a model for other labor disputes, particularly those involving large-scale technological displacements. Earlier President Kennedy had reacted strongly to the steel industry when it had raised prices, and Senator Dirkson at one point stated that he hoped President Kennedy would be as firm with the flight engineers as he had been with steel management. These kinds of unfortunate comparisons come forward when an Administration is anxious to intervene in labor disputes.

Clearly the Administration had its greatest success in getting the settlement at TWA and its greatest failure in not getting a settlement at Eastern. It is interesting that the two places where the government pressure produced settlements, TWA and Pan American, involved international carriers whose international routes are given out by the U.S. State Department. Where such additional pressure was not available to the government, it was unable to muster the pressure necessary to get a settlement. At Eastern the animosity between the local flight engineer and pilot groups and the economics and job employment situation proved too strong.

This analysis raises the question as to whether the government should set job qualifications when a carrier is being forced to assign particular work to employees in a particular labor organization or to establish qualifications which are in the midst of a jurisdictional dispute. The results at a number of these carriers raise the question of whether equity was obtained by the individual flight engineers who lost their jobs. In one sense, one can argue that these engineers freely elected their leaders; they and their leaders chose to strike, and they should be content to live with the results. One trouble with that reasoning is that given the economic and employment pressures acting on these industrial relations systems one could at least conjecture that regardless of the course taken by the local FEIA chapters, they could not have obtained settlements which would have protected their memberships and equally important their chapters so that they could continue to protect their memberships. Looking at the matter more broadly, should the results of a jurisdictional dispute be allowed to vary with the particular pressures at each company so that some employee groups lose their jobs while others continue to work? The government must regulate various aspects of the airline industry in order to protect the flying and nonflying populace. The question then becomes what type and amount of regulation are optimum. If the government is empowered to require the use of flight engineers, should it not also have the additional power to assign work among employee groups which end up competing for the flight engineer job?

Fundamentally the question is: does one want to have the job rights of individuals dependent upon such things as the personal relationship between local labor leaders, the employment situation or the economic picture at individual carriers, or even the wisdom of their duly elected representatives? In other words, does one want to have such job rights hinge on "muddling through" by means of relatively free collective bargaining, which in some cases produces equity for the individual and in other cases may not. Or, is one willing to reduce a little further the scope of free collective bargaining in a government-regulated industry through increasing the power of the government to solve jurisdictional disputes, and thereby to help guarantee equity to the individual? The author, laying stress on equity, would be willing to give the government such power to help guarantee such results.

PART III

The Ramifications of Flight Crew Grievance Handling and Contract Negotiating Processes

IN PART III the emphasis shifts from the detailed analyses of substantive contract areas of Part II to concentration on the impacts of the processes by which these parties handle grievances and arrive at new contract terms. At the end of Part III some concluding observations are given which it is hoped will tie together the characteristics of this industrial relations system given in Part I, the evolution of substantive contract areas of Part II, and the important effects of processes by which grievances are handled and new contract terms are created yet to be described in Chapters 9 and 10.

CHAPTER 9

Grievance Handling and Arbitration

IN THIS CHAPTER several questions are considered regarding the procedures which the airlines and ALPA use to process grievances. The principal questions are:

Is the grievance area a relatively important part of this industrial relations system?

What factors tend to make it an important part or not?

What are the grievance procedures used by the airlines and ALPA?

Do the airlines use them effectively?

Does ALPA use them effectively?

This chapter is divided into six sections. The first section presents statistics of the numbers and types of grievances filed annually by pilots. The second section contains a description of the grievance procedures and some evaluation of their effectiveness. The third and fourth sections focus, respectively, on the ways in which the airline managements and ALPA use the grievance procedures. The fifth section contains an analysis of the relationship between airline negotiations and grievance procedures. The sixth section summarizes the evidence brought out in the chapter in answer to the questions posed above.

NUMBERS AND TYPES OF GRIEVANCES

Relative to unionized employee groups in general, pilots submit few grievances. For most unionized employee groups, "a rate of about 10 to 20 grievances per 100 employees per year, if grievances are written at the first step, is frequently encountered."[1] As

[1] S. H. Slichter, J. J. Healy, and E. R. Livernash, *The Impact of Collective Bargaining on Management* (Washington: The Brookings Institution, 1960), p. 698.

will be derived below, pilots submit grievances in writing at the first step at rates of about 1.8 to 2.8 per 100 pilots per year.

The data to support these statements about pilot grievance rates are found in ALPA and ATA sources. For the periods of time between its conventions (typically two years), ALPA collects grievance data and publishes them in a document called "The State of the Association." These data, which are presented in Table 9.1, indicate that during the three two-year periods between 1954 and 1960, all pilots filed between 380 and 691 first-step grievances.

TABLE 9.1.   DISPOSITION OF PILOT GRIEVANCES: 1954–1962

	11/1/54– 10/30/56	11/1/56– 10/30/58	11/1/58– 10/30/60	11/1/60– 3/15/62
Pending at the beginning of the period	N.A.	215	314	323
Opened during the period	380	691	559	420
Closed during the period	N.A.	592	550	433
Pending at the end of the period	215	314	323	310

SOURCE: ALPA, "The State of the Association," 1956, 1958, 1960, and 1962.

For the 17.5-month period ending March 15, 1962, all pilots filed 420 first-step grievances. On an annual basis, as shown in Table 9.2, all pilots submitted on the average between 190 and 345.5 grievances per year during these years.

Two measures of the numbers of pilots were available which can be used to derive per capita figures: (1) the average number

TABLE 9.2.   ANNUAL RATE OF PILOT GRIEVANCES FILED:
1954–1962

	11/1/54– 10/30/56	11/1/56– 10/30/58	11/1/58– 10/30/60	11/1/60– 3/15/62
Annual filing rate	190	345.5	279.5	288

SOURCE: Derived from Table 9.1.

TABLE 9.3. ANNUAL PER CAPITA PILOT GRIEVANCE RATES: 1954–1962

	No. of Active ALPA Members*	Weighted Average No. of Active ALPA Members	ATA No. of Pilots & Copilots as of 12/31†	Weighted Average No. of ATA Pilots & Copilots	No. of Pilot Grievances Opened per Period*	Annual Rate of Pilot Grievances	No. of Pilot Grievances Filed per 100 Members per Year	No. of Pilot Grievances Filed per 100 ATA Pilots & Copilots per Year
11/1/54–10/30/56	11/1/54 9,422 11/1/55 9,781	9,975	1954 9,495 1955 10,857 1956 11,386	10,649	380	190	1.9	1.8
11/1/56–10/30/58	11/1/56 10,914 11/1/57 12,837	12,534	1957 13,286 1958 12,897	12,714	691	345.5	2.8	2.7
11/1/58–10/30/60	11/1/58 13,545 11/1/59 13,690	13,623	1959 14,471 1960 13,535 1961 13,936	13,844	559	279.5	2.0	2.0
11/1/60–3/15/62	11/1/60 13,569 11/1/61 13,842 3/15/62 13,955	13,770	1962 13,820	13,764	420	288	2.1	2.1

* Compiled from ALPA, "The State of the Association," 1956, 1958, 1960, and 1962.
† Compiled from ATA, "Air Transport Facts and Figures" for 1959 and 1964.

of active ALPA members as published periodically by the Association's Secretary, and (2) the employment figures for pilots and copilots published annually by the ATA. In Table 9.3 grievance rates per 100 pilots per year have been derived using both the ALPA and the ATA figures. As shown in the last two columns of Table 9.3, for the period November 1, 1958, through March 15, 1962, the pilot grievance rate varied only between 2.0 and 2.1 per 100 pilots per year.

The rates of pilot grievances vary carrier by carrier. For example, an airline industry study indicated that in 1958 for the trunk lines which reported the rates of first-step pilot grievances varied from 0.10 to 1.99 per 100 pilots per year, while averaging 1.1 per 100 pilots per year. The same study indicated that for nine local service lines which reported, the comparable rates varied from 0.0 to 21.3 per 100 pilots per year, while averaging 2.5 per 100 pilots per year.

Pilot grievance rates also vary at some carriers over time. Occasionally some circumstance or a combination of circumstances will cause the grievance rate to increase markedly for a period of months before subsiding. For example, the pilots of one major carrier filed 8 first-step grievances during 1958 and 91 during 1959. As will be discussed more fully later in this chapter, the pilots of two of the carriers which were studied intensively during this study filed many more grievances in 1963 than they had in previous years.

In attempting to find out what subjects pilots grieve and in what proportions, the author analyzed reports published by ALPA during the period 1958–1960 of decisions reached in the final steps of the pilot grievance procedure. Dividing these grievance reports among topics under which they logically appeared to fall produced the results presented in Table 9.4. Based on this analysis, 57% of pilot grievances decided in the final steps of the grievance procedure concerned the interrelated areas of compensation and scheduling. As shown in Table 9.4, the next two most frequently grieved subjects were training and discharge, which accounted for 12% and 10%, respectively, of the grievance reports. Seven other topics divided the remaining 22% of the grievance reports.

TABLE 9.4. TYPES OF CASES REPORTED IN ALPA SYSTEM BOARD REPORTS: 1958–1960

Type of Grievance	1958		1959		1960		Total 1958–1960	
	No.	*%*	*No.*	*%*	*No.*	*%*	*No.*	*%*
Compensation and scheduling	75	64%	31	57%	10	30%	116	57%
Training	7	6	8	15	9	27	24	12
Discharge	11	9	6	11	4	12	21	10
Expenses and facilities	11	9	2	4	1	3	14	7
Discipline	3	3	5	9	3	9	11	5
Vacation	6	5	1	2	2	6	9	4
Sick leave	2	2	1	2	1	3	4	2
Retirement	1	1	0	0	2	6	3	2
Furlough and leaves	2	2	0	0	0	0	2	1
Insurance	0	0	0	0	1	3	1	1

NOTE: Percentages do not add to 100% because of rounding.

SOURCE: Compiled from ALPA reports of System Board actions as listed in issues of the *ALPA News Bulletin*, 1958–1960.

The Grievance Procedures

The grievance procedures typically used by the airlines and the pilots involve four steps: an initial hearing, an appeal, a joint four-man board, and the joint board augmented with a neutral arbitrator. Usually before filing a grievance a pilot will discuss it informally with his immediate supervisor. Under some contracts such a discussion is obligatory.

Establishment of the Airline Grievance Procedures

After the formation of ALPA in 1931 its leaders under President Behncke were anxious to get some forum with the power to protect pilots from arbitrary discipline and discharge, particularly in the cases of pilots who were being disciplined or discharged for union activities. Since the first pilot labor contract was not negotiated until 1939, the disputes or grievances in the 1930's were not over the interpretation or application of contracts, but over actions by the managements which the pilots believed were unjust or were designed to prevent union recognition. During the life of the National Labor Board under the National Industrial Recovery Act from August 1933 to July 1934, a few pilot disputes were submitted to it for settlement. For example, the National Labor Board reinstated a pilot of one carrier who had been discharged allegedly for buzzing an airport. At that time the carrier was trying to establish a company union. In the mid-1930's Mr. Behncke succeeded in getting another carrier to hold a hearing in the case of a pilot who had been disciplined for causing an accident by landing short of a runway. The hearing was held before the president of the airline.

The major accomplishment of the ALPA leadership in getting a forum with the power to protect pilots from arbitrary discipline and discharge came in its successful effort to get Congress to enact Title II of the Railway Labor Act, which for the first time placed the airlines and their employees under the purview of this act. Title II, which was approved on April 10, 1936, affected the grievance area because it made mandatory a specific form of final and binding arbitration of disputes over "grievances or out of interpretation or application of agreements concerning rates of pay, rules, or working conditions."

According to an early ALPA official who worked closely with Behncke during this period in Washington, the latter at first had favored legislation which would have required the creation of a National Air Transport Adjustment Board to give final and binding answers on a national basis to airline employee grievances. Such a board would have been similar to the National Railroad Adjustment Board, which had been created by a 1934 amendment to the Railway Labor Act. Under the advice of the then Chairman of the National Mediation Board, however, President Behncke decided to favor the type of amendment which was in fact enacted, under which the creation of a National Air Transport Adjustment Board would be left to the discretion of the National Mediation Board and under which the powers of final and binding arbitration of grievances would reside in boards of adjustment with jurisdictions limited to one carrier, a group of carriers, or a region of the country.

Since the enactment of Title II, as will be discussed in detail in this section, airlines and their employees have relied exclusively for the final and binding resolution of grievances on boards of adjustment limited in jurisdiction to individual carriers and to individual classes or crafts of airline employees at individual carriers. Thus, for example, the pilots at a carrier will have their own board of adjustment, while the mechanics at the same carrier will have a separate board of adjustment. No attempt has been made to have the National Mediation Board create a National Air Transport Adjustment Board.

The pertinent language of Title II of the Railway Labor Act reads as follows:

> Sec. 204. The disputes between an employee or group of employees and a carrier or carriers by air growing out of grievances, or out of interpretation or application of agreements concerning rates of pay, rules, or working conditions, including cases pending and unadjusted on the date of approval of this Act before the National Labor Relations Board, shall be handled in the usual manner up to and including the chief operating officer of the

carrier designated to handle such disputes; but, failing to reach an adjustment in this manner, the disputes may be referred by petition of the parties or by either party to an appropriate adjustment board, as hereinafter provided, with a full statement of the facts and supporting data bearing upon the disputes.

It shall be the duty of every carrier and of its employees, acting through their representatives, selected in accordance with the provisions of this title, to establish a board of adjustment of jurisdiction not exceeding the jurisdiction which may be lawfully exercised by system, group, or regional boards of adjustment, under the authority of section 3, Title I, of this Act.

Such boards of adjustment may be established by agreement between employees and carriers either on any individual carrier, or system, or group of carriers by air and any class of classes of its or their employees; or pending the establishment of a permanent National Board of Adjustment as hereinafter provided. Nothing in this Act shall prevent said carriers by air, or any class or classes of their employees, both acting through their representatives selected in accordance with provisions of this title, from mutually agreeing to the establishment of a National Board of Adjustment of temporary duration and of similarly limited jurisdiction.

The Initial Grievance Steps

As the above quotation indicates, the Railway Labor Act dictates that the grievance steps prior to appeal to the board of adjustment "shall be handled in the usual manner up to and including the chief operating officer of the carrier designated to hear such disputes." The "usual manner" comprises an initial hearing and an appeal.

The first step of the grievance procedure typically proceeds as follows. To initiate the process, a pilot with a grievance is required to write a letter to his supervisor or, perhaps, the line official next above his supervisor, in which he states the nature of his grievance and requests a hearing on the matter. The company official writes back acknowledging the letter and setting a time for a hearing, which is the first step of the grievance procedure.

Typically the atmosphere at the hearing is informal. Its purpose is simply to allow the pilot to describe his grievance and the conditions surrounding it as he sees them. The company official generally does not present a counter case for the company. His role rather is to hear the pilot's story. Generally the pilot and the company official are the only people present, although the pilot may be accompanied by a member of his local executive council or his local grievance chairman. Generally the only records maintained during the hearing are notes made by the pilot and the company official.

After the hearing the company official will usually investigate the grievance. For example, if it involved a claim for additional flight pay, he might check with the people in scheduling and payroll.

The authority to settle grievances granted by airline managements to hearing officials apparently varies carrier by carrier. ALPA lawyers stated that only rarely do such first-step officials have a significant amount of authority because the airlines cannot afford to have them make costly errors. Some airline officials indicated also that such authority is limited. An official of a major carrier, however, stated that its first step hearing officers were free to discharge their responsibilities as they saw fit. If they made wrong decisions, they would be reversed at the second step without recriminations. An industrial relations staff member of the same carrier said that for local grievances which did not involve an interpretation of the contract, a first-step official would probably give his answer without checking with the people in industrial relations. If the grievance carried implications beyond the local domicile or involved contract interpretation, however, he would check with industrial relations because he had been trained to see the need for consistent first-step answers.

The contract language which establishes the grievance procedure between the airlines and the pilots is interesting primarily for two reasons: (1) it is essentially standard throughout the industry, and (2) it stresses the procedures to be followed for discipline and discharge grievances and adds on, almost as an afterthought, a paragraph to the effect that grievances on other matters are to be similarly processed. The standard nature of contract language indicates the willingness of the airlines to accept patterns set by their competitors and the success of ALPA in having standard contract language accepted across the industry. The major emphasis of the language on discipline and discharge cases reflects Mr. Behncke's original goal in having grievance procedures established: obtaining some protection for the pilots against arbitrary and unjust disciplinary actions.

The standard contract language in regard to discipline and non-discipline cases as well as to the hearing step reads as follows:

INVESTIGATION AND DISCIPLINE:

SECTION 29. (a) Hearing.

(1) A pilot shall not be disciplined or dismissed from the Company without notification in writing as to any such action, and such pilot shall not be disciplined or dismissed without an investigation and hearing, provided that the pilot makes written request for an investigation and hearing within seven (7) days after receiving such notification.

(2) Nothing in this Section shall be construed to prevent the Company from holding a pilot out of service prior to written notification of charges preferred against him, and such written notification stipulated in Paragraph (a) (1) of this Section shall be furnished the pilot with reasonable expeditiousness.

(3) Such investigation and hearing shall be held by a junior operating official of the Company designated by the Company for that purpose, and shall be held within seven (7) days after the Company receives the written notification from the pilot for an investigation and hearing as stipulated in Paragraph (a) (1) of this Section.

(4) Prior to such investigation and hearing the Company shall furnish such pilot a copy of the precise charge or charges against him, and he shall not be required to give testimony or furnish evidence prior to the actual time of the investigation and hearing. He shall be given the necessary time in which to prepare and to secure the presence of witnesses and shall have the right to be represented by an employee of the Company of his choice or by his duly accredited representative or representatives.

(5) Within seven (7) days after the close of such investigation and hearing, the Company shall announce its decision in writing and shall furnish the pilot, or his duly accredited representative, a copy thereof.

(6) Any pilot or group of pilots hereunder who has a grievance concerning any action of the Company affecting them shall be entitled to have such grievance handled in accordance with the procedure established in . . . this Agreement for investigating and hearing cases of discipline and dismissal.

As the above contract language indicates, a time limit is clearly set regarding the time a pilot has to request a hearing after receiving notification that he has been disciplined or discharged. Whether the same time limit applies to the requesting of a hearing on grievances concerning other matters is in dispute at some carriers. The dispute revolves around the question of whether the language of the last paragraph of Section 29(a) above requires a pilot to submit a nondiscipline grievance within seven days after the situation causing the grievance arises. The carriers generally maintain that the time limit applies. ALPA, on the other hand, maintains that it does not apply, but advises that non-discipline-or-discharge grievances "must be filed within a reasonable period."[2] Some airlines and their pilot groups have eliminated the dispute by writing contract language explicitly setting time limits on the filing of all grievances.

As the above contract language also indicates, the time limits apply to the scheduling of the hearing and the issuing of the first-step decision.

If the pilot does not agree with the decision of the hearing officer, he has the right to appeal the case to a more senior company official.

Time limits also are generally established for the appeal procedures. Usually a pilot must file an appeal within seven days after receiving word of the first-step decision, the appeal hearing must be held within seven days after the company official designated to hear appeals receives notice of the appeal, and his answer must come within ten days after he hears the appeal. If the pilot fails to appeal within the time limit, the first-step decision of the company stands.

The appeal hearing is generally as informal as the initial hearing. The aggrieved pilot presents his grievance to the appeal officer, who generally is the senior flight operating official. His title will usually be something like senior vice president of flying, vice president—operations, director of flying, or vice president—flight. Although usually the pilot and the appeal officer will be the only people present, it is not uncommon for the pilot to be accompanied by a member of his master executive council or for a member of the carrier's industrial relations staff to sit in during the appeal

[2] ALPA, *Guide for Processing Grievances,* 1955, p. 2.

hearing as an observer. At one carrier at least, the pilot's supervisor may be present to present the company's side of the grievance to the appeal officer, but such a practice is rare.

During the appeal hearing all the facts of the grievance may be brought out anew.

The standard contract language on appeal procedures reads as follows:

Appeal.

(1) When a copy of such decision has been received by the pilot or his duly accredited representative and such pilot is dissatisfied with the Company's decision, he shall have the right to appeal to the senior operating official of the Company, provided such appeal request is filed by the pilot in writing with the senior operating official within seven (7) days from the date of the pilot's receipt of the decision of the investigation and hearing conducted by the junior operating official. Such appeal hearing shall be held within seven (7) days after the receipt of the pilot's request therefor by a senior operating official of the Company designated by the Company for that purpose.

(2) Within ten (10) days after the close of such appeal hearing the Company shall announce its decision in writing and shall furnish the pilot, or his duly accredited representative, a copy thereof.

(c) General.

(1) If any decision made by the Company under the provisions of this Section is not appealed by the pilot affected within the time limit prescribed herein for such appeals, the decision of the Company shall become final and binding.

According to ALPA statistics, the proportion of pilot grievances resolved during the hearing and the appeal steps of the grievance procedure increased during the period from late 1954 to early 1962. As shown in Table 9.5, ALPA data indicated that for the two-year period starting November 1, 1954, some 26.6% of the grievances disposed of were resolved in the hearing and appeal steps. During the next four years the comparable percentage had increased to about 65%. And for the period from November 1, 1960, to March 15, 1962, the comparable percentage had climbed to 80.1%. These percentages, of course, do not indicate one way or another whether

TABLE 9.5. NUMBERS AND PROPORTIONS OF PILOT GRIEVANCES SETTLED AT VARIOUS LEVELS OF THE GRIEVANCE PROCEDURES: 1954–1962

Disposition of Grievances	11/1/54–11/30/56		11/1/56–10/30/58		11/1/58–10/30/60		11/1/60–3/15/62	
	No. of Grievances	Per Cent of Total	No. of Grievances	Per Cent of Total	No. of Grievances	Per Cent of Total	No. of Grievances	Per Cent of Total
Number of grievances disposed of in 1st & 2nd steps	44	26.6%	386	65.2%	351	63.8%	347	80.1%
Number of grievances disposed of by the four-man boards of adjustment	115	69.8	139	23.5	147	26.8	64	14.8
Number of grievances disposed of by the five-man boards of adjustment	6	3.6	67	11.3	52	9.4	22	5.1
Total number of grievances disposed of	165	100%	592	100%	550	100%	433	100%

SOURCE: ALPA records.

sound resolutions of these grievances were being made from either the pilot's or the airline management's points of view. At least a qualitative appraisal of this latter question will be presented later in this chapter.

The Four-Man Board of Adjustment

If a pilot does not agree with a decision at the appeal level, in the great majority of cases his next step is to have his grievance appealed to a joint- four-man board of adjustment. Such boards are termed "system boards of adjustment" because their jurisdictions are limited to one system, i.e., one airline. "All system boards are uniform in organization and fairly uniform in procedure."[3]

On rare occasions the four-man board will be by-passed, and a grievance will be sent from the appeal step directly to a five-man system board of adjustment which is the four-man board augmented by an arbitrator. In such rare cases the members of the four-man board may all sign a letter concurring that the four-man board is to be by-passed.

A pilot has 30 days from receipt of the appeal decision to have his grievance appealed to the four-man board. The actual submission itself must be made either by the President of ALPA, or in the infrequent case of a company grievance by the operating officer of the company. An individual pilot or group of pilots, therefore, cannot submit grievances to a system board of adjustment. This is because the Railway Labor Act states that disputes will be "referred by petition of the parties or by either party" (as opposed to by an individual or individuals) to an appropriate adjustment board.

The standard contract language covering the submission of grievances to the four-man system boards reads in part as follows:

> If, after the appeal provisions herein before have been complied with, further appeal by the pilot if made, shall be made to the . . . Airlines pilot's system board of adjustment as provided in the agreement between . . . Airlines, Inc., and the airline pilots in the service of . . . Airlines, Inc., as represented by the Air Line Pilots Association, International, covering the establishment and maintenance of a system board of adjustment, . . . provided such an

[3] ALPA, *Negotiators' Guide,* Vol. 2, Sect. I, p. 2 (1964).

appeal is made within thirty days from the date of receipt by the pilot, or his duly accredited representative of the appeal hearing decision of the company . . . The Board shall consider any dispute properly submitted to it by the President of the Association or by the Chief Operating Officer of the Company, when such dispute has not been previously settled in accordance with the terms provided in the Pilots Agreement.

For ease of presentation, the following discussion of the four-man system board of adjustment will be divided into four subtopics: the makeup of the board, the people presenting grievances to the board, general board procedures, and statistics pertaining to the board's resolution of grievances.

The Makeup of the Board

A system board of adjustment is made up of two ALPA and two company members. They serve for a minimum of one year or until replacements are appointed. Typically, board members serve for several years. Each party tries to stagger appointments so that at all times one of its members will have at least a year's experience on the board.

The two ALPA members are appointed by the President of ALPA from lists of nominees submitted to him by each Master Executive Council. They are line pilots who carry on their duties as board members in addition to their regular flying assignments. Occasionally an ALPA board member will be a lawyer as well as a pilot. The ALPA Legal Department is responsible for keeping a current roster of ALPA board members and for informing the President when a replacement or substitute member is needed.

Practice varies among airline managements as to the type of individuals they appoint to system boards. Some carriers use only active members of the management group; others use retired company executives or persons who worked for the airline's consulting firm or industrial relations firm. Most carriers assign duties as system board members as an added duty to an executive's regular job; one carrier has appointed the same two individuals to all seven system boards at that carrier and they spend full time as system board members. Usually one of the board members is an executive in the Operations Department of the airline. The other board member may be also from the Operations Department or from such departments as Personnel, Administration, or Legal.

The company board members of three trunk lines which were studied intensively were as follows: (1) two permanent, full-time system board members (both of whom had flying and personnel backgrounds), (2) the retired vice-president—personnel and the vice president—administration and finance, and (3) a retired former head of the airline's flight operations training center and a member of an outside law firm which handled much of the airlines' legal work.

According to some airline executives, one of the important reasons for this variation is that airline managements differ fundamentally in their views concerning the proper role of a system board. The predominant view at some airlines is that the four-man system board should properly fill a mediatory role and attempt to mediate settlements to grievances. Thus they view the four-man system board in effect as an extension of the negotiation process. The predominant view among other airline managements is that the four-man system board is a form of adjudication. This difference in philosophy reflects itself in the appointment of company board members in the following way. Managements viewing the board as fulfilling a mediatory role tend to appoint their top operating people to the board, whereas managements with the opposing view tend to appoint persons who they believe might be able to take a more neutral position such as lawyers and persons not part of the active management team.

On the matter of neutrality, system board members are in a somewhat untenable position. According to their mandate, as shown in the following standard contract language, they are supposed to be independent:

> It is understood and agreed that each and every board member shall be free to discharge his duty in an independent manner, without fear that his individual relations with the company or the employees may be affected in any manner by any action taken by him in good faith in his capacity as board member.

Executives and system board members at airlines where the view prevails that a system board member should fulfill an adjudicatory role complain that ALPA system board members tend not to be neutral. They point to instances in which ALPA board members have actively helped in the presentation of the pilot's case. They state that the company board members play a much less active role, if any, in helping the company present its case and take the position that if a decision hurts the company, it should not have agreed to contract language under which it could be hurt.

ALPA, for its part, does not expect its system board members to be neutral as the following quotation indicates:

> Must a board member be unbiased?
> Certainly not in the sense that he should not argue the merits of the case of the party he represents. Since the board is composed of two pilot members and two company members, it is contemplated that the members will be sympathetic, if not prejudiced, to the viewpoint of their respective constituents. This is not to say that a board member is instructed, not that he is not entirely free to decide a case as his conscience may dictate. But it goes without saying that the company members of the board will champion the arguments and the evidence in the case which is favorable to the company, and, by the same token, the pilot members of the board will champion the arguments and evidence most favorable to the grieving pilot. The association must rely on the fact that its appointees are interested in the pilot's welfare to see that the interests of its members are properly protected before the system board, and that if the evidence is available, the pilot's case will be fairly decided.[4]

People Presenting Grievances to the System Board

Both ALPA and the airlines use staff people to present and argue grievances before system boards of adjustment. This represents a shift in primary responsibility for handling grievances for both sides from the line to the staff. For ALPA, this responsibility shifts from the aggrieved pilot to an ALPA lawyer. For the airline managements, which normally make no presentations in the first two steps, the presentation to the system board is generally made by a man from the personnel or legal staffs.

[4] ALPA, *Guide for System Board Members,* 1957, p. 5.

The ALPA lawyers form a legal department which is based at ALPA headquarters in Chicago. As of mid-1963 this department consisted of six lawyers, and a seventh was being sought. As is the case with most ALPA staff members, these lawyers go out from Chicago to handle problems wherever they are needed. Not infrequently, prior to becoming ALPA lawyers, these men will have had some connection with the airline industry and/or familiarity with the Railway Labor Act. A number of them were former private or military pilots. Each is assigned more or less permanently to handle the work-related legal problems of the pilots at about six airlines. The lawyer assigned to handle the work at a particular airline will argue all the pilot grievance cases before the pilot system board at that carrier.

Most carriers are represented before system boards by a personnel specialist; some carriers are represented by in-company lawyers; and a relatively few carriers are represented by outside legal counsel. Of the four trunk lines studied closely, two were represented by personnel specialists; one was represented by a lawyer in the airline's legal department who worked closely with the personnel department; and one was represented by outside legal counsel.

General System Board Procedures

ALPA and the managements of every airline at which it represents the pilot group have negotiated system board agreements. Generally the agreement is a separate document from the basic labor contract. The system board agreements, which contain essentially identical language, establish the procedures to be followed by the boards.

Under these procedures each year the four board members select a chairman and a vice chairman. If the chairman is an ALPA board member, the vice chairman will be a company member, and vice versa. The two positions alternate annually between the two parties.

In general, the costs incurred by each side are paid by that side, while joint costs are shared equally. An airline typically will offer free transportation over its routes to persons taking part in system board hearings, such as aggrieved pilots, pilot representatives, and witnesses in the airline's employ.

The jurisdiction of system boards is spelled out in two sections of the system board agreements. As shown below, in one paragraph the jurisdiction is limited to disputes arising under the terms of the pilot agreement and in the other paragraph it is limited to grievances or interpretations or applications of the pilot agreement. In practical terms, the jurisdiction of system boards is comparable to that generally found under labor contracts, with disputes as to jurisdiction settled by the arbitrator.

> In compliance with Section 204, Title II, of the Railway Labor Act, as amended, there is hereby established a system board of adjustment for the purpose of adjusting and deciding disputes which may arise under the terms of the pilot agreement.
>
> . . . . .
>
> The board shall have jurisdiction over disputes between any employee covered by the pilots' agreement and the company growing out of grievances or out of interpretation or application of any of the terms of the pilots' agreement. The jurisdiction of the board shall not extend to proposed changes in the hours of employment, rates of compensation or working conditions covered by existing agreements between the parties thereto.

Under ALPA procedures, the aggrieved pilot decides whether his grievance will be submitted to a system board. If the decision is in the affirmative, he sends to the ALPA Legal Department a complete record of the grievance, including the appeal and hearing decisions as well as a statement of his position on the case.[5]

The ALPA lawyer assigned to represent pilots at his airline will draft a letter of submission concerning the grievance to the system board, but, as previously mentioned, the President of ALPA or another ALPA official he designates will sign the letter.

The standard system board agreement calls for joint company and association submission of grievances, but joint submissions are rare because the parties generally disagree as to the facts or issues involved in grievances and because the persons drafting letters of submission may be hundreds of miles apart and therefore not conveniently located to work on a joint submission.

The standard language pertaining to the letter of submission reads in part as follows:

[5] ALPA, *Guide for Processing Grievances*, p. 5.

All disputes properly referred to the board for consideration shall be referred to the chairman. . . .

Each case submitted shall show:
1. Question or questions at issue.
2. Statements of facts.
3. Position of employee or employees.
4. Position of company.

When possible, joint submission should be made, but if the parties are unable to agree upon a joint submission then either party may submit the dispute and its position to the board. No matter shall be considered by the board which has not first been handled in accordance with the appeals provision of the pilot's agreement, including the rendering of a decision thereon by the chief operating officer of the company.

Four-man system boards usually meet at regularly scheduled times twice a year to consider any grievances which have been submitted. If two board members request a special meeting to consider a grievance they consider urgent, however, the chairman must convene the system board within the ensuing 15 days.

System board hearings are more formal than hearings of the earlier steps of the grievance procedure but not as formal, for example, as a court of law. Grievances are presented and argued by ALPA lawyers and company representatives. All the facts of the case and new facts may be brought out. A verbatim transcript is usually taken. Both sides may call witnesses who may give oral or written testimony.Witnesses are cross-examined. Fairly relaxed rules of evidence are applied. Usually if a question arises as to the admissibility of certain evidence, the board will hear the evidence and consider its admissibility before rendering a decision. If a serious question of admissibility arises, the four-man board may send the case directly to the five-man board level for the arbitrator to decide the question.

The great majority of the people connected with the system board procedures find them satisfactory. Some of these people, however, particularly some who have had experience with the more formal procedures used in the comparable railroad board hearings, voice at least the following complaints. They believe that by permitting all facts of a grievance to be brought out at the system board level, regardless of whether they had been presented during

the initial grievance steps, the airline procedure results in grievances arriving at the system board level without the facts of the
case clearly understood. They believe that the airline procedure
counts too heavily on oral testimony which they believe to be both
of uncertain validity and too lengthy. And as a corollary point, they
believe that the rules of evidence are too relaxed under the airline
procedure.

A majority of the four-man system board is competent to make
a decision. Board decisions are final and binding upon the parties.

A four-man system board can take four types of actions in regard to a grievance: allow, modify, deny, or deadlock. The actual
decisions tend to be short. ALPA advises its system board members
to have their boards issue decisions as short as "grievance allowed" or "grievance denied" and to avoid giving accompanying
opinions which it believes lead to endless argument, to questioning
the board's ability, and to doubt as to the validity of the decision.
According to the company system board members at one airline,
the decisions of their board have at least been complete enough
so that a person reading one of them can learn what happened.

The system board agreements at all but four airlines contain
language to the effect that if the four-man board deadlocks on a
grievance and cannot agree on a procedure to break the deadlock,
either side may petition the National Mediation Board to appoint
a neutral to augment the board and to decide the case. At four
trunk lines the system board agreements are "open-ended" in that
they do not provide a procedure to break a deadlock at the four-
man level if the parties fail to agree on a procedure to break it. The
purpose was to avoid having an outsider rule on the proficiency
of pilots. According to some company system board members, this
difference in language makes no difference in practice because the
four-man boards at the four carriers regularly agree to obtain an
arbitrator to decide deadlocked cases.

The Proportion of Cases Resolved at the Four-Man Level

During the years 1956–1962 the four-man system boards were
resolving roughly between one-half and three-quarters of the grievances submitted to them. Figures of this order were estimated by
both airline and ALPA officials. For example, a vice president—
personnel for a major carrier estimated that about five or six cases

out of ten were resolved by the pilot system board. An ALPA official and some company board members estimated that the figure was about two-thirds resolved by the four-man boards.

According to ALPA data, as presented in Table 9.6, during the years 1956–1962 pilot system boards throughout the industry were resolving between 67.5% and 74.4% of the grievances submitted to them. Table 9.6 also indicates that for the two-year period ending September 30, 1956, the four-man boards were resolving 95.0% of the grievances submitted to them. This would indicate that the efficiency of the four-man level dropped markedly about 1957.

Similar data and information about individual four-man system boards revealed that they vary in their ability to resolve grievances and that a trend is in evidence in the direction of a lower proportion of grievances being resolved at the four-man level. At one extreme, a carrier reported that its pilot four-man system board had reached the point at which it was resolving no grievances. Data pertaining to another trunkline's system board indicated, as shown in Table 9.7, that from 1959 to 1962 the percentage of pilot grievances submitted to the four-man level which were resolved at that level dropped from 87.5% to 45.5%.

Several reasons were given for the decline. At the airline to which Table 9.7 pertains, a company official conjectured that because the 1959–1960 period followed a new agreement, it was a time when a number of trivial grievances were raised concerning that new agreement. Because they were trivial, they could be resolved at the four-man level. By mid-1961, this official believed hard core issues had arisen on which the four-man level could not agree.

At the carrier where the pilot system board was resolving no cases, the company and ALPA people gave the following reasons. Management reported that neither side was willing to give in on grievances; that both sides were holding back "ammunition" for the arbitrator, and thus were shifting their defenses between the four- and five-man levels; and that the pilots were taking all cases to arbitration, hoping for a 50–50 split. A pilot at this carrier who was active in ALPA affairs reported that pilot system boards were increasingly being given grievances to decide which did not conform to the type of grievances four-man boards were created to resolve. His point was that system boards had been created mainly to resolve

TABLE 9.6. NUMBERS AND PROPORTIONS OF GRIEVANCES REACHING THE
FOUR-MAN SYSTEM BOARD LEVEL WHICH WERE RESOLVED AT THE
FOUR- AND FIVE-MAN LEVELS: 1954–1962

Disposition of Grievances	11/1/54–10/30/56		11/1/56–10/30/58		11/1/58–10/30/60		10/30/60–3/15/62	
	No. of Grievances	Per Cent	No. of Grievances	Per Cent	No. of Grievances	Per Cent	No. of Grievances	Per Cent
Grievances reaching the four-man level	121	100%	206	100%	199	100%	86	100%
Cases resolved at the four-man level	115	95.0	139	67.5	147	73.9	64	74.4
Cases resolved at the five-man level	6	5.0	67	32.5	52	26.1	22	25.6

SOURCE: ALPA records.

TABLE 9.7. THE EXPERIENCE OF ONE DOMESTIC TRUNK LINE IN RESOLVING
GRIEVANCES AT THE FOUR- AND FIVE-MAN LEVELS: 1959–1962

Disposition of Grievances	1959 No.	1959 Per Cent	1960 No.	1960 Per Cent	1961 No.	1961 Per Cent	1962 No.	1962 Per Cent
Grievances reaching the four-man level	16	100%	20	100%	6	100%	22	100%
Cases resolved at the four-man level	14	87.5	14	70.0	3	50	10	45.5
Cases resolved at the five-man level	2	12.5	6	30.0	3	50	12	54.5

SOURCE: Records of a domestic trunk line.

discipline and discharge cases, many of which involved a question of a pilot's proficiency. He said that in recent years more and more grievances involved questions of management's judgment in operating the airline, particularly in the scheduling area. He believed that the four-man board could not be expected to resolve many grievances of the latter type. This line of reasoning coincides with that of one industry spokesman who reported that four-man boards will frequently be able to resolve grievances involving pilot proficiency where it is clear a pilot has failed to measure up to flight standards. He reported that in such cases the pilot system board member will frequently join with the company members in advising a pilot to resign quietly in order to enhance his chances of getting a job elsewhere. Of course, essentially all discipline cases will be carried to arbitration when a pilot's proficiency is not clearly below standards or when the pilots believe the company is being arbitrary.

The Five-Man System Board of Adjustment

Once the four-man board deadlocks on a grievance, the members in general utilize one of the following methods of obtaining a neutral: (1) they may have listed a few arbitrators by name in their system board agreement and will call in one of them; (2) they may agree to call in a mutually acceptable arbitrator on an *ad hoc* basis; or (3) either side or both sides may petition the National Mediation Board to select an arbitrator for them again on an *ad hoc* basis. The NMB maintains a list of suitable arbitrators and makes appointments from it. The NMB made the following numbers of such appointments in recent years: 12 in 1958; 13 in 1959; 7 in 1960; 9 in 1961; 18 in 1962; and 19 in 1963. Unlike the railroad grievance procedures under which the costs of arbitration are borne by the government, such costs are divided equally between the two parties.

When the board members are selecting an *ad hoc* arbitrator, the ALPA board members are advised to contact the ALPA home office, which maintains a list of acceptable arbitrators. They are advised never to agree to an arbitrator until the association has had an opportunity to investigate and to consent to his selection.[6]

Once he is selected, the arbitrator normally decides whether he will decide the grievance in conjunction with the four board

[6] ALPA, "Guide for System Board Members," pp. 6–7.

members based on the transcript of the four-man level and the other material concerning the grievance, or whether he desires to have a hearing at which the facts will be brought out anew. More often than not, arbitrators in this situation desire the hearing.

The nature of these hearings varies among arbitrators. Some run fairly formal hearings and adhere closely to rules of evidence; others do not. Grievances are argued for each party by the same individuals who argued them at the four-man level.

After the hearing, the arbitrator may or may not meet in executive session with the other board members. Later, the parties may or may not file post-hearing briefs.

Typically, the arbitrator will hear a case, return to his office, and, after some period of time, make his decision. Then, the board members whose side it favors will join him to form a three-man majority. All decisions must be by majority and if an arbitrator were unable to reach a decision on which he could get a majority, he would be replaced on that case.

Occasionally a grievance will occur which both parties believe requires an immediate decision. They will ask an arbitrator to hear the grievance and to render an oral decision within 24 hours.

The grievance procedures used by the airlines and their pilot groups have handled the grievances as they have arisen and have not developed large backlogs of unresolved cases. As shown in Table 9.1, the backlog of such cases for the entire pilot group has been holding steady over the last several years at about 310 to 323.

The same type of pattern exists at each of the airlines studied. For example, at a major trunkline, the backlog of grievances as of the end of the years 1959 through 1962 and as of November 30, 1963, ranged from 5 to 16 and averaged 10.2. The managements of two other trunklines expressed concern that the backlog of unresolved pilot grievances awaiting system board action had reached about 12. In other words, a problem involving a backlog of pilot grievances or of the pilot grievance procedure becoming bogged down simply has not existed.

A BROADER PERSPECTIVE

In actual practice, the processing of grievances is only one aspect of an interconnected chain of activities which includes as well the negotiation, interpretation, and administration of a labor agreement. Therefore, in order to present a more complete picture of the processing of pilot grievances, it is necessary to describe how an airline management combines the four types of activities in this chain. The following paragraphs describe how these activities are handled at a major domestic trunkline. Particularly in the area of contract administration this description is representative of the best kinds of practice found in this study.

At the carrier in question the departments primarily concerned with this chain of activities were the personnel and flight departments. Although the management had found it almost impossible to draw sharp lines of responsibility between these two departments for some of these activities, to the extent that it was possible the personnel department was responsible for the negotiation and interpretation of the pilot agreement and the system board steps of the grievance procedure, while the flight department was responsible for administering the pilot agreement and the first two steps of the grievance procedure.

In order to understand how the responsibility for these activities was divided, at least parts of the organizations of these departments must be understood. An abbreviated organization chart presenting such information is given in Exhibit 9.1.

During contract negotiations with the pilots, for example, the company is represented by a bargaining team made up of personnel and flight executives. The vice president—personnel and the vice president—flight attend and participate in sessions when important issues are under discussion. Such an issue has been the crew complement situation. In routine negotiations involving simple changes in wages, rules, and working conditions, a flight official under the vice president—flight is designated to represent the latter on the negotiating committee.

Turning to contract administration, once a recent contract had been negotiated, the personnel department retained the ultimate responsibility for interpreting it. In practice, however, the director of labor relations—flight and the manager of flight administration discussed questions of interpretation and made joint decisions on them.

The flight department was responsible for administering the pilot agreement. Specifically, the bulk of the administration workload

EXHIBIT 9.1. ABBREVIATED ORGANIZATION CHART SHOWING THOSE PRIMARILY
RESPONSIBLE FOR ADMINISTERING THE PILOT AGREEMENT

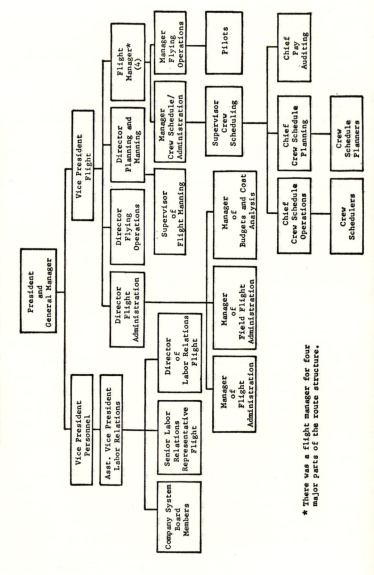

* There was a flight manager for four
major parts of the route structure.

devolved on the director—flight administration and his three assistants and the scheduling group at four major domiciles. Each of these scheduling groups was under the direction of a manager crew schedule—administration. In addition, the director—planning and manning, under whose direction flying time and flight sequences were assigned among the airline's ten domiciles, carried some of the burden of contract administration. One company official estimated that 95% of contract administration in regard to the pilots devolved on the scheduling people at the four major domiciles. Another executive estimated that pilot contract administration divided as follows: 70% to the director—flight administration, 20% to the director—planning and manning, and 10% to the director—flying operations. This latter estimate probably considered the crew scheduling operations at the bases as coming under the authority of the director—flight administration, although they each formally reported to a flight manager. The organizational relationship between these scheduling operations and the director—flight administration was described as "a heavy dotted line."

The handling of pilot grievances also showed the merging of responsibilities between the flight and personnel departments. If a purely local grievance arose that did not involve an interpretation of the contract, it would be heard at the first step by the flight manager and at the second step by the vice president—flight without personnel being told about it. If, however, the grievance involved more than one domicile or called for an interpretation of the contract, the flight manager would contact the director of labor relations—flight directly or the manager of flight administration who would in turn contact the director of labor relations—flight. As previously indicated, on matters of interpretation these two men would make joint decisions, although the ultimate authority rested with personnel.

Once a grievance reached the four-man system board level, it became the responsibility of the personnel department. Pilot grievances were generally presented to the system board by the senior labor relations representative—flight. At this carrier the two company system board members were assigned to all seven of the airline's system boards on a full-time basis. They reported to the assistant vice president—labor relations.

With so many people involved in contract negotiation, interpretation, and administration as well as in grievance handling, having the pilot contract administered in a fair and consistent manner without being undermined day-by-day was a formidable task. This task was made more difficult by a number of factors related to the nature of the job and the characteristics of pilots. As to the job, the operations of an airline are spread over as many cities as its routes cover and more. The pilots who fly between these cities have a work place that actually moves, unlike the work places of most workers. In addition, operating an airline involves continual changes in schedules as mechanical problems develop, traffic is encountered en route, and weather affects flights. The requirements of safety are unusually demanding. In addition, pilots are in absolute command of their work places and out of immediate contact with supervision. As to the pilots themselves, they are in general vitally concerned with their working conditions and as a group unusually knowledgeable concerning the rules and regulations, both governmental and contractual, which affect their working conditions.

The principal contact between pilots and airlines comes in the crew scheduling area where most of the pilot working conditions are determined and where the pilot contract is most intensively administered on a day-by-day basis. At this point of contact airlines are represented by staff personnel well down the management hierarchy who are devoid of the authority usually awarded, for example, to foremen. All these factors combine to make proper contract administration and the activities related to it difficult to achieve.

For at least eight years the management of the carrier in question had been working to develop a positive, aggressive program of contract administration. As it has evolved, the primary elements of this program consist of determining right after a pilot contract is negotiated exactly what it contains and how it is to be interpreted, disseminating that information quickly to interested company officials and to the entire pilot group, developing cooperation among all the company officials who administer and interpret the contract, and in a real sense developing cooperation between the management and the pilots.

Working out what the new contract means and how it is to be interpreted is done jointly with the pilot representatives. As a first step, the parties have tried to write clear contract language. As a second step, they agreed in negotiating their latest agreement that the various changes it embodied would be implemented slowly and carefully in eleven steps over a nine-month period.

The most important technique used both to work out exactly what the new contract entails and to disseminate that information is the use of so-called "road shows." They involve tours of the domiciles made by a joint team on which the pilots are represented by their negotiators and the company is represented by the assistant vice president—labor relations, the director of labor relations—flight, and the director—flight administration. At each domicile the members of this joint team make a several-hour presentation of the contents of the new contract to the company officials who will be administering it and to all pilots wishing to attend. During the presentations the members of the joint team sharpshoot each other concerning the exact meaning and intent of the contract and they accept all questions from the floor. Questions to which the answers are clear are answered on the spot. Answers to some of the more complex questions are published shortly after the completion of the tour of the domiciles, after answers have been worked out jointly. Thus, about two months after the latest contract had been signed, the assistant vice president-labor relations published the answers to 53 questions which had been considered too complex to answer orally during the tour.

The management of this airline has found these tours so valuable in developing detailed agreement and in getting information out to the field that they in effect ran two road shows regarding the latest pilot agreement. Within a week after it was signed, a joint team had made presentations at the four major domiciles to the company's flight administration personnel. For these discussions a mimeographed version of the new contract was used. During the ensuing few weeks the joint team then made its presentation at every pilot domicile to interested pilots and company officials. For these meetings the personnel department, which carries the primary responsibility for disseminating the terms of the new contract, had expedited the publication of the contract in booklet form.

Once the tours are over, the parties spend several weeks evaluating the operation of the new contract. When particularly thorny problems arise, the director—flight administration and the director of labor relations—flight will arrange for an all-day session with representatives of the pilots to thrash the problem out. Thus, eight months after the latest contract had been signed they were scheduling such a session to work out in detail how the new duty-time rigs were to be applied.

As a further step to improve contract administration, the flight administration staff had been writing, revising, and expanding a Crew Schedule Manual which explained in detail, for example, under what conditions pilots would accrue flight time credit, how much credit, and what the proper entries were on the payroll forms. By 1964 the Crew Schedule Manual contained 316 pages.

All these techniques had brought about some positive results, but they had not turned contract administration into an exact science, eliminated all disputes, or insured that the pilot contract would not be undermined somewhat in its daily administration. As to the positive results, the director—flight administration stated that achieving wide understanding of the contract had reduced the number of pilot pay claims "because facts win out." Although many factors in addition to improved contract administration were involved, during 1963 the number of grievances submitted to the pilot system board was less than one-third of what it had been in previous years. An important positive aspect of this situation was the development of an expert concerning the pilot contract in both the personnel and the flight departments and the line/staff cooperation between them. The manager of flight administration and the director of labor relations—flight, who himself had formerly been in flight administration, together knew what the contract contained as well as what it did not contain. They also knew the intent of the company during the negotiations leading to the contract. Thus they were able to judge whether a pilot grievance was valid or not. If a grievance lacked merit, they so informed the pilot. Similarly, where the company had erred in administering the contract, they advised that the aggrieved pilot be "made whole."

That improved contract administration does not solve all problems regarding the integrity of pilot contract results from the far-flung and fluid nature of airline operations and from the large number of people who are involved in its administration. Some extra-contract practices arise out of a sincere concern for safety. For example, the manning people place self-imposed restrictions on the frequency with which pilots are scheduled to be shifted back and forth between day and night flying or on the conditions under which flight crews are assigned long overnight flights which take them through several time zones because of the difficulty of getting a meaningful rest under those circumstances.

On balance, it may be said that the work of this airline in improving contract administration has placed its management more on top of the situation than it formerly was. Fewer extra-contractual practices are likely to arise because more management personnel know what the contract contains. Whether a situation calls for a cooperative arrangement to be made with the pilots to keep the airline operating or whether an issue has been raised on which management should stand on principle, at least management is more aware than it was formerly of exactly what it is doing.

NEGOTIATIONS AND GRIEVANCE PROCESSING

The amounts of emphasis parties place on the negotiating of grievances and the filing and processing of grievances are presumably interrelated. Parties can tend to negotiate out their differences more or less as they arise or they can tend to stand by their labor agreements and increase their activities in the grievance area. These are proclivities, not a complete emphasis on one to the exclusion of the other.

Indications are that the airline managements and the pilots tend to emphasize the negotiation of agreements and to de-emphasize the filing and processing of grievances. As was pointed out at the beginning of this chapter, all pilots have been filing first-step grievances in recent years at a rate of about 280 per year (see Table 9.2). A remarkable fact is that during the same period the airline parties have been negotiating agreements and amendments of all types at a rate of about 160 per year! Thus, for every two first-step grievances pilots file, they negotiate at least one new document. The numbers of documents the parties have negotiated during different periods since the founding of ALPA are presented in Table 9.8. As an example of what type of documents are included in these totals, the 1961 figure of 113 comprised 13 renewal agreements, 15 supplementary agreements, 25 miscellaneous letters, 31 letters of agreement, 8 letters of understanding, 9 miscellaneous amendments, 7 amendments to pension plans, 2 amendments to system board agreements, and 1 definitive fixed benefit pension plan.

It appears as though the principal reason that pilots file relatively few grievances is that most of their disputes (other than individual claims involving flight time, pay, or discipline) are handled through the negotating process rather than through the grievance procedure. Airline officials support this notion. They state that only rarely are

TABLE 9.8.   DOCUMENTS OF ALL KINDS NEGOTIATED
BY ALPA: PRE-1940–1963

Time Period	No. of Documents	Time Period	No. of Documents
Prior to 11/29/40	16	11/10/54–11/5/56	214
11/30/40–12/1/42	31	1957	118
12/2/42–12/4/44	38	1958	139
12/5/44–2/18/47	51	1959	168
2/19/47–11/9/48	57	1960	173
11/10/48–10/1/50	75	1961	113
10/2/50–10/20/52	130	1962	212
10/21/52–11/9/54	148	1963	153

SOURCE: ALPA, *The Airline Pilot,* February 1957, p. 13 for 11/30/40–11/5/56; *ALPA News Bulletin,* January 29, 1962, for 1957–1961; *ALPA News Bulletin,* January 14, 1963, for 1962; and *ALPA News Bulletin,* February 10, 1964, for 1963.

important matters tested in the grievance procedure. Such an exception at one carrier was the question of whether the management could make retirement at age 60 mandatory, and even that question was in the end decided by government regulation, not through the grievance procedure.

The organization and policies of ALPA also tend to support the idea of an emphasis on negotiations. By ALPA policy labor agreements cannot be for a duration longer than 18 months. This means that in addition to frequent supplementary agreements on a variety of matters the basic contract is continually being rewritten. Also negotiations usually last several months. To handle the negotiating workload ALPA maintains a staff of about 11 negotiators, all but 2 of whom spend full time on negotiations. In contrast ALPA has a staff of about six lawyers to handle grievance cases along with a number of other important and time-consuming duties.

The converse to frequent negotiations keeping down the number of pilot grievances is apparently also in evidence. At two airlines where the volume of grievances had increased markedly, the company officials stated that the primary reason was that the parties had been unable to reach a new agreement for months after the former one had been due to expire, and therefore pilots were filing more grievances because the old contract did not cover new working conditions which had not existed or been anticipated when it was written.

By ALPA policy, when a question arises under a pilot agreement concerning the intent of the parties, the ALPA negotiators have the responsibility for answering it. This is a responsibility they are loath to perform because it may cause them to testify before a system board of adjustment in opposition to a company negotiator. The ALPA negotiators believe such confrontations adversely affect future negotiations. They much prefer not to testify and to accept whatever ruling an arbitrator renders as to apparent intent, then resolve the problem in the next set of negotiations.

Summary Comments

Basically, having grievances resolved on a carrier-by-carrier basis is sound because it conforms to the way pilot labor agreements are negotiated. In this situation system boards of adjustment appear to be better suited to the job than would be a National Air Transport Adjustment Board.

Pilots place more emphasis on the negotiating of agreements than on the filing of grievances. As a result the pilot grievance procedures are not overly burdened and can handle grievances as they arise. The available data indicate that a great majority of all pilot grievances are resolved in the early grievances steps, a significant but declining proportion are resolved by the four-man boards, and relatively few are left for arbitration. Thus it would appear that in the area of grievance handling the airlines and the pilots, working within the confines of the Railway Labor Act, have devised workable procedures for the prompt and just elimination of grievances.

CHAPTER 10

An Analysis of Bargaining Power and Its Ramifications

THIS CHAPTER is divided into four parts as follows: (1) an analysis of the bargaining power of ALPA and the domestic airlines;[1] (2) a hypothesis as to the relative bargaining power of the parties; (3) a review of the material in the earlier chapters for signs of an imbalance of bargaining power; and (4) some concluding observations regarding the imbalance of bargaining power and its ramifications.

ANALYSIS OF THE BALANCE OF POWER

Analyzing bargaining power is not an exact science. Even a simple assessment of the strength of the parties requires consideration of a number of factors which do not lend themselves to quantitative analysis. It is not enough to say that some condition or variable may affect bargaining power. One must then decide which of the bargaining parties it aids, and how much. Each step in the analysis is open to question and more than one interpretation. These difficulties, however, should not preclude an attempt to analyze bargaining power. It is an important concept. Even a very tentative conclusion that one bargaining team possesses a relative power advantage is worth drawing because it may explain many of the things that are transpiring in an industrial relations system. If it does seem to explain some of what is going on, perhaps the conclusion itself can be preferred less tentatively.

In analyzing bargaining power one may take at least two approaches, which complement one another. First, one can ask what

[1] Brief mention will be made of the bargaining power of FEIA in the third section of this chapter in regard to the work assignment area.

institutional factors tend to give or to remove bargaining power from a bargaining group. For example, if a union has totally organized a highly skilled group whose services are essential and not easily replaceable in the short run and if the union bargains against one company at a time rather than against the industry, one would say that these institutional factors tend to give bargaining power to the union. Second, one can state a more or less formal definition of bargaining power and analyze a particular industrial relations system in relation to such definition. In this chapter a mixture of both approaches will be used. The choice of institutional factors will be this author's; the definition of bargaining power will be Professor Neil W. Chamberlain's.[2]

Chamberlain states a useful definition of bargaining power as follows: ". . . we may define bargaining power (of A, let us say) as being the cost to B of *disagreeing* on A's terms relative to the cost of *agreeing* on A's terms." Translating this definition into the airline situation, one can say that if agreeing with ALPA's terms would not cost an airline very much, ALPA's bargaining power (its ability to get what it wanted) would be stronger than if its terms would cost an airline dearly. One can say also that if disagreeing with ALPA's demands (and causing a pilot strike) would be very costly for an airline, ALPA's bargaining power would be greater than if disagreeing would not be very costly to the airline.

In order to state whether one party has more or less bargaining power than a party with which it is bargaining, one must consider their relative bargaining powers. Thus in Chamberlain's terms, ". . . if the cost to B of disagreeing on A's terms is greater than the cost of agreeing on A's terms, while the cost to A of disagreeing on B's terms is less than the cost of agreeing on B's terms, then A's bargaining power is greater than that of B."[3]

At first glance, Chamberlain would appear to be stating that if a union asked for a penny its bargaining power would be greater than

[2] Neil W. Chamberlain, *Collective Bargaining* (New York: McGraw-Hill Book Company, 1951), pp. 220–221. For an excellent discussion of the impacts of institutional factors on bargaining power, see E. Robert Livernash, "The Relation of Power to the Structure and Process of Collective Bargaining," *The Journal of Law and Economics,* Vol. VI, October 1963, pp. 18–24.

[3] Chamberlain, *op. cit.* p. 221.

if it asked for a quarter. Such would not necessarily be the case, however, because the union members might not be willing to strike for a penny while they might be willing to strike for some time with the prospect of winning a quarter. In other words, from the company's viewpoint if the union's demand is a quarter, making the cost of agreement relatively high, the cost of disagreement (a strike of some duration and its consequences) also tends to be high. From the company's viewpoint, if the union's demand is a penny, making the cost of agreement relatively low, the cost of disagreement (no strike, but perhaps some ill will) also tends to be low. Similar statements apply from the union's viewpoint. Thus, Chamberlain's definition relates to the relative cost of agreement and disagreement for each party, and such costs vary as the terms of each party vary.

There seem to be six institutional factors which are particularly important regarding the bargaining power of the pilots' association and the airlines. They are:

(a) The People Involved
(b) The Economic Considerations
(c) The Effect of Bargaining Carrier-by-Carrier
(d) The Short-Run Force of Public Opinion
(e) The Effect of Mutual Aid Agreements
(f) The Desire for a "Good" Relationship

In the following analysis they will be analyzed as institutional factors affecting bargaining power and they will be related to Chamberlain's definition.

The People Involved

To some degree, the industrial relations work of each of the airlines studied was influenced by members of management who were pilots. This influence most often came from pilots filling any one, or all, of the following management positions: the presidency, supervisory positions in the operations department, or members of the negotiating team which bargained with the pilots. For example, of the five airlines originally studied, four had pilots as presidents. Most of the supervisory positions in the operations department of each airline are filled by pilots, as the pilot group is a natural source of informed talent for such positions. Of the airlines studied, three have pilots on the negotiating team, and all the teams seek advice from pilots somewhere in the management hierarchy.

The wide prevalence of pilots in supervisory positions is certainly not surprising, nor does their presence immediately lead to any conclusion concerning the bargaining power of the airlines when they negotiate with the pilot group. It could be argued that their presence gives management an advantage because they provide the management team with valuable information about the details of a pilot's work and about the thinking of the pilot group. It could be argued equally that the presence of members of the same highly skilled and proud profession on both sides of the bargaining table gives the Air Line Pilots Association an advantage simply because both teams may be more concerned with advancing the profession than with protecting the interests of the stockholders. Before either conclusion can be drawn, a more thorough analysis must be made.

There are two very interesting aspects of this situation. One is the frequency with which a significant number of pilots move back and forth between flying the line as one of the pilots, and flying or working in some supervisory position. The other point is that pilots do not lose their places on the pilot seniority list when they move into a supervisory job. They not only continue to accrue seniority but they also remain members in good standing of ALPA, merely shifting their membership from an "active" status to an "executive inactive" status.

These facts lead to interesting industrial relations situations. For example, at one small trunk line a review of the pilot seniority list revealed that there were 18 pilots included in a total of 321 who, at the time of the review or formerly, were or had been members of management. The first figure did not include any check pilots whose inclusion would probably have added another 20 names to the list of pilots who had served in a supervisory capacity. Of the 18 pilots, 12 were at the time of the review holding down supervisory jobs, as follows: the manager of operations, the chief pilot, three assistant chief pilots, the director of training, and six flight instructors. Of the remaining six pilots, two had been general managers of operations for the company, and a third was the vice president of operations for more than ten years. One of these general managers led the company's negotiating team in 1947 and signed the contract for the company. Shortly thereafter he was replaced, and during most of the ensuing years he has been the chairman of the ALPA Master Executive Council at this airline. As such, he has led almost every succeeding ALPA bargaining team. The pilot who was the vice president of operations for so many years led all the company bargaining teams during that period. Then he was replaced as vice president and is back flying the line as one of the most senior pilots.

This carrier does not represent an extreme in this regard. Throughout the industry a good deal of movement by pilots in and out of supervisory positions is the norm.

Another factor that should be considered in this analysis of the people involved is the direct tie between pilot pay and the pay of some supervisory pilots. When they are filling supervisory positions, pilots are paid more than they could earn with their seniority and qualifications if they were flying the line. They have to be paid at least this much in order for most of them to be interested in accepting supervisory positions. This means that when the pilot group negotiates higher wage rates, the pay of supervisory pilots is increased. It is not unusual for these supervisory pilots to be on the company negotiating team which grants the wage increase, and it is common for these supervisory pilots to be consulted on proposed work rule changes.

During the last two decades a shift has occurred in the make-up of bargaining teams for the airlines. In the past negotiations were typically carried on between the pilot group and the airline president, or at least the vice president of operations. Since that time the trend has been toward the development of industrial relations staffs at many airlines. As a result the bargaining teams have more and more technically trained industrial relations experts. These men may be lawyers, accountants, experienced negotiators, or industrial engineers.

The development of industrial relations staffs has not proceeded evenly throughout the industry. In most cases, the men who handle the entire area of personnel include industrial relations among their many duties. Some of the largest carriers have distinct industrial relations staffs headed by a vice president or assistant vice president who report to a senior vice president of personnel or vice president of personnel, respectively. Where the industrial relations function was headed by a vice president, his staff consisted of five men including himself. In the case of one staff of this size, all the men were lawyers and two were former military pilots. A similar staff consisted of five men none of whom were pilots and only one of whom was a lawyer. For the most part, they were all men with industrial relations backgrounds in other industries.

Except for the few very large airlines, the industrial relations function is typically carried on by the two men who form the personnel department. For example, both the local service line and the small trunk line studied had a vice president of personnel and one assistant.

The arrival of these industrial relations specialists throughout the industry has affected the negotiations with the pilots. In the first place, the presence of lawyers may tend to lead to more documentation and more legalism. Where the industrial relations staff is large enough, the negotiations may be based on a more thorough investigation of the facts. Industrial engineers may have detailed information concerning work loads, cost accountants may have careful cost analyses of company and union proposals, and professional negotiators may conduct the direct negotiations in such a way that they will be in a strong position in the later steps of the Railway Labor Act procedure. Perhaps the most important effect of the technically trained staff has been the buffer it throws up between the pilots and the president of the airline. Immediately, the company bargaining shifts to a contingent basis in which the actual negotiators are unable to reach an agreement without checking with the top administration of the company. This has the beneficial effect for the company in that it gains time to study any proposed changes carefully under the pretext of checking with the top executives. The buffer has also been a considerable irritant to the pilots who were accustomed to negotiating directly with the top man.

This discussion leads directly to the central questions concerning the effect which the people involved in the management hierarchy have on the bargaining power of the company. To what extent are company negotiators dominated by the president and the operations department? To what extent is the company's bargaining power weakened because the president and the operations department officials are usually pilots, and thus share an esteemed profession with the men with whom their company is negotiating?

Pilot thinking influences negotiations to a remarkable degree. For example, at a local service line the president was a young man and former pilot. He was particularly interested in the matter of scheduling and was reported to be very sympathetic when the pilot negotiators described monthly lines of flying which represented relatively poor working conditions. This control by a pilot president occurred in spite of the fact that the head of the operations department was not permitted to negotiate with the pilot group. This particular local service line adopted a policy to the effect that the individual who directly supervised a department might not take part in the negotiations with a union which represented employees in that department. Thus, the vice president of maintenance would not negotiate with the mechanics, nor would the vice president of operations negotiate with the pilots. In each case, however, the company would have a representative of the pertinent department in the negotiations. Ostensibly, the purpose of this policy was to eliminate just the type of influence we have been discussing. When a pilot president made the final decisions concerning concessions to the pilot group, however, and he happened to be very sympathetic with their professional problems, the pilot influence did not appear to have been eliminated. This seemed true in spite of the fact that the vice president of personnel led the formal negotiating team *vis-à-vis* the pilots.

The occurrence of pilot domination was even more marked at one trunk line. The bargaining team for the carrier consisted of five members, three of whom were pilot members of the operations department, and two of whom were the carrier's two personnel department officials. The team was led by the vice president of operations, while the personnel staff men only served in an advisory capacity. Both the personnel staff members testified to the complete domination of negotiations by the pilots in the operations department. One of them resigned from the company, in part because he could make no headway against the pilot control over his department. To make the situation more one-sided, this was the carrier in which two former general managers and a long-time vice president of operations are now back flying the line as pilots.

Pilot domination at the major carriers has become less clear-cut during the last several years with the development of large industrial relations staffs. In some instances the staff members are former pilots. For example, until recently the vice president—personnel of a major carrier had previously been the head of the operations department. At another major carrier the head of the industrial relations staff was a former nonairline pilot and he was in the process of renewing his private license at the time of the field research. Most importantly, pilot domination at the major airlines comes through the use of top pilot members of the operations departments to lead, staff, or advise concerning the collective bargaining between the carriers and ALPA.

When one asks management officials in the industry directly about the pilot influence on negotiations, one receives two types of replies. The most frequent answer is that there is no influence because supervisory pilots are honest men who do a conscientious job in protecting their company's interest. Less frequently, an official will say that the pilot influence is definitely a factor which weakens management's bargaining position. While allowing that supervisory pilots may be consciously trying to do a good job for their carriers, these officials feel that subconsciously, at least, supervisory pilots are concerned about their profession. One top industrial relations official said that with the occasional exception of a former line pilot who, when he becomes a management official, leans over backwards to be tough on the pilots, the general idea of pilot domination of company/ALPA negotiations is valid.

Before one should reach a conclusion about the effect of the people involved on the balance of power at the bargaining table, one should consider the people on the other side.

A typical bargaining team for the Air Line Pilots Association is made up of from three to five members employed by the carrier in question, and a professional, nonpilot negotiator from the ALPA home office employment agreement division. The professional negotiator is generally not a lawyer, although his knowledge of pilot contracts and Railway Labor Act procedures is thorough.

The ALPA bargaining team has complete authority to reach a final agreement. It includes first pilots, copilots, and, where applicable, a pilot-engineer, who have either been elected by the membership at that airline or have been appointed by the Master Executive Council. Although there is no rule that the three groups must be represented on the bargaining team, they normally are all included because the men in each category are sensitive about their representation and are quick to complain that a new contract favors the other two categories. In recent years the bargaining teams have included more and more of the less senior members of the association primarily for two reasons. They now outnumber the pre-World War II members. More importantly, they are the members with relatively poor wages and working conditions and are, therefore, the ones who are interested in pushing through changes during negotiations.

In contrast to the supervisory pilots, the members of the ALPA negotiating teams are not very likely to have divided loyalties. They have been elected to represent a group of their associates in the piloting profession. Concern on their part for the protection of the stockholders is minimal. As will be emphasized later, their concern is not increased by the availability to the company of government subsidy which would tend to keep it solvent regardless of the cost of any new labor contract.

Also, without belaboring the point, it should be stated that these pilots are members of a strong clique—bordering on an aristocracy. As a group, pilots represent excellence in most of the qualities an employer would seek in a skilled worker. Pilots know these facts and act accordingly. Finally, with the notable exception of the Allied Pilots' Association at American Airlines, the Air Line Pilots Association is firmly entrenched within the pilot group. It represents the pilots at virtually every commercial airline in the country and well over 90% of those eligible for membership have joined the Association. As a result of these factors, an analysis of the people involved on the pilots' side of the bargaining table reveals factors which represent bargaining strength.

Four aspects of this analysis of the people involved bear directly on Chamberlain's definition of bargaining power. The solidarity of pilots across the industry and within any given company puts them in a position to make the cost to a carrier of disagreeing with ALPA's terms relatively high. In addition, when company negotiators are pilots in the same profession as their adversaries at the bargaining table, the cost of disagreeing with the pilots' terms tends to be high on a personal basis. In the normal situation in which supervisory pilots move back and forth between flying as line pilots and filling supervisory roles and in which the pay of supervisory pilots is tied directly to the pay of line pilots, the cost of agreeing with ALPA's demands are not only low, but in fact the cost is negative. In other words, supervisory pilots benefit as line pilots benefit. Because the people involved tend to make the cost to the company's pilot negotiators of agreeing with ALPA's demands low and to make the cost to the company of disagreeing with ALPA's terms high, this factor tends to give relative bargaining power to ALPA.

Economic Factors

Several economic factors have a bearing on the relative bargaining power of the airlines and ALPA. These will be analyzed primarily from the viewpoint of an airline. First analyzed will be those economic factors which affect an airline's cost of disagreeing with ALPA's terms. Then those factors which affect a carrier's cost of agreeing with ALPA's terms will be discussed. Finally, some factors which affect ALPA's cost of disagreeing with an airline's terms will be mentioned.

An Airline's Cost of Disagreeing. From an airline's point of view, the costs of disagreeing with ALPA's terms are associated with the strike which would be expected to ensue. Of great importance, therefore, is the key role played by pilots in the operation of an airline. Without the service of the pilots an airline cannot operate. Because of the skilled nature of their job, the detailed governmental requirements they must continually meet, and the relative shortage of fully qualified pilots in the labor market, they are essentially irreplaceable in the short run in numbers sufficient to operate more than a small part of a major airline. Thus, pilots are basically in a position to make an airline's cost of disagreeing with their terms relatively high by closing it down.

The next question is how costly do airline strikes tend to be.

During strikes the ability of airlines to reduce operating expenses varies widely. As Table 10.1 shows, during ten airline strikes in

TABLE 10.1. DATA COMPARING ACTUAL TO NORMAL OPERATING
EXPENSES DURING TEN STRIKES: 1958–1961

Carrier	Date	Per Cent Operations Shut Down	No. of Days Strike Lasted	Actual Operating Expense as Per Cent of Normal Operating Expense
Capital	1958	100%	37	23.2%
TWA	1958	100	16	39.5
Eastern	1958	100	38	25.0
American	1958–9	100	22	51.5
Eastern	1960	67	12	84.4
Northwest	1960–1	33	137	71.4
American	1961	100	6	32.8
Eastern	1961	75	8	67.4
Pan American	1961	70	6	68.8
TWA	1961	100	7	56.3

SOURCE: CAB, Docket 9977, *Initial Decision of Hearing Examiner S. Thomas Simon,* p. 124.

the period 1958–1961 actual operating expenses as a percentage of normal operating expenses varied from 23.2% to 84.4%.

Although the actual operating expenses are not normally reduced below 25% of normal, evidence indicates that the cash drain on an airline is relatively low during a strike. For example, Table 10.2 shows the actual operating expenses of Eastern Air Lines during a strike period in which the company gradually started up operations. Thus, the actual expenses, particularly in the cash items, were higher than they could have been had a complete shutdown been continued. The important figure to note in Table 10.2 is the $11.2 million depreciation and amortization expense. Had the strike kept operations closed this noncash item probably would have remained the major portion of actual operating expenses.

Turning to the question of financial reserves, one gets a different perspective. Repeatedly throughout the years the airline industry has needed new funds with which to purchase new equipment. Periodically this need has made the airlines in a sense strapped for funds. It is not that they were insolvent, but that they had to plan their cash flows very closely in order to meet debt repayments, or to pay dividends when equity financing was involved. During those times the airlines would be anxious to avoid strikes. The loss of

TABLE 10.2.   EASTERN AIR LINES REVENUES AND EXPENSES
FROM JUNE 23 THROUGH SEPTEMBER 12, 1962, WHILE A
FLIGHT ENGINEER STRIKE WAS IN PROGRESS

(000)

Total Revenues		$ 8,800
Flying operations	$ 6,300	
Maintenance	3,500	
Passenger service	900	
Aircraft and traffic servicing	3,700	
Promotion and sales	3,100	
General and administrative	1,600	
Depreciation and amortization	11,200	
Total Operating Expenses		30,300
Net Nonoperating Income and Expense		1,900
Total Expenses		32,200
Loss		$23,400

SOURCE: CAB, Docket 9977, *Statement of Eastern Air Lines, Inc.,
with respect to 1962 Flight Engineer Strike*, Exhibit 63, p. 2.

revenue which a strike entails, coupled with the cash drain, however small, would be likely to force an airline to replan its needs
for new capital. A strike might force the postponement of new
aircraft purchases, or the seeking of additional funds. The tight
financial position of the air carriers when re-equipping makes
strikes very uncomfortable and thereby weakens the carriers' ability
to withstand them. It makes the cost to the airline of disagreeing
with ALPA's terms relatively high. At other times, such as the
mid-1960's, this factor is not so important.

Some interesting aspects of strikes in the airline industry weaken
management's bargaining position. As with service industries generally, the nature of an airline's product does not permit building
up inventories from which to sell during a strike. If an airline loses
business during a strike, it loses it forever. Very little, if any,
pent-up demand exists for travel after a strike. In fact, carriers
attest to severe strike aftermaths caused by deteriorating competitive positions in their markets, large added expenses in restoring

operations, and, not infrequently, disrupted transitional training schedules which delay the introduction of new equipment.[4]

A separate point is the loss of business an airline suffers from the mere threat of a strike. When a strike is threatened, a significant percentage of a carrier's potential passengers will make other travel arrangements in order to be certain their travel plans will not be cancelled. For example, Eastern reported losing $1.0 million in revenues during a week while under a strike threat from the FEIA in June 1962. Even the air shuttle where no reservations were required experienced a 20% reduction in traffic. Eastern reported that operating under a strike threat would result in a $300,000 to $400,000 loss per day.[5]

Losing business while under a strike is in direct contrast to the build-up of inventory by the customers of a manufacturing firm when a strike looms. In that sense a strike threat spurs their sales. For these reasons airlines are particularly vulnerable to union pressure in the forms of a strike or a strike threat. This analysis means that the cost to an airline of disagreeing with ALPA's terms tends to be relatively high.

Pilots are able to control the lengths of flights through countless decisions in the air, not the least of which is how fast to run the engines. Should the pilots at an airline make a concerted effort to lengthen flights at every possible opportunity, the ramifications to a carrier's costs would be very grave indeed.

Direct operating costs per flight hour[6] of several aircraft types are as follows:

DC-3	$139.10
CV-340	205.95
DC-6B	349.72
CV-880	893.28
707-120	822.92
DC-8	830.87

[4] CAB, Docket 9977, *Statement of Position of the Carrier Parties,* p. 15.
[5] CAB, Docket 9977, Eastern Exhibit 63, p. 23.
[6] FAA, "Direct Operating Costs and Other Performance Characteristics of Transport Aircraft in Airline Service: Calendar Year 1962," Table I.

For this analysis a rough estimate must be made of the costs which actually do vary directly with the length of each individual flight. Primarily those would be flight crew wages and fuel. They constitute about 40% of the above figures.[7] But using very conservative estimates the costs of a pilot slowdown would be serious. For example, suppose a major carrier had 700 flight crews with a monthly utilization of 60 flight hours each per month. Using those figures, the carrier would have 42,000 aircraft flight hours per month. If the pilots increased the time of all flights by as little as 5%, they would generate 2,100 additional flight hours. Then assuming that direct costs were as low as $200 per hour for the average of all the aircraft in the fleet, the additional 2,100 flight hours would cost $420,000 per month, or $5,040,000 per year. When one realizes that the largest total operating profit of any of the trunks for the 12 months ending September 30, 1964, was only $56,024,000, one can judge how important a pilot slowdown in this form could be.[8]

It must be emphasized immediately that, as a group, pilots take great pride in their jobs and almost nothing is more important to them than completing a flight on schedule. Therefore the thought of slowing down would be anathema to them. The threat of a slowdown, however, as an economic weapon cannot be dismissed entirely.

While the pilots would be unlikely to institute a concerted slowdown, another very effective economic weapon of this nature in which they have on occasion indulged is the refusal to take training on a new piece of equipment. This technique places the carrier at a great disadvantage because the pilots can continue to fly the old equipment while exerting pressure on the carrier to come to terms on the new equipment. By using either of these factors pilots could make the cost to an airline of disagreeing with ALPA's terms relatively high.

On balance, one can say that a number of economic factors tend to make the cost to an airline of disagreeing with ALPA's terms relatively high. Therefore they tend to give relative bargaining

[7] *Ibid.*, Table II.

[8] CAB, *Air Carrier Financial Statistics,* quarter ending September 30, 1964, Table 1.

power to ALPA. One economic factor which potentially could have the opposite effect will be discussed in a later section. It is the airlines' mutual aid pact under which a number of carriers have agreed to help financially any one of the participating carriers when it is struck under certain circumstances. In approving such an arrangement the CAB noted the vulnerability of the air carriers to strikes. The CAB majority stated:

> Air carriers are particularly vulnerable to strikes, and the industry has, in the recent past, been plagued by strikes. . . .[9]

An Airline's Cost of Agreeing. Of fundamental importance to the cost of an airline's agreeing with ALPA's terms have been the size and nature of the growth of the airline industry, which was described in Chapter 1. During the last three decades the airline industry has been expanding at the expense of such other forms of transportation as first class railroad passenger service. With demand for airline services relatively inelastic and with competition among airlines based more on service than on price, the airline managements could give wage increases, confident that increased costs, even if reflected in airline fares, would not hamper the industry's growth. Also, as will be detailed in the next section, the bargaining structure is such that ALPA bargains against individual airlines any one of which can be fairly certain that the concessions it makes to its pilots will be matched by each of its competitors. In fact, as was shown in Table 4.7 concerning the wage increases during the first round of jet negotiations, a carrier may expect its competitors to more than match any pattern it may set. The trucking industry in the post-World War II period experienced a similar type of growth. In such cases the costs to managements of agreeing to a union's demands are quite low, and thus the relative bargaining power of the union tends to be high.

Two other economic factors which bear on the cost to an airline of agreeing with ALPA's terms are the increased productivity of new, larger aircraft and the proportion which pilot pay is of total operating costs. As to the first point, while the purchase of new airplanes has periodically strapped the airlines for funds, their

[9] CAB, Docket 9977, *Opinion of the Board,* July 10, 1964, p. 4.

arrival on the property has introduced important reductions in unit costs. As shown in Table 10.3, in general, the direct operating costs per available seat-mile and per available ton-mile are lower the larger and faster the aircraft type. These savings in unit costs have been one reason why airlines have moved rapidly in purchasing new equipment. The other important reason, of course, has been the need to stay competitive in terms of aircraft speeds. The effect of these reductions on the bargaining power of the pilot group is apparent. They have been in the position of demanding a share of the productivity increases, while the carriers have been under pressure to yield, knowing that unit costs could probably be reduced if they could only get a settlement that would allow them to put the new equipment into operation.

TABLE 10.3. DIRECT OPERATING COSTS OF
DOMESTIC TRUNK LINE OPERATIONS: CALENDAR 1962

Aircraft Type	Direct Operating Cost per Available Seat-Mile (cents)	Direct Operating Cost per Available Ton-Mile (cents)
2-engine piston	2.61	22.07
4-engine piston	2.75	21.85
Turboprops	2.35	19.22
4-engine jet	1.64	12.15

SOURCE: FAA, "Direct Operating Costs and Other Performance Characteristics of Transport Aircraft in Airline Service: Calendar Year 1962," Table I.

As to the second point, data in Chapter 1 indicated that pilot payroll was 19.9% of total payroll which was in turn 43.4% of total operating revenue. Thus, pilot payroll was about 8.6% of total operating revenue.

Applying Chamberlain's definition, both the availability of lower unit costs and the relatively small proportion of total operating revenues represented by pilot pay tend to make the cost to an airline of agreeing with ALPA's terms low, and this tends to increase ALPA's relative bargaining power.

The Civil Aeronautics Board exerts an economic influence on

the bargaining parties, particularly in negotiations carried on by the local service lines. Its influence stems from its power to grant subsidies to the carriers. During the 12 months ending September 30, 1964, for example, all the local service lines received some subsidy from the federal government. For that 12-month period these lines received $66.7 million in federal subsidy.[10] The payments to individual local service lines ranged from $3.4 million to $8.0 million.

In determining the amount of subsidy to which a carrier is entitled, the Civil Aeronautics Board is required by law to ensure that such carrier is being run under "honest, efficient, and economical management." Presumably, a carrier is not entitled to a subsidy which may be required because its management is dishonest, inefficient, or uneconomical. Therefore if a carrier for some reason signed a labor agreement which diminished its efficiency, it would seem that the CAB would be required not to raise its subsidy to cover the inefficient use of manpower. Such is not the case. The CAB assumes that any labor agreement was negotiated by honest men who did the best job possible under the circumstances. Thus, if a carrier agrees to a work rule which causes an inefficient use of pilots, in a sense it need not worry about paying for it. The CAB stands ready to subsidize the results of these bargains between honest men. The point is that the very knowledge that the CAB will provide the necessary funds undermines the carrier's determination to take a strike and, conversely, strengthens the position of the Air Line Pilots Association In short, the CAB is failing to force efficient settlements in the industrial relations area. It is making the cost of a local service line's agreeing to ALPA's terms relatively low.

The analysis in this section indicates that again the relative bargaining power of ALPA tends to be high because the cost to an airline of agreeing to ALPA's terms tends to be low.

The Cost to Pilots of Disagreeing. Turning to the economic position of the pilot group, one finds some indications of bargaining strength. In the first place, pilots make high enough incomes so

[10] CAB, *Air Carrier Financial Statistics,* quarter ended September 30, 1964, Table 1.

that they can build up their personal reserves to carry them through a strike. Of course, many of them may not manage their personal finances in this way. Even if they do have reserves, they may not desire to use them up in a strike. Fortunately for the pilots they will not have to use reserves in a strike unless their current expenses are high and fixed. Otherwise their strike benefits will keep them comfortably provided for during a strike. The Air Line Pilots Association pays monthly strike benefits amounting to 5% of each pilot's annual income with a minimum benefit of $350 per month and a maximum of $650 per month. The funds to provide these benefits come from assessments levied on the remainder of the membership. For example, during a pilot strike against Southern Airways, ALPA paid about $2.6 million in strike benefits.[11] These factors apply to the other side of Chamberlain's definition. They tend to make the cost to the pilots of disagreeing with an airline's terms relatively low. Thus they tend again to give relative bargaining power to the pilots.

In summary, the economic factors in this industrial relations system give considerable relative bargaining power to ALPA.

The Effect of Carrier-by-Carrier Bargaining

The carrier-by-carrier bargaining which is practiced by the airlines and the pilots is perhaps the most important cause of an imbalance of bargaining power. This method of bargaining allows the Air Line Pilots Association to bring its full force against one carrier at a time.

Under the provisions of the Railway Labor Act, neither party may be forced to negotiate on a joint basis. This right stems from the language of the Act which reads in part as follows:

> Representatives—shall be designated by the respective parties without interference, influence or coercion by either party over the designation of representatives of the other; and neither party shall in any way interfere with, influence or coerce the other in its choice of representatives.

The practical effect of this quotation is that the pilots are free to designate bargaining representatives at each carrier, and that the

[11] CAB, Docket 9977, *Brief of Union Parties,* p. 112. From 1958 to 1962 airline unions paid $5,041,612 in strike benefits.

pilots on one carrier may not be forced to accept representatives on a joint basis. At the same time, the carriers are free to establish a committee to do the bargaining for all of them; i.e., the same men could move from one carrier to another to bargain with the individual pilot bargaining teams. Except for a period of time after ALPA was organized in 1930, it has been completely opposed to any form of industry-wide or joint bargaining. Under the protection of the Railway Labor Act, it has succeeded in preventing any joint bargaining since the early thirties.

The principal attempt by the carriers to obtain joint bargaining came right after the war in 1945. They realized that they all faced a common problem in negotiating pilot wages and working conditions on the new DC–4 and Constellation equipment. They also knew that they could have brought more bargaining pressure to bear on the Air Line Pilots Association if they could have successfully instituted industry-wide bargaining. To reach this goal, they formed the Airlines Negotiating Committee, which was composed of representatives of the 13 major carriers. This committee was given the power to negotiate for all these carriers.

For its part, ALPA adamantly refused to bargain on any basis other than with an individual carrier. Thus the 1945–1946 negotiations became the real test of the industry's ability to force industry-wide negotiations. As will be seen, their attempt failed completely and negotiations with the pilots have been on an individual carrier basis to this day. The right to have individual negotiations is still jealously guarded by the Air Line Pilots Association.

The situation in 1945–1946 developed in this way. The head of the Airlines Negotiating Committee notified the pilot association of its desire to negotiate jointly on the new contracts. Mr. Behncke, the president of ALPA, simply refused to meet on that basis. Without an agreement covering their wages and working conditions, one of the major carriers put the new four-engine equipment into service. Its pilots flew the planes for a few weeks under the old formula and then set a strike deadline for May 7, 1946. This strike threat forced President Truman to establish a Presidential Emergency Fact Finding Board.[12] His order, creating the board,

---

[12] *12th Annual Report of the National Mediation Board,* fiscal year ended June 30, 1946, p. 49.

indicated that he wanted the disputes with all 13 carriers included in the investigation. However, ALPA maintained its position that it would only enter into talks with one carrier at a time. A compromise solution, to get the board's work accomplished, was worked out in which the board agreed to hear first the facts surrounding ALPA's dispute with the strike-threatened carrier. That dispute was fully aired by the company and ALPA. Then the remaining 12 carriers made brief presentations. In the main, they rested their cases on the facts already before the board. ALPA refused to discuss the merits of any of the other 12 disputes. Instead, it pointed out in each case wherein the parties had not gone through all the required Railway Labor Act procedures and claimed those cases therefore were not properly before the board.

On July 8, 1946, the board issued its report. It did not recommend that ALPA bargain on an industry-wide basis, but at the same time it made clear the right of all the employers to be represented by the Airlines Negotiating Committee. In effect, each side could be represented by whomever it pleased. The practical effect of this recommendation was to say that a party cannot be forced to negotiate on a joint basis but may do so voluntarily.

Although ALPA refused to accept the economic recommendations of the board's report, they were put into effect by most of the carriers in the fall of 1946.[13] This action caused some futile negotiations at the previously strike-threatened carrier. When the talks failed, the pilots struck this carrier on October 21, 1946. The strike forced the carrier to cease operations.

Ten days later the National Mediation Board proffered arbitration to which both parties agreed in principle. It was not until November 15, however, that the parties reached agreement on the arbitration stipulation and ended the strike. Getting an arbitration agreement with one carrier was an important victory for ALPA because it meant that the industry's joint approach had been broken. Since that date all negotiations between the airlines and the association have been on an individual carrier basis.

Why has individual system bargaining increased the bargaining

[13] Mark L. Kahn, "Wage Determination for Airline Pilots," *Industrial and Labor Relations Review*, Vol. 6, No. 3, April 1953, p. 329.

power of the pilot group? Generally, it may be said that ALPA has been able to divide and conquer the airline industry. The technique has been to force one carrier under a strike threat, or an actual strike, to make a new concession to the association. Then the next carrier will be forced to make the same concession or another new one. Finally, the third carrier will be forced to accept both of the previous concessions, and so it goes, higher and higher. This is generally known as "pattern plus" bargaining. This has been the "whipsawing" pattern ALPA has followed successfully.

ALPA recognizes the success of its whipsawing approach. Its Wage and Working Conditions Policy Committee, in writing of the successive wage increases ALPA had negotiated in the first round of jet negotiations, stated:

> This steady progress, in moderately sized increments, is, of course, an excellent example of ALPA's collective bargaining technique. It is recognized by the ATA [Air Transport Association of America], most people in other industries and some pilots. Speaking for the air line industry, Mr. Stuart Tipton, President of the Air Transport Association . . . had this to say about ALPA's collective bargaining. "The technique calls for playing one air line against another. At a later date concessions made by the various individual carriers are consolidated into an agreement embodying all the objectives that the union originally set out to attain."

Why doesn't the industry get together to hold the line against ALPA? The answer to this question involves many of the factors already discussed in this chapter. For example, the airlines are very competitive—they are continually trying to outsell each other. This competition has been made increasingly more severe by the CAB's policy since the war of granting numerous route certifications over the same routes. It has also been intensified by the governmental red tape carriers must go through if they wish to cooperate with each other in even the simplest way. For example, carriers must receive governmental permission before they may share one of the movable stairs which are rolled up to most planes at the ramp. For these reasons, carriers have developed a fiercely competitive spirit which makes it extremely difficult for them to cooperate in the labor relations area.

History abounds with examples in which the carriers could not maintain a united front *vis-à-vis* the pilots. The normal pattern of their behavior is the reverse: carriers typically move into a market with renewed rigor when one of their competitors is halted with a strike.

Another aspect of this problem is that once a carrier agrees to a new contract which sets a higher pattern, it is interested in seeing its competitors follow suit. Therefore, generally it will not take steps to aid competitors to maintain an advantage. ALPA only has to win the pattern-setting contract at one carrier and the others are practically forced to follow suit. The carrier mutual aid fund, which is a form of strike insurance, represents the only move of the airlines to support each other. It will be discussed shortly.

Other factors lead to individual bargains. Important among them are the differences among carriers which cause identical contract clauses to have markedly different impacts. In general, these differences involve route structure, type of equipment, operating practices, and company policies. For example, in the scheduling area one carrier could agree to a certain type of on-duty ratio and never give up any pay and flight time credit under it. Another carrier could agree to the same clause only to find it very costly.

A good example of differences in operating procedures can be found in the matter of domicile policy. Some carriers try to limit the number of bases at which their flight crews live. This is in part an attempt to keep down the number of families who have to move. Other carriers maintain a relatively large number of domiciles and open or close them as business shifts. This is no condemnation of the latter policy—the economics of the situation may demand it. Identical contract language, however, may have markedly different cost impacts on carriers with different domicile policies. For example, a trip-time ratio would be likely to cost the carrier with few domiciles more than a carrier with many of them simply because on the average the latter carrier will have a better chance of getting more crews home oftener.

The important point about these differences among carriers is that they tend to foster individual bargaining because in that way an airline believes it may stand a chance of getting a tailor-made settlement which will keep its costs down.

At least one major carrier opposes any move toward industry-wide bargaining because it believes it would be forced to accept in a joint approach the most costly agreement among the participating carriers. The Vice President—Personnel of this carrier has written:

> Actually, the airlines now have such different provisions in their labor agreements that I believe our differences prevent us from arriving at industry-wide bargaining on any basis other than going down to the level of the weakest agreement in the industry.[14]

Airlines have tended to develop over the years as "one-man shows." At least, many of them have been dominated by strong presidents, each of whom has had his own convictions concerning the way his airline should be run. In some cases these individualistic presidents are still in control of their respective airlines. The strong convictions of these presidents and the particular characteristics they impart to each airline are also factors which hinder joint efforts among the carriers.

In summary, many reasons may be found why the airlines fail to present a united front to the Air Line Pilots Association. By giving in for these reasons, however, the airlines give the pilots one of their greatest sources of bargaining strength.

Before translating these facts to Chamberlain's definition of bargaining power, two implicit aspects of this type of bargaining structure should be made explicit. First, any given carrier in weighing whether to agree to ALPA's terms or not is aware that if a strike occurs its operations will be shut down while its competitors will be operating. Similarly, ALPA in weighing whether to accept an airline's terms or not is aware that a strike would involve only the pilots at one airline and that they could be supported by the rest of the membership which would be working. These facts mean that the relative cost to an airline of disagreeing with ALPA's terms tends to be very high, while the cost to the pilots either at that carrier or across the industry of disagreeing with an airline's terms tends to be quite low. Thus, the pilots gain relative bargaining power from the bargaining structure.

---

[14] CAB, Docket 9977, *Joint Exhibits of the Airline Parties,* Vol. I, p. 53.

The Short-Run Force of Public Opinion

When an airline halts operations because of a pilot strike, the public is quick to condemn both parties. The pilots have grown accustomed to the fact that they will receive what they consider to be a very bad press. They feel that the press usually quotes the highest wage possible in the industry, as if it were the average earned by most pilots. The press is also fond of pointing out that a pilot can fly only 85 hours per month and can easily accrue that in ten days of work. ALPA feels that these statements fail to present a fair or accurate picture of the situation, which of course is true. Another typical press story about a pilot strike will describe how such-and-such a pilot drove up to the picket line in a Cadillac and, following his picket duties, returned to his suburban home for a refreshing dip in his private pool. This type of press and a certain amount of public censure for halting a vital transportation service lead ALPA to feel under considerable pressure to reach a settlement.

An airline is under no less pressure from a bad press when a strike is in process. Essentially, an airline has a responsibility to the public to provide convenient air service over its routes. When it is unable to settle its labor problems and is struck, it is failing to serve the public in the transportation sense. The public and the press are not slow to express their wrath at being inconvenienced.

This leads to the question of what is the force of public opinion in a strike situation? Clearly, the public is most concerned with seeing the operation get started again so that it can get where it wants to go. The costs of the settlement in lower earnings for the stockholders, or even in the possibility of a slightly more expensive fare, are of less concern to the traveling public. Primarily, they want the air service to recommence as soon as possible. This fact weakens the carrier's bargaining power with which to withstand a strike. Conversely, the public indifference to the cost of the settlement strengthens the hand of the Air Line Pilots Association. It makes the cost of disagreement with the other parties' terms relatively higher for an airline than for ALPA.

The Effect of Mutual Aid Agreements

Both parties have sought to use mutual aid agreements to aid their bargaining strength. The unions have successfully used agreements with other airline unions to ensure that a struck carrier was forced to halt all operations. Of course, the primary goal is to have the other unions honor picket lines. A secondary source of interunion support has been the borrowing of funds with which to pay strike benefits. The fact that airline unions paid over $5 million in strike benefits, a form of mutual aid, from 1958 to 1962 has already been mentioned.

The Air Line Pilots Association for the most part does not need to get assistance from other unions to make its strikes effective in closing an airline. The pilots hold such a key role in the operations, and so many of them are needed relative to the short-run supply, that carriers generally do not attempt to continue operating by replacing their struck pilots. One exception occurred in which a struck line did replace its pilots and succeeded in operating. In this case, ALPA had failed to obtain the support of the other unions. Since that time ALPA has reached a mutual aid agreement with the International Association of Machinists. If both of these unions cease working concurrently, an airline would practically be forced to close down.

The most important instance of interunion mutual aid uncovered in the field research has been described in Chapter 8. FEIA was able to obtain the support of the local chapters of IAM and ALSSA (Air Line Stewards and Stewardesses Association) when the flight engineers were fighting their key battle for a place on the turbojets. In this situation, the machinists and the stewardesses both respected the FEIA picket lines and forced the carrier to cease operations. The teamsters also lent FEIA important funds for strike benefits, and would probably have stopped deliveries of fuel and supplies had that been necessary. Under these conditions the carrier was forced to capitulate and to agree to a four-man turbojet crew. The added bargaining power the mutual aid agreements gave FEIA cannot be overestimated. Without them there is every reason to believe that the pilots would have replaced the striking flight engineers, thereby defeating the FEIA strike.

Another example of mutual aid among unions came in a 1961 strike by flight engineers against Western. In that case the mechanics and the navigators refused to cross the engineers' picket lines and precluded "any further substantial operations by the company." Similarly, during a strike by 12 navigators against Flying Tiger in 1960 ALPA and FEIA members interrupted operations by refusing to cross the picket line. In 1960 pilots of Mohawk Airline refused to cross a stewardess picket line.[15]

Union mutual aid can come from nonairline unions. In a 1962 FEIA strike against Eastern, the National Maritime Union indicated its intention to respect water-borne FEIA pickets and cut off fuel deliveries, and Miami Building Trade Unions halted construction of Eastern's jet overhaul base.[16] Thus it may be said that interunion mutual aid agreements are potentially one of the union's greatest bargaining strengths in the airline industry.

Mutual aid agreements among airlines are potentially no less important for the other side of the bargaining table. Effective October 20, 1958, six carriers established a mutual aid pact which was designed to bolster the financial strength of a member carrier when its flight operations were shut down as a result of a strike (1) to enforce demands in excess of or opposed to recommendations of a Presidential Emergency Board; (2) called before exhaustion of the procedures of the Railway Labor Act; or (3) otherwise unlawful. When a member carrier was struck under one of those conditions, the other carriers would remit to it any increased "windfall" revenues they received as a result of handling the struck carrier's business less the additional expense of handling such increased business. As first executed any air carrier could become a member. The original six members were American, Capital, Eastern, Pan American, TWA and United.[17]

On March 7, 1960, the terms of the pact were amended so that payments would be called for in the case of strikes called in the absence of a Presidential Emergency Board as long as the struck carrier had acted in full compliance with the Railway Labor Act.[18]

[15] CAB, Docket 9977, *Brief of the Carrier Parties,* p. 23.
[16] *Ibid.*
[17] CAB, Docket 9977, *Initial Decision of Hearing Examiner S. Thomas Simon,* p. 131.
[18] *Ibid.*

This amendment was designed to make the pact attractive to carriers which because of their size could not expect the appointment of a Presidential Emergency Board when they were struck. As a result in March and April 1960 Braniff, Continental, National, and Northwest joined the Mutual Aid Pact. In 1961, however, National and Continental withdrew from membership.[19]

On March 22, 1962, the pact was amended so that payments would be required in the case of a strike after a Presidential Emergency Board had reported without making specific recommendations on the merits of the dispute. In addition membership was limited to the trunk lines. The terms of payments were broadened so that as a minimum a struck carrier would receive 25% of its normal operating expenses for the operations shut down. If "windfall" payments were less than that 25%, the other carriers were liable for the difference up to 0.5% of their air transport operating revenues of the previous calendar year. Regardless of amount, a struck carrier would continue to receive all the "windfall" payments for which it was eligible.[20] The CAB at various times approved these features of the Mutual Aid Pact.

As shown in Table 10.4, from October 1958 to January 1, 1962, payments of over $16 million had been made by ten carriers to eight carriers under the terms of the Pact.

When one evaluates the Mutual Aid Pact, one is led to the conclusion that for a variety of reasons, although it may have added to the bargaining power of member carriers at times, it has not approached its full potential. In the first place, at no time have all the trunk lines been participating members. Indeed, during most of its existence five of the trunk lines have stayed out of it. As a result, although a member carrier while struck may receive payments under the Pact, competing nonmember carriers will keep their "windfall" profits and will enhance their market image at the expense of the struck carrier. For example, when Eastern was struck in 1962, its three major competitors were not in the Pact and benefited greatly from Eastern's position. Second, while payments may be helpful, they do not cover actual strike losses. Thus for 11 strikes during the period 1958–1962 member carriers re-

[19] *Ibid.*, p. 8.
[20] *Ibid.* p. 132.

TABLE 10.4. SUMMARY OF MUTUAL AID PAYMENTS UNDER "WINDFALL" AGREEMENTS: OCTOBER 1958 TO JANUARY 1, 1962

(000)

Carrier	Total Received	Paid by									
		AAL	BNF	CAP	CAL	EAL*	NAL	NWA	PAA	TWA	UAL
American	$ 4,431	$ —	$169	$ 353	$41	$ —	$ —	$ —	$ —	$1,260	$2,608
Braniff	†	—	—	—	—	†	—	—	—	419	992
Capital	2,620	908	—	—	—	301	—	—	—		
Continental	—	—	—	—	—	—	—	—	—	—	—
Eastern	2,209	306	66	714	2	—	411	116	328	183	83
National	107	4	1	26	—	74	—	—	—	1	1
Northwest	3,601	177	—	796	—	115	—	—	650	43	1,820
Pan American	121	—	7	—	44	1	—	—	—	—	114
TWA	3,071	727	25	195	—	—	—	—	319	—	1,760
United	—	—	—	—	—	—	—	—	—	—	—
Total	$16,160	$2,122	$268	$2,084	$87	$491	$411	$116	$1,297	$1,906	$7,378

* In addition, Eastern estimated payments for a 1962 FEIA strike amounting to $5.9 million for "windfall" payments and supplemental payments.

† Payment less than $500.

SOURCES: CAB, Docket 9977, *Initial Decision of Hearing Examiner S. Thomas Simon*, p. 150, and *Statement of Eastern Air Lines, Inc., with respect to 1962 Flight Engineers' Strike*, Exhibit 63.

ported losses of $74.8 million (not including $5.8 million in lost profits) and Mutual Aid payments of $31.8 million, leaving a net loss of $42.9 million.[21] The Pact "has not led to coordination of bargaining positions among the parties."[22]

Another weakness of the Pact is that local service lines are excluded. While these lines do not in general set patterns for the trunk lines to follow because they usually trail the trunks on wages and working conditions, nevertheless such a possibility is not out of the question. A local service line was recently very much involved in establishing the crew complement on the BAC–1–11. At a minimum, the local service lines are presently individually on their own when negotiating with their unions and are therefore ripe for being "whipsawed."

A final weakness of the mutual aid pact is that it will not automatically prevent unions from winning a new concession from a carrier to which it is not important. A carrier may be willing to set a very high pegged speed on an aircraft type because it has very few of them in its fleet or is about to sell all of them. For example, pegging the DC–3 at 300 mph, a high rate for that aircraft, might be unimportant to a particular carrier. It may, however, be setting a pattern to which the pilots of other airlines will point and those airlines may have a large fleet of this aircraft type. To match the pattern therefore would be extremely costly. The point is that differences among carriers may undermine the effectiveness of mutual aid agreements.

A trial examiner for the CAB made an exhaustive examination of the evolution and effect of the Mutual Aid Pact. Based on this study he reported to the CAB in part as follows:

> The examiner, nevertheless, is of the opinion that the Pact has had little or no recognizable authority upon the course which labor relations has taken during this period. Even in the case of the recent strikes, there is no substantial evidence to more than suggest that the financial assistance of the Pact was a determinative factor in the decisions of Eastern, and none to indicate that the Pact influenced the manner in which this troublesome controversy evolved. . . .

[21] CAB, Docket 9977, Simon, *op. cit.,* p. 95.
[22] *Ibid.,* p. 10.

There is no substantial evidence in the record that the Pact has had any material effect upon the collective bargaining process in the industry. . . .[23]

In summary, the airlines and the unions can increase their bargaining power if they make mutual aid agreements. Mutual aid which provides funds to one side or the other during a shutdown decreases the cost to the party receiving it of disagreeing with the other party's terms. Mutual aid which binds unions together in terms of honoring picket lines tends to increase the cost to the airline of disagreeing with the union's terms.

To date both parties have only begun to exploit this potential. It is not possible to predict which party will gain more from this factor in the future.

The Desire for a "Good" Relationship

The management of each airline studied was anxious to maintain or to develop a "good" relationship with its pilot group. This was an important management goal which permeated many operations and industrial relations decisions. For example, in the middle of pilot negotiations at the local service line, the president was writing a series of personal letters to the pilots in an attempt to re-establish a "good" relationship with them. The relationship, he felt, had been suffering from the impersonalization rapid expansion may bring.

Another carrier was concerned about its relationship with its pilots following a strike. The new contract called for further negotiations over the rates for the third pilots on the jets. During the supplementary negotiations the company suggested that in return for a ten months' extension of the basic contract it would give further increases to the first pilots and copilots in addition to setting the third pilot rates. Aside from the primary purpose of getting the extension, the carrier also hoped that the additional wage increases would help to improve its relationship with its pilot group. After the signing of the supplementary agreement, company and union negotiators made concurrent visits to each base at which pilots were domiciled in order to explain every aspect of the new

---

[23] The trial examiner did not see an imbalance of bargaining power between ALPA and the airlines.

contract to them and to express the hopes of both sides for a better relationship in the future.

Another major carrier is convinced with some justification that it has the "best" relationship with a pilot group of any carrier. It believes that the relationship is the result of hard work and careful planning throughout the years. In order to maintain this relationship, this carrier refuses to consider any joint bargaining approach, fearful lest that type of bargaining will tend to bring its relationship down to the poorest relationship of the carriers jointly bargaining. This may be a good policy for this individual carrier. From an industry or a public viewpoint, however, it does nothing to limit the whipsawing capability of the Air Line Pilots Association.

Several other reasons exist why the carriers seek a "good" relationship so avidly. Many of them have been discussed in other contexts. A major airline will have over 1,500 pilots who, as a group, are accustomed to command, are relatively well educated, and are individualistic. Their job places them in absolute control of many lives and very costly pieces of equipment. It also gives them some degree of control over a carrier's costs and its relations with the public. Under these circumstances it is natural for a carrier to desire to have the pilots in a cooperative mood and ready to give their wholehearted effort to the job. Carriers equate these goals with a "good" relationship. From an airline's viewpoint this factor tends to make the cost of disagreeing with ALPA high.

HYPOTHESIS

Of the six factors which have been considered, five would appear to lend bargaining strength to the Air Line Pilots Association. The sixth, concerning mutual aid pacts, is more or less inconclusive at present but represents real potential for both parties. On the basis of this analysis, the following hypothesis is made: The Air Line Pilots Association possesses a high degree of relative bargaining power.

REVIEWING FOR SIGNS OF A RELATIVE IMBALANCE

We are in a position to look for signs of a relative imbalance of bargaining power in the four contract areas covered in detail in Chapters 4 through 9.

In the compensation area, the pilots at each airline have been able to maintain the basic wage formula in spite of management opposition to it. In addition, the pilots have refused to simplify the formula although as the years have passed its applications have become more and more complex and confusing. A further indication of the relative bargaining power of the pilots has been their ability to extend the importance of the mileage component of the formula although the carriers would have preferred to put what wage increases as were necessary in hourly pay.

Concerning the general level of pilot pay, ALPA has apparently been able to exert an independent influence which resulted in higher pilot wages than would have occurred if the pilots had bargained as individuals. ALPA has been able to hold its approximate differential with all production workers during years of generally declining differentials between skilled and less skilled employee groups. ALPA was able to hold this differential while journeymen in the building trades, for example, apparently did not have the relative bargaining power to do so.

ALPA has also been able to maintain large differentials among pilots of the same rank (captains, copilots, and flight engineers) which the companies probably would have wished to reduce to obtain a wage structure based more on valid occupational differences and less on personal differentials based on seniority.

ALPA's relative bargaining power is also indicated by its ability to maintain an ideal position as to wages in which to whipsaw the airlines. ALPA is able to maintain earnings for the same aircraft type within a narrow range throughout the industry but yet the individual earnings are almost never identical. Table 10.5 shows the range of monthly earnings of senior captains at various airlines flying DC–6B, DC–8, and Boeing 707 equipment for 85 hours, one half day, one half night as of July 1, 1961. It shows how rates are closely bunched but not identical. For example, the monthly earnings on the DC–6B averaged $1,773 and ranged from $1,671 to $1,838. Such a pattern represents an ideal "whipsawing" position for a union.

A final indication of ALPA's relative bargaining strength in the compensation area is its apparent ability to employ "pattern plus" bargaining. This was most clearly seen in the compensation chapter

TABLE 10.5. COMPARATIVE RATES OF
COMPENSATION FOR SENIOR CAPTAINS, 85 HOURS
(ONE-HALF DAY, ONE-HALF NIGHT), ON THREE
TYPES OF AIRPLANES: AS OF JULY 1, 1961

Carrier	DC–6B	DC–8	B–707
American	$1,809	$2,516	$ —
Braniff	—	—	2,468
Capital	1,797	—	—
Continental	1,778	—	2,481
Delta	1,680	2,392	—
Eastern	1,838	2,548	—
National	1,801	2,534	2,516
Northeast	1,785	—	2,679
Northwest	1,800	2,584	—
Trans World	—	—	—
United	1,775	2,482	—
Western	1,671	—	2,463
Average	$1,773	$2,509	$2,521

SOURCE: ALPA records.

in the wage rates which resulted from the first round of jet negotiations. Almost without exception each new contract contained higher rates than the preceding one. In this situation, even responsible airline officials are thinking about the philosophy that "he who settles first, settles cheapest." This pattern plus bargaining demonstrates ALPA's ability to whipsaw the airline industry and to adhere to a policy of not letting a new contract represent a retrogression in terms of its latest pattern.

In the area of scheduling the strongest indication of a relative imbalance of power is the continual loss of pilot utilization that has been suffered by the airline managements. Work rules have proliferated to the point where airlines are unable to obtain a reasonable amount of flying from each pilot. Under most of these work rules flight crew members received credit for flight time, although they did not actually fly during that time. The five types of work rules which stood out in this study were flight credit for one half of the time spent deadheading; for scheduled or actual time, whichever was greater, on a leg-by-leg basis; for guaranteed time under the on-duty ratios; for guaranteed time under the trip-time ratios; and direct reductions in monthly flight time limitations. The justifications for or against these work rules may be argued in terms of featherbedding or establishing minimum working conditions. The fact remains that airline administrators have lost flexibility in the scheduling of flight crew members and have had to hire extra men in large numbers because they have not been able to get as much actual flight time from their flight crew members.

Part of the reductions in scheduling efficiency has come through the duty-time ratios and through direct reductions in hours. The trend in the ratios was pointed out in Chapter 5. Here two further points about them should be made. In the first place the airlines would not have agreed to these ratios originally or to their being made more stringent unless a relative imbalance of power existed at the bargaining table. They make scheduling much more difficult and they reduce manning efficiency. Second, most of the carriers certainly would not have agreed to essentially one form of duty-time ratio if they had the relative power to resist. The differences between carriers would normally demand tailor-made ratios. Thus, the pilots not only have been able to force the ratios into their contracts; they have also been able to force standard ratios in most cases, although their cost impact on different carriers has been by no means standard. In this area, it was in part the lack of discrimination that hurt efficiency and indicated the pilots' relative bargaining power.

The advent of the direct reduction in hours was bitterly opposed by the airline managements for years. That it has come about at all indicates managements' lack of relative bargaining strength. It was first introduced on two carriers, where, as was pointed out in Chapter 8, it was given as part of package solutions in the face of the managements' great desire to obtain the three-man jet crew. Once such a pattern has been set on two carriers, the balance of the industry is being forced either to reduce hours or to improve significantly the duty-time ratios. This dual pattern puts ALPA once again in an ideal whipsawing position. Its negotiators can now look to get the improved duty-time ratios from the carriers that have already reduced hours, and reduced hours from those carriers which have improved the ratios.

The area of pensions provides an excellent example of how ALPA was able to adopt a pension philosophy, overcome the resistance of airline managements to negotiating on pensions, and push through the industry the ALPA pension plan which represents uniquely high costs and benefits. ALPA was able to obtain pension features which were particularly costly or unpalatable to managements. For example, the carriers were forced to pick up more and more of the pilot contributions and to have such additional payments treated for cash vesting purposes as if the pilots had made them. Additionally, the pilots have been winning a very loose definition of "disability" which has many industry experts worried. These developments indicate ALPA's relative bargaining power.

In the work assignment area a number of important flight crew developments have taken place. The pilots' union was effective in having the government require a flight engineer on four-engine aircraft weighing over 80,000 pounds. This ruling which came in 1948 was bitterly opposed by the air carriers. It is an example of ALPA's turning to the government to obtain a goal involving working conditions and employment opportunities.

In order to discuss bargaining power in regard to the crew complement dispute, one must assess the bargaining power relationship between the airlines and the FEIA. In those situations in which ALPA and FEIA were not making opposing demands upon an airline, a number of the factors discussed in regard to ALPA's relative bargaining power pertained also to FEIA. Essentially from an airline's point of view the cost of agreeing with FEIA tended to be low while the cost of disagreeing tended to be high. Thus FEIA possessed enough relative bargaining power, for example, to negotiate the general mechanic's qualification at a number of carriers.

Even in 1958 when ALPA and FEIA were making opposing demands on the airlines, FEIA's bargaining power was enough to have half of the trunk lines agree to the four-man jet crew. When the other half of the trunk lines gained the distinct competitive advantage of flying jets with three-man crews, the cost to the other carriers of continuing to agree with ALPA's demand for three pilots and with the FEIA's demand for a general mechanic increased significantly. In this situation what became important was ALPA's bargaining power relative to an airline as compared with FEIA's

352 *The Effects of Negotiations*

bargaining power relative to the airline. In this comparison of bargaining power ALPA was the clear victor for one fundamental reason: the technologies of the pilot and flight engineer jobs were such that an airline management could not operate without its pilots while it could operate in the near short run without its flight engineers, particularly with pilots generally willing and able to replace flight engineers. Thus the cost to a carrier of disagreeing with ALPA remained high, while the cost of disagreeing with FEIA went down. Also the cost to an airline of agreeing to FEIA's terms regarding the elimination of the fourth crew member went up because it was tied automatically to a high cost of disagreement with ALPA.

The work assignment area therefore gave further indication of ALPA's relative bargaining power in relation to the airlines. ALPA's strength was indicated also in that where the pilots were intransigent, equitable solutions were not possible; where they were tractable, equitable solutions ensued.

This review of the developments in four substantive areas reinforces the hypothesis that the pilots have possessed a relative bargaining power advantage *vis-à-vis* airline managements. The latter simply would not have allowed such developments to take place had the bargaining power been more evenly divided.

Some Concluding Observations

The industrial relations system between the domestic airlines and the pilots is viable. Its decentralized negotiation, contract administration, grievance handling, and use of arbitration have worked reasonably well and have disposed of problems as they have arisen. The exception has been the dispute involving work assignment and the threat of technological unemployment on the jet aircraft.

The grievance and arbitration machinery is not overly used, and has certainly not bogged down. Disputes are handled as they arise on each property with reasonable informality and dispatch.

As to the general level of pilot wages, pretty clearly the pilots have done well. No objective way exists to say that they have done "too well." Several aspects of the economics of the situation have combined, however, to keep down the cost and damage to the airlines of the relatively high pilot earnings. Such aspects have been the growth of the airline industry at the expense of other forms of transportation, the inelastic demand for airline travel based on price and the relative de-emphasis of price competition, the pattern bargaining, the increasing productivity of the aircraft, and the low ratio of pilot payroll to total operating costs.

Similarly, the costs of the pilot pension plans have not hurt the carriers very much. Certainly adequate pensions which are available at an early age and in cases of forced early retirement are appropriate for pilots, given the nature of their occupation.

Toward the purely economic aspects of this industrial relations system one can take a fairly sanguine attitude.

As to some of the "noneconomic" aspects of this system, however, more cause for concern exists. The concessions which airline managements have made in the scheduling area have brought about an unrealistically low month's work for a significant percentage of pilots. While no data are available, it is generally known that many pilots have enough free time to carry on full-time occupations apart from their flying careers.

Similarly, in the work assignment area managements have yielded at the bargaining table and through daily concessions a great deal of manning flexibility regarding setting of qualifications, training, and assigning duties. Reason exists to be concerned that in these areas the companies have given away too much. The airlines and the pilots have been setting themselves up for difficult adjustments should the time arrive when the airline industry should stabilize or decline. The flight engineer dispute gives an indication of the trouble potentially involved in a declining situation in which unemployment was threatened as a result of technological change.

Pilots have strong relative bargaining power. In the "noneconomic areas managements continue to lose manning flexibility and utilization. What is the answer? If the airline managements should decide to increase their bargaining power by moving as close to industry-wide bargaining as possible with the pilots opposing such a change, they will surely invite heavy government involvement and a consequent breakdown in the ability and freedom of the parties to devise and interpret their own wages, hours, and working conditions. If the airline managements do not move toward industry-wide bargaining, each management will continue to be vulnerable to ALPA's relative bargaining power and to declining manning flexibility and utilization. Thus, the unique setting of this industrial relations system, particularly its close involvement with government regulation and interest in uninterrupted service, causes a dilemma with which the airlines must continue to live.

APPENDICES

Appendix 1

APPENDIX 1

SELECTED PENSION INFORMATION REPORTED BY THE TRUNK LINES AND THE LOCAL SERVICE LINES IN ANNUAL REPORTS TO THE U.S. DEPARTMENT OF LABOR ON "FORM D–2" AS REQUIRED BY THE WELFARE AND PENSION PLANS DISCLOSURE ACT

(1)

AMERICAN AIRLINES
RETIREMENT BENEFIT PLAN FOR PILOT PERSONNEL

Year	Employer Contribution	Employee Contribution	Number Covered	Number Retired	Benefits Paid	Current and Past Service Liabilities	Balance in Fund
1959	$2,502,775	$1,566,548	1,475	24	N.A.	$26,275,520	N.A.
1960	3,131,023	2,211,212	1,598	32	N.A.	30,410,644	N.A.
1961	2,748,729	2,080,413	1,602	38	N.A.	51,747,822	N.A.
1962	2,434,431	2,157,439	1,606	42	$164,765	55,485,262	$36,913,849

(2)

BRANIFF AIRWAYS
RETIREMENT PLAN FOR PILOTS

Year	Employer Contribution	Employee Contribution	Number Covered	Number Retired	Benefits Paid	Current and Past Service Liabilities	Balance in Fund
1959	$372,088	$501,641	424	0	0	$1,427,181	$1,851,872
1960	853,800	543,024	427	0	0	2,039,878	3,397,426
1961	909,946	519,003	443	5	$17,309	N.A.	5,525,594

(3A)

CONTINENTAL AIR LINES
FIXED PENSION PLAN FOR PILOTS

Year	Employer Contribution	Employee Contribution	Number Covered	Number Retired	Benefits Paid	Current and Past Service Liabilities	Balance in Fund
1959	$260,794	$119,830	221	0	0	$1,562,523	$1,060,808
1960	327,653	148,435	269	0	$ 1,897	1,961,845	1,594,159
1961	420,040	14,247	288	2	12,319	2,652,149	2,070,041
1962	449,833	– 0 –	292	6	15,760	3,174,963	2,599,604

(3B)

CONTINENTAL AIR LINES
VARIABLE PENSION PLAN FOR PILOTS

Year	Employer Contribution	Employee Contribution	Number Covered	Number Retired	Benefits Paid	Current and Past Service Liabilities	Balance in Fund
1959	$135,550	$163,558	221	0	0	$ 271,030	$ 605,399
1960	157,318	206,371	269	0	$ 194	605,399	1,028,492
1961	283,100	89,193	288	2	2,327	1,001,051	1,720,771
1962	382,807	107,449	292	6	4,705	1,828,869	1,987,867

(4)

DELTA AIR LINES
EMPLOYEES' VARIABLE ANNUITY RETIREMENT INCOME PLAN

Year	Employer Contribution	Employee Contribution	Number Covered	Number Retired	Benefits Paid	Current and Past Service Liabilities	Balance in Fund
1959	$ 338,790	$197,006	509	2	$ 396	$2,513,589	$2,507,475
1960	341,662	219,474	543	6	3,150	3,117,709	3,087,660
1961	575,715	214,631	576	8	6,378	4,697,404	4,666,002
1962	1,369,957	14,639	738	14	11,076	4,953,455	5,278,129

(5)

EASTERN AIRLINES
VARIABLE BENEFIT RETIREMENT PLAN FOR PILOTS

Year	Employer Contribution	Employee Contribution	Number Covered	Number Retired	Benefits Paid	Current and Past Service Liabilities	Balance in Fund
1959	$728,235	$ 943,252	1,380	0	$ 2,217	$1,679,246	$1,679,246
1960	830,636	1,034,533	1,563	3	6,135	3,847,475	3,847,475
1961	981,635	1,148,771	1,614	7	16,329	7,333,880	7,333,880
1962	916,616	1,047,583	1,615	14	26,653	7,030,990	7,030,990

(6)

NATIONAL AIRLINES
VARIABLE ANNUITY PLAN FOR PILOTS

Year	Employer Contribution	Employee Contribution	Number Covered	Number Retired	Benefits Paid	Current and Past Service Liabilities	Balance in Fund
1959	$155,573	$155,573	285	0	$3,120	N.A.	$682,139

(7A)

NORTHEAST AIRLINES
FIXED BENEFIT PLAN (PILOTS AND OTHER EMPLOYEES)

Year	Employer Contribution	Employee Contribution	Number Covered	Number Retired	Benefits Paid	Current and Past Service Liabilities	Balance in Fund
1959	$295,597	0	1,482	6	$1,544	$1,727,066	$1,149,865
1960	518,875	0	1,910	8	2,550	2,210,384	1,711,361
1961	0	0	1,916	8	3,046	2,147,629	1,939,435
1962	0	0	2,199	9	4,462	2,375,703	2,005,838
1963	0	0	2,374	11	4,616	3,329,274	2,079,173

(7B)

NORTHEAST AIRLINES
VARIABLE ANNUITY PLAN FOR PILOTS

Year	Employer Contribution	Employee Contribution	Number Covered	Number Retired	Refunds	Current and Past Service Liabilities	Balance in Fund
1959	$ 90,981	$108,986	208	N.A.	($ 1,942)	N.A.	$ 539,302
1960	104,965	135,831	254	N.A.	(577)	N.A.	800,759
1961	133,991	176,948	274	N.A.	(30)	N.A.	1,142,891
1962	130,761	176,331	294	N.A.	(2,299)	N.A.	1,465,659
1963	127,173	169,442	253	N.A.	(32,243)	N.A.	1,777,151

(8)

NORTHWEST AIRLINES
PILOTS' PENSION PLAN

Year	Employer Contribution	Employee Contribution	Number Covered	Number Retired	Benefits Paid	Current and Past Service Liabilities	Balance in Fund
1959	$795,593	$581,553	478	3	$ 713	$4,195,555	$4,199,033
1960	894,050	716,998	597	4	1,046	5,895,889	5,849,390
1961	N.A.	N.A.	N.A.	N.A.	N.A.	N.A.	N.A.
1962	446,464	818,900	597	12	16,535	8,629,417	8,629,417

(9)

TRANS WORLD AIRLINES
TRUST ANNUITY PLAN FOR PILOTS

Year	Employer Contribution	Employee Contribution	Number Covered	Number Retired	Benefits Paid	Current and Past Service Liabilities	Balance in Fund
1959	$1,560,606	$1,014,967	1,598	5	$ 44,834	$ 8,027,679	$ 8,027,679
1960	2,024,125	1,405,120	1,598	7	39,939	11,334,817	11,334,817
1961	2,052,541	1,419,626	1,574	10	113,832	16,197,323	16,197,323
1962	2,436,345	1,480,484	1,558	18	208,522	18,513,356	18,513,356

(10A)

UNITED AIR LINES
FIXED BENEFIT PART OF UAL PENSION PLAN FOR PILOTS

Year	Employer Contribution	Employee Contribution	Number Covered	Number Retired	Benefits Paid	Current and Past Service Liabilities	Amount of Accumulated Reserves
1959	$1,361,373	$ 791,468	1,390	7	$32,261	$16,660,577	$17,871,600
1960	1,551,992	857,405	1,375	9	40,836	19,216,703	18,997,417
1961	N.A.	N.A.	N.A.	N.A.	N.A.	N.A.	N.A.
1962	1,717,068	1,008,086	1,379	16	71,994	31,431,455*	28,127,191

*Amount of current and past service liabilities of the entire (pilot and nonpilot) plan.

(10B)

UNITED AIR LINES
VARIABLE BENEFIT PLAN FOR PILOTS

Year	Employer Contribution	Employee Contribution	Number Covered	Number Retired	Benefits Paid	Current and Past Service Liabilities	Balance in Fund
1959	$ 940,327	$ 989,305	1,390	7	$ 3,693	$303,842	$ 7,952,502
1960	1,006,146	1,071,753	1,375	9	5,366	246,280	10,311,252
1961	1,079,675	1,162,173	1,352	12	23,450	184,753	13,264,750
1962	1,148,126	1,260,111	1,379	16	32,444	120,268	16,214,149

(11)

WESTERN AIR LINES
PILOT VARIABLE PENSION PLAN

Year	Employer Contribution	Employee Contribution	Number Covered	Number Retired	Benefits Paid	Current and Past Service Liabilities	Balance in Fund
1960	$104,160	$104,160	212	4	$1,007	$ 759,629	$ 742,362
1961	104,932	108,665	214	4	2,539	1,174,820	1,158,126
1962	122,372	122,372	223	4	1,169	1,305,530	1,290,991

(12)

PAN AMERICAN WORLD AIRWAYS
COOPERATIVE RETIREMENT INCOME TRUST PLAN FOR PILOTS

Year	Employer Contribution	Employee Contribution	Number Covered	Number Retired	Benefits Paid	Current and Past Service Liabilities	Balance in Fund
1959	$2,504,145	$1,938,994	1,447	9	$23,871	0	$19,049,641
1960	975,832	1,906,731	1,330	11	20,552	0	22,648,263
1961	2,322,564	2,009,428	1,305	11	28,063	0	28,096,353
1962	3,422,722	1,872,448	1,342	13	34,458	0	34,283,960

(13A)

ALLEGHENY AIRLINES
FIXED RETIREMENT PENSION PLAN FOR PILOTS

Year	Employer Contribution	Employee Contribution	Number Covered	Number Retired	Benefits Paid	Current and Past Service Liabilities	Amount of Accumulated Reserves
1959	$ 74,244	$ 38,213	106	0	0	$417,650	$ 61,079
1960	132,729	51,245	112	0	0	550,349	331,483
1961	76,923	142,054	121	1	$3,927	687,502	392,053
1962	75,425	154,960	140	1	3,881	861,401	794,469

(13B)

ALLEGHENY AIRLINES
VARIABLE ANNUITY PLAN FOR PILOTS

Year	Employer Contribution	Employee Contribution	Number Covered	Number Retired	Benefits Paid	Current and Past Service Liabilities	Balance in Fund
1959	$35,119	$90,761	106	0	0	$132,292	$132,292
1960	49,903	50,364	112	0	0	237,251	237,251
1961	80,397	94,126	121	1	0	420,935	420,935
1962	87,530	89,759	140	1	$378	611,584	611,584

(14)

BONANZA AIR LINES
PILOTS' VARIABLE ANNUITY RETIREMENT PLAN

Year	Employer Contribution	Employee Contribution	Number Covered	Number Retired	Benefits Paid	Current and Past Service Liabilities	Balance in Fund
1960	$11,001	$13,418	58	0	0	$26,131	$26,131
1961	20,817	28,045	60	0	0	80,397	80,397

(15A)

FRONTIER AIRLINES
FIXED PENSION PLAN FOR PILOTS

Year	Employer Contribution	Employee Contribution	Number Covered	Number Retired	Benefits Paid	Current and Past Service Liabilities	Amount of Accumulated Reserves
1959	$55,537	$41,669	95	0	$ 330	$272,709	$220,149
1960	62,090	47,290	104	0	0	635,920	341,878
1961	79,428	49,837	118	0	1,996	635,920	525,630
1962	46,200	59,698	141	0	2,580	962,400	627,760

(15B)

FRONTIER AIRLINES
VARIABLE PENSION PLAN FOR PILOTS

Year	Employer Contribution	Employee Contribution	Number Covered	Number Retired	Benefits Paid	Current and Past Service Liabilities	Balance in Fund
1959	$35,502	$50,185	95	0	$ 139	0	$132,523
1960	41,455	57,155	104	0	0	$239,427	239,427
1961	49,087	60,705	118	0	4,358	453,932	399,657
1962	69,651	72,300	141	0	13	530,502	530,502

(16)

LAKE CENTRAL AIRLINES
FIXED PENSION PLAN FOR PILOTS

Year	Employer Contribution	Employee Contribution	Number Covered	Number Retired	Benefits Paid	Current and Past Service Liabilities	Total Assets
1959	$26,649	$18,087	47	0	$441	$131,761	$113,303
1960	33,659	20,528	47	0	34	177,963	105,448
1961	46,821	29,051	55	0	0	233,524	171,977

(17)

LAKE CENTRAL AIRLINES
VARIABLE PENSION PLAN FOR PILOTS

Year	Employer Contribution	Employee Contribution	Number Covered	Number Retired	Benefits Paid	Current and Past Service Liabilities	Balance in Fund
1959	$12,281	$19,255	46	0	$282	$ 24,393	$113,303
1960	13,270	30,616	38	0	34	56,704	92,392
1961	25,063	28,226	47	0	0	101,868	148,236

(18A)

MOHAWK AIRLINES
FIXED BENEFIT RETIREMENT PLAN FOR PILOTS

Year	Employer Contribution	Employee Contribution	Number Covered	Number Retired	Benefits Paid	Current and Past Service Liabilities	Balance in Fund
1959	$45,084	$29,451	93	0	0	$112,200	$ 99,101
1960	44,374	32,768	100	0	0	294,969	182,769
1961	44,374	39,750	96	0	0	294,969	179,751
1962	37,936	14,232	126	0	0	493,463	N.A.

(18B)

MOHAWK AIRLINES
VARIABLE BENEFIT RETIREMENT PLAN FOR PILOTS

Year	Employer Contribution	Employee Contribution	Number Covered	Number Retired	Benefits Paid	Current and Past Service Liabilities	Balance in Fund
1959	$15,825	$26,956	93	0	0	$ 45,947	$ 43,279
1960	31,172	38,672	100	0	0	161,009	115,062
1961	48,000	48,160	96	0	0	161,009	111,737
1962	66,665	66,409	130	0	0	364,509	N.A.

(19A)

NORTH CENTRAL AIRLINES
PILOTS' RETIREMENT PLAN

Year	Employer Contribution	Employee Contribution	Number Covered	Number Retired	Benefits Paid	Current and Past Service Liabilities	Balance in Fund
1959	$ 73,516	$47,045	179	0	0	$389,784	$ 77,542
1960	107,934	62,192	192	0	0	551,796	113,421
1961	134,945	69,305	204	0	0	756,714	134,998
1962	126,200	92,598	223	0	0	911,109	130,963
1963	114,719	8,459	281	0	0	886,635	110,499

(19B)

NORTH CENTRAL AIRLINES
PILOTS' EQUITY ANNUITY PLAN

Year	Employer Contribution	Employee Contribution	Number Covered	Number Retired	Benefits Paid	Current and Past Service Liabilities	Balance in Fund
1959	$ 12,969	$ 26,471	153	0	0	N.A.	$40,647
1960	37,031	76,441	161	0	0	N.A.	10,971
1961	41,977	88,658	173	0	0	N.A.	11,643
1962	117,267	106,767	190	0	0	N.A.	13,029
1963	109,697	116,212	205	0	0	N.A.	19,374

(20A)

OZARK AIRLINES
FIXED PENSION PLAN FOR PILOTS

Year	Employer Contribution	Employee Contribution	Number Covered	Number Retired	Benefits Paid	Current and Past Service Liabilities	Amount of Accumulated Reserves
1959	$ 31,682	$24,598	103	0	0	$273,844	$175,352
1960	67,364	40,261	106	0	0	391,396	288,084
1961	73,722	40,834	113	0	$ 43	508,073	410,643
1962	96,312	49,131	122	0	1,353	642,764	566,321
1963	132,742	33,188	168	0	0	809,116	761,452

(20B)

OZARK AIRLINES
VARIABLE PENSION PLAN FOR PILOTS

Year	Employer Contribution	Employee Contribution	Number Covered	Number Retired	Benefits Paid	Current and Past Service Liabilities	Balance in Fund
1960	$ 5,541	$36,814	63	0	0	N.A.	$ 42,355
1961	18,056	33,074	68	0	0	$ 98,645	98,645
1962	33,246	44,645	83	0	$1,062	192,252	192,252

(21A)

PACIFIC AIRLINES
RETIREMENT PLAN FOR PILOTS

Year	Employer Contribution	Employee Contribution	Number Covered	Number Retired	Benefits Paid	Current and Past Service Liabilities	Balance in Fund
1959	$ 75,534	$30,742	74	0	0	$134,087	N.A.
1960	96,796	41,074	79	0	0	120,721	N.A.
1961	105,091	40,476	79	0	$5,354	108,618	N.A.

(21B)

PACIFIC AIRLINES
VARIABLE BUDGET RETIREMENT PLAN FOR PILOTS

Year	Employer Contribution	Employee Contribution	Number Covered	Number Retired	Benefits Paid	Current and Past Service Liabilities	Balance in Fund
1961	$27,632	$43,930	85	0	0	0	$71,843

(22A)

PIEDMONT AVIATION
PILOT RETIREMENT PLAN

Year	Employer Contribution	Employee Contribution	Number Covered	Number Retired	Benefits Paid	Current and Past Service Liabilities	Balance in Fund
1959	$ 86,506	$36,229	145	0	$ 312	$ 563,279	$ 305,210
1960	96,216	46,883	143	0	1,207	697,744	460,269
1961	110,876	63,692	146	0	1,355	868,647	726,632
1962	123,146	59,341	147	0	0	1,064,271	945,011
1963	180,159	47,546	156	0	1,150	1,334,246	1,210,940

(22B)

PIEDMONT AVIATION
PILOT VARIABLE ANNUITY RETIREMENT PLAN

Year	Employer Contribution	Employee Contribution	Number Covered	Number Retired	Benefits Paid	Current and Past Service Liabilities	Balance in Fund
1959	$26,312	$57,796	143	0	0	$ 84,108	$ 84,108
1961	48,382	78,211	146	0	$203	211,008	211,008
1962	67,419	78,287	147	0	0	333,362	333,362

(23)

SOUTHERN AIRWAYS PILOTS' RETIREMENT PLAN

Year	Employer Contribution	Employee Contribution	Number Covered	Number Retired	Benefits Paid	Current and Past Service Liabilities	Balance in Fund
1959	$44,300	$20,941	65	0	0	N.A.	N.A.
1960	43,890	21,690	71	0	0	N.A.	N.A.
1961	28,324	15,859	71	0	0	$351,824	$220,140
1962	1,262	1,027	71	0	0	395,682	277,328
1963	29,015	7,283	206	0	0	414,767	286,377

(24A)

TRANS-TEXAS AIRWAYS FIXED PENSION PLAN FOR PILOTS

Year	Employer Contribution	Employee Contribution	Number Covered	Number Retired	Benefits Paid	Current and Past Service Liabilities	Amount of Accumulated Reserves
1959	$108,000	0	101	0	0	$452,559	0
1960	N.A.	0	101	0	0	550,358	$102,155
1961	1,000	0	103	0	$ 499	656,673	450,794
1962	102,992	0	116	1	15,270	642,909	293,093

(24B)

TRANS-TEXAS AIRWAYS
VARIABLE PENSION PLAN FOR PILOTS

Year	Employer Contribution	Employee Contribution	Number Covered	Number Retired	Benefits Paid	Current and Past Service Liabilities	Balance in Fund
1960	$ 8,177	$63,421	100	2	$ 387	$ 79,841	$ 79,841
1961	12,714	70,390	118	0	2,209	184,259	184,259
1962	13,335	90,307	122	0	1,977	278,184	278,184

APPENDIX 2

NUMBER OF PILOTS AND COPILOTS AND THEIR COMPENSATION, DOMESTIC TRUNK LINES: 1940–1962

Carrier	As of 6/30/40		As of 6/30/41		As of 12/31/42		As of 12/31/43	
	No.	Total Monthly Compensation	No.	Total Monthly Compensation	No.	Total Monthly Compensation	No.	Total Monthly Compensation
American	413	$175,595	480	$218,444	460	$224,886	427	$190,671
Braniff	78	32,842	106	39,290	44	24,421	74	29,591
Capital	76	32,796	108	44,610	105	38,523	58	25,700
Continental	20	7,702	22	8,316	22	8,334	31	13,050
Delta	37	14,878	48	19,735	33	14,675	59	24,935
Eastern	230	110,806	295	134,388	206	93,783	215	107,713
National	17	6,325	21	8,413	22	7,998	39	16,680
Northeast	21	7,110	25	10,019	12	3,741	23	9,143
Northwest	101	43,234	104	49,319	299	94,717	265	41,869
Trans World	255	108,671	311	140,074	375	120,888	345	127,814
United	358	172,925	450	187,084	326	135,358	387	180,154
Western	38	22,139	51	22,416	85	27,179	49	17,205

Carrier	As of 12/31/44		As of 12/31/45		As of 12/31/46		1947	
	No.	*Total Monthly Compensation*	*No.*	*Total Monthly Compensation*	*No.*	*Total Monthly Compensation*	*No.*	*Total Annual Compensation*
American	700	$290,330	960	$438,342	1,052	$581,389	785	$6,397,552
Braniff	121	52,125	171	75,455	208	98,283	162	1,279,699
Capital	127	51,414	309	110,336	348	159,633	819	5,850,551
Continental	43	19,155	71	31,765	82.9	36,798	88	549,825
Delta	66	29,161	119	51,370	208	95,990	203	1,436,772
Eastern	340	147,553	578	271,470	755	374,138	715	5,312,677
National	58	25,189	97	44,582	160	78,139	100	748,675
Northeast	20	11,874	57	24,920	86	41,333	66.5	456,267
Northwest	146	67,567	368	127,655	339	180,598	228	2,135,297
Trans World	437	178,235	998	362,267	791	281,238	819	5,850,551
United	562	247,119	758	350,326	996	541,514	941.5	5,893,999
Western	64	29,075	110	51,821	138	65,319	97	726,611

Carrier	1948		1949		1950		1951	
	No.	*Total Annual Compensation*	*No.*	*Total Annual Compensation*	*No.*	*Total Annual Compensation*	*No.*	*Total Annual Compensation*
American	723	$6,545,926	726	$6,736,544	819	$7,381,752	1,103	$9,190,680
Braniff	168	1,340,908	172	1,355,279	169	1,456,368	188	1,558,908
Capital	—	—	304	2,527,913	375	2,955,940	429	3,149,706
Continental	91	619,760	82	620,862	90	711,067	115	987,660
Delta	203	1,438,912	224	1,604,896	234	1,788,534	268	2,177,065
Eastern	708	6,295,822	732	5,885,970	752	6,462,026	861	7,694,518
National	164	880,546	172	1,336,690	186	1,446,462	210	1,722,045
Northeast	69	460,035	80	573,051	85	640,089	91	673,059
Northwest	248	2,102,356	316	2,904,519	375	3,246,449	333	3,273,240
Trans World	858	6,257,748	637	5,496,541	711	6,195,152	745	6,727,621
United	930	6,896,622	759	6,601,111	768	7,037,064	953	7,540,252
Western	95	761,536	109	926,690	119	993,384	137	1,398,376

Carrier	1952 No.	1952 Total Annual Compensation	1953 No.	1953 Total Annual Compensation	1954 No.	1954 Total Annual Compensation	1955 No.	1955 Total Annual Compensation
American	1,159	$12,403,968	1,226	$14,450,928	1,196	$14,606,616	1,393	$16,849,788
Braniff	358	3,541,347	311	3,475,300	318	3,502,324	343	3,468,400
Capital	419	3,878,851	461	4,614,014	454	5,142,566	491	5,463,213
Continental	118	1,047,124	114	1,211,152	116	1,251,363	206	2,121,779
Delta	282	2,606,041	462	4,621,386	443	4,957,267	465	5,194,835
Eastern	895	8,971,968	967	11,366,103	971	12,506,944	1,185	14,359,812
National	240	2,250,698	242	2,564,845	293	3,124,253	292	3,305,636
Northeast	93.5	780,678	108	944,111	110	1,001,348	112.5	1,041,023
Northwest	376	4,302,187	315	4,125,057	360	4,601,303	297	3,746,728
Trans World	816	8,715,771	999	10,793,208	1,007	11,074,010	1,020	12,330,733
United	1,099	10,718,642	1,245	13,438,662	1,209	14,772,134	1,446	17,171,004
Western	206	1,955,975	212	2,203,687	220	2,477,351	243	2,752,799

Carrier	1956 No.	1956 Total Annual Compensation	1957 No.	1957 Total Annual Compensation	1958 No.	1958 Total Annual Compensation	1959 No.	1959 Total Annual Compensation
American	1,539	$19,105,440	1,602	$20,032,380	1,490	$20,075,677	1,650	$27,029,930
Braniff	382	4,537,194	417	5,412,056	451	5,988,013	438	7,637,743
Capital	722	7,615,692	827	9,660,850	829	10,328,572	775	11,435,455
Continental	206	2,199,510	230	2,498,439	228	2,946,806	253	3,952,249
Delta	465	5,194,835	696	7,335,372	724	8,985,105	719	10,677,547
Eastern	1,452	18,067,579	1,748	20,618,801	1,700	22,808,841	1,899	25,918,981
National	350	3,879,323	356	4,126,808	334	5,009,576	356	5,669,681
Northeast	156.5	1,406,827	177	2,043,796	270	3,018,778	295	3,657,778
Northwest	321	4,041,236	440	6,069,684	500	7,567,490	594	8,804,509
Trans World	1,263	14,894,351	1,630	22,117,484	1,443	20,701,781	1,489	24,698,057
United	1,448	18,564,887	1,517	21,526,332	1,439	22,100,145	1,465	25,163,251
Western	235	2,625,670	283	3,375,215	257	3,545,080	293	4,291,373

Carrier	1960		1961		1962	
	No.	*Total Annual Compensation*	*No.*	*Total Annual Compensation*	*No.*	*Total Annual Compensation*
American	1,550	$27,381,939	1,446	$26,582,456	1,504	$28,316,681
Braniff	423	7,540,514	389	6,808,863	375	7,901,848
Capital	708	11,523,817	—	—	—	—
Continental	315	4,344,797	279	4,726,101	271	4,947,244
Delta	741	11,200,440	826	13,475,660	879	15,100,973
Eastern	1,526	23,231,003	1,706	30,802,817	1,256	24,454,988
National	287	4,957,630	275	5,228,291	250	5,210,941
Northeast	302	4,274,351	321	4,978,220	260	4,245,487
Northwest	434	7,817,473	481	9,303,550	487	9,618,744
Trans World	1,401	24,144,783	1,330	24,386,219	1,394	28,632,377
United	1,463	26,412,260	2,244	40,148,437	2,155	40,393,662
Western	258	4,134,913	199	4,061,145	344	5,847,356

SOURCE: CAB, Rates and Audits Division, *Annual Airline Statistics, Domestic Carriers.*

APPENDIX 3

NUMBER OF PILOTS AND COPILOTS AND THEIR COMPENSATION, LOCAL SERVICE LINES: 1947–1962

Carrier	1947 No.	1947 Total Annual Compensation	1948 No.	1948 Total Annual Compensation	1949 No.	1949 Total Annual Compensation	1950 No.	1950 Total Annual Compensation
Allegheny	18	$141,792	17	$147,595	57	$334,663	60	$398,612
Bonanza					16	62,820	16	96,000
Central					16	91,405	23	128,371
Frontier							79	506,393
Lake Central					6	27,561	40	213,331
Mohawk			15	85,197	22	132,669	29	182,298
North Central			23	123,672	39	227,330	40	254,004
Ozark							27	121,343
Pacific	39	192,108	48	269,764	45	271,690	42	278,728
Piedmont			40	218,820	55	301,359	63	374,148
Southern					33	154,560	38	211,338
Trans Texas	21	83,639	36	199,687	53	287,670	51	302,205
West Coast	28	141,904	27	164,288	25	143,766	24	160,688

Carrier	1951 No.	Total Annual Compensation	1952 No.	Total Annual Compensation	1953 No.	Total Annual Compensation	1954 No.	Total Annual Compensation
Allegheny	77	$461,229	64	$483,259	72	$601,954	87	$751,426
Bonanza	16	99,888	28	208,440	31	236,556	31	260,174
Central	29	162,052	36	227,335	37	304,236	53	391,008
Frontier	85	562,262	86	709,894	78	721,064	87	809,991
Lake Central	21	112,378	25	168,965	40	287,518	35	309,141
Mohawk	45	299,969	41	309,498	54	390,818	58	479,595
North Central	36	258,089	69	446,202	84	622,741	95	647,088
Ozark	50	314,684	55	378,606	63	472,668	62	490,410
Pacific	58	423,114	57	419,235	46	420,564	48	451,800
Piedmont	74	460,970	96	768,190	112	884,944	104	899,184
Southern	58	423,114	60	430,235	53	432,199	55	458,887
Trans Texas	52	313,074	47	375,164	78	599,244	77	610,599
West Coast	30	193,491	66	530,625	62	577,842	61	554,519

Carrier	1955		1956		1957		1958	
	No.	*Total Annual Compensation*	*No.*	*Total Annual Compensation*	*No.*	*Total Annual Compensation*	*No.*	*Total Annual Compensation*
Allegheny	95	$877,808	114	$1,020,003	125	$1,249,440	132	$1,347,804
Bonanza	52	409,921	51	441,271	73	573,872	72	614,262
Central	52	439,764	64	542,314	70	617,033	80	703,077
Frontier	90	861,233	105	994,085	103	999,989	119	1,188,037
Lake Central	45	366,417	49	403,104	61	575,560	64	580,778
Mohawk	77	689,371	94	861,029	109	1,113,462	102	1,020,768
North Central	127	1,014,362	157	1,434,225	208	1,682,956	230	2,390,890
Ozark	92	710,263	109	823,309	112	887,447	127	1,137,797
Pacific	61	587,741	71	667,524	83	787,020	96	974,107
Piedmont	120	1,053,016	138	1,199,724	144	1,276,572	147	1,483,176
Southern	57	524,334	67	596,449	73	641,124	84	784,991
Trans Texas	81	656,160	114	940,536	106	940,512	104	1,002,312
West Coast	74	668,927	78	699,624	88	794,731	92	829,214

Carrier	1959 No.	1959 Total Annual Compensation	1960 No.	1960 Total Annual Compensation	1961 No.	1961 Total Annual Compensation	1962 No.	1962 Total Annual Compensation
Allegheny	147	$1,622,112	196	$2,274,488	188	$2,440,004	199	$2,755,020
Bonanza	71	776,786	60	777,724	59	834,200	74	1,030,422
Central	80	767,485	84	840,289	126	1,466,212	140	1,417,846
Frontier	176	1,769,021	167	1,913,436	166	2,031,636	179	2,285,623
Lake Central	74	719,757	105	978,343	134	1,374,564	137	1,564,075
Mohawk	138	1,411,400	141	1,584,300	196	2,293,651	217	2,558,697
North Central	283	2,807,976	290	3,013,794	273	3,321,732	277	3,550,032
Ozark	165	1,557,598	155	1,649,532	161	1,812,976	195	2,242,881
Pacific	107	1,073,667	107	1,277,107	81	1,129,337	100	1,256,896
Piedmont	147	1,646,676	135	1,945,846	157	1,997,433	184	2,427,612
Southern	102	988,388	149	1,337,232	139	1,444,316	165	1,695,984
Trans Texas	135	1,222,536	133	1,300,752	132	1,486,525	128	1,573,800
West Coast	125	1,239,419	122	1,355,202	120	1,558,488	120	1,464,626

SOURCE: CAB, Rates and Audits Division, *Annual Airline Statistics, Domestic Carriers.*

Index

Advisory Committee to the President (ALPA) on Retirement Problems, formation of, 160–161; report recommendations of: bargaining for fixed employer contributions as if for straight wage increase, 165; contingent annuitant options, 163; deferred vesting and vesting for retirement purposes, 162; equal voice for ALPA in pension plan administration, 163; fundamental aim of retirement at 55, 163; negotiated variable annuity plans, 161; plans fully funded in advance to be thought of as deferred wages, 162; "realistic income at a realistic age," 162; recommended pilot and employer contributions, 163; use of actuarial experts for data, 164–165; variable annuity combined with fixed benefit plan as devised by TIAA, 163–164; withdrawal of pilots from the current pension plans, 165

agreement, costs of in economic terms, 331–333, 339; costs of in terms of people involved, 325–326; costs of to airlines, 319; costs of to airlines in jurisdictional dispute, 351–352; influence of public opinion on costs of, 340

Air Carrier Flight Engineers Association, 204; demand of AF of L for disassociation from ALPA, 213; subchartered by ALPA, 211.

Air Commerce Act, 27

aircraft, number in operation, 9, 10

airline employees, number of, 12, 14; salaries of, 14, 16; types of, 12–13; unionization of, 17–18

Airline Flight Engineer Association, 201

airline industrial relations, effect of federal subsidy to local lines on, 99; effect of nature of airline operations on, 50–51, 53; effect of new equipment on, 49

airline industrial relations system, conclusions on economic aspects of, 352–353; conclusions on non-economic aspects of, 353, 354; environmental determinants of, 38; influence of Railway Labor Act on, 39

airline industry, competition in, 46; early statistics of, 28; equipment investment of, 47–48; expansion of after World War II, 35; fare changes of, 47; government control of through CAB, 42–43, 45–47; government control of through FAA, 43–45; growth of certificated, 7–9; rate of return to, 45–48; regulation of under Air Mail Act of 1934, 32–33; regulation of under Civil Aeronautics Act of 1938, 34; total payrolls of, 16; unionization of, 17–18

airline management, costs to in jet crew reduction, 264–265; loss of freedom of in manning flexibility, 265; recommendations to with regard to job qualifications and jurisdictional disputes, 224–225

Airline Mechanics Association, 210

airline operations, effect of nature of, 50–51, 53; far flung nature of, 22, 50; organization of, 9–11

Air Line Pilots Association (henceforth called ALPA), early influence on legislation, 33–34; effect on of 1933 wage changes, 78–79; establishment of, 29–30; first collective bargaining of, 34; first labor agreement of, 83; first limitation through collective bargaining of monthly mileage, 35, 37; impact on general level of pilot pay, 107–110; importance of efforts of to gain and maintain basic wage formula, 102–103, 110; insistence of on Decision #83 formula but not rates, 83–84; other monthly mileage limitation attempt, 91–92; pension policy

236–237; aid to FEIA from nonairline unions in strike at, 342;
certification of ALPA as engineers' representative at, 256; costs
of threatened strike at, 329; flight
engineer union representation at,
201; failure at of attempts for
tripartite settlement because of
threatened pilot layoffs from Martin equipment, 254; later agreement with ALPA for three-man
jet crew, 236; order of to engineers to return, 255; petition of
ALPA in October 1963 to represent engineers at, 256; pressure
on in 1958 to settle because of
competition, 236; recommendation
of for simplified wage structure,
231; rejection by of proposal by
Secretary Goldberg to end 1962
strike, 255; requirement of for
A & E ratings for flight engineers,
206; revenue and expenses of
while flight engineers' strike in
process, 328; strikes by FEIA
against, 235, 248, 254; strike by
machinists against, 235; use of
nonpilots as flight engineers, 205
Edwards, Leverett, National Mediation Board Chairman, 255
Electra, weight, 94; pay of National
captain on, 234
employees, all airlines, 14
equipment, airline investment in,
47–48
equity, obtaining of through collective bargaining, 276; through government policy, 276–277

fares, passenger, CAB control over,
46–47; major changes in for
domestic trunks, 47
Federal Aviation Act of 1958, 43,
44
Federal Aviation Agency (FAA),
Administrator's control over airline industry through safety regulations, 43, 52; control over
aircraft industry through other
certificates for manufacture, 44;
control of navigable air space by,
44–45; development and operation
of air facilities by, 45; influence of
on labor relations through control
of airman certificates, 43, 52; ruling of that only flight engineer's
certificate needed for jet flight
engineers, 233, 269

federal airways system, development
of, 44–45
federal subsidies to airlines, direct,
42; through federal airways system, 45; through grants to local
governments for airports, 45; to
local service lines, 49
Feinsinger, Nathan, Chairman of
Kennedy Presidential Commission, 250, 255
financial reserves, airline, effect of
strikes on, 327–328
flight deck crew members, number
employed, 13–14
flight engineer certificate, first CAB
regulations for, 191; requirement
by CAB for flight engineer on aircraft of over 80,000 lbs. or over
30,000 lbs. if needed for safety
(later amended to four-engine
planes of those weights), 192;
views of ALPA and FEIA as to
experience necessary for, 217
flight engineer duties, before and
after big pistons, 197; complexity
of, 197–198; dispute over in
1950's, 210; not specified by CAB,
196
flight engineering nature, effect of
regulations of CAB on, 191; impact of postwar pistons on, 188–
189; work of, 186
Flight Engineering Officers Association, 201, 204
flight engineers, age distribution of,
15; first use of, 187; job requirements for, 50; number employed,
13, 14; pay computation for, 63–
64, 97–98; pilots' argument for on
DC-6, 195; regulation of CAB
establishing certificate for, 191;
regulations of CAB requiring presence on aircraft of specified size,
192–193; salaries of, 14, 16;
unions representing, 17–18, 201–
204; use of in international flights,
188
Flight Engineers' International Association, 17, 204 (henceforth called
FEIA); chartered by AF of L,
211; concept of job assignment of,
212; jurisdiction granted to, 212
FEIA bargaining power, weak due to
internal organization, 265–266;
weak due to nature of job, 265;
weakened by attempt to overturn
class or craft determination at
United, 266; weakened by fear of